DATABASE AND DATA COMMUNICATION NETWORK SYSTEMS

Techniques and Applications

VOLUME 1

DATABASE AND DATA COMMUNICATION NETWORK SYSTEMS

Techniques and Applications

VOLUME 1

Edited by

Cornelius T. Leondes
Professor Emeritus
University of California
Los Angeles, California

ACADEMIC PRESS
An imprint of Elsevier Science

Amsterdam   Boston   London   New York   Oxford   Paris
San Diego   San Francisco   Singapore   Sydney   Tokyo

Front cover: Digital Image © 2002 PhotoDisc.

This book is printed on acid-free paper. ∞

Copyright © 2002, Elsevier Science (USA).

All Rights Reserved.
No part of this publication may be reproduced or transmitted in any form or by any means, electronic or mechanical, including photocopy, recording, or any information storage and retrieval system, without permission in writing from the publisher.

Requests for permission to make copies of any part of the work should be mailed to: Permissions Department, Harcourt Inc., 6277 Sea Harbor Drive, Orlando, Florida 32887-6777

Academic Press
An imprint of Elsevier Science
525 B Street, Suite 1900, San Diego, California 92101-4495, USA
http://www.academicpress.com

Academic Press
84 Theobalds Road, London WC1X 8RR, UK
http://www.academicpress.com

Library of Congress Catalog Card Number: 20016576

International Standard Book Number: 0-12-443895-4 (set)
International Standard Book Number: 0-12-443896-2 (volume 1)
International Standard Book Number: 0-12-443897-0 (volume 2)
International Standard Book Number: 0-12-443898-9 (volume 3)

PRINTED IN THE UNITED STATES OF AMERICA
02 03 04 05 06 07 MM 9 8 7 6 5 4 3 2 1

CONTENTS

CONTRIBUTORS xiii
FOREWORD xvii
PREFACE xxi

CONTENTS OF VOLUME I

1 Emerging Database System Architectures
TIMON C. DU

    I. Introduction 2
   II. History 6
  III. Relational Data Model 8
  IV. Next Generation Data Model 10
   V. Hybrid Database Technologies 22
  VI. Future Study Related to Database Technologies 26
 VII. Future Database Applications 31
VIII. Summary 38
      References 38

2 Data Mining
DOHEON LEE AND MYOUNG HO KIM

    I. Introduction 41
    II. Overview of Data Mining Techniques 46
    III. Data Characterization 47
    IV. Classification Techniques 67
    V. Association Rule Discovery 72
    VI. Concluding Remarks 74
        References 75

3 Object-Oriented Database Systems
HIROSHI ISHIKAWA

    I. Introduction 77
    II. Functionality 78
    III. Implementation 87
    IV. Applications 103
    V. Conclusion 119
        References 120

4 Query Optimization Concepts and Methodologies in Multidatabase Systems
CHIANG LEE

    I. Introduction 124
    II. Semantic Discrepancy and Schema Conflicts 126
    III. Optimization at the Algebra Level 130
    IV. Optimization at the Execution Strategy Level 151
    V. Conclusions 170
        References 171

5 Development of Multilevel Secure Database Systems
ELISA BERTINO AND ELENA FERRARI

    I. Introduction 175
    II. Access Control: Basic Concepts 178
    III. Mandatory Access Control 180
    IV. Multilevel Security in Relational DBMSs 183
    V. Multilevel Security in Object DBMSs 188
    VI. Secure Concurrency Control 194
    VII. Conclusions 199
        References 200

6 Fuzzy Query Processing in the Distributed Relational Databases Environment

SHYI-MING CHEN AND HSIN-HORNG CHEN

   I. Introduction   203
  II. Fuzzy Set Theory   205
 III. Fuzzy Query Translation Based on the α-Cuts Operations of Fuzzy Numbers   207
  IV. Fuzzy Query Translation in the Distributed Relational Databases Environment   214
   V. Data Estimation in the Distributed Relational Databases Environment   217
  VI. Conclusions   231
      References   231

7 Data Compression: Theory and Techniques

GÁBOR GALAMBOS AND JÓZSEF BÉKÉSI

   I. Introduction   233
  II. Fundamentals of Data Compression   235
 III. Statistical Coding   243
  IV. Dictionary Coding   255
   V. Universal Coding   269
  VI. Special Methods   271
 VII. Conclusions   273
      References   273

8 Geometric Hashing and Its Applications

GILL BAREQUET

   I. Introduction   277
  II. Model-Based Object Recognition   278
 III. Principles of Geometric Hashing   279
  IV. Examples   281
   V. Implementation Issues   284
  VI. Applications   284
      References   286

9 Intelligent and Heuristic Approaches and Tools for the Topological Design of Data Communication Networks

SAMUEL PIERRE

   I. Introduction   289
  II. Basic Concepts and Background   291

III. Characterization and Representation of Data Communication Networks   294
IV. Intelligent and Hybrid Approaches   305
V. Heuristic Approaches   312
    References   325

CONTENTS OF VOLUME 2

10 Multimedia Database Systems in Education, Training, and Product Demonstration
TIMOTHY K. SHIH

I. Introduction   328
II. Database Applications in Training—The IMMPS Project   333
III. Database Applications in Education—A Web Document Database   341
IV. Future Directions   350
    Appendix A: The Design and Implementing of IMMPS   350
    Appendix B: The Design and Implementation of MMU   353
    References   364

11 Data Structure in Rapid Prototyping and Manufacturing
CHUA CHEE KAI, JACOB GAN, TONG MEI, AND DU ZHAOHUI

I. Introduction   368
II. Interfaces between CAD and RP&M   376
III. Slicing   395
IV. Layer Data Interfaces   400
V. Solid Interchange Format (SIF): The Future Interface   409
VI. Virtual Reality and RP&M   410
VII. Volumetric Modeling for RP&M   412
    References   414

12 Database Systems in Manufacturing Resource Planning
M. AHSAN AKHTAR HASIN AND P. C. PANDEY

I. Introduction   417
II. MRPII Concepts and Planning Procedure   418
III. Data Element Requirements in the MRPII System   433
IV. Application of Relational Database Management Technique in MRPII   452

V. Applications of Object-Oriented Techniques in MRPII   457
References   494

13 Developing Applications in Corporate Finance: An Object-Oriented Database Management Approach
IRENE M. Y. WOON AND MONG LI LEE

I. Introduction   498
II. Financial Information and Its Uses   499
III. Database Management Systems   505
IV. Financial Object-Oriented Databases   508
V. Discussion   515
References   516

14 Scientific Data Visualization: A Hypervolume Approach for Modeling and Rendering of Volumetric Data Sets
SANGKUN PARK AND KUNWOO LEE

I. Introduction   518
II. Representation of Volumetric Data   520
III. Manipulation of Volumetric Data   525
IV. Rendering Methods of Volumetric Data   538
V. Application to Flow Visualization   540
VI. Summary and Conclusions   546
References   547

15 The Development of Database Systems for the Construction of Virtual Environments with Force Feedback
HIROO IWATA

I. Introduction   550
II. LHX   554
III. Applications of LHX: Data Haptization   557
IV. Applications of LHX: 3D Shape Design Using Autonomous Virtual Object   563
V. Other Applications of LHX   570
VI. Conclusion   571
References   571

16 Data Compression in Information Retrieval Systems
SHMUEL TOMI KLEIN

I. Introduction   573
II. Text Compression   579

III. Dictionaries 607
IV. Concordances 609
V. Bitmaps 622
VI. Final Remarks 631
References 631

CONTENTS OF VOLUME 3

17 Information Data Acquisition on the World Wide Web during Heavy Client/Server Traffic Periods
STATHES HADJIEFTHYMIADES AND DRAKOULIS MARTAKOS

I. Introduction 635
II. Gateway Specifications 637
III. Architectures of RDBMS Gateways 643
IV. Web Server Architectures 655
V. Performance Evaluation Tools 656
VI. Epilogue 659
References 660

18 Information Exploration on the World Wide Web
XINDONG WU, SAMEER PRADHAN, JIAN CHEN, TROY MILNER, AND JASON LOWDER

I. Introduction 664
II. Getting Started with Netscape Communicator and Internet Explorer 664
III. How Search Engines Work 670
IV. Typical Search Engines 679
V. Advanced Information Exploration with Data Mining 686
VI. Conclusions 689
References 690

19 Asynchronous Transfer Mode (ATM) Congestion Control in Communication and Data Network Systems
SAVERIO MASCOLO AND MARIO GERLA

I. Introduction 694
II. The Data Network Model 697
III. A Classical Control Approach to Model a Flow-Controlled Data Network 701
IV. Designing the Control Law Using the Smith Principle 703

V. Mathematical Analysis of Steady-State and Transient Dynamics 707
VI. Congestion Control for ATM Networks 709
VII. Performance Evaluation of the Control Law 711
VIII. Conclusions 715
References 716

20 Optimization Techniques in Connectionless (Wireless) Data Systems on ATM-Based ISDN Networks and Their Applications
RONG-HONG JAN AND I-FEI TSAI

I. Introduction 719
II. Connectionless Data Services in ATM-Based B-ISDN 724
III. Connectionless Data System Optimization 727
IV. Solution Methods for the Unconstrained Optimization Problem 733
V. Solution Methods for the Constrained Optimization Problem 739
VI. Construction of Virtual Overlayed Network 745
VII. Conclusions and Discussions 748
References 749

21 Integrating Databases, Data Communication, and Artificial Intelligence for Applications in Systems Monitoring and Safety Problems
PAOLO SALVANESCHI AND MARCO LAZZARI

I. Setting the Scene 751
II. Data Acquisition and Communication 757
III. Adding Intelligence to Monitoring 758
IV. A Database for Off-Line Management of Safety 770
V. Integrating Databases and AI 771
VI. Conclusions 781
References 782

22 Reliable Data Flow in Network Systems in the Event of Failures
WATARU KISHIMOTO

I. Introduction 784
II. Flows in a Network 789
III. Edge-δ-Reliable Flow 800
IV. Vertex-δ-Reliable Flow 804
V. m-Route Flow 810

VI. Summary   821
   References   823

23 Techniques in Medical Systems Intensive Care Units
BERNARDINO ARCAY, CARLOS DAFONTE, AND JOSÉ A. TABOADA

I. General Vision on ICUs and Information   825
II. Intelligent Data Management in ICU   827
III. Knowledge Base and Database Integration   838
IV. A Real Implementation   844
   References   856

24 Wireless Asynchronous Transfer Mode (ATM) in Data Networks for Mobile Systems
C. APOSTOLAS, G. SFIKAS, AND R. TAFAZOLLI

I. Introduction   860
II. Services in ATM WLAN   861
III. Fixed ATM LAN Concept   863
IV. Migration from ATM LAN to ATM WLAN   869
V. HIPERLAN, a Candidate Solution for an ATM WLAN   872
VI. Optimum Design for ATM WLAN   881
VII. Support of TCP over ATM WLAN   891
VIII. Mobility Management in ATM WLAN   896
IX. Conclusion   898
   References   899

25 Supporting High-Speed Applications on SingAREN ATM Network
NGOH LEK-HENG AND LI HONG-YI

I. Background   902
II. Advanced Applications on SingAREN   903
III. Advanced Backbone Network Services   905
IV. SingAREN "Premium" Network Service   908
V. Key Research Contributions   911
VI. Proposed Design   913
VII. Multicast Service Agent (MSA)   915
VIII. Scaling Up to Large Networks with Multiple MSAs   921
IX. Host Mobility Support   928
X. Conclusions and Future Directions   931
   References   932

INDEX   935

CONTRIBUTORS

Numbers in parentheses indicate the pages on which the authors' contributions begin.

C. Apostolas (859) Network Communications Laboratory, Department of Informatics, University of Athens, Panepistimioupolis, Athens 15784, Greece

Bernardino Arcay (825) Department of Information and Communications Technologies, Universidade Da Coruña, Campus de Elviña, 15071 A Coruña, Spain

Gill Barequet (277) The Technion—Israel Institute of Technology, Haifa 32000, Israel

József Békési (233) Department of Informatics, Teacher's Training College, University of Szeged, Szeged H-6701, Hungary

Elisa Bertino (175) Dipartimento di Scienze dell'Informazione, Università di Milano, 20135 Milano, Italy

Hsin-Horng Chen (203) Department of Computer and Information Science, National Chiao Tung University, Hsinchu, Taiwan, Republic of China

Shyi-Ming Chen (203) Department of Computer Science and Information Engineering, National Taiwan University of Science and Technology, Taipei 106, Taiwan, Republic of China

Jian Chen (663) Department of Mathematical and Computer Sciences, Colorado School of Mines, Golden, Colorado 80401

Carlos Dafonte (825) Department of Information and Communications Technologies, Universidade Da Coruña, Campus de Elviña, 15071 A Coruña, Spain

Timon C. Du (1) Department of Industrial Engineering, Chung Yuan Christian University, Chung Li, Taiwan 32023; and Department of Decision Sciences and Managerial Economics, The Chinese University of Hong Kong, Shatin, NT Hong Kong

Elena Ferrari (175) Dipartimento di Chimica, Fisica e Matematica, Università dell'Insubria - Como, Italy

Gábor Galambos (233) Department of Informatics, Teacher's Training College, University of Szeged, Szeged H-6701, Hungary

Jacob Gan (367) School of Mechanical and Production Engineering, Nanyang Technological University, Singapore 639798

Mario Gerla (693) Computer Science Department, University of California—Los Angeles, Los Angeles, California 90095

Stathes Hadjiefthymiades (635) Department of Informatics and Telecommunications, University of Athens, Panepistimioupolis, Ilisia, Athens 15784, Greece

M. Ahsan Akhtar Hasin[1] (417) Industrial Systems Engineering, Asian Institute of Technology, Klong Luang, Pathumthani 12120, Thailand

Li Hong-Yi (901) Advanced Wireless Networks, Nortel Research, Nepean, Ontario, Canada K2G 6J8

Hiroshi Ishikawa (77) Department of Electronics and Information Engineering, Tokyo Metropolitan University, Tokyo 192-0397, Japan

Hiroo Iwata (549) Institute of Engineering Mechanics and Systems, University of Tsukuba, Tsukuba 305-8573, Japan

Rong-Hong Jan (719) Department of Computer and Information Science, National Chiao Tung University, Hsinchu 300, Taiwan

Chua Chee Kai (367) School of Mechanical and Production Engineering, Nanyang Technological University, Singapore 639798

Myoung Ho Kim (41) Department of Computer Science, Korea Advanced Institute of Science and Technology, Taejon 305-701, Korea

Wataru Kishimoto (783) Department of Information and Image Sciences, Chiba University, Chiba 263-8522, Japan

Shmuel Tomi Klein (573) Department of Computer Science, Bar-Ilan University, Ramat Gan 52900, Israel

Marco Lazzari[2] (751) ISMES, Via Pastrengo 9, 24068 Seriate BG, Italy

Doheon Lee (41) Department of BioSystems, Korea Advanced Institute of Science and Technology, Daejon, Republic of Korea

---

[1] Current address: Industrial and Production Engineering, Bangladesh University of Engineering and Technology (BUET), Dhaka-1000, Bangladesh

[2] Current address: Dipartimento de Scienze della Formazione, Università di Bergamo, Bergamo 24029, Italy

Chiang Lee (123) Institute of Information Engineering, National Cheng-Kung University, Tainan, Taiwan, Republic of China

Mong Li Lee (497) School of Computing, National University of Singapore, Singapore 117543

Kunwoo Lee (517) School of Mechanical and Aerospace Engineering, Seoul National University, Seoul 151-742, Korea

Ngoh Lek-Heng (901) SingAREN, Kent Ridge Digital Labs, Singapore 119613

Jason Lowder (663) School of Computer Science and Software Engineering, Monash University, Melbourne, Victoria 3145, Australia

Drakoulis Martakos (635) Department of Informatics and Telecommunications, University of Athens, Panepistimioupolis, Ilisia, Athens 15784, Greece

Saverio Mascolo (693) Dipartimento di Elettrotecnica ed Elettronica, Politecnico di Bari, 70125 Bari, Italy

Tong Mei (367) Gintic Institute of Manufacturing Technology, Singapore 638075

Troy Milner (663) School of Computer Science and Software Engineering, Monash University, Melbourne, Victoria 3145, Australia

P. C. Pandey (417) Asian Institute of Technology, Klong Luang, Pathumthani 12120, Thailand

Sangkun Park (517) Institute of Advanced Machinery and Design, Seoul National University, Seoul 151-742, Korea

Samuel Pierre (289) Mobile Computing and Networking Research Laboratory (LARIM); and Department of Computer Engineering, École Polytechnique de Montréal, Montréal, Quebec, Canada H3C 3A7

Sameer Pradhan (663) Department of Mathematical and Computer Sciences, Colorado School of Mines, Golden, Colorado 80401

Paolo Salvaneschi (751) ISMES, Via Pastrengo 9, 24068 Seriate BG, Italy

G. Sfikas[3] (859) Mobile Communications Research Group, Center for Communication Systems Research, University of Surrey, Guildford, Surrey GU2 5XH, England

Timothy K. Shih (327) Department of Computer Science and Information Engineering, Tamkang University, Tamsui, Taipei Hsien, Taiwan 25137, Republic of China

José A. Taboada (825) Department of Electronics and Computer Science, Universidade de Santiago de Compostela, 15782, Santiago de Compostela (A Coruña), Spain

R Tafazolli (859) Mobile Communications Research Group, Center for Communication Systems Research, University of Surrey, Guildford, Surrey GU2 5XH, England

I-Fei Tsai (719) Wistron Corporation, Taipei 221, Taiwan

---

[3]Current address: Lucent Technologies, Optimus, Windmill Hill Business Park, Swindon, Wiltshire SN5 6PP, England

Irene M. Y. Woon (497) School of Computing, National University of Singapore, Singapore 117543

Xindong Wu (663) Department of Computer Science, University of Vermont, Burlington, Vermont 05405

Du Zhaohui (367) School of Mechanical and Production Engineering, Nanyang Technological University, Singapore 639798

FOREWORD

Database and Data Communication Network Systems: Techniques and Applications is a significant, extremely timely contribution to the emerging field of networked databases. Edited by Cornelius T. Leondes, a leading author in the areas of system analysis and design, this trilogy addresses three key topics: (1) database query, organization, and maintenance; (2) advanced database applications, and; (3) data communications and network architectures. This landmark work features 25 authoritative and up-to-date expositions from world-renowned experts in industry, government, and academia.

The two most valuable features of this work are the breadth of material covered and the alignment of the many diverse topics toward a common theme—the integration of database and data communications technologies. This work provides an extremely valuable reference for researchers and practitioners interested in the analysis, design, and implementation of distributed, networked databases. Collectively, the 25 chapters will assist the reader in building the necessary background and in acquiring the most advanced tools to effectively engage in the evaluation of existing network and database systems and in the design/development of new ones. Volume I covers data processing techniques and includes 9 chapters that describe the architectural characteristics of a modern database system (including object-oriented structure, multilevel organization, data compression, and security aspects) as well as the most efficient methods to query a database (e.g., data mining, query optimization, fuzzy query processing, and geometric hashing). Volume II covers database application techniques and includes 7 chapters that describe challenging applications that rely on advanced database concepts and technologies. In these chapters, database practitioners describe their experience in adapting and often extending state-of-the-art technology to support several demanding applications. The applications range from scientific (data visualization, virtual environments) to manufacturing and engineering support (training, product demonstration, prototyping, manufacturing, resource planning), and corporate (finance, management information systems). Volume III covers data communications networks and closes the loop, introducing the third key component (next to database technology and applications) in modern database design, namely, the network. Of the 9 chapters in this volume, some cover the key design issues in a data communications network (ATM congestion control; ATM connectionless service optimization; fault tolerant network design; heuristic tools for network topology optimization; wireless ATM). Other chapters address the efficient use of the web (web access during heavy traffic periods; web information exploration). The balance of the chapters brings networks, databases, and applications together in vertically integrated system designs (integration of database, network, and AI to support monitoring and safety applications; networks and databases for hospital intensive care units; high-speed, multimedia application support over ATM). Collectively, this material represents a tremendous resource of methodologies, examples, and references to practitioners engaged in the development of networked database systems for advanced applications.

The publication of this work could have not been better timed. Let us take a look back in history to study the evolution and interplay of data communications, computer processors, and databases. A little over 30 years ago the ARPANet was born. The packet switching technology introduced by the ARPANet made it possible to integrate computers and communications in a common fabric, where the cycles and software of remote machines could be shared and parallelized to achieve results unthinkable on a single machine. Since then, the concept of opportunistic sharing of computers across the Internet has come a long way, as witnessed by the all powerful "computational grid," where intelligent middleware steers real time cycle hungry applications to idle computer resources. Ten years ago, the web revolution propelled a new key player to the stage—the data files and the data information bases stored across the network. It immediately became clear that databases and network will grow hand in hand to form a distributed information fabric. In this fabric, data will be stored in a hierarchical fashion, from the tiniest sensors monitoring a patient's heartbeat or the traffic on a freeway to the largest servers storing the economic parameters of the universe and the models to forecast the future of the world economy. This massively distributed database environment will require radically new technologies for efficient data organization, data query, security, and load balancing.

The trilogy by Cornelius T. Leondes addresses precisely the issue of synergy between databases and data networks. It provides the ideal foundation and set of tools for the professional that wants to venture into the field of networked databases. Across the chapters, the reader will find a wealth of information and advice on how to select the database organization, the query strategy, and the network architecture and how to best match the architecture choices to the target application.

Mario Gerla
Computer Science Department
University of California, Los Angeles

PREFACE

The use of databases and data communication networks (the Internet, LAN/Local Area Networks, and WAN/Wide Area Networks) is expanding almost literally at an exponential rate and in all areas of human endeavor. This illustrates their increasing importance and, therefore, the strong need for a rather comprehensive treatment of this broad area with a unique and well-integrated set of volumes by leading contributors from around the world, including 12 countries in addition to the United States.

It is worth noting that this subject is entirely too broad to be treated adequately in a single volume. Hence, the focus of **Database and Data Communication Network Systems: Techniques and Applications** is broken into three areas: database processing techniques are covered in Volume 1, database application techniques are covered in Volume 2, and data communication networks are covered in Volume 3.

The result is that each respective contribution is a remarkably comprehensive and self-contained treatment of major areas of significance that collectively provides a well-rounded treatment of the topics in these volumes. The authors are all to be highly commended for their splendid contributions to this three-volume set, which will provide an important and uniquely comprehensive reference source for students, research workers, practitioners, computer scientists, and others for years to come.

C. T. Leondes

EMERGING DATABASE SYSTEM ARCHITECTURES

TIMON C. DU

Department of Industrial Engineering, Chung Yuan Christian University, Chung Li, Taiwan 32023; and
Department of Decision Sciences and Managerial Economics, The Chinese University of Hong Kong, Shatin, NT Hong Kong

I. INTRODUCTION   2
II. HISTORY   6
III. RELATIONAL DATA MODEL   8
IV. NEXT GENERATION DATA MODEL   10
   A. Deductive Data Model   10
   B. Object-Oriented Database   12
   C. Distributed Database   18
   D. Active Database   19
   E. Other Database Models   21
V. HYBRID DATABASE TECHNOLOGIES   22
   A. Deductive and Object-Oriented Database (DOOD)   22
   B. The Joining of Active Databases and Object-Oriented Databases   24
VI. FUTURE STUDY RELATED TO DATABASE TECHNOLOGIES   26
   A. Software Engineering   26
   B. Artificial Intelligence   27
   C. Data Mining   29
   D. User Interfaces   30
VII. FUTURE DATABASE APPLICATIONS   31
   A. Data Warehousing   31
   B. On-line Analytic Processing (OLAP)   34
   C. Decision-Support System   35
   D. Engineering and Production Applications   36
VIII. SUMMARY   38
   REFERENCES   38

A database is a repository that collects related data, and is different from the traditional file approach, which is only responsible for data maintenance. Instead, a database should have the characteristics of maintaining persistent data, preserving a self-describing nature, controlling insulation between programs and data, supporting multiple views of data, and sharing data among multitransactions. From the 1970s to 1990s, the relational database model has replaced the hierarchical database model and network database model in most application areas. Section II briefly describes the database system in historical perspective, and Section III presents the relational data model. Then other database models such as the deductive data model, object-oriented data model, distributed data model, active database, and other databases are discussed in Section IV. Moreover, Section V shows the hybrid system, e.g., deductive and object-oriented database (DOOD) and the joint of active databases and object-oriented databases, which integrates the advantages of individual database models. For example, researchers in DOOD have attempted to combine the merits of the deductive database and the object-oriented database. The future study of database technology will concentrate on design perspectives, knowledge exploration, and system interfaces. These topics are covered in Section VI. Section VII introduces several important database applications, such as data warehousing, on-line analytic processing, decision-support system, and engineering and production applications. Finally, Section VIII presents a summary.

I. INTRODUCTION

The database system is a system to support compact, speedy, ease-of-use, and concurrent databases. Therefore, a database system includes hardware, software, data, and users. A database management system (DBMS) is software that interacts with the operating system and is responsible for creating, operating, and maintaining the data. A DBMS has several responsibilities [19]:

(a) *Redundancy control*. Duplicated data require data to be stored many times, and thus there are problems of duplication of effort, waste storage, and more importantly, data inconsistency.

(b) *Restriction of unauthorized access*. Some data may only be permitted to be retrieved, or updated by specific users. A DBMS should provide a database security and authorization subsystem to maintain data in either (1) a discretionary security mechanism, granting privileges to users, or (2) a mandatory security mechanism, enforcing multilevel security toward various security classes.

(c) *Database inference*. New information may be needed to be deduced from the data. The deductive database, data mining, and other technologies, explained later, can produce new information from existing data.

(d) *Representation of complex relationships among data*. The relationships between data reveal a lot of information. To well represent relationships in a database model for efficient usage is an important duty of a DBMS. An entity-relationship (ER) model is normally adopted for data modeling.

(e) *Retrieveval and update of related data easily and efficiently*. Since the data are maintained for future usage, the file organization, such as indexing structure, is critical for retrieval and updating easily and efficiently.

(f) *Enforcement of integrity constraints*. The DBMS provides the capabilities to define and maintain the data integrity. The DBMS evaluates the data states and triggers actions if the constraint is violated. In general, the data are maintained in the ways of *must be* and *must not be*. Defining the data integrity means that the data *must be* in certain states. For example, domain constraints specify the value of attributes *must be* the domain values while the key constraints assert each table in the relational database *must have* the primary key and entity integrity constraints affirm the key value cannot be null. Similarly, the referential integrity constraint maintains the data consistency between tables. On the other hand, the DBMS can make sure the data *must not be* in specified states. For example, the basic salary *must not be* lower than a certain amount and the employees' salary *must not be* increased higher than their immediate supervisor. Most of these types of constraints are considered as business rules and are preserved by the semantic constraints.

(g) *Concurrency control.* Concurrency control is a mechanism to allow data to be accessed by many users concurrently so that the lost update problem, the dirty read problem, and the incorrect summary problem will not happen [19]. Most DBMS use a locking mechanism, timestamp protocol, multiversion control, optimistic protocol, or any combination of them to achieve concurrent data access. The higher degree of concurrency, the more heavier the operations are on the DBMS.

(h) *Backup and recovery.* Data transaction may fail because of system crash, transmission errors, local errors, concurrency control enforcement, or catastrophes. The recovery process is a mechanism for recovering the committed data without losing any data. The recovery process can be done by DBMS automatically or through restoring from backup copies by users.

In order to meet these responsibilities, a DBMS has several components to define (specify the data types, structures, and constraints), construct (store the data itself on some storage media), and manipulate (query, update, generate report) the data. The components include data definition language (DDL), data manipulation language (DML), data security and integrity subsystem, data recovery and concurrency mechanism, query optimization algorithm and performance monitoring functions.

It is an important job of a DBMS to respond to user requests. A query language is a normal tool for processing a request. The ad hoc query languages are a structured query language (SQL)-like language. SQL is a kind of declarative language, which specifies what the user wants instead of how the job is done. The language is easy to use, and is composed of several key words, i.e., select, from where, group by, having, order by, insert, update, delete, that most relational DBMS have adopted the query standard. Corresponding to the SQL language, relational algebra and relational calculus are also well-known query languages. Any query can be written in either relational algebra, relational calculus, or SQL, and can be transformed from one to the other. The combination of these three methods provides a strong tool set for theoretical analysis or computing implementations. Furthermore, both relational algebra and relational calculus support the query optimization and SQL is easy to comprehend.

As an example, find which options are unavailable on a 2002 Ford Explorer using the database represented by the ER model. If the relational schema (tables) is

> option (CODE, DESCRIPTION, PRICE)
> avail_opt (MAKE, MODEL, YEAR, OPTCODE, STD_OPT),

The relational algebra is written as

$$option_{(CODE, DESCRIPTION, PRICE)} - \pi_{(CODE, DESCRIPTION, PRICE)} (\sigma_{MAKE='Ford', MODEL='Explorer', YEAR='2002'} (avail\_opt \bowtie_{OPTCODE=CODE} option)),$$

where two relational tables, *option* and *avail_opt*, are joined ($\bowtie$) based on attribute $OPTCODE = CODE$, then select (σ) using the conditions of *Make = Ford*, *Model = Explorer*, and *Year = 2002*, then projected (π) to leave only three attributes CODE, DESCRIPTION, and PRICE. Finally, values for the resulting tuples are returned from the *option* table.

Similarly, the SQL is written as

> select   CODE, DESCRIPTION, PRICE
> from   option
> where   not exists
>   (select *
>   from   avail_opt
>   where CODE = OPTCODE and
>   MAKE = 'FORD'
>   MODEL = 'Explorer'
>   YEAR = '2002');

The tuple relational calculus is

$$O \begin{vmatrix} option(O) \text{ and not } (exist\ A)(avail\_opt(A) \text{ and } A.OPTCODE = O.CODE \\ and\ A.MAKE = \text{'Ford' and } A.MODEL = \text{'Explorer' and } A.year = \text{'2002'} \end{vmatrix}$$

There are several kinds of users using a DBMS: database administrators, database designers, and end users. A database administrator oversees and manages the database and secondary storage resources (hard disk, tapes, etc.), authorizes access to the database, coordinates and monitors database usage, and acquires software and hardware resources. He/she is the key person responsible for the success of implementing a DBMS. The database designer identifies the data to be stored and chooses appropriate structures to represent data. He/she can be the system analyst who communicates with end users and interacts with application programmers to develop a database system. A database system is built to support the needs of different kinds of end users, such as causal end users, naïve end users, and sophisticated end users. Causal end users normally are middle-or high-level managers who access the database for querying, updating, and generating reports occasionally. Therefore, an appropriate interface with higher flexibility is required for the causal users. Naïve end users, e.g., bank tellers and reservation clerks, use standard types of queries and updates.

EMERGING DATABASE SYSTEM ARCHITECTURES

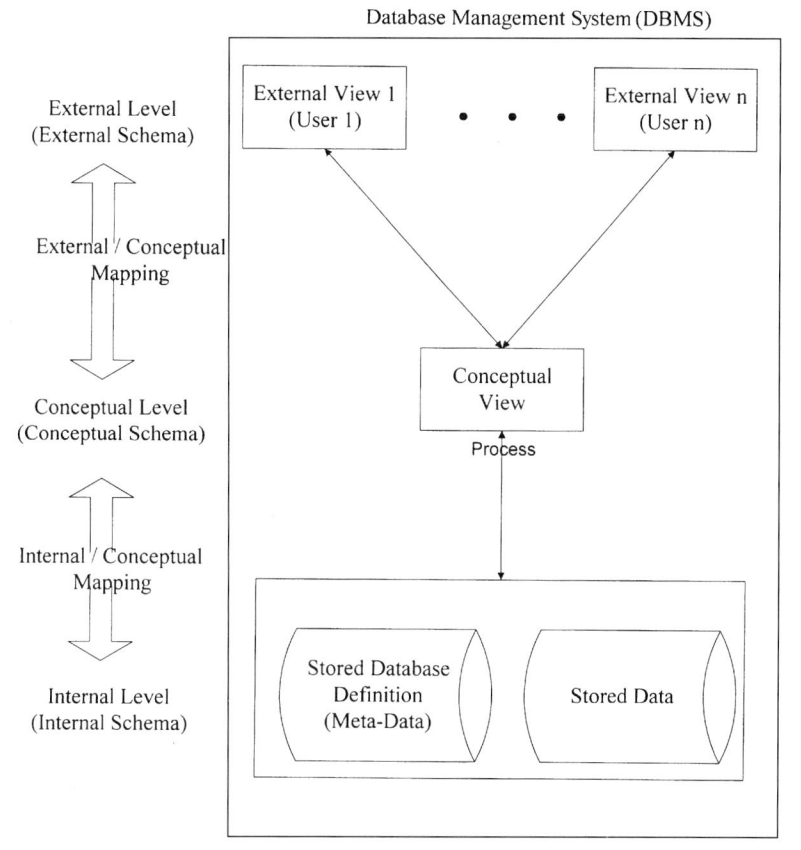

FIGURE 1 The three-schema architecture and two-mapping independence.

A designated interface with canned query transactions is needed. Sophisticated end users, e.g., engineers, scientists, and business analysts, know the database system very well. They use tools to meet their complex requirements.

As has been stated, a DBMS has several functions. However, the most important concept of building a database is the three-schema architecture and two mapping independents. As shown in Fig. 1, the three schemas are external schema, internal schema, and conceptual schema. The internal schema describes the structure of the physical data storage and the access path while the external schema portrays the database from the user's point of view and hides the detailed information from users. The conceptual schema describes the structure of the whole database just like the entity types, relationship types, and constraints in the ER model. Two mapping independents, logical data independence and physical data independence, make the database design and implementation possible. Logical data independence means any change of the conceptual schema will not affect the external views of users, and physical data independence means any change of the internal schema will not change the conceptual schema. That is, the reorganization of the physical structure and modification of the conceptual design will not affect the database user's perspective. This feature allows the database to be improved.

II. HISTORY

The first computer was invented in 1942 by Dr. John V. Atanasoff, a professor of University of Iowa, and his graduate student Clifford E. Berry for solving physics problems [24]. The computer was named ABC, which stands for "Atanasoff Berry Computer." The computer used an electronic medium and vacuum tubes to operate binary computation. However, the era of the first generation of computers is considered from 1951 to 1959, characterized by the computers using vacuum tubes. The IBM 701 was the first commercialized computer. The second generation of computers was triggered by the invention of transistors in 1959. Computers with transistors were compact, more reliable, and cheaper than the vacuum tube computers. Integrated circuits, the most important invention in the history of computers, created the era of the third generation of computers in 1964. In 1971 more circuits were able to be confined in a unit of space, called very large scale of integrated circuits, VLSI, and the age of the fourth generation of computers was declared. However, the commonness of information technologies is due to the announcement of IBM personal computers, PCs, in 1981. From then on, the use of computers grew and the requests for data storage prevailed.

Corresponding to the movement of computer technology, the trend of information system can also be divided into five generations [19,28] (see also Fig. 2). In the 1950s, the information system was responsible for simple transaction

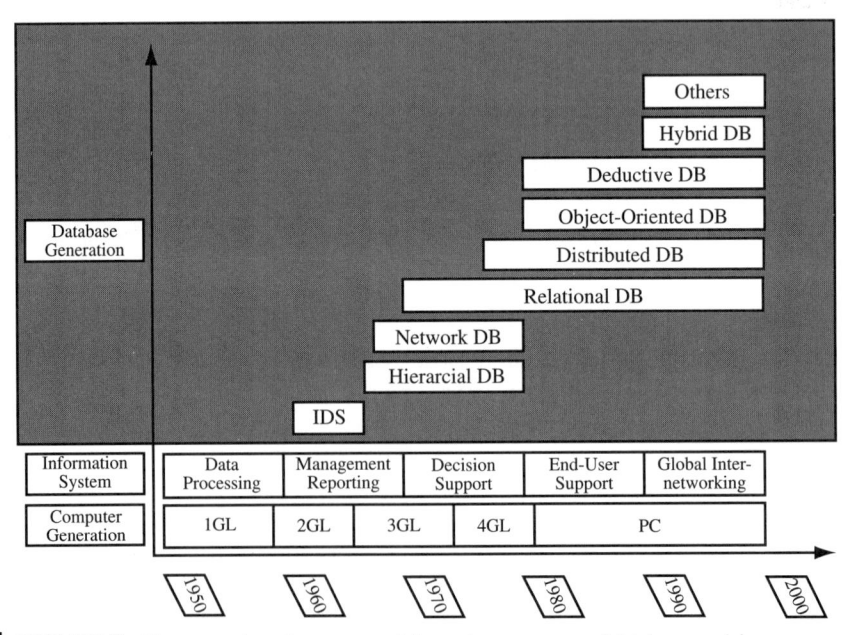

FIGURE 2 The generation of computers, information systems, and database models.

processing and record-keeping. At that time, database technologies were too far ahead to think about. In the 1960s, the concept of a management information system (MIS) was initiated. During that time, the information system provided the data and information for management purposes. The first generation database system, called Integrated Data Store (IDS), was designed by Bachman of GE. Two famous database models, the network data model and the hierarchical data model, were also proposed during this period of time. The network data model was developed by the Conference on Data Systems Languages Database Task Group (CODASYL DBTG) and the basis of the hierarchical data model was formed by joint development groups of IBM and North American Aviation. Note that the innovation of the hierarchical data model is earlier than both the network data model and the relational data model [25]. The implementation of information systems grew rapidly in various areas in the 1970s. Therefore, information technologies were proposed for specific implementation topics. For example, the decision support system (DSS) provides decision-making style information for managers when he/she confronts problems in the real world. Related to the database technologies in this period of time, the relational data model proposed by Ted Codd and the ER model introduced by Chen are the most significant achievements. These technologies have prevailed for decades. The use of SQL, a declared data definition language and data manipulation language, is another push for the database population growth. Several famous relational database management systems were built from academic research projects, such as INGRES from University of California, Berkeley, Austin's System 2000 from University of Texas, Austin, and computer companies, such as System R from IBM. In 1980, the popularity of personal computers awakened the need for end-user computing. For example, executive information systems (EIS), expert systems, strategic information systems, and the personal DBMS i.e. DBASE, PARADOX, etc., were developed. The main stream of database technologies moved from hieararchical and network database to the relational database. Several prominent commercial DBMS are DB2, ORACLE, SYBASE, and INFORMIX. On the other hand, the computer network technology and the artificial intelligent technology pushed the database system toward a new perspective of implementation. That is, the computer network technology enhanced the relational database into the distributed database, and the artificial intelligent technology integrated the database system into the deductive database. Some famous prototypes of the deductive databases are NAIL! (Not Another Implementation of Logic) by Standard University in 1985, the CORAL system by University of Wisconsin at Madison, the LDL (Logic Data Language) project by Microelectronics and Computer Technology Corporation (MCC) in 1984, and the Datalog language, a subset of Prolog language. The distributed database distributes data over multiple sites and communicates with one another via computer networks. Thus, there are several advantages to the distributed database, such as local autonomy, improved performance, improved reliability and availability, economics, expandability, and shareability [31]. There are numbers of experimental distributed DBMS, such as distributed INGRES by Epstein *et al.* in 1978, DDTS by Devor and Weeldreyer in 1980, SDD-1 by Rothnie *et al.* in 1980, System R* by Lindsay *et al.* in 1984, SIRIUS-DELTA by Ferrier and Stangret in 1982, MULTIBASE by Smith *et al.* in

1981, and OMNIBASE system by Rusinkiewicz *et al.* in 1988 [19]. However, since the developing time of the distributed database technology is matched to the maturity of the relational database, most commercial function-complete relational DBMS offer some degree of database distribution capabilities. The example can be found in ORACLE, SYBASE, and SQL Server. It is worth noting that the client/server architecture can also be considered as a kind of distributed database with limited distributed functions.

The object-oriented database was another important landmark in the 1980s since the need for data-intensive applications, such as the Office Information System (OIS), Computer-Aided Design and Manufacturing (CAD/CAM), Computer Aided Software Engineering (CASE), and Computer-Integrated Manufacturing (CIM). The object-oriented database integrated the technologies of object-oriented concepts and database concepts. There were several prototypes of the object-oriented database: O2, GemStone, ONTOS, ORION, Iris, POSTGRES, Versant, and ObjectStore [18].

In the 1990s, the main trend of database technologies is building hybrid DBMS since the individual database tools have matured. For example, the importance of the object-oriented database increased in the 1990s and were even admired as the next generation database system. Since that time some researcher tried to integrate the deductive database and the object-oriented database for obtaining the advantages of both systems. Therefore, a new system, called the deductive and object-oriented database (DOOD), has been proposed. Examples can also be found on integrating the distributed system and object-oriented database into the distributed object-oriented database, and integrating the distributed system and the knowledge base system into the distributed knowledge bases [31]. Another trend of information technologies is that the database is expected to play more important roles and store more complicated data types. For example, the active database tries to monitor environmental conditions than just be a passive data storage. The multimedia database stores complicated datatypes, such as documented, musical, pictorial, and knowledge-related data. Others database systems, including scientific, statistical, spatial, temporal, etc., will be discussed in the later sections.

III. RELATIONAL DATA MODEL

As discussed under History, Ted Codd, an IBM research fellow, proposed the relational data model in 1970. Not surprisingly, the relational data model soon became the most successful database architecture because of its simple and uniform data structure. A relational database represents data in tables, called relations. A table means it is an entity class, which is composed of a set of homogeneous instances, such as students class, courses class, instructors class, and department class. In each table the columns stand for attributes, defined in domains, of these entities and the rows, also called tuples, are the instance set.

In the relational data model, the data are organized in the fashion of tables, and the data consistency is secured by integrity constraints. Constraints can be categorized into *class constraints* and *operational constraints*. The class constraints include ISA class constraints, disjoint class constraints, property induction constraints, required property constraints, single-valued property constraints, and unique property constraints. In the list, both the key constraints and referential integrity are the kernel components for the relational database. The key constraints assure that all instances of a table are distinct and the referential integrity constraints maintain consistency among instances of two tables. For example, if a student in a student class intends to take a course, we must assure that this course is actually offered in a course class. A DBMS should maintain the data consistency when data insertion, deletion, and modification are requested.

To successfully design a relational database, a designer could start from two approaches: relational normalization or semantic data modeling. The relational normalization process allocates facts based on the dependencies among attributes. In a well-designed database, two kinds of dependencies exist among attributes: functional dependency and multivalued dependency. The attribute A is functionally dependent on attribute B if the value of attribute A is dependent on the value of attribute B. Otherwise, the attribute A is multivalued dependent on attribute B.

Both the ER model and the extended-ER (EER) model are semantic data modeling tools. This approach is called the synthesis process. The semantic data modeling technique starts from small tables. In the graphical representation, the designer identifies the primary key and foreign key of each table, and uses integrity constraints, e.g., entity integrity constraints and referential integrity constraints, to maintain the consistency and relationships. The entity integrity constraints require that no null is allowed in the primary key, while the referential integrity constraints state the relationships in tables and tuples. The relationship between tables is represented by the relationship entity and cardinality ratio. This ratio is a constraint that specifies the number of participating entities. It is recommended that the designer first uses the relational normalization process to generate the elementary tables and then revises them using a semantic data model. At the beginning, the designer may be confronted with a large source table that includes many entities with several kinds of attributes that relate to different candidate keys. Structured guidelines were developed to decompose (normalize) a source table into smaller tables so that update anomalies are avoided. Loomis [25] listed the following five steps of normalization (each step results in a level of normal form):

1. A table can only have one single value in the same attribute and the same tuple.
2. Every nonkey attribute has to be fully functionally dependent on the key attribute or attributes.
3. A table cannot have any nonkey attributes that are functionally dependent on other nonkey attributes.
4. A table cannot have more than one multivalued dependency.
5. A table cannot be decomposed into smaller tables then rejoined without losing facts and meaning.

IV. NEXT GENERATION DATA MODEL

From the 1970s to 1990s, the relational database model replaced the hierarchical database model and network database model in most application areas. However, the constraints on simple and uniform data types and normalization requirements of the relational database model limited the implementation scopes, such as the operations on version maintenance, long transaction time, quick and complex data retrieval, evolutionary nature, and knowledge generation. Therefore, other database models have emerged to fulfill these needs. The examples below include the deductive data model, object-oriented data model, distributed data model, active database, and other databases, which will be discussed in the later sections.

A. Deductive Data Model

A deductive database uses facts and rules, which are concepts from the artificially intelligent arena. Unlike other database systems, the deductive database defines what a database process wants to achieve rather than specifying the details of how to achieve it.

The facts are a collection of ground predicates in the first-order logic manner. For example, *Mother (John, Mary)* can be used to describe that John's mother is Mary. Rules are the core of a deductive database. They describe the relationships among facts. For example,

if x is y's mother, then x is y's parent.

New facts are generated by interpreting the rules through the inference engine. This interpretation can be by way of either the bottom-up or top-down inference mechanism.

The bottom-up inference mechanism (forward chaining) starts by checking the facts and then applies the rules to generate the new facts to achieve the query goal. The top-down mechanism (backward chaining) starts with the query goal by matching one condition after another until valid facts are obtained. *Prolog* is the most famous artificial programming language that utilizes backward chaining [19]. The drawback of this inference mechanism is that the order of facts and rules can significantly affect the query results. An example will illustrate the point.

Consider the query: *James is whose ancestor?*, written as: ?*Ancestor (James, Y)*, the database in which contains these facts

Parent(Franklin, John),
Parent(Franklin, Tom),
Parent(Franklin, Joyce),
Parent(Jennifer, Alicia),
Parent(Jennifer, Mary),
Parent(James, Franklin), and
Parent(James, Jennifer),

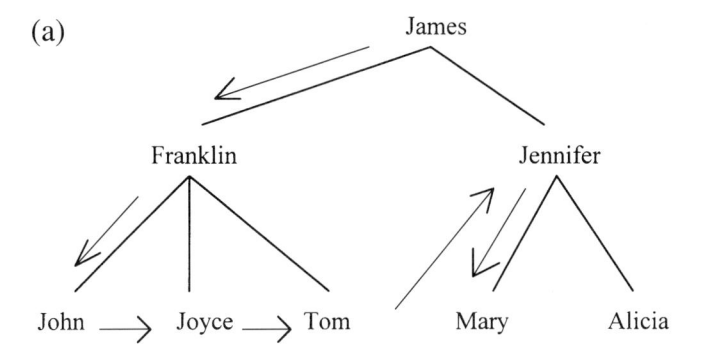

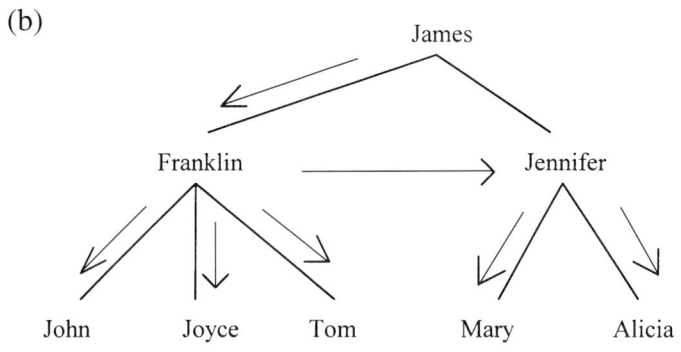

FIGURE 3 Backward and forward inference mechanism search paths [17]. (a) The search path of backward chaining inference and (b) the search path of forward chaining inference.

and these rules

> rule 1: Ancestor(X, Y):- Parent(X, Y), and
> rule 2: Ancestor(X, Y):- Parent(X, Z), Ancestor(Z, Y).

There are no facts of Ancestor(James, Y). However, using the rules, both the backward and forward inference mechanism generates new facts, such as Ancestor(James, Franklin). This permits the query to be answered. They are: Y = Franklin and Y = Jennifer. The backward chaining inference will stop after finding one answer, e.g., Franklin, and will find other answers only when requested. Therefore, the sequence of rules and facts is important. Figure 3 shows the backward and forward chaining paths.

When the inference mechanism generates new facts by applying the individual rules, higher level of facts may be generated several times. Therefore, it is important to have a mechanism for duplication elimination. Consequently, this is also an important issue in the deductive and object-oriented database architecture.

A deductive database would use a forward chaining inference mechanism, such as *Datalog*, rather than a backward chaining inference mechanism such as *Prolog*. Datalog is a bottom-up evaluation mechanism in which the order is not important. Datalog requires that rules be written as a Horn Clause. Such a clause can have at most one positive atom formula (literal). For example, a rule can be written as, if P_1 and $P_2 \ldots$ and P_n are true, then Q is true (it can be written formally as $Q\text{:-}\ P_1, P_2, \ldots, P_n$) where Q is the only positive literal. If there is no positive literal, the rule is used for integrity control, referential integrity, and entity integrity, such as $P_1, P_2, \ldots, P_n$.

Another important feature of a deductive database is that only facts and rules are physically stored in the database. However, the new facts for query process will not be stored in the database permanently. In other words, after finishing the execution of a query, the new facts will be eliminated from the database. This feature can minimize memory requirements, especially when recursive rules are used and the same recursive predicate occurs in the antecedent and consequence. An example can be written as

unavail_Ford_Explorer (CODE, DESCRIPTION,PRICE)
:- option (CODE,DESCRIPTION,PRICE),
not (avail_opt('Ford', 'Explorer', '2002', CODE,--)).

Deductive database research projects started in the 1970s. Since then, several prototypes have been developed, such as the LDL prototype from MCC in Austin, NAIL! from Stanford, the Aditi project at University of Melbourne, the CORAL project at University of Wisconsin, the LOLA project at Technical University Muenchen, and the Starburst project at IBM [33]. However, it should be noted that few of these prototypes have been implemented in the industry.

B. Object-Oriented Database

Recently, as a result of hardware improvement, more application designs and implementations of data-intensive applications have occurred. Many of these implementations require complex data structures, which bring out the following issues: (1) object version maintenance, (2) long transaction time operations, (3) quick and complex object retrieval, (4) communication protocols, (5) evolutionary nature, (6) primitive and component manipulation, (7) protection mechanisms, and (8) rules and integrity constraints [8].

Since the object-oriented database model has been praised as the next generation database model, this section will present it thoroughly [18]. An object-oriented database management system integrates concepts of object-oriented and database technologies. The core concepts of an object-oriented technology include identity of objects, complex objects, encapsulation, classes, and inheritance. On the other hand, integrity constraints, data organization (update, read, deletion, etc.), schema design, rules, queries, and associations are important in designing databases. However, some of these concepts are not congruent. Therefore, building an object-oriented database management system requires making compromises. This section examines the important issues in designing object-oriented database prototypes from three perspectives: object-oriented technologies, database technologies, and application environments. The discussion from these three perspectives will explain object-oriented database fundamentals. In the object technologies, the focus will be on issues related to object-oriented databases, which include (1) class methods and attributes, (2) multiple inheritance, (3) exceptional instances, (4) class extent, (5) versions, and (6) object identifier. The data technology topics are (1) composite objects, (2) association, (3) persistence, (4) deletion of instance, (5) integrity constraints, and (6) object migration. Many of these issues are also relevant to other database management architectures, such as relational, deductive, and active databases. Application environment topics discussed include (1) application program interface, (2) transactions, (3) object sharing/concurrency, (4) backup, recovery, and logging, (5) adhoc queries, and (6) constraints and triggers.

1. The Object-Oriented Technologies

Object-oriented programming is an accepted approach for large scale system development. The important concepts include class, object, encapsulation, inheritance, and polymorphism. An object can be any kind of conceptual entity. Object-oriented technologies build on the concept of classes.

A class represents a group of objects with conceptual similarities. For building a solid class structure, a class maintains private memory areas (called *attributes*), and the memory is accessed only through some designated channels (the channel is called *method*). This mechanism is called encapsulation. The outsider uses *messages* to communicate through methods to access the private memory. A class can inherit properties from other classes (called *class inheritance*), thereby forming a class hierarchical structure. A subclass can extend the information from a superclass (called *class exception*). By means of the class inheritance, unnecessary specifications and storages can be avoided. However, a class can only inherit properties from its immediate superclasses. Fortunately, more than one superclass is allowed (called *multiple inheritance*).

The same name can be assigned in the class hierarchy. If the contents of the class are different, the specification in the subclass can override the one in the superclass (called *overloading* or *overriding*). If two attributes with the same names but different contents appear in the superclasses in multiple inheritance, the name conflict can be resolved by assigning a higher priority to the default superclass or the first superclass.

In object-oriented technologies, both classes and their instances are treated as objects. Although the object-oriented technology appears promising, Banerjee *et al.* [5] asserts that lack of consensus on the object-oriented model is the most important problem to be resolved in object-oriented technologies, a fact born out by the different interpretations appearing in different object-oriented prototypes.

In designing an object-oriented database, there are several important issues that should be addressed:

1. *Class methods and attributes*. A class consists of methods and attributes. The method is the mechanism to manipulate stored data in an object. It includes two parts, *signature* and *body*. The signature is encapsulated in a class and describes the name of the method, the name of entities to be manipulated, and the return entities. The body consists of a sequence of instructions for implementing the method.

In an object-oriented design, the concept of encapsulation forbids the attributes in a class to be accessed from the outside without using the assigned methods. However, the database management system does allow values and definitions of attributes to be read and written in order to increase the implementation efficiency. A trade-off between these two conflicting goals must be made in the design phase.

Several recommendations have been proposed for resolving this conflict:
  (1) Provide a "system-defined" method for reading and writing the attributes.
  (2) Allow users to decide which attributes and methods can be modified from outside.
  (3) Allow all attributes and methods to be accessed from the outside, but use the authorization mechanisms to limit the access level.

2. *Multiple inheritance.* The inheritance property supports object reusability. This is done by inheriting attributes, methods, and messages from superclasses. Furthermore, a subclass can have its own attributes, methods, and messages. The multiple inheritance focuses on whether a subclass can inherit properties from more than one superclass. If the system allows multiple inheritance, several conflicts may happen:
  (1) The subclass has the same names for attributes and methods within superclasses that are within different domains. In this case, the solution is either to warn the user or simply not to inherit the functions. The overloading property takes advantage of this conflict by assigning the same function names to different domains.
  (2) More than two superclasses have the same function name but with different domains. In this case, the system needs to maintain rules for resolving the conflict.
  (3) An inheritance structure might have cyclic inheritance relationships. Therefore, the system needs to detect the cycle automatically. If the cycle exists when the new inheritance is assigned, the inheritance assignment should be forbidden.

3. *Exceptional instances.* Objects are generated through instantiation from classes and prototype objects. When instantiation from classes occurs, the class is used as a template to generate objects with the same structure and behaviors. When instantiation from other prototype objects occurs, new objects are generated from the old objects through modification of their existing attributes and methods. Modifying the attributes and methods of an object during the generation process is called *exceptional instances.* The features of late-binding and overloading are accomplished through exceptional instantiation.

4. *Class extent.* The object-oriented systems interpret classes and types in several different ways. Generally speaking, the purpose for differentiating types and classes is to avoid assigning object identifiers (OIDs) to some kinds of objects, i.e., types. A type represents a collection of the same characteristics (integers, characters, etc.) of a set of objects, while a class is its implementation. From this point of view, a class encapsulates attributes and methods, and its instances are objects while the instances of types are values.

5. *Versions.* Multiple-version is a necessary property in some application areas, such as the design version in CAD, but not all prototypes allow more

than one version to exist. When multiple-versioned objects are allowed, systems must resolve referential integrity problems.

6. *Object identifier.* The OID is used to identify objects. There should not be any two objects with the same OID. A system assigns OIDs according to how the system manages objects and secondary storage. Two approaches are used in assigning OIDs:

(1) The system assigns the logical OIDs (surrogate OIDs) and uses a table to map the OIDs to the physical locations, or

(2) The system assigns persistent OIDs; the OIDs will point directly to their physical locations.

2. Database Technologies

A database management system is a tool for organizing real world data into a miniworld database. To create a good database management system, several important issues need to be considered:

1. *Composite objects.* A composite object in an object-oriented database is equivalent to an aggregation relationship in a relational database. Several component objects can be grouped into a logical entity, a composite object. As discussed by Bertino and Martino [8], locking, authorization, and physical clustering are achieved efficiently through this process. The relationship between a composite object and its component objects is described by the composite reference. The component objects are called dependent objects. The structure of dependent objects is used to maintain the integrity constraints. Thus, the existence of a dependent object depends on the existence of its composite object.

Composite references can be implemented in two ways: shared and exclusive. A shared composite reference means that a component object can belong to more than one composite object, while an exclusive composite reference can only belong to one. The composite reference can also be distinguished as dependent and independent. This aspect is used to analyze the existence between the composite object and the component object. It is called a dependent composite reference if the component objects cannot exist when the corresponding composite object is deleted. However, in the independent composite reference, the component objects can exist no matter whether the composite object exists.

2. *Associations.* An association is a link, i.e., a relationship, between related objects. For example, a manager is associated with employees in his research department through the project relationship. Therefore, the project number can be an attribute of manager entities that link with employee entities. The number of entities involved in an association is indicated by a degree value. The minimum and maximum number of associations in which an entity can participate is defined in the cardiality ratio.

The function of association is not explicitly implemented by most object-oriented prototypes. One approach is to use a separate attribute to indicate each participating entity. For example, if an *order* entity is associated with three other entities, *customer*, *supplier*, and *product*, then three attributes, say *to_customer*, *to_supplier*, and *to_product*, can be added to indicate the associations.

Furthermore, for more efficient reverse traversal, adding reverse reference attributes is necessary. The reverse reference attribute is an additional attribute in the associated entity and points back to the original entity. The consistency of such an attribute can be controlled by users or the system.

3. *Persistence.* The persistent design issue deals with whether the objects should permanently and automatically exist in the database. There are three kinds of approaches to deal with the existence of instances:

(1) Persistence is automatically implied when an instance is created.
(2) All the instances created during the execution of a program will be deleted at the end of execution. If the user wants to retain the instances in the database, he or she needs to insert the instance into the collection of objects.
(3) Classes are categorized into temporary objects and permanent objects. The instances created through the permanent classes are permanent instances, while those created through temporary classes are temporary objects.

4. *Deletion of instance.* The issue of deletion of an instance is related to persistence. There are two approaches to deleting instances:

(1) Provide a system-defined deletion function. When an instance is deleted, the reference integrity constraint is violated. The system can totally ignore the violation or maintain a reference count. The reference count records the number of references connected to other objects. An object can be deleted when the count is zero.
(2) An object will be removed automatically when no references are associated with it.

5. *Integrity constraints.* Integrity constraints are used to maintain the consistency and correctness of data by domain and referential integrity constraints. The domain constraints specify the legalization and range of data, while the referential integrity constraints control the existence of referenced entities.

Integrity constraints can be implemented as static or dynamic constraints. Whether the state values of objects are legal is controlled by the static constraints, and the state transactions of objects are controlled by the dynamic constraints. Integrity constraints in an object-oriented database prototype is defined imperatively in methods. This approach is different than a relational database. However, the declarative approach in the relational database seems to be superior to the object-oriented database approach.

6. *Object migration.* The migration of instances through classes is an important function in object-oriented databases. For example, when a student goes from undergraduate to graduate school, the student instance should be able to migrate from an undergraduate class to a graduate class without deleting the instance from one class and recreating it in another.

3. Application Environments

To successfully implement an object-oriented database on different platforms, consideration needs to be given to several issues:

1. *Transactions.* If a prototype is implemented in a client/server architecture, the maintenance of data transaction becomes important. Using a network

to transfer large data files, e.g., bipmap files, can result in a long transaction period, which can create unexpected problems such as system or network crashes during the transaction.

There are two kinds of transactions: short and long. The short transaction is designed for an atomic transaction, one that can either commit or rollback completely. The long transaction has similar behavior but is used for checking-out objects from a group database to a personal database with a persistent write or read lock on source database to decrease the network traffic. Therefore, a long transaction can continue for an extended period.

2. *Object sharing/concurrency.* Concurrency control is a critical issue in the multiuser environment. Some prototypes choose an optimistic approach, which means that no lock is requested when updating the data. However, whether the new data can overwrite the old data depends on successful commitment. The other, pessimistic approach requires all transactions to grant locks before doing any processing. This approach is more conservative but reliable.

The locking strategy is dependent upon the transaction type. As has been discussed before, there are two kinds of transactions. The short transaction has four kinds of lock: write, read, updating, and null. The write lock needs to be granted before updating the objects. If an object is locked by the write lock, it cannot be read or written by other transactions. The read lock is useful when the user only wants to read the data of objects. For preventing the data to be changed at the moment of reading, the write lock and updating lock are not allowed if an object has a read lock. The updating lock stands between the write lock and the read lock and is useful when updating is expected after the reading. Therefore, any other write and updating locks should be rejected when an object has an updating lock. The long transaction is designed for checking out objects from the group database to the personal database. Therefore, the updating lock is not appropriate in the long transaction. The write lock in the long transaction is used to lock the object in the source database to prevent other transactions from checking out the object. Since the data will be changed only when an object is checked back into the group database, the read lock allows the object to be checked out by other transactions. The null lock for both short and long transactions is only a snapshot of the object, not a real lock. When the null lock is used for checking out an object in the long transaction, the object is actually being copied from the group transaction to the short transaction with an assigned new OID. If this object is checked-in back to the source database, it will be treated as a new object.

3. *Backup, recovery, and logging.* These are important issues when transferring data in a network. Some prototypes provide transaction logs, but some do not.

Logging can be used either for backing up values or for recovering from a crash. For example, logging provides a place for temporarily storing values when the savepoint is chosen in a short transaction. Logging is even important for long transactions in the following situations:

(1) To maintain the status (e.g., locks, creation/deletion, or updating) of source copies and duplicated copies when objects are checked-out or checked-in between a personal database and a group database.

(2) To reconstruct a long transaction if the personal database crashes after objects have been checked-out.

(3) To reconstruct the locks and links of the source objects between the duplicated objects in the personal database if the group database recovers from the crash.

4. *Ad hoc queries.* The ad hoc query function provides a declarative query, e.g., SQL, for retrieving data. It is difficult to declare a query in an object-oriented database management system. Stonebreaker *et al.* [36] insisted that a third-generation database must provide an ad hoc queries capability. To query an object-oriented database, the user needs to navigate from one object to another through links. Also, to not violate the rule of encapsulation, the only way to access data is through designated methods in objects. This is one of the major criticisms of an object-oriented database.

5. *Constraints and triggers.* Constraints and triggers are not mandatory concepts in an object-oriented database. Gehani and Jagadish [20] identified the difference between triggers and constraints. Generally speaking, constraints are used to ensure the consistency of the states and can be implemented in two ways: (1) to serve as constraints to protect the integrity, and (2) to implement query functions. Triggers are the active alert systems for detecting integrity violations whenever the specified conditions are satisfied. Normally, constraints and triggers are declaratively stated in the relational database and deductive database.

C. Distributed Database

When the computer network technologies matured in the late 1980s, distributed database concepts prevailed. Research focused on placing the existing centralized databases into networks so that these databases could utilize advantages provided by the networks, such as local autonomy, improved performance, improved reliability and availability, economics, expandability, and sharability [31]. Through the networks the processing logic, functions, data, and controls could be distributed to local processing nodes. By interconnecting the networks, the local processing elements could achieve an assigned task cooperatively.

The design of a distributed database system can start from either a top-down or a bottom-up approach. The top-down approach fragments the global schema into local schema, while the bottom-up approach emphasizes the integration of local conceptual schema. The latter approach creates a multidatabase architecture that compromises the existing heterogeneous database architectures. In this approach, the different local conceptual schema are transformed by a translator modular for schema integration. Since the local schema are different, the data of a local processing node are unable to be backed-up from one processing node to another in the multidatabase architecture. Fortunately, most approaches focus on the top-down approach while using the concepts of a relational database for the design phase. This approach has been successfully commercialized.

The system designer must carefully select the process used to fragment a source table into small tables and replicate them in local processing nodes. The process used should be carefully combined with relational normalization. There are two kinds of fragmentation schema: vertical and horizontal fragmentation. The vertical fragmentation process cuts the source table into several fragments (tables) with different attributes. For joining purposes, the key attributes should be included in all fragments. The horizontal fragmentation slices the tuples of a source table into smaller tables with the same schema. The tuples in different fragments should not be overlapped.

Bochmann [9] proposed the following set of criteria for classifying distributed databases even though the degree of distribution may vary greatly:

1. Degree of coupling of the processing nodes, e.g., strong or weak.
2. Interconnection structure of the nodes, e.g., point-to-point.
3. Independence of data components.
4. Synchronization between data components.

For increasing availability and reliability, some distributed databases maintain multiple copies in different sites. However, updating the data is a difficult job. For example, when a processor wants to update the data in one site, it needs to update all copies to maintain data consistency. The intercommunication among sites for granting the data locks and the permissions for data access increases the network loading. Related issues are the handling of updates when one site crashes at the moment of updating and finding the most current copy when recovering. Therefore, timestamping, locking, updating, recovering, and deadlock, weave a complex web for a distributed database. Also, the reliability of networks creates an obstacle in using a distributed database. Many questions, such as how many copies should be kept and where they should be kept, affect cost and performance. Too many replicates may decrease the system performance since the network communication among nodes for maintaining the data consistency will increase.

D. Active Database

The earliest active database research was associated with System R. Eswaran and Chamberlin described this work at the first International Very Large Database Conference in 1975 [38]. The concepts of triggers and assertions were added to System R [26]. Briefly speaking, an active system is a database system with intelligence. It allows users to specify the actions that will be executed automatically when the expected conditions are satisfied. These actions are defined by specifying *assertions (or constraints)*, *triggers*, or *rules*. These three kinds of actions are written in Horn Clause form but have different behaviors. For example, a constraint for the relationship of advisor and advisee can be written as

$$advisor(x,y) \rightarrow advisee(y,x).$$

In some research, the terminology of constraints, triggers, and rules is confusing. A distinction between constraints and triggers was presented by Gehani and Jagadish [20]:

1. Constraints are used to ensure the consistency of the states. Triggers do not concern the consistency of states. They are simply triggered whenever conditions are true.

2. The actions of triggers can be separated from system transaction while the actions of constraints are parts of system transactions.
3. Triggers are evaluated after the events have been completed while constraints are evaluated at the moment of events processing.
4. Constraints are applied to all objects, but different triggers may be activated by different objects.

Both constraints and triggers are mainly used for active maintenance of database consistency. Gehani and Jagadish also suggested three kind of triggers:

1. *Once-only triggers.* The once-only triggers are deactivated after the triggers are fired and the actions are completed. If they are going to be used later, they need to be reactivated. For example, if the inventory is lower than the reorder level, a trigger is fired to place a new order. Then this trigger needs to be deactivated. Otherwise, the trigger will place orders several times. After the order products are received, the trigger should be reactivated.
2. *Perpetual triggers.* Unlike the once-only triggers, the perpetual triggers will be activated whenever the conditions are satisfied.
3. *Timed triggers.* The timed triggers will be fired by system clock.

Constraints can also be divided into two kinds of categories: hard constraints and soft constraints. The hard constraints will be checked right after any part of the predicate is completed, while the soft constraints will defer the constraint checking until all the predicates are completed.

Rules are different from constraints and triggers. Rules are used for knowledge deduction; therefore, the rules are able to propagate more rules and knowledge (facts).

There is some disagreement as to whether the rules, constraints, and triggers should be embedded within the application codes or declared outside the application. From a coding point of view, it is easy to write the codes if they are embedded within the application. However, both deductive reasoning and query optimization cannot be achieved if the rules, constraints, and triggers are embedded, because the deductive mechanism cannot infer from program codes. Another advantage of using the declarative approach is the ease of explaining the behaviors [38].

Today, the most important project in active database management system research is HiPac, which was supported by the 1987 Defense Advances Research Project [26]. HiPac proposed the event–condition–action (ECA) model. This model has been used in several consecutive research projects. The basic concept is simple: after the event occurs the conditions will be evaluated; if the conditions are satisfied, the corresponding actions will be applied. However, the most significant contributions of this work were the definitions of the attributes of ECA.

There are five attributes: *event, condition, action, E–C coupling,* and *C–A coupling.* E–C and C–A coupling can be executed in immediate, separate, or deferred modes. Therefore, a transaction can be divided into several subtransactions. Dayton and Hsu [16] used this idea for long-running activities and multiple transactions. Beeri and Milo [6] proceeded further to allow a programmer to specify an execution interval between condition evaluations and their corresponding actions. The interval can be written as

execution-interval: [start-event, end-event].

Therefore, the triggered action can be executed between the start time and end time. This design alleviates system loading and increases parallelism. Moreover, a structure for storing the information about triggered actions until they are executed is provided. The events can come from database operations, temporal events, or external notifications. The database operations include all operations on the database such as data definition, data manipulation, and transaction control. The temporal events are based on the system clock and can be absolute, relative, or periodic. Any sources other than internal hardware or software events can be considered as external notification.

E. Other Database Models

There are other databases also appraised as the next generation databases. The following briefly explains the concepts.

1. *Scientific database.* The science-used data have the characteristics of rarely discarded data, low update frequencies, and large volume. Most of the time, the scientific data need to be analyzed by statistic analysis, time-series analysis, or pattern search. That is, the conventional database cannot be used for science data because the sequence of data and their characteristics are unable to be represented.

2. *Spatial database.* The spatial database models spatial data such as engineering design, cartography, and geological data. Lacking the appropriate data model is a problem for using the spatial database. The spatial database also needs to be able to support the query on the spatial data. For example, the queries can be "the line that intersects a given line segment?" or "the nearest point to a given point?"

3. *Temporal database.* The temporal database stores the temporal data and supports the queries for time points, time intervals, or the relationships between time points, i.e., before, after, during, simultaneously.

4. *Multimedia database.* There are several areas expect the support of the multimedia database, such as documents management, education, advertising, traveling, and system control. The multimedia database stores data in the format of numeric data, text, bitmap, video, or audio. Some issues of designing the multimedia database needs to be addressed: (a) The conventional database focuses on the schema design rather than on the data contents since the data have a rigid structure and the meaning of data can refer to the schema. However, the importance of data contents is greater in the multimedia database than in the conventional database. The meaning of data content cannot rely on the schema but on the application system. Therefore, a linkage between applications and data is needed. (b) The conventional keyword search cannot be used in bitmap, video, or audio types of data. From this perspective, the design process, data model, index structure, query processing, and performance should have different approaches. These remain for further study.

V. HYBRID DATABASE TECHNOLOGIES

New database models solve the deficiency of the conventional database model. However, further studies have proposed that the hybrid system needs to integrate the advantages of individual database models. The following presents two types of approaches: DOOD and the joining of active and object-oriented databases.

A. Deductive and Object-Oriented Database (DOOD)

Combining the merits of both deductive and object-oriented database architecture is called a deductive and object-oriented database (DOOD). There are two approaches being proposed for the database architecture: (1) adding the inference capability and rules into an object-oriented database architecture to and (2) adding the object-oriented concepts into a deductive database architecture. However, Ullman [37] asserted that both object-oriented and deductive database philosophies cannot be combined because of object identity and declarative programming problems. These two issues are explained below.

1. *Object identity.* Zaniolo [40] tried to incorporate object identity into a deductive database. He presented a set of steps to transform a rule into a new form. To the original rule

grandpa(Child, Gpa) <-- mother(Child, Mother), father(Mother, Gpa),

he added the OID so that the rule is transformed into

grandpa(Child, Gpa) <-- int (I), -: mother (Child, Mother), -: father(Mother, Gpa).

By following the new rule, when an atom is generated it will be assigned a new ID. Unfortunately, there are three problems in this process:

1. One atom should have only one ID. The new model will generate more than one ID for the same atom in the recursive rule evaluation.
2. The atom cannot permanently exist in the deductive database. (It will lose the objective of deduction if the atom exists permanently.)
3. Since the atom (object) is identified by an ID, if one atom is generated with a different ID, it is treated as a different atom. In this case, the function of duplication delimitation will not work.

Hence, Ullman's first assertion is valid.

However, such rigid constraints of OID also created some difficulties for the object-oriented database architecture. For example, in order to process data efficiently, an object-oriented database distinguishes the objects into persistent objects and transient objects. The persistent objects are the objects that will be stored permanently while the transient objects will be deleted after processing. From this perspective, the transit objects will face the same kinds of problems as the deductive database did. Another example can be found in the version issue of concurrent engineering. Therefore, it is necessary to relax the severe object identity constraint.

One way is to distinguish between identification and equality. That is, two objects are said to be identical if all the values and OID are the same. If the values are the same but with different OIDs, the two objects are said to be equal. As discussed in the deductive database section, a major advantage of a deductive database is the recursive predicate. If the equality concept can be accepted (not necessarily identical), then the previous problems would no longer be an issue. Actually, the recursive function can help an object-oriented database generate structured complex objects.

A query in both deductive and relational models uses declaration with high level abstraction. The optimization process and semantics in both models are clear and lead to relatively simple strategies for producing optimal results as the relational algebra does. The object-oriented model, however, does not use declaration. Manipulation and query of data are defined in the methods of a class. Even though the query in the object-oriented database can be written in SQL mode, it is still necessary to specify which method is going to be used. Furthermore, complex objects in an object-oriented database include structured and unstructured complex objects. A structured complex object is defined by specifying the data types, and the type of inheritance operates as usual. An unstructured complex object is for binary large objects (e.g., a bitmap file for graphical representation). However, since the data and its implementation software are stored in another object, an unstructured complex object cannot be queried in a declarative way. Thus, Ullman's second assertion is valid.

2. *Declarative programming.* Associated with the deductive database structure is the declarative programming approach, in which data are grouped by properties. Controversially, the object-oriented database architecture uses imperative programming, and data are grouped by properties. Controversially, the object-oriented database architecture uses imperative programming, and data are grouped by objects. Kifer and co-workers [10] presented a criteria for classifying future database prototypes. In this classification, the prototypes Pascal-R and GLUE represent imperative and relational approaches. The deductive object-oriented database architecture, such as F-logic, O-logic, and C-logic, stands between object-oriented and deductive database architectures. It utilizes declarative programming, grouping data by objects.

Based on Kifer's point of view, "pure object-oriented relational languages are not flexible enough; some knowledge is naturally imperative whereas some is naturally declarative." Therefore, even though some problems exist, the DOOD will become important if those problems can be solved, because DOOD can combine the advantages of a deductive databases structure, such as explicit specification, high-level abstraction, extendibility, modifiability, and easy comprehension, with the merits of an object-oriented structure, such as the richness of object structure and the potential of integration. However, Bancilhon in [10] insisted that it is too early to combine object-oriented and deductive database concepts since there are still some difficulties in implementing object-oriented concepts into an object-oriented database itself. He proclaimed that the object-oriented database and deductive database systems need to be developed separately rather than abruptly combining them. Moreover, in the long term, research efforts should focus on a deductive database approach, since it transfers more work to machines. Ullman agrees with this view point. Furthermore,

Ullman predicted that if it is necessary to combine these two architectures, some object-oriented features should be added to the deductive database but not vice versa.

In conclusion, as Ullman addressed earlier, the full integration between object-oriented database and deductive database is impossible. However, if some concepts in these two approaches can be removed or relaxed, it is possible to combine the merits of the two approaches. Still to be solved are the questions: should we add deductive functions into object-oriented databases or add object-oriented functions into deductive databases? and which approach will provide the greatest promise for the next database generation?

B. The Joining of Active Databases and Object-Oriented Databases

An object-oriented database organizes data and the static relationship of data into class hierarchies and provides superior complex data structure manipulation, data reusability, and the potentiality of integration and distribution. Recently, some research projects attempted to combine artificial intelligence and database management technologies with object-oriented databases so that the object-oriented database can have intelligence and operate dynamically.

Based on Dayal's opinion [15], an active database system can automatically respond to satisfied conditions and recover from constraint violation. To achieve this objective, the active database system should include rules, constraints, and triggers [26]. By definition, rules are used for deducing new knowledge from existing facts, as in a deductive database [27]. The distinction between constraints and triggers is that constraints are used for internal integrity maintenance while the triggers are used for external operations, and both can be evaluated at the moment of event processing or after finishing processing, and can apply to all objects or selected objects in the database.

However, an active object-oriented database should (1) organize and maintain data with class hierarchies, i.e., object-oriented approaches, and (2) process internal or external operations automatically. This should be done by adding constraints and triggers but not rules.

1. *Rules.* In a deductive database, rules and facts are used to represent static knowledge. The deductive database uses an inference engine to generate new facts from existing facts and rules. Unlike other database management systems, the deductive database system does not specify how to achieve but what to achieve. The deduced facts are not physically stored in the database. In fact, the new facts will be eliminated from the database after finishing the query operation. Therefore, a deductive database can provide a concise database model and high-level abstract operations.

Researchers in DOOD have attempted to combine the merits of the deductive database and the object-oriented database. Generally speaking, there are two approaches: (1) adding inference capacities into the object-oriented database [1,39], and (2) adding the object-oriented technologies into the deductive database [12,41]. However, the object-oriented technology which provides rich class structure for organizing similarities of instances conflicts with the concise data model target in the deductive database. Furthermore, declarative programming in the deductive database versus imperative programming in the object-oriented database is the essential difference between these two database systems. Other than that, the strategy of assigning object identification in the object-oriented database also resists the approach of deducing new facts in the deductive database. From this point of view, there are rudimentary differences which create difficulties of adopting DOOD [10,37]. Therefore, the opinions of Ullman [37] and Brodie *et al.* [10] are adopted in this research. Consequently, rules are not included in the active object-oriented database.

2. *Constraints.* A constraint is used for internal consistency maintenance. Unlike the static knowledge of rules, a constraint is the representation of either *static* (state variable x) or *dynamic* (state changing variable Δx) knowledge. For example, the statement that an employee's salary must not be below the minimum salary is a static constraint while the statement that an employee's salary cannot decrease is a dynamic constraint [8]. Constraints can also be categorized into *class constraints* and *operational constraints*. The class constraints include ISA class constraints, disjoint class constraints, property induction constraints, required property constraints, single-valued property constraints, unique property constraints, inverse property constraints, keys constraints [38], and referential integrity constraints [23]. The operational constraints mainly focus on maintaining relative circumstances of objects; for example, the inventory level of component A should never be lower than 300 if the throughput is higher than 400. From this point of view, joining an active database and an object-oriented database requires both class and operational constraints.

3. *Triggers.* A trigger provides the means for an active database to respond with satisfied conditions automatically. Since a trigger can work in consonance with an object-oriented database (triggers can retrieve data from object-oriented databases without violating encapsulation), this capability should be added into the object-oriented database. Roughly speaking, a trigger is used for external control and will be activated only when state variables change (Δx). In other words, a trigger is the representation of dynamic knowledge. Unlike constraints, the conditions of triggers are unsatisfied all the time. If the conditions of events (transactions) are satisfied, the actions can be applied right away or wait for further instructions, depending on how the ECA rules are written. Also, a trigger is independent of transactions. Therefore, if the trigger is aborted, the transaction should not be aborted [20].

As has been stated, there are three kinds of triggers: once-only triggers, perpetual triggers, and timed triggers. A once-only trigger will be disabled after the action is completed and requires reactivation for the next usage. For example, if a trigger is used for ordering new parts while the inventory is lower than a certain level, the trigger should be disabled after one order has been triggered. Otherwise, the conditions will keep being satisfied in the ordering lead time. In contrast, the perpetual triggers will always be activated whenever the conditions are satisfied. Triggering alarms or alerts are the examples of applications. Timed triggers are activated by a system clock. For example, a trigger can be set for examining the inventory level every three weeks.

Adding constraints and triggers into an object-oriented database creates an active object-oriented database that has the advantages of object-oriented database and dynamic behavior. However, when the knowledge is too complex for analysis by conventional quantitative techniques or when the available data sources are qualitative, inexact, or uncertain, the fuzzy logic controller can provide better performance than conventional approaches [22]. This is done by replacing fuzzy if–then rules with triggers or constraints and is especially useful in dynamic knowledge representation, i.e., operational constraints and triggers. Unfortunately, there is no systematic approach for finding membership functions for triggers and constraints. Fortunately, a neural network utilizes a simple computing algorithm for optimization with adapting, learning, and fault-tolerance properties. By combining fuzzy logic controllers and neural networks, the triggers and constraints are able to process many kinds of data for an active object-oriented database.

VI. FUTURE STUDY RELATED TO DATABASE TECHNOLOGIES

Section 5 presented the new database model of DOOD, and the joining of different database models. The advanced database models integrate the data models of the deductive database, the distributed database, the object-oriented database, the active database, and the multimedia database. Other than the integration of different database models, future study of the database technology will concentrate on design perspectives, knowledge explores, and system interfaces. Section A discusses the issues in software engineering. Artificial intelligence and data mining topics are presented in Sections B and C. The user-interface issues will be covered in Section D.

A. Software Engineering

The classical system development life cycle (SDLC) includes five stages: system planning, system analysis, system design, system implementation, and system maintenance. System planning analyzes company strategically level issues for developing the information system while system analysis concentrates on specific system requirements. System design describes the detailed components to meet the requirements specified in the previous stage, and then the actual coding process is completed in the system implementation stage. The operations of customer service and system testing belong to system maintenance. In SDLC, the procedure of requirements gathering and refinement, quick design, building prototyping, customer evaluation of prototype, prototype refinement, and engineer product development are critical. Therefore, how to develop ways to make the software development process easier, more effective, and more efficient are important. On the other hand, the database is designed corresponding to program development. A large centralized relational database system, which is hierarchically decomposed into smaller components, is normally adopted. However, when each component evolved and design specifications changed, a new design alternative is expected. In this situation, the existing relational database has difficulty meeting the current needs. Therefore, other database models, such as object-oriented models and deductive models, can provide a new paradigm.

In system engineering, CASE tools support application generation from high level specification and can reduce the effort and cost in application development. A integrated case environment provides (1) common user interface, (2) utilities, (3) trigger mechanism, (4) metadata, i.e., object definitions, relationships, and dependencies among objects of arbitrary granularity, design rules, etc., and (5) shared project data repository [32]. The software utilities (1) can reduce the work of certain tasks for people using requirements specification and analysis tools, conceptual design tools, tools for view integration, tools for schema mapping among models, tools for physical design and optimization, and partitioning/allocation tools; (2) improve the performance of certain machines using performance monitoring, tuning, reorganizing, and reconstructing tools along with requirement tracing, configuration management, audits trails, dependency tracking, and data versioning. The shared project data repository is a database that must be able to control a wide variety of object types including text, graphics, bit maps, complex documents, report definitions, object files, test data, and results.

B. Artificial Intelligence

How to implement the knowledge in the database is always important. The knowledge comes in various forms: (a) structural knowledge: knowledge about dependencies and constraints among the data; (b) general procedural knowledge: knowledge described only by a procedure or a method; (c) application-specific knowledge: knowledge determined by the rules and regulations applicable in a specific domain; and (d) enterprise-directing knowledge: adding artificial intelligent functions into the database and generating a knowledge base for storing intentional knowledge are still substantial topics. For example, creating intelligent agents to retrieve correct data at the right time requires further study.

Thus, neural network technology is a keen tool for developing the intelligent agents. A neuron has two phase computations: input phase and output phase. The input phase computation, called *basic function*, is used to process the input signals such as weights w_{ij} and input data x_i. The weights are assigned arbitrarily at the beginning stage of the training process and are later tuned up through algorithms. The input data of the neurons can either come from environment or neurons. Two kinds of basic functions are commonly used: linear and radial. The output of basic function computation is the net value u_j. This value will become the input data for the output phase computation called *activation function*. Therefore, a neuron output value is obtained from $a_j(\mathbf{W}, \mathbf{X}) = f(u_j(\mathbf{W}, \mathbf{X})) = a_j(u_j(\mathbf{W}, \mathbf{X}))$. A neuron network, also called *connectionist*, is a collection of neurons synapticly connected. The types of connection structures are also an important factor in the neural network designing because they decide the data transmission direction. Three major connections are the following:

1. *Feedforward connections*. The data are passed from input nodes to output nodes. In other words, the data are propagated from the lower level to the higher level.

2. *Feedback connections.* The data are passed in the opposite direction of feedforward connection networks. However, they are the complementary connections of the feedforward networks.

3. *Lateral connection.* The lateral connections allow the data to be passed laterally. The winner-take-all network is a typical application.

Another important factor in designing neural networks is the size of the network. The size factor is measured through the number of layers or the number of hidden nodes. The system with the hidden layer can be used to simulate the nonlinear model. However, the number of hidden layers and nodes can only be decided through experiments. Therefore, more than one network with different hidden neurons should be trained simultaneously at the early design stages. Then the best performance can be picked.

1. *Fixed-weight networks.* The weights of fixed-weight networks are assigned early and will not be changed in the training process. A set of threshold values will be assigned to neurons and plays an important role for pattern retrieval. The connection of this kind of network can be feedforward, feedback, auto-associate, or hetero-associate. The most successful models are the Associative Memory Model, Hamming Net, and Hopfield Net.

2. *Unsupervised networks.* The training data in unsupervised networks are only composed of input data. There is no expected output data for teaching. The learning capacity comes from the experience of previous training patterns. The weights for both unsupervised and supervised networks are updated through $w_{ij}^{(\kappa+1)} = w_{ij}^{(\kappa)} + \Delta w_{ij}^{(\kappa)}$. The training period of unsupervised networks is longer than supervised networks, and less accurate results may be obtained. The most commonly used unsupervised networks are Neocognitron, Feature Map, Competitive Learning, ART, and Principal Component.

3. *Supervised networks.* To build a supervised network, two steps are required: training and retrieving. In the training step, the weights are learned (adjusted) to classify training patterns till no more adjustment is needed. Then the networks are trained appropriately and ready for retrieving patterns. The output of the retrieving step is a function, called *discriminate function*, of weights and input values. The training data set is composed of input and expected output. These types of networks have been the mainstream of the neural network arena. The examples of famous supervised networks are Percetron, Decision-Based NN, ADALINE (LMS), Multilayer Perceptron, Temporal Dynamic Models, Hidden Markov Model, Back-propagation, and Radial-Basis Function (RFB) Models. Basically, there are two kinds of teaching patterns in supervised networks: decision-based formulation and approximate-based formulation. In the decision-based formulation, telling the system correctness of training patterns and finding a set of weights to yield the correct output are the training objectives. The Percetron is one such example and will be discussed later. The purpose of the approximate-based formulation is to find the optimal set of weights that can minimize the error between the teaching patterns and the actual output. The most famous example in this category is the back-propagation algorithm.

C. Data Mining

Since more and more data are stored in the database, e.g., data generated from science research, business management, engineering application, and other sources, finding meaning from data becomes difficult. Therefore, assistance to help find meaning from data is expected urgently. Data mining technology can discover information from data, and has drawn more attention recently. Data mining, also called knowledge discovery, knowledge extraction, data archaeology, data dredging, or data analysis in a database, is a terminology of nontrivial extraction of implicit, previously unknown, and potentially useful information from data in a database. The discovered knowledge can be applied to areas such as information management, query processing, decision making, and process control.

The data mining techniques can be classified based on [13]:

1. What kinds of database to work on. Normally, the relational data model is the focal point. Not surprisingly, data mining technologies on other database models, such as object-oriented, distributed, and deductive databases, require further exploration and should have astonishing results.

2. What kind of knowledge to be mined. There are several kinds of data mining problems: classification, association, and sequence. The classification problems group the data into clusters while association problems discover the relationships between data. The sequence problems focus on the appeared sequence of data [3]. For solving these problems, there are several well-known data mining techniques, such as association rules, characteristic rules, classification rules, discriminate rules, clustering analysis, evolution, deviation analysis, sequences search, and mining path traversal [6]. Other than that, machine learning approaches are also being adopted, such as neural network, genetic algorithm, and simulated annealing [7]. The following introduce several techniques:

(a) *Association rules*. An association rule discovers the important associations among items such as that the presence of some items in a transaction will imply the presence of other items in the same transaction. Several famous algorithms of the association rule approach are Apriori [2], DHP (Dynamic Hash Pruning) [6], AIS (Agrawal, Imielinski, and Swami) [2], Parallel Algorithms [3], DMA (Distributed Mining of Association Rules) [14], SETM (Set-Oriented Mining) [21], and PARTITION [34].

(b) *Characteristic rules*. Characteristic rules are also called data generalization. It is a process of abstracting a large set of relevant data in a database from a low concept level to relatively high ones since summarizing a large set of data and presenting it at a high concept level is often desirable. The examples of characteristic rules are data cube approach (OLAP) and attribute-oriented induction approach. OLAP will be discussed later, and the attribute-oriented induction takes a data mining query expressed in an SQL-like data mining query language and collects the set of relevant data in a database.

(c) *Classification rules*. A classification rules technique is a kind of supervised training that finds common properties among a set of objects in a database and classifies them into different classes according to a classification model. Since it is a supervised training algorithm, training sets of data are needed in advanced. First, analyze the training data using tools like statistics, machine learning, neural networks, or expert systems to develop an accurate description. The classification variables can be categorical, ranking, interval, or true measure variables. Categorical variables tell to which of several unordered categories a thing belongs. Ranking variables put things in order, but don't tell how much larger one thing is than another. Interval variables measure the distance between two observations, and true variables, e.g., age, weight, length, volume, measure from a meaningful zero point.

(d) *Clustering analysis.* Unlike classification rules, the clustering analysis technique is an unsupervised training. It helps to construct meaningful partitioning by decomposing a large scale system into smaller components to simplify design and implementation. Clusters are identified according to some distance measurement in a large data set. Normally, the process takes a longer time than the classification rules.

(e) *Pattern-based similarity search.* The pattern-based similarity searches for similar patterns in a database. Different similarity measures such as Euclidean distance, distance between two vectors in the same dimension, and the correlation, linear correlation between data, are normally used.

(f) *Mining path traversal pattern.* The mining path traversal pattern captures user access patterns and path. The information can be used to analyze the user's behavior, such as the tendency of depth-first search, breadth-first search, top-down approach, and bottom-up approach.

3. What kind of techniques to be utilized. Data mining can be driven based on an autonomous knowledge miner, data-driven miner, query-driven miner, or interactive data miner. Different driven forces trigger different mining techniques, and the database is also used in different ways. The techniques can also be identified according to its underlying data mining approach, such as generalization-based mining, pattern-based mining, statistics- or mathematical theories-based mining, and integrated approaches.

D. User Interfaces

The user interfaces of a database system is also another topic that can be improved. A database user needs (1) customized languages for easily fitting their problem domain and (2) alternative paradigms for accessing the database. In the future, data can be presented in different formats such as three-dimensional, visualization, animation, and virtual reality. Therefore, a new concept of the user interface is expected. A natural language interface is one of the choices. The natural language interface demands multilingual support to interact between people and computers, and would allow complex systems to be accessible to everyone. People would be able to retrieve data and information using a natural language without the need of learning complicated query languages. The new technology would be more flexible and intelligent than is possible with current computer technology. The applications can be divided into two major classes [4]:

1. *Text-base applications.* The text-based interface uses documented expression to find appropriate articles on certain topics from a database of texts,

extract information from messages on certain topics, translate papers from one language to another, summarize texts for certain purpose, etc.

2. *Dialogue-based applications.* The dialogue-based application would resolve the problems of communication between human and machine firstly. The system is not just process speech recognition. Rather, it provides smooth-flowing dialogue; therefore, the system needs to participate actively in order to maintain a natural dialogue. A simple system can use a question-and-answer system to query a database. A complete system should be able to automate operations, such as customer service over the telephone, language control of a machine, and general cooperative problem-solving systems.

VII. FUTURE DATABASE APPLICATIONS

There are several applications that will increase the importance of database systems, such as data warehousing, on-line analytic processing (OLAP), decision-support system, and engineering and production applications.

A. Data Warehousing

The business automation of diverse computer systems and the increasing of service quality for a flexible marketplace have requested large data amounts. On the other hand, the computer and network technology have improved to support requests on the large data amounts and versatile data types. Also the user-friendly interface eases the difficultly of using computers and therefore increases the degree of user dependence on computers. The data warehousing technology is the process of bringing together disparate data from throughout an organization for decision-support purposes [7]. The large amount of data comes from several sources such as (a) automated data input/output device, i.e., magnetic-ink character recognition, scanner, optical mark recognition, optical character recognition, bar code, and voice input [11], and (b) data interchange, i.e. electrical bank, point-of-sale, POS, electronic data interchange, EDI, ATM machine, adjustable rate mortgages, just-in-time inventory, credit cards, and overnight deliveries.

The data warehouse stores only data rather than information. Therefore, for getting the right information at the right time, the data warehousing technology is normally implemented with data analysis techniques and data mining tools. In order to implement data, the different levels of abstraction show that data exists on several interdependent levels. For example, (1) the operational data of whom, what, where, and when, (2) the summarized data of whom, what, where, and when, (3) the database schema of the data, tables, field, indexes and types, (4) the logical model and mappings to the physical layout and sources, (5) the business rules of what's been learned from the data, and (6) the relationship between data and how they are applied can help to support different levels of needs [7]. When applying analysis and mining tools, the actionable patterns in data is expected. That is, the consistent data are required. In this case, a database management system is the heart of the data warehousing. However, the current research on data mining technology is only limited to RDBMS. Further study on other data models are needed.

There are some common types of the data warehousing system: (1) operational data warehouse which stores raw data, (2) departmental data warehouse which stores summarized representations of interest to a single application area, (3) interdepartmental data warehouse which uses downloads and uploads to exchange the data between departments and does not have a logical data model.

The data warehouse can locate three different types of architecture: client/server networks, 3-tier networks, and distributed networks (Fig. 4).

1. *Client/server network*. The client/server network allows disparate source systems to talk to each other via middleware tools. The middleware does not include the software that provides the actual service. There are three types of middleware.

(a) *General middleware*. The middleware is responsible for processing the communication stacks, distributed directories, authentication services, network time, remote procedure calls, and queuing services. Products that fall into this category are OSF's DCE, Netware, Name Pipes, LAN Server, LAN Manger, Vines, TCP/IP, APPC, and NetBIOS.

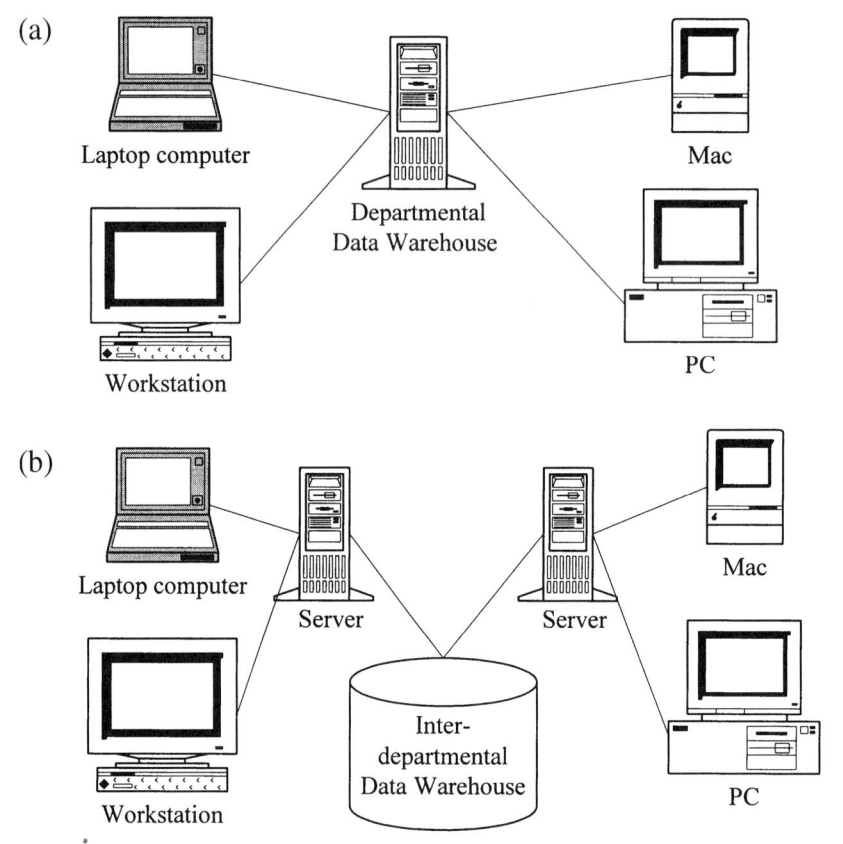

FIGURE 4 The data warehouse can be located in different types of architecture such as client/server networks, 3-tier networks, and distributed networks. (a) Departmental data warehouse, (b) interdepartmental data warehouse, (c) middleware approach, and (d) multitiered approach.

(b) *Service-specific middleware.* The middleware accomplishes a particular client/server type of service. Examples for database-specific middleware are ODBC, IDAPI, DRDA, EDA/SQL, SAG/CLI, and Oracle Glue; for OLTP-specific middleware are Tuzedo's ATMI, Encina's Transactional RPC, and X/Open's TxRPC and XATMI; for groupware-specific middleware are MAPI, VIM, VIC, and Lotus Notes calls; for object-specific middleware are OMG's ORB and Object Services and ODMG-93; and for system management-specific middleware are SNMP, CMIP, and ORBs [30].

There are several different types of client/server architectures:

(a) *File servers.* The server is only responsible for managing data as files. The files are shared across a network.

(b) *Database server.* The server uses its won processing power to find the requested data instead of singularly passing all the records to a client and letting it find its own data as was the case of the file server.

(c) *Transaction servers.* The client invokes remote procedures who reside on the server with an SQL database engine to accomplish jobs.

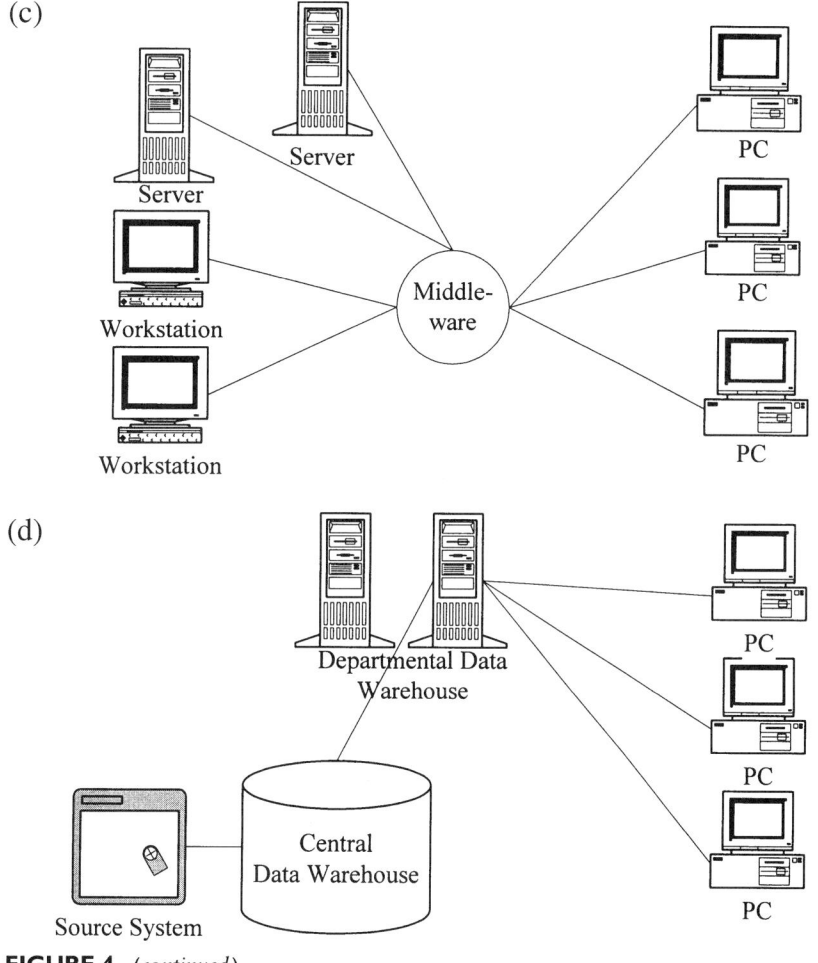

FIGURE 4 (*continued*)

(d) *Groupware*. Groupware, also called collaborative software, is a kind of software used for documents, imaging, and workflow management. The software lets a group of people share information or track information together [11]. Therefore, to work together effectively on a project, the data can be stored in a central place or in a distributed manner. Again, most of the data depository of the groupware is limited to the relational database, or simply a data storage. The integration between other data models with the groupware remains for further study.

(e) *Object servers*. In an object server, the client objects communicate with server objects using an object request broker (ORB). The ORB is located at the middleware and interacts with the instance of object server class, invokes the requested method, and returns the results back to the client object. Examples of object servers are DSOM from IBM, DOMS HyperDesk, DOMF from HP, and DOE from Sun.

2. *3-tier approach*. The 3-tier approach separate the architecture into three levels: source systems, data transport, and central repository. The first tier, source systems, belongs to the client such as the visual aspects of the business object. The second tier, data transport, belongs to traditional servers, such as common object requested broker architecture (CORBA) objects, who act as the middle-tier application servers. CORBA encapsulates the business logic, interacts with the client, implements the logic of the business object, and extracts their persistent state from multiple data sources. The object management model (OMG) has published standards for 16 object services: life cycle, persistence, naming, event, concurrency control, transaction, relationship, externalization, query, licensing, properties, time, security, collection, and startup. The third tier, central repository, provides an integrated model of disparate data source and back-end applications, i.e., TP Monitors, MOM, DBMS, ODBMS, Lotus Notes [29]. It is also worth noting that the central repository can be any kind of database model and will be changed to meet the modeling requirements thereafter.

3. *Distributed system*. A distributed system shares the load of processes data, providing services, and storing data from client/server and 3-tier architectures toward architecture. The responsibilities of data warehousing are shared from a central repository to many computers. It is clear that the advantages of economics and reliability can also be found in the distributed data warehouse. The distributed system has gradually drawn more and more attention.

B. On-line Analytic Processing (OLAP)

On-line analytic processing is a presentation tool for providing different views of large sets of data to end users no matter whether the data resides in a single centralized data warehouse, in virtual distributed warehouses, or on operational systems. The OLAP is a fast and powerful way of reporting data and can enable manual knowledge discovery. Therefore, the human intelligence for knowledge discovery is important. The data can be presented in a powerful and efficient representation, called a cube, through an advanced graphical interface. The cube is ideally suited for queries that allow users to look for specific targets for decision-support purposes (as shown in Fig. 5). The cube itself is stored either

EMERGING DATABASE SYSTEM ARCHITECTURES

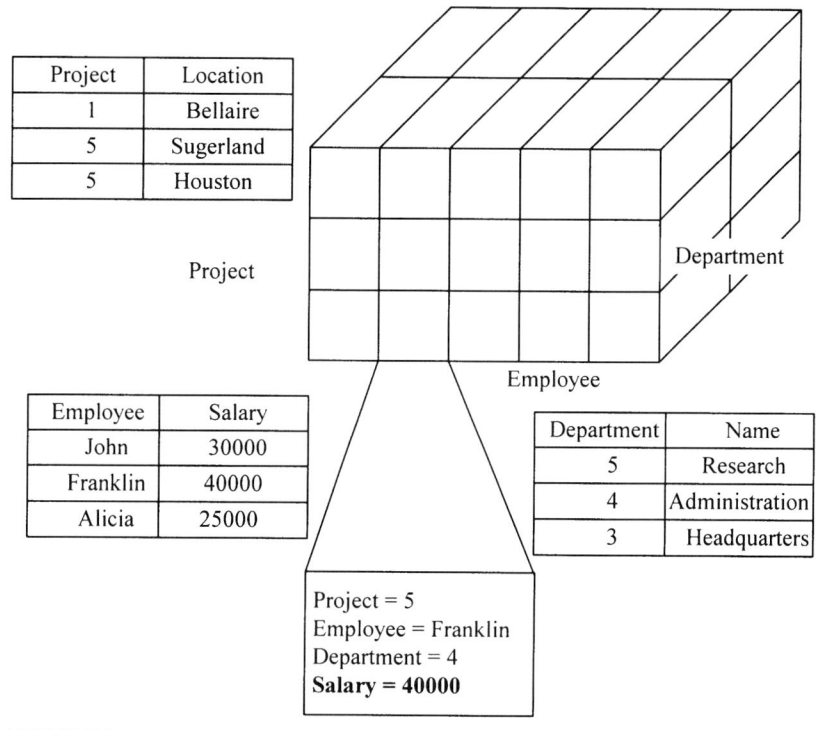

Project	Location
1	Bellaire
5	Sugerland
5	Houston

Employee	Salary
John	30000
Franklin	40000
Alicia	25000

Department	Name
5	Research
4	Administration
3	Headquarters

Project = 5
Employee = Franklin
Department = 4
Salary = 40000

FIGURE 5 The cube used for OLAP is divided into subcubes. Each subcube can contain the calculations, counts, and aggregations of all records landed on it.

in a relational database or in any other kind of database that optimizes OLAP operations.

The most famous of OLAP representation is the star schema by Ralph Kimball [7]. The star schema starts with central fact tables that correspond to facts about a business issue. Each row in the central fact table contains some combination of keys that make it unique (again, a concept of the relational database) and these keys are called dimensions. The central facts table also has other columns to contain its own information. Associated with each key are auxiliary tables called dimension tables. Any query on the central fact table would require multiple joins of the dimension tables. Since many joining operations are required, indexing is important with the key attributes. Other than star schema, the multidimensional database (MDD) is also an important representation of OLAP. The MDD is a way of representing data that comes in relational tabular form. Each record is exactly represented in a subcube. Inside a subcube are calculations, counts, or aggregations of all the records that belong to it. Therefore, the useful information can be revealed to users quickly.

C. Decision-Support System

A decision support system (DSS) improves the performance of users through implementing information technology to increase knowledge level. The system is comprised of three components: database management software (DBMS), model base management software (MBMS), and dialogue generation and management software (DGMS) [35]. The MBMS integrates data access and decision models to provide (1) creation generation functions, (2) maintenance update functions, and (3) manipulation use functions. The decision model is embedded in the MBMS of an information system, and uses the database as the integration and communication mechanism between strategic models, tactical models, and operational models. The output of MBMS is generated toward decision makers or intellectual processes. The model should have the functions of:

(a) the ability to create new models quickly and easily,
(b) the ability to catalog and maintain a wide range of models, supporting all levels of management,
(c) the ability to interrelate these models with appropriate linkage through the database,
(d) the ability to access and integrate model "building blocks", and
(e) the ability to manage the model base with management functions analogous to database management.

The DGMS has three parts: (1) active language, (2) display or presentation language, and (3) knowledge base (what the user must know). The DGMS has the knowledge base to interact with the active language to instruct what the user can do and with the presentation language to show what the user can see. In this situation, a good man/machine interface for interactive applications is required. Therefore, the interface should have:

(a) the ability to handle a variety of dialogue styles,
(b) the ability to accommodate user actions in a variety of media,
(c) the ability to present data in a variety of formats and media, and
(d) the ability to provide flexible support for the user's knowledge base.

The DBMS can be any data model as previous discussed. The distributed database model can generate distributed decision support systems, and an active system can increase the alive operations. Moreover, the deductive database can produce an intelligent decision support environment.

D. Engineering and Production Applications

Engineering and production applications are a structured approach to integrate production functions. This approach can result in significant savings in both time and cost. The application topics include financial functions, order processing and accounting functions, capacity requirements planning, inventory management, manufacturing performance planning, production data management, production monitoring and control, purchasing, sale forecasting, order processing, product planning, production control, inventory control, and material resource planning (MRP). An engineering application is a tedious and complicated procedure in which designers need to manage a large amount of data into applications, and the data needs to be maintained for specific applications. The engineering design has the characteristics of (1) long duration, (2) complex design object, (3) hierarchical object architecture, (4) multiple versions, and (5) cooperation. A database management system has been adopted for sharing information and data management among applications. In order to integrate different applications, several protocols for data exchange have been proposed. An example can be the Standard for Exchange of Product model, abbreviated as STEP. However, conventional engineering applications employ a relational database system to manage data. There are obstructions in a relational database system [19]:

1. Engineering design requires complex data types. A relational database system is suitable for processing a high degree of similarity among data. The complex data type cannot be supported effectively by the relational database.
2. A relational database system is more appropriate for using in short-string or fixed-length types of data. Engineering applications, e.g., engineering design, require large data type.
3. Temporal and spatial data are important in planning, assembly, or allocating. The examples can be found in the topics such as facility layout production scheduling and solid modeling.
4. A database schema must be evolved frequently in the engineering applications for improving design quality.
5. A designer may need to edit designs for a long period of time, which requires a long transaction in the database. This approach places a locking mechanism on data and prevents other designers from working simultaneously.
6. The old and new versions of the same data need to be retained for reference. The key constraints of a relational database prohibit it from storing the same data twice.

In contrast to the obstructions in relational database systems, an object-oriented database has characteristics which are important in engineering usage [19]:

1. *Common model.* A common model allows designers to map real-world objects into a data object directly.
2. *Uniform interface.* Objects generated from the same class will have the same interface in operation.
3. *Complex objects.* Complex data types and relationships, including hierarchies and lattices, are supported by an object-oriented database.
4. *Information hiding and abstraction.* The abstraction process focuses on the generalization and aggregation of objects, which hides internal detailed differences to simplify the architecture.
5. *Versions.* Multiple versions of the same object are permitted in an object-oriented database.
6. *Modularity, flexibility, extensibility, and tailorability.* Adding new objects or editing old objects are simple procedures through the schema evolution function.

In the future, the database must support areas such as computer-aided design (CAD), computer-aided manufacturing (CAM), computer-aided engineering (CAE), manufacturing requirement planning (MRPII), computer-integrated manufacturing (CIM), computer-aided logistical system (CALS), and enterprise-resource planning (ERP). In order to meet such a diversified environment, the distributed and heterogeneous environment and active database should be adopted.

VIII. SUMMARY

In this chapter, we presented the techniques and applications of emerging database system architecture. The history of computers, information systems, and database systems are covered. The relational data model, deductive data model, object-oriented data model, distributed data model, active database model, deductive and object-oriented database (DOOD), and the joining of active databases and object-oriented databases are discussed. It is worth noting that different data models can satisfy different needs, and future system requirements are diversified. In the future, database performance can be increased because of the improvement of system engineering, artificial intelligence, data mining, and user interface. Many techniques will also enhance the application of database systems, such as data warehousing, on-line analytic processing (OLAP), decision-support systems, and engineering and production applications.

REFERENCES

1. Abiteboul, S. Towards a deductive object-oriented database language. *Deductive and Object-Oriented Database*, 453–472, 1990.
2. Agrawal, R., Imielinshi, T., and Swami, A. Mining association rules between sets of items in large databases. In *Proc. of the 1993 International Conference on Management of Data (SIGMOD-93)*, pp. 207–216, 1993.
3. Agrawl, R., and Shafer, J. Parallel mining of association rules. *IEEE Trans. Knowledge Data Engrg.* 8(6), 962–969, 1996.
4. Allen, J. *Natural Language Understanding*. Benjamin/Cummings, Redwood City, CA, 1995.
5. Banerjee, J. *et al.* Data model issues for object-oriented applications. In *Readings in Database Systems*, (M. Stonebreaker, Ed.), 2nd ed., pp. 802–813. Morgan Kaufmann, San Mateo, CA, 1994.
6. Beeri, C., and Milo, T. A model for active object oriented database. In *Proceedings of the 17th International Conference on Very Large Data Bases*. (Sep.), pp. 337–349, 1991.
7. Berry, M., and Linoff, G. *Data Mining Techniques: For Marketing. Sales, and Customer Support*. Wiley, New York, 1997.
8. Bertino, E., and Martino, L. *Object-Oriented Database Systems: Concepts and Architecture*. Addison-Wesley, Reading, MA, 1993.
9. Bochmann, G. *Concepts for Distributed Systems Design* Springer-Verlag, New York, 1983.
10. Brodie, M. L., Bancilhon, F., Harris, F., Kifer, M., Masunada, Y., Sacerdoti, E., and Tanska, K. Next generation database management systems technology. *Deductive and Object-Oriented Database* 335–346, 1990.
11. Capron, H. L. *Computers: Tools for an Information Age,* 5th ed. Addison-Wesley, Reading, MA, 1998.
12. Caseau, Y. Constraints in an object-oriented deductive database. *Deductive and Object-Oriented Database* 292–310, 1991.
13. Chen, M., Han, J., and Yu, P., Data mining: An overview from a database perspective. *IEEE Trans. Knowledge Data Engrg.* 8(6): 866–883, 1996.

14. Cheung, D. W., Vincent, T., Fu, W., and Fu, Y. Efficient mining of association rules in distributed databases. *IEEE Trans. Knowledge Data Engrg.* **8**(6): 911–922, 1996.
15. Dayal, U. Active database management systems. In *Proceedings of the Third International Conference on Data and Knowledge Base,* Jerusalem, pp. 150–170, 1988.
16. Dayton, U., and Hsu, M. Organizing long-running activities with triggers and transactions. In *Readings in Database Systems,* (M. Stonebreaker, Ed.), 2nd. ed., pp. 324–334. Morgan Kaufmann, San Mateo, CA, 1994.
17. Du, T., and Wolfe, P. Overview of emerging database architectures. *Comput. Indust. Engrg.* **32**(4): 811–821, 1997.
18. Du, T., and Wolfe, P. An implementation perspective of applying object-oriented database technologies. *IIE Trans.* **29**: 733–742, 1997.
19. Elmasri, R., and Navathe, S. B. *Fundamentals of Database Systems,* 3rd ed. Addison-Wesley, Reading, MA, 2000.
20. Gehani, N., and Jagadish, H. V. Ode as an active database: Constraints and triggers. In *Proceedings of the 17th International Conference on Very Large Data Bases,* pp. 327–336, 1991.
21. Houtsma, M., and Swami, A. Set-oriented data mining in relational databases. *Data Knowledge Engrg.* **17**: 245–262, 1995.
22. Lee, C. C. Fuzzy logic in control systems: Fuzzy logic controller—Parts I and II. *IEEE Trans. Systems Man Cybernet.* **20** (2): 404–418, 419–435, 1990.
23. Little, D., and Misra, S. Auditing for database integrity. *J. Systems Manage.* 6–10, 1994.
24. Long, L., and Long, N. *Brief Edition of Computers,* 5th ed. Prentice-Hall, Upper Saddle River, NJ, 1998.
25. Loomis, M. *The Database Book.* Macmillan, New York, 1987.
26. McCarthy, D., and Dayal, U. The architecture of an active data base management system. In *Reading in Database Systems* (M. Stonebreaker, Ed.), 2nd ed., pp. 373–382. Morgan Kaufmann, San Mateo, CA, 1994.
27. Minker, J. *Fundations of Deductive Databases and Logic Programming.* Morgan Kaufmann, Los Altos, CA, 1988.
28. O'Brien, J. A. *Introduction to Information Systems,* 8th ed. Irwin, Chicago, 1997.
29. Orfali, R., and Harkey, D. *Client/Server Programming with JAVA and CORBA.* Wiley, New York, 1997.
30. Orfali, R., Harkey, D., and Edwards, J. *Essential Client/Server Survival Guide.* Van Nostrand Reinhold, New York, 1994.
31. Ozsu, T. M. *Principles of Distributed Database Systems.* Prentice-Hall, Englewood Cliffs, NJ, 1991.
32. Pressman, R. *Software Engineering: A Practitioner's Approach,* 3rd ed. McGraw-Hill, New York, 1992.
33. Ramakrishnan, R., and Ullman, D. A survey of deductive database systems. *J. Logic Programming* 125–148, 1995.
34. Savaere, A., Omiecinski, E., and Navathe, S. An efficient algorithm for association rules in large databases. In *Proc. Int'l Conf. Very Large Data Bases,* Zurich, pp. 432–444, 1995.
35. Sprague, R., and Watson, H. *Decision Support Systems: Putting Theory into Practice,* 3rd ed. Prentice-Hall, Englewood Cliffs, NJ, 1993.
36. Stonebreaker and the Committee for Advances DBMS Function. Third-generation database system manifesto. In *Reading in Database System,* pp. 932–945. Morgan Kaufmann, San Mateo, CA, 1994.
37. Ullman, J. A comparison between deductive and object-oriented database systems. In *Proceedings Deductive and Object-Oriented Database Conference,* pp. 7–24, 1990.
38. Urban, S., and Lim, B. An intelligent framework for active support of database semantics. *Int. J. Expert Systems.* **6**(1): 1–37, 1993.
39. Wong, L. Inference rules in object oriented programming systems. *Deductive and Object-Oriented Database* 493–509, 1990.
40. Zaniolo, C. Object identity and inheritance in deductive databases—An evolutionary approach. *Deductive and Object-Oriented Database* 7–24, 1990.

2
DATA MINING

DOHEON LEE

Department of BioSystems, Korea Advanced Institute of Science and Technology, Daejon, Republic of Korea

MYOUNG HO KIM

Department of Computer Science, Korea Advanced Institute of Science and Technology, Taejon 305-701, Republic of Korea

- I. INTRODUCTION 41
  - A. Definition of Data Mining 41
  - B. Motivation of Data Mining 42
  - C. Comparison with Machine Learning 43
  - D. Steps of the Data Mining Process 45
- II. OVERVIEW OF DATA MINING TECHNIQUES 46
  - A. Classification of Data Mining Techniques 46
  - B. Requirements for Effective Data Mining 46
- III. DATA CHARACTERIZATION 47
  - A. Top-Down Data Characterization 48
  - B. Bottom-Up Data Characterization 64
  - C. Comparison of Top-Down and Bottom-Up Approaches 67
- IV. CLASSIFICATION TECHNIQUES 67
  - A. Decision Tree Induction 68
  - B. Artificial Neural Network-Based Classification 70
- V. ASSOCIATION RULE DISCOVERY 72
  - A. Definition of the Association Rule 72
  - B. Association Rule Discovery Algorithms 72
- VI. CONCLUDING REMARKS 74
  - REFERENCES 75

This chapter introduces the concept and various techniques of data mining. Data mining is defined as the nontrivial extraction of implicit, previously unknown, and potentially useful knowledge from a large volume of actual data. Various techniques including data characterization, classification, and association rule discovery are discussed. Especially, the treatment of fuzzy information in data characterization is explained in detail. Finally, the relationship between data mining and data warehousing is briefly addressed.

I. INTRODUCTION

A. Definition of Data Mining

According to the Oxford dictionary, "mining" means the activity of digging for useful mineral resources such as coal and ores from the ground. In the context of data mining, "mineral resources" and "the ground" are mapped into "knowledge" and "data," respectively. That is, data mining is the activity of exploring data for useful knowledge. Although there are several precise definitions of data mining in the recent literature, we adopt the definition as "the nontrivial extraction of implicit, previously unknown, and potentially useful knowledge from large volume of actual data" since it represents essential attributes of data mining comprehensively [1]. There are several terms in the literature to represent the same or similar area with data mining such as knowledge discovery in databases, data archeology, and data visualization, to name a few. However, we adopt the term, "data mining," in this chapter since it is the most common term in recent days.

One typical example of data mining might be as follows. After exploring sales records in a point-of-sales system for a large retail shop, a marketing manager may discover a fact such that "customers who purchase baby diapers are likely to purchase some bottles of beer." This example is famous among data mining practitioners, since it is an unpredictable knowledge before the data mining is actually performed. Who can expect the relationship between diapers and beer? However, once such a pattern is discovered in actual data, the marketing manager could exploit it for redesigning the self-layout and deciding a target customer list for advertisement of new products. He/she is very likely to achieve competitive advantages over others without such knowledge.

Let us examine each phrase of the definition in detail with counterexamples to get more concrete insight for data mining. Firstly, the phrase "implicit" means that information stored explicitly in the database or the system catalog is not the subject. The results for ordinary database queries and the schema information such as column names and data types are examples of explicit knowledge. Secondly, the phrase "previously unknown" means that we are not looking for well-known knowledge. Suppose we come to know that "most adult men are taller than five feet" by exploring the national health information records. It is rarely worth the effort of exploration since the information is common sense. Thirdly, "potentially useful" implies that the data mining process is driven by application requirement. The cost of data mining should be rewarded by the business benefit. The last phrase, "from a large volume of actual data," distinguishes data mining from experimental machine learning. Since data mining is performed on a large volume of data, it is hard to adopt such algorithms whose execution times increase fast as the data size grows. In addition, missing or corrupted values in actual data require a more sophisticated treatment of data.

B. Motivation of Data Mining

As a variety of disciplines including business automation, engineering support, and even scientific experiments have begun to rely on database systems, the advance of database system technology has become faster, and in turn, the volume of data stored in databases has increased rapidly in recent days. It has been estimated that the amount of information in the world doubles every 20 months, and the total number of databases in the world was estimated at five million in 1989. Earth observation satellites, planned for the 1990s, are expected to generate one terabyte of data every day and the federally funded Human Genomc project will store thousands of bytes for each of the several billion genetic bases. The census databases are also typical examples of a large amount of information [1]. As an example around our daily life, several millions of sales records in retail stores are produced every day.

What are we supposed to do with this flood of raw data? It is no longer helpful to make direct exposure of raw records to users. If it is be understood at all, it will have to be analyzed by computers. Although simple statistical techniques for data analyses were developed long ago, advanced techniques for intelligent data analyses are not yet mature. As a result there is a growing gap between data generation and data understanding [1]. At the same time, there is a growing realization and expectation that data, intelligently analyzed and presented, will be a valuable resource to be used for a competitive advantage [1].

The necessity of data mining capability is emphasized by this circumstance. A National Science Foundation workshop on the future of database research ranked data mining among the most promising research and engineering topics [2]. Decision support systems (DSS), executive information systems (EIS), and strategic information systems (SIS) are also typical examples that solicit knowledge through data mining techniques rather than scatter-brained, raw data chunks through simple SQL queries.

C. Comparison with Machine Learning

In the context of machine learning, there are four levels of learning situations as follows [3].

1. *Rote learning:* The environment provides the learning entity with how-to-do information precisely. Conventional procedural programs written in C language are typical examples. In such programs, the learning entity, i.e., the processor, is given step-by-step instructions to accomplish the goal. The learning entity does not have to infer anything. It just follows the instructions faithfully.

2. *Learning by being told:* The environment provides the learning entity with general information such as rules. For example, suppose that a rule is given as "if A is a parent of B, and B is a parent of C, then A is a grandparent of C." When there are facts such as "Tom is a parent of John" and "John is a parent of Mary," the learning environment is able to deduce a new fact that "Tom is a grandparent of Mary." Many expert systems and query processors for deductive databases have adopted this level of learning. This level of learning is also called deductive learning.

3. *Learning from examples:* The environment provides the learning entity with a set of detail facts. Then the learning entity has to infer general rules representing common properties in the set of given facts. For example, suppose that we have the facts such as "a pigeon can fly" and "a swallow can fly." From these facts, the learning entity can induce a rule that "a bird can fly" based on the knowledge that "a pigeon and a swallow are kinds of birds." Once the learning entity obtains the knowledge, it can utilize the knowledge to deduce new facts such as "a sparrow can fly." This level of learning is also called inductive learning.

4. *Learning from analogy:* The environment provides the learning entity with a set of facts and/or rules. When an unknown problem is given, the learning entity looks for known facts or rules similar to them. For example, the most effective treatment for a given patient is probably the treatment that resulted in the best outcomes for similar patients. This level of learning is also called memory-based reasoning (MBR).

The former two levels have been already well understood and exploited in actual applications. Most computer programs around us are primarily based on the first level, i.e., rote learning. Success stories about expert systems such as chemical analyses and medical diagnoses mostly belong to the second level of learning, i.e., deductive learning. However, the latter two levels have been at the stage of research activities and prototyping experiments.

Since data mining is the activity of learning patterns or general knowledge from a large volume of data, it can be regarded as a sort of the third level of machine learning, i.e., inductive learning. However, note that some data mining practitioners use the term, "data mining," in a broader meaning that includes most conventional data analysis techniques. For example, software packages for statistical hypothesis test and visual data analysis are often claimed as data mining tools. In this chapter, we limit the scope of data mining to the level of inductive learning in order to concentrate on the technical aspects of data mining.

Frawley *et al.* have distinguished data mining techniques from conventional inductive learning with respect to the input data to be explored [1]. It is summarized in Table 1.

While the learning data set for conventional inductive learning is typically predefined, the input data for data mining is apt to be dynamically changed. This difference raises both the possibility and challenge of incremental algorithms; i.e., algorithms take the changed portion of the data instead of the whole as their inputs. Actual databases are likely to include erroneous data, uncertain data, and missing data due to mistakes in database construction or genuine deficiency of information. Since data mining is performed on actual databases rather than test data sets, it must cope with such problems. It should be robust in noisy data while it should not miss important exceptions. Whereas test data sets are

TABLE I The Differences between Data Mining and Conventional Inductive Learning with Respect to the Characteristics of Input Data

Data mining	Conventional inductive learning
Dynamic data	Static data
Erroneous data	Error-free data
Uncertain data	Exact data
Missing data	No missing data
Coexistence with irrelevant data	Only relevant data
Immense size of data	Moderate size of data

collected carefully to contain only data relevant to the learning process, actual databases also include irrelevant data. Data mining techniques must identify relevant data before and/or in the middle of the learning process. Since data mining is performed on the immense size of data, it is unrealistic to directly apply inductive learning algorithms whose execution times increase fast as the data size grows.

In consequence, data mining can be regarded as the application of the inductive learning paradigm to an actual environment. Although many conventional inductive learning techniques such as classification and clustering can be adopted as starting points for data mining techniques, we must modify and supplement them for actual environment.

D. Steps of the Data Mining Process

Data mining techniques should be integrated into the business process in order to maximize its usefulness. The following six-step procedure is given for typical data mining processes. Although the procedure is not a panacea for all situations, it might be a helpful reference [4, 5].

1. *Identify the business problem*: As the first step, we must identify the business problem precisely, and define it in a formal manner. This is an essential gradient in data mining processes. Although it sounds intuitive and straightforward, it may not be in practice. Data mining for the sake of data mining itself is rarely successful.

2. *Prepare and transform the data to be explored*: There can be many internal and external sources of data for the data mining application. We must identify them and prepare access methods to them. In addition, we must transform the data to the proper format for the data mining application. It is seldom for them to be already in the proper format, since they are collected for their own operational purposes not for data mining.

3. *Apply specific data mining techniques*: We apply a specific data mining technique or a combination of several techniques on the prepared data.

4. *Act based on the obtained knowledge*: At this step, we exploit the obtained knowledge for our business problems. For example, customer purchase patterns can be used to plan an advertisement program for a new product.

5. *Measurement of the business benefit*: It is quite important to measure the business benefit that is gained from applying the knowledge.

6. *Assimilation of the knowledge*: Finally, we must incorporate the business insights gained so far into the organization's business and information systems.

It is quite interesting to note that the major effort for a data mining process is concentrated on the data preparation rather than the application of specific data mining techniques. It has been reported that the cost of data preparation is over 50% among the total process [5]. Actually, many data mining practices suffer from the difficulty of data preparation. However, we will concentrate on the third step, i.e., the application of specific data mining techniques, since other steps have many managerial aspects beyond the scope of this chapter.

II. OVERVIEW OF DATA MINING TECHNIQUES

A. Classification of Data Mining Techniques

Recently, there have been a large number of works on data mining in universities, research institutions, and commercial vendors. There are several criteria to classifying those works. The most common criterion is the type of knowledge to be obtained. According to the criterion, data mining techniques are classified into characterization, classification, clustering, association discovery, sequential pattern discovery, prediction, and so on.

Characterization is the activity of obtaining generalized descriptions to represent a large number of detail data records [6–9]. Classification is the activity of finding out rules to discriminate a group of objects from others [10–12], whereas clustering is grouping similar objects based on certain similarity measures [13, 14]. Association rules represent the co-occurrence tendency of multiple events [15, 16]. A rule such as "if an event A occurs, it is very likely for an event B to occur simultaneously" is an example of the association rule. The sequential pattern is a variation of the association rule, which considers relative orders of occurrence [17]. Prediction is the activity of interpolating or extrapolating an unknown value of interest based on known values. Linear regression is a typical example of prediction. To the best of our knowledge, there does not exist any notion of completeness for types of knowledge to be obtained. It means that it is quite possible to develop new types of knowledge according to the application requirements evolved continuously.

The other criteria for classification of data mining techniques can be types of input data. Even though many input data are stored in relational databases currently, useful data can reside in legacy file systems, object-oriented databases, object-relational databases, spatial databases, multimedia databases, Internet information-base, and so on. According to the type of input data, it may be required to differentiate data mining techniques. Especially, Internet information-base is regarded as the fruitful resource for data mining recently [18].

Meanwhile, since various techniques in several disciplines such as machine learning, statistics and database management are combined to provide data mining solutions, we can classify data mining techniques based on the types of adopted techniques. For example, techniques based on symbolic artificial intelligence are likely to produce human-understandable knowledge while neural network techniques may not.

B. Requirements for Effective Data Mining

When we design and utilize data mining techniques, we must consider the following requirements.

1. The technique should have sufficient efficiency and scalability: As we mentioned earlier, the input data of data mining is of immense size over hundreds of *giga*bytes in many cases. Thus, algorithms with exponential or high-order polynomial time complexity are seldom useful. Commonly, we try to achieve the time complexity to be linear or less than quadratic in the worst cases.

2. It is desirable to provide chances of user interaction in the middle of the process at various levels of abstraction: Since data mining is the activity of exploration, it is hard to expect the result before the exploration process. Thus, it is effective to allow the user interaction in the middle of the process in order to drill down or change the exploration focus.

3. It should handle various types of data in an integrated way: It is apt to have disparate sources of input data for the specific data mining. Thus, the technique should handle multiple types of data such as categorical data and continuous data in an integrated way.

4. It should be possible to measure the usefulness and the risk of the results: Since all the data mining results are not necessarily useful with respect to the application requirement, we should have proper measures of usefulness to distinguish better ones. In addition, some data mining results may include the degrees of genuine uncertainty. Careless adoption of uncertain results could come up with negative effects on the business operation. Thus, we should have proper measures of uncertainty to avoid it.

5. It should be possible to represent the results in understandable ways: The result of data mining activities is the subsequent input for the next step, i.e., business actions on the result. In many cases, business actions are performed by human entity. The data mining results need to have understandable forms.

6. It should consider the issue of data security: In many application domains, the result of data mining is highly sensitive to the security of the organization. For example, fraud detection techniques for credit card companies should be hidden for effective operations. In addition, likely to the cases of statistical databases, there are situations where individual information can be deduced from multiple aggregated information stuffs. It could violate the security policy of the organization.

III. DATA CHARACTERIZATION

Data characterization provides the user with comprehensive information for grasping the essence of a focused database portion in an understandable manner. It also establishes a starting point to make useful inferences from large collections of data, and facilitates easy communication of observations about the problem domain [8].

Informally, our definition of data characterization is a task that reduces a large number of actual database records into a relatively small number of generalized descriptions, i.e., generalized records. For example, a computer usage log table whose attribute scheme is (PROGRAM, USER, TIME), containing thousands of usage log records such as ⟨vi, John, 23:20⟩ and ⟨emacs, Tom, 23:31⟩, could be reduced into a few generalized records, say, ⟨editor, programmer, around midnight⟩. It delivers an assertion that programmers have executed editor programs around midnight.

In this section, we introduce two approaches for data characterization. One is top-down characterization [6, 7] and the other is bottom-up characterization [9]. The top-down approach introduced herein also accommodates fuzzy information. The bottom-up characterization is called attributed-oriented induction.

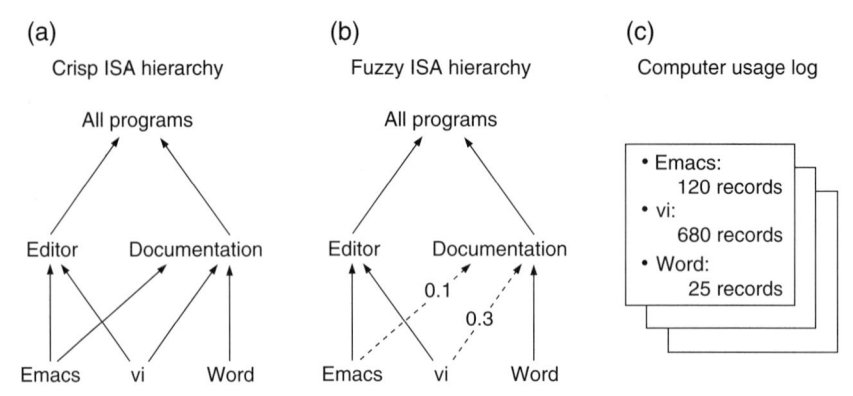

FIGURE 1 (a) and (b) show crisp and fuzzy ISA hierarchies: Dotted lines represent partial ISA relationships as strong as the augmented fraction numbers between two incident concept nodes, while solid lines denote complete ISA relationships. (c) depicts a situation where database summarization is to be done.

A. Top-Down Data Characterization[1]

Since data characterization can be regarded to summarize the content of a database, we use the terms "database summarization" and "data characterization" interchangeably herein. Among several requirements for effective data characterization techniques, we concentrate on the following ones: Firstly, it must be allowed to represent data characteristics in terms of fuzzy concepts, i.e., concepts with fuzzy boundaries, since crisp concepts are occasionally too restrictive to express complex situations [19, 20]. Secondly, it must be possible to utilize fuzzy domain knowledge, since actual domain knowledge is apt to include fuzziness inherently. Thirdly, users must be able to interact with a characterization process to reflect their own discovery purposes.

ISA hierarchies are commonly used to exploit "specialization" relationships among domain concepts. However, ISA hierarchies including only crisp ISA relationships are not sufficient to express actual domain knowledge. For example, suppose we know that programs "emacs" and "vi" are used to edit source codes, and a program word is used to write documents. In addition, suppose we also know that some users execute 'emacs' and 'vi' to write documents only on rare occasions. With only crisp relationships, there is no other way to represent the above-mentioned domain knowledge except as shown in Fig. 1a. If fuzzy relationships can be expressed, however, we would have an ISA hierarchy as shown in Fig. 1b.

Let us consider how different are the results these two ISA hierarchies yield, in data characterization. Suppose a computer usage log table during a certain period contains 120, 680, and 25 log records of "emacs," "vi," and "word" executions, respectively, as shown in Fig. 1c, and we want to determine whether "editor" or "documentation" programs are mainly executed in that period. With the crisp ISA hierarchy, we cannot identify the majority of usage since $120 + 680 = 800$ records are for "editor" programs, and $120 + 680 + 25 = 825$ records are for "documentation" programs. On the other hand, if we exploit

---

[1] Based on "Database Summarization Using Fuzzy Hierarchies" by Doheon Lee and Myoung Ho Kim, which appeared in IEEE Transactions on Systems, Man, and Cybernetics, vol. 27, no. 4, pp. 671–680 ©1997 IEEE.

the fuzzy ISA hierarchy, we can conclude that "editor" programs have been mostly executed, since 120 and 680 records of "emacs" and "vi," respectively, are known mainly for editing source codes not for writing documents.

1. Representation of the Database Summary

Herein, we define a generalized record as a representational form of a database summary, and elaborate how to evaluate the validity of a generalized record with respect to a given database. We assume that all attributes appear in a single table, i.e., the universal relation assumption, without loss of generality, to avoid unnecessary complexity of the presentation. However, this work can be applied to any other data models where a database record can be regarded as a series of attribute values.

a. Generalized Records

There are many domain concepts having fuzzy boundaries in practice. For example, it is difficult to draw a crisp boundary of documentation programs in a set of programs since some programs such as "vi" and "emacs" can be thought as source code editors for some programmers but as word processors for some manual writers. It is more natural and useful to express such domain concepts in terms of fuzzy sets rather than crisp sets [20]. Thus, we use a vector of fuzzy sets to effectively represent a database summary.

A fuzzy set f on a domain D is defined by its membership function $\mu_f(x)$, which assigns a fraction number between 0 and 1 as the membership degree to each domain value [19]. Since $\mu_f(x)$ represents the degree to which an element x belongs to a fuzzy set f, a conventional set is regarded as a special case of a fuzzy set whose membership degrees are either one or zero. Given two fuzzy sets, f_1 and f_2, on a domain D, f_1 is called a *subset* of f_2 and denoted as $f_1 \subseteq f_2$, iff $\forall x \in D, \mu_{f_1}(x) \leq \mu_{f_2}(x)$. In this paper, a special fuzzy set f such that $\forall x \in D, \mu_f(x) = 1$, is denoted as ω.

Definition 1 (Generalized Record). A *generalized record* is defined as an m-ary record $\langle f_1, \ldots, f_m \rangle$ on an attribute scheme $(A_1, \ldots, A_m)$, where f_j's are fuzzy sets and A_j's are attributes. Given two different generalized records $g_1 = \langle f_{11}, \ldots, f_{1m} \rangle$ and $g_2 = \langle f_{21}, \ldots, f_{2m} \rangle$, on the same attribute scheme, g_1 is called a *specialization* of g_2 iff $\forall_j, f_{1j} \subseteq f_{2j}$.

A generalized record $\langle f_1, \ldots, f_m \rangle$ on an attribute scheme $(A_1, \ldots, A_m)$ is interpreted as an assertion that "each record has $f_1, \ldots, f_m$ for attributes $A_1, \ldots, A_m$, respectively." Note that an ordinary database record is also regarded as a generalized record whose fuzzy sets are singleton sets. A singleton set is a set having a unique element. An example of a generalized record with respect to an attribute scheme (PROGRAM, USER) is ⟨editor programmer⟩. It implies an assertion that "the program is an editor and its user is a programmer"; in other words, "programmers have executed editor programs."

b. Validity of Generalized Records

From the viewpoint of inductive learning, a given database (or a part of it) and a set of possible generalized records are regarded as an instance space and a pattern space respectively [3]. Our summarization process searches a pattern space to choose valid generalized records with respect to a given instance space, i.e., a given database. Recall that the goal of database summarization is to generate representative descriptions embracing as many database records as possible. Thus, the validity of a generalized record is determined by the number of database records that are compatible, i.e., of statistical significance. In the following this notion is formulated as the support degree.

Definition 2 (Support Degree). The *support degree* of a generalized record $g = \langle f_1, \ldots, f_m \rangle$ with respect to a given collection of database records C whose attribute scheme is $(A_1, \ldots, A_m)$ is defined as

$$SD(g|C) = \left\{ \sum_{t_i \in C} \otimes [\mu_{f1}(t_1.A_1), \ldots, \mu_{fm}(t_1.A_m)] \right\} \Big/ |C|,$$

where $\otimes$ is T-norm operator [20]. $\mu_{fj}(t_i.A_j)$ denotes the membership degree of an attribute A_j of a record t_i with respect to a fuzzy set f_j, and $|C|$ denotes the cardinality of the collection C. We call generalized records with support degrees higher than a user-given threshold value *qualified generalized records*.

Note that we do not use the term, a set of database records or a database relation, because a collection of database records is allowed to have duplicates. We will denote $SD(g/C)$ as $SD(g)$ for simplicity as long as the data collection C is obvious in the context. T-norm operators are used to obtain conjunctive notions of membership degrees in the fuzzy set theory [20]. Examples include MIN and probabilistic product operators. Since the usage of T-norm operators in the fuzzy set theory is analogous with that of the product operator in the probability theory, the symbol $\otimes$, which is analogous with $\times$, is commonly used to denote a specific instance of a T-norm operator.

Since $\mu_{fj}(t_i.A_j)$ denotes the membership degree of an attribute A_j of a record t_i with respect to a fuzzy set f_j, a *T-norm* value over membership degrees of all attributes of a record t_i, i.e., $\otimes[\mu_{fi}(t_1.A_1), \ldots, \mu_{fm}(t_1.A_m)]$, represents how strongly the record t_i supports the assertion of a generalized record $\langle f_1, \ldots, f_m \rangle$. As a result, the support degree of a generalized record is the normalized sum of such support strength of individual database records. In other words, the support degree implies the fraction of supporting database records to the total data collection.

The defined support degree has the following properties:

- Boundary conditions:
  Given a generalized record g,
  — $0 \leq SD(g) \leq 1$.
  — If all fuzzy sets in g are ω, $SD(g) = 1$.
- Monotonicity:
  Given two generalized records, g_1 and g_2 on the same attribute scheme,
  $SD(g_1) \leq SD(g_2)$ if g_1 is a specialization of g_2.

While boundary conditions are self-evident by definition, the monotonicity property needs some explanation. The following theorem shows the monotonicity property.

Theorem 1 (Monotonicity of the support degree). Given two generalized records, $g_1 = \langle f_{11}, \ldots, f_{1m} \rangle$, and $g_2 = \langle f_{2l}, \ldots, f_{2m} \rangle$, on an attribute scheme

DATA MINING

TABLE 2 The Support Strength of Example Data Records

Record	A_1	A_2	$\mu_{f_1}(A_1)$	$\mu_{f_2}(A_2)$	t_i supports $\langle f_1, f_2 \rangle$ as strong as
t_1	a	α	1.0	0.3	$\otimes(1.0, 0.3) = 0.3$
t_2	b	β	0.1	1.0	$\otimes(0.1, 1.0) = 0.1$
t_3	c	α	0.1	0.3	$\otimes(0.1, 0.3) = 0.1$

$(A_1, \ldots, A_m)$,

$$SD(g_1) \leq SD(g_2) \quad \text{if } \forall j \in \{1, \ldots, m\},\ f_{1j} \subseteq f_{2j},$$

Proof. The premise of the theorem implies that $\forall j \in \{1, \ldots, m\}, [\forall x \in DOM(A_j), \mu_{f_{1j}}(x) \leq \mu_{f_{2j}}(x)]$, where $DOM(A_j)$ denotes the domain of an attribute A_j.

When a collection of database records is C,

$$SD(g_1) = \left\{ \sum_{t_1 \in C} \otimes_{j \in \{1,\ldots,m\}} [\mu_{f_{1j}}(t_i.A_j)] \right\} \Big/ |C|$$

$$\leq \left\{ \sum_{t_1 \in C} \otimes_{j \in \{1,\ldots,m\}} [\mu_{f_{2j}}(t_i.A_j)] \right\} \Big/ |C|, \text{ since}$$

$$\mu_{f_{1j}}(t_i.A_j) \leq \mu_{f_{2j}}(t_i.A_j) = SD(g_2).$$

Thus, $SD(g_1) \leq SD(g_2)$.

Let us look at an example of support degree computation. Suppose a generalized record g on an attribute scheme (A_1, A_2) is $\langle f_1, f_2 \rangle$, where fuzzy sets f_1 and f_2 are $\{1.0/a, 0.1/b\}$ and $\{0.3/\alpha, 1.0/\beta\}$, respectively. If a data collection C is given as Table 2, $SD(g)$ is computed as follows: The first record t_1 supports g as strong as 0.3, since its first and second attribute values, a and α, belong to fuzzy sets, f_1 and f_2, to the degrees, 1.0 and 0.3, respectively. Note that we use the MIN operator for the T-norm operation just for illustration throughout this paper. Similarly, both the second and third records support g as strong as 0.1. As a result, we can say that the generalized record g is supported by $0.3 + 0.1 + 0.1 = 0.5$ records out of a total of three records, i.e., 17% of the data collection.

2. Fuzzy Domain Knowledge

An ISA hierarchy is an acyclic digraph (N, A), where N and A are a set of concept nodes and a set of ISA arrows, respectively. If there is an ISA arrow from a concept node n_1 to another concept node n_2, we say that n_1 ISA n_2; in other words, n_1 is a specialized concept of n_2. While conventional ISA hierarchies have only crisp ISA arrows, fuzzy ISA hierarchies include fuzzy ISA arrows. The meaning of a fuzzy ISA arrow from n_1 to n_2 can be interpreted as n_1 is a partially specialized concept of n_2. Without loss of generality, we suppose that the root node of any fuzzy ISA hierarchy is the special fuzzy set ω, and each terminal node is a singleton set whose unique element is an atomic domain value, i.e., a value appearing in actual database records.

TABLE 3 Level-*k* Fuzzy Sets

Set label	Membership function	Level
engineering	{1.0/editor, 1.0/docu. 0.8/spread}	3
business	{1.0/docu, 1.0/spread}	3
editor	{1.0/emacs, 1.0/vi}	2
documentation	{0.1/emacs, 0.3/vi, 1.0/word}	2
spreadsheet	{0.1/word, 1.0/wright}	2
emacs	{1.0/emacs}	1
vi	{1.0/vi}	1
word	{1.0/word}	1
wright	{1.0/wright}	1

Fuzzy ISA hierarchies are too flexible of a structure to be used directly in database summarization. Thus, we provide a method to resolve a given fuzzy ISA hierarchy into a collection of fuzzy sets defined on the same domain, and a fuzzy set hierarchy that focuses on the complete inclusion relationships.

Definition 3 (Fuzzy Set Hierarchy). A *fuzzy set hierarchy* is a partially ordered set $(\Gamma, \subseteq)$, where Γ is a set of fuzzy sets defined on the domain D. The binary relation $\subseteq$ is the (complete) set inclusion relationship between two fuzzy sets. A fuzzy set f_1 is called a direct subset of another fuzzy set f_j if $f_i \subseteq f_j$ and there is no other f_k such as $f_i \subseteq f_k \subseteq f_j$.

Recall that a fuzzy set f_i is said to be (completely) included by a fuzzy set f_j in the same domain, if for each domain element x, $\mu_{f_i}(x) \le \mu_{f_j}(x)$.

a. Transforming a Fuzzy ISA Hierarchy to a Fuzzy Set Hierarchy

In fuzzy set theory [21], the elements of a fuzzy set can themselves be fuzzy sets, rather than atomic domain values. Ordinary fuzzy sets whose elements are atomic values are called level-1 fuzzy sets. Fuzzy sets whose elements are level-$(k-1)$ fuzzy sets are called level-k fuzzy sets. Table 3 depicts some level-k fuzzy sets. If two fuzzy sets have different levels, we cannot directly determine the inclusion relationship between them, since the domains are different. However, the level of a fuzzy set can be either upgraded or downgraded by some fuzzy set-theoretic treatments. Thus, if we want to determine the inclusion relationship between two fuzzy sets with different levels, we must adjust their levels to the same through upgrading or downgrading levels.

Upgrading the level of a fuzzy set is trivial, since a level-k fuzzy set can be simply rewritten as a level-$(k + 1)$ singleton set whose unique element is the original level-k fuzzy set. For example, a level-2 fuzzy set editor in Table 3 can be thought as a level-3 fuzzy set such as {1.0/editor}.

Downgrading the level of a fuzzy set is done by a support fuzzification technique based on the extension principle [20]. Rather than spending a large space to explain support fuzzification precisely, we will explain it by example. Interested readers are recommended to refer to Zadeh's orginal paper [22].

The transformation procedure of a fuzzy ISA hierarchy to a fuzzy set hierarchy is composed of three steps as follows:

1. Downgrade several levels of fuzzy sets in a fuzzy ISA hierarchy to level-1 fuzzy sets.

DATA MINING

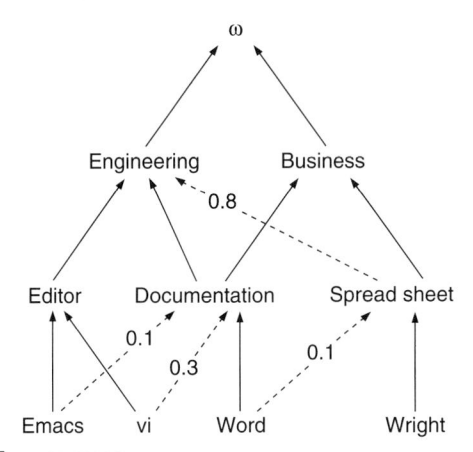

FIGURE 2 A fuzzy ISA hierarchy on computer programs.

2. By probing pairwise inclusion relationships, elicit partial order relation on those level-1 fuzzy sets obtained in the previous step.
3. Draw arrows between fuzzy sets and their direct subsets based on the partial order relation.

Let us demonstrate the transformation procedure step by step with an example. Figure 2 shows an example fuzzy ISA hierarchy on computer programs that could be used in computer usage analysis. Note that a fuzzy set f in a fuzzy ISA hierarchy is a level-k fuzzy set, if the maximal path length from f to terminal nodes is k-1. The several levels of fuzzy sets in the fuzzy ISA hierarchy of Fig. 2 are in Table 3.

In the first step, all level-k ($k > 1$) fuzzy sets are downgraded to level-1 fuzzy sets through support fuzzification. For example, a level-3 fuzzy set engineering in Table 3 is transformed to a level-2 fuzzy set as follows:

$$\begin{aligned}
\text{engineering} &= \{1.0/\text{editor}, 1.0/\text{documentation}, 0.8/\text{spreadsheet}\} \\
&= \{1.0/\{1.0/\text{emacs}, 1.0/\text{vi}\}, 1.0/\{0.1/\text{emacs}, 0.3/\text{vi}, 1.0/\text{word}\}, \\
&\quad 0.8/\{0.1/\text{word}, 1.0/\text{wright}\}\} \\
&= \{\otimes(1.0, 1.0)/\text{emacs}, \otimes(1.0, 1.0)/\text{vi}, \otimes(1.0, 0.1)/\text{emacs}, \\
&\quad \otimes(1.0, 0.3)/\text{vi}, \otimes(1.0, 1.0)/\text{word}, \otimes(0.8, 0.1)/\text{word}, \\
&\quad \otimes(0.8, 1.0)/\text{wright}\} \\
&= \{1.0/\text{emacs}, 1.0/\text{vi}, 0.1/\text{emacs}, 0.3/\text{vi}, 1.0/\text{word}, 0.1/\text{word}, \\
&\quad 0.8/\text{wright}\} \\
&= \{\oplus(1.0, 0.1)/\text{emacs}, \oplus(1.0, 0.3)/\text{vi}, \oplus(1.0, 0.1)/\text{word}, \\
&\quad 0.8/\text{wright}\} \\
&= \{1.0/\text{emacs}, 1.0/\text{vi}, 1.0/\text{word}, 0.8/\text{wright}\},
\end{aligned}$$

where $\otimes$ and $\oplus$ are a T-norm and a T-conorm operator, respectively. In contrast with T-norm operators, T-conorm operators are used to obtain disjunctive combinations of membership degrees. Herein, we use MIN and MAX for T-norm and T-conorm operations just for illustration. However, there are also several alternatives for T-conorm operators.

TABLE 4 Level-1 Fuzzy Sets Obtained through Support Fuzzification from Level-k ($k>1$) Fuzzy Sets

Value	editor	docu	spread	engi	busi	ω
emacs	1.0	0.1	0.0	1.0	0.1	1.0
vi	1.0	0.3	0.0	1.0	0.3	1.0
word	0.0	1.0	0.1	1.0	1.0	1.0
wright	0.0	0.0	1.0	0.8	1.0	1.0

Note. The leftmost column enumerates atomic domain values and other columns represent membership degrees of atomic domain values for the fuzzy sets listed in the first row.

To envisage the implication of support fuzzification, let us consider why the membership degree of the element word is determined as 1.0. Since documentation is a member of engineering, and word is a member of documentation, word is also regarded as a member of engineering. By this transitivity, the membership degree of word to engineering is determined as $\otimes(\mu_{engineering}(\text{documentation}), \mu_{documentation}(\text{word})) = \otimes(1.0, 1.0) = 1.0$. Meanwhile, the alternative transitivity that spreadsheet is a member of engineering, and word is a member of spreadsheet, also implies that word is regarded as a member of engineering. If we follow the latter transitivity, the membership degree of word to engineering is determined as $\otimes(\mu_{engineering}(\text{spreadsheet}), \mu_{spreadsheet}(\text{word})) = \otimes(0.8, 0.1) = 0.1$. Note that as far as either of such two transitivity relationships exists, i.e., the disjunctive combination of two facts, the membership of word to engineering holds. Thus, the membership degree of word to engineering is concluded as $\oplus(1.0, 0.1) = 1.0$.

Note that the elements, "emacs," "vi," "word," and "wright" appearing in the final line of the above formula are not atomic domain values. They are level-1 fuzzy sets as depicted in Table 3. That is, they can be rewritten as {1.0/emacs},{1.0/vi},{1.0/word}, and {1.0/wright}. If we downgrade again the obtained level-2 fuzzy set engineering to level-1, we have the same looking fuzzy set such as {1.0/emacs}, {1.0/vi}, {1.0/word}, and {0.8/wright}. However now, the elements are atomic domain values. The reason we treat the terminal nodes in a fuzzy ISA hierarchy as level-1 singleton sets rather than just atomic domain values is in order to achieve a unified representation of domain concepts and domain values. As a result of this first step, we have a collection of level-1 fuzzy sets as in Table 4.

In the second step, we compare the obtained level-1 fuzzy sets in a pairwise manner to probe the inclusion relationships. Finally, we draw arrows between fuzzy sets and their direct subsets based on the obtained partial order relation. Figure 3 depicts the fuzzy set hierarchy obtained.

3. Data Characterization Process

Now we present a process for discovering qualified generalized records based on given fuzzy domain knowledge, i.e., fuzzy set hierarchies. In short, our summary discovery process looks for qualified generalized records in a top-down manner. It initially hypothesizes the most generalized record, i.e., a generalized record whose fuzzy sets are all ω's. The process specializes the most

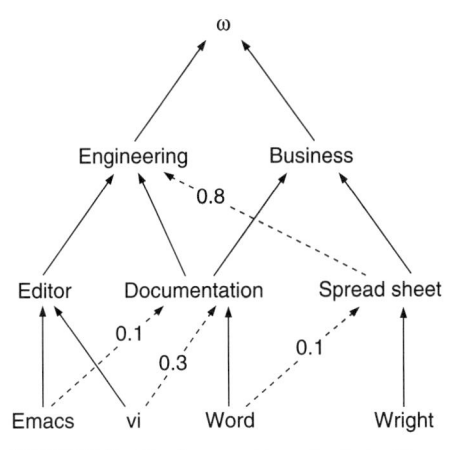

FIGURE 3 The fuzzy set hierarchy derived from a fuzzy ISA hierarchy.

generalized record, i.e., $\langle \omega, \ldots, \omega \rangle$, based on the given fuzzy set hierarchies to search for more specific generalized records while remaining qualified. The specialization is done minimally in the sense that only one fuzzy set is specialized into its direct subset. By evaluating support degrees of those specializations with respect to a given collection of database records, qualified generalized records are identified. At this point, human users can interact with the discovery process.

They might choose only some qualified generalized records for further consideration if they are not interested in the others or want to trade in the search completeness for reducing the search cost. The process minimally specializes again only user-chosen qualified generalized records. Those specializations become hypotheses for the next phase. After some repetitive steps of such specialization, the process yields a specialization hierarchy of qualified generalized records i.e., significant database summaries. Figure 4 diagrams the process, and Fig. 5 depicts the steps in detail.

Note that the monotonicity property of the support degree in Theorem 1 guarantees that any specializations of unqualified generalized records cannot be qualified, and as a result, the process never misses qualified generalized records, even though it does not specialize unqualified generalized records.

In Fig. 5, the support degree of each generalized record is computed from Line 5 to Line 7. This is the most time-consuming part of the process except the user interaction (Line 12), since the process must scan disks to read each database record. In Line 9, qualified generalized records with respect to τ are identified, and they are put into the result. After users choose only interesting generalized records in Line 12, they are minimally specialized in the sub-function specialize(). The process comes back to Line 4 with those specializations to repeat the steps.

Let us consider the efficiency of the process in terms of the number of disk accesses. Because it is hard to estimate how much time it takes to interact with human users, let us assume that users choose all qualified generalized records in Line 12 for the efficiency analysis. It is common to analyze the efficiency of most disk-based database applications in terms of disk access costs [23]. It is because the cost of disk accesses is much more expensive than that of in-memory

Cf. GR: generalized record

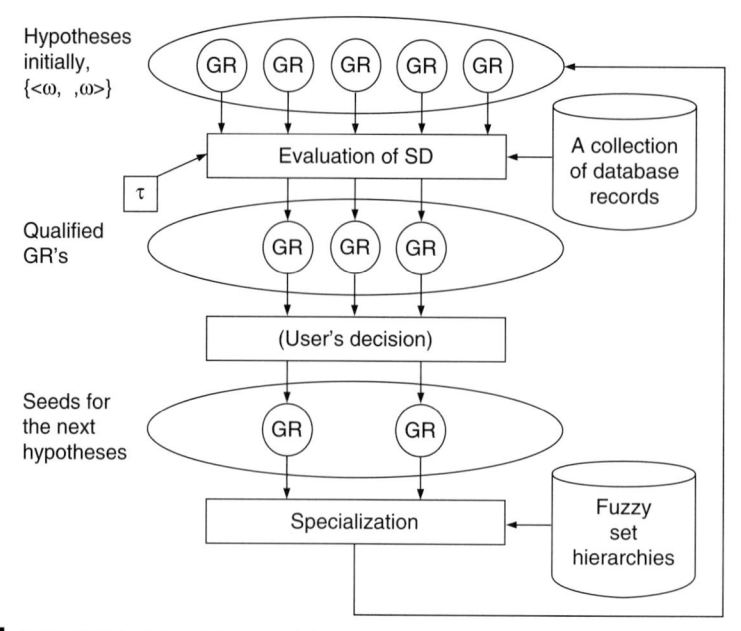

FIGURE 4 A brief diagram of the summary discovery process.

```
INPUT:
    (i) A collection of database records C.  (ii) fuzzy set hierarchies for attributes,
    (iii) a support degree threshold value τ
OUTPUT:
    A specialization hierarchy of qualified generalized records
(1)     SPGR()
(2)     {
(3)         result = Ø ; curr = { < ω , ..., ω > } ;
(4)         while(curr = Ø ){
(5)             for each t in C
(6)                 for each g in curr
(7)                     accumulate SD(g);
(8)             for each g in curr
(9)                 if SD(g) > r, then result = result U g,
(10)                else curr = curr – g;
(11)            for each g in curr {
(12)                if the USER marks g then specialize(curr,g);
(13)                curr = curr – g;
(14)            }
(15)        }
(16)    }

(17)    specialize (set, g = < a₁,..., aₘ >)
(18)    {
(19)        for i = 1 to m
(20)            for each direct subset saⱼ of aⱼ
                    (in the fuzzy set hierarchy for the jth attribute)
                        set = set U < a₁, ... ,saⱼ , ... aₘ >)
(22)    }
```

FIGURE 5 A specialization process of generalized records (SPGR).

operations. The disk access cost actually determines the efficiency of a process if the number of in-memory operations does not increase exponentially along with the input size, and no external network-based communication is involved.

The number of generalized records whose support degrees are evaluated in one specialization phase, i.e., the size of "curr" in Line 6, has nothing to do with the number of database records. Rather, it is determined by the average fan-outs of given fuzzy set hierarchies. Empirically, we expect that the system memory buffer space can hold all those generalized records in one specialization phase.

Then the total number of disk accesses is the number of specialization phases multiplied by the number of disk accesses to read database records in C. Let us denote the maximal path length of a fuzzy set hierarchy on the jth attribute as l_j. Since the specialization of generalized records are done attribute by attribute (see line 16 to 21), the number of specialization phases cannot be greater than $\sum_j (l_j)$. As a result, the number of disk accesses is no greater than $\sum_j (l_j) \times p$, where p denotes the number of disk pages containing the collection C of database records. Note that like the size of curr, $\sum_j (l_j)$ is also determined by given fuzzy set hierarchies not by the number of database records. Thus, we claim that the average cost of our summary discovery process increases linearly along with the number of database records in a collection if we ignore a human user's interaction.

Let us see the behavior of the algorithm with an example. Suppose that we have a collection of computer usage records whose attributes are PROGRAM and USER as shown in Table 5. Given fuzzy ISA hierarchies on attributes, PROGRAM and USER are supposed to be resolved to fuzzy sets in Table 6 and fuzzy set hierarchies in Fig. 6. The fuzzy sets in Table 6 are represented in the form of semantic relations [23]. Semantic relations represent several fuzzy sets on the same domain in the relational form. If the domain is a continuous

TABLE 5 An Example Collection of Computer Usage Records

Program	User	Program	User
emacs	John	emacs	Tom
vi	Tom	gcc	John
emacs	Tom	wright	Steve
vi	John	emacs	Jane
word	Kimberly	emacs	Mary
emacs	John	tetris	John
word	Mary	emacs	Jane
emacs	John	ultima	Mary
word	Kimberly	emacs	John
word	Kimberly	emacs	John
emacs	John	ultima	Mary
word	Mary	emacs	Jane
emacs	John	tetris	John
word	Kimberly	emacs	Mary
vi	John	emacs	Jane
emacs	Tom	wright	Steve
vi	Tom	gcc	John
emacs	John	emacs	Tom

TABLE 6 Semantic Relations Representing Fuzzy Sets in the Fuzzy Set Hierarchies

Value	compiler	editor	docu	spread	engi	busi	game	ω
			For PROGRAM_01					
gcc	1.0	0.0	0.0	0.0	1.0	0.0	0.0	1.0
cc	1.0	0.0	0.0	0.0	1.0	0.0	0.0	1.0
f77	1.0	0.0	0.0	0.0	1.0	0.0	0.0	1.0
emacs	0.0	1.0	0.1	0.0	1.0	0.1	0.0	1.0
vi	0.0	1.0	0.3	0.0	1.0	0.3	0.0	1.0
word	0.0	0.0	1.0	0.1	1.0	1.0	0.0	1.0
wright	0.0	0.0	0.0	1.0	0.0	1.0	0.0	1.0
tetris	0.0	0.0	0.0	0.0	0.0	0.0	1.0	1.0
ultima	0.0	0.0	0.0	0.0	0.0	0.0	1.0	1.0

Value	prog	writer	seller	account	develop	market	ω
			For USER_01				
John	1.0	0.0	0.0	0.0	1.0	0.0	1.0
Tom	1.0	0.0	0.0	0.0	1.0	0.0	1.0
Mary	0.2	0.8	0.0	0.0	1.0	0.8	1.0
Kimberly	0.0	1.0	0.1	0.0	1.0	1.0	1.0
Steve	0.0	0.0	1.0	0.0	0.0	1.0	1.0
Jane	0.0	0.0	0.4	1.0	0.0	1.0	1.0
Bob	0.0	0.0	0.0	1.0	0.0	1.0	1.0

interval, a semantic relation partitions the domain into disjoint subintervals and assigns a representative membership degree to each subinterval. Semantic relations are treated in the same way as ordinary database tables, and as a result, we do not have to deviate from the framework of conventional data models. Even though we adopt and recommend semantic relations as a proper representation of fuzzy sets for the benefit homogeneity, our discovery process is not tied to a specific fuzzy set representation in principle.

Figures 7 to 10 shows the behavior of the summary discovery process SPGR along with the specialization phases. The threshold value of support degrees is given as 0.4. Each figure corresponds to a single while loop in Fig. 5. In the first specialization, among six generalized records derivable from the root generalized record, only three depicted in Fig. 7 are qualified. If users are interested in the computer usage of developers, they would mark the middle one, i.e., ⟨-, developer⟩, for further consideration. By specializing the marked one and evaluating support degrees of derived hypotheses, the process yields qualified generalized records as shown in Fig. 8. Figures 9 and 10 show subsequent specializations.

From the final hierarchy of generalized records in Fig. 10, we can conclude that developers used engineering programs mostly. In particular, programmers have been using heavily executed editor programs.

4. Informativeness of Generalized Records

This section derives a measure for informativeness of generalized records based on Shannon's information theory [24]. Although the proposed data characterization process comes up with several qualified generalized records, the

PROGRAM_01

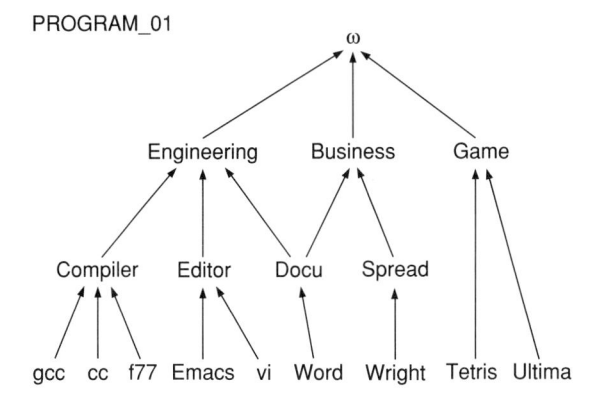

```
                    ω
                   ↗↑↖
        Engineering  Business   Game
           ↗↑         ↑↖          ↑
      Compiler Editor Docu Spread
       ↗↑↖    ↗↑↖     ↑    ↑      ↑
      gcc cc f77 Emacs vi Word Wright Tetris Ultima
```
cf. Doc: Documentation, Spread: Spreadsheet

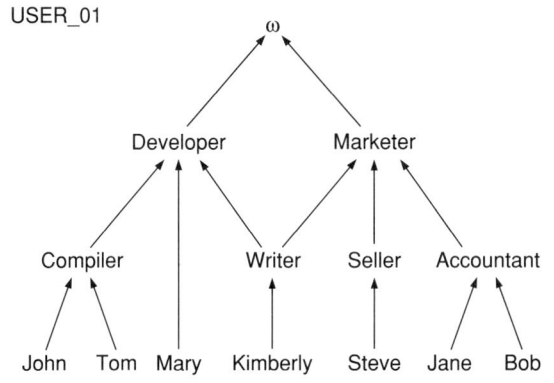

USER_01

```
                    ω
                   ↗↖
            Developer  Marketer
             ↗↑          ↑↖
       Compiler  Writer Seller Accountant
        ↗↑↖       ↑      ↑      ↗↖
       John Tom Mary Kimberly Steve Jane Bob
```

FIGURE 6 Fuzzy set hierarchies for PROGRAM and USER. As different users have different ISA relationships between domain concepts in mind, there can be several fuzzy set hierarchies for an attribute domain. Thus, we postfix "_number" to each fuzzy set hierarchy name to denote that it is chosen among several available ones.

quantity of information we can obtain from each generalized record may be different.

In the previous example, ⟨editor, programmer⟩ seems more informative than ⟨engineering, programmer⟩. The reason is that since a fuzzy set editor is more specific than a fuzzy set engineering, we have less uncertainty to figure out the original collection of database records from ⟨editor, programmer⟩ than from ⟨engineering, programmer⟩.

$\tau = 0.4$

```
              ⟨-, -⟩
              1.000
           ↙    ↓    ↘
⟨engineering, -⟩  ⟨-, developer⟩  ⟨-, marketer⟩
     0.833            0.833            0.411
```

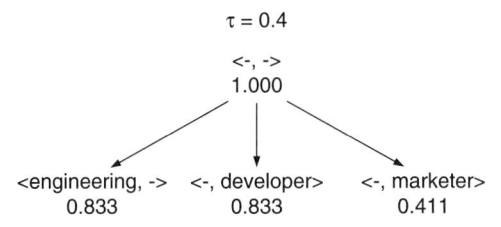

FIGURE 7 The first specialization of the root generalized record.

$\tau = 0.4$

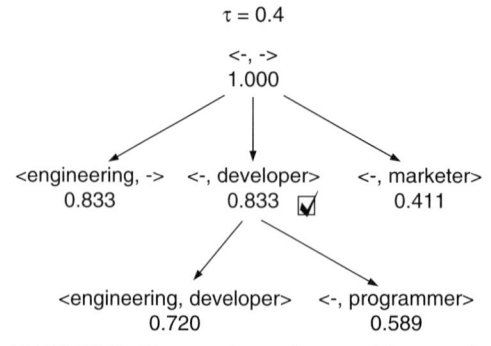

```
            <-, ->
            1.000
      ╱       ↓       ╲
<engineering,->  <-, developer>  <-, marketer>
   0.833          0.833 ☑         0.411
              ╱      ╲
   <engineering, developer>  <-, programmer>
          0.720                  0.589
```

FIGURE 8 The second specialization of the generalized records.

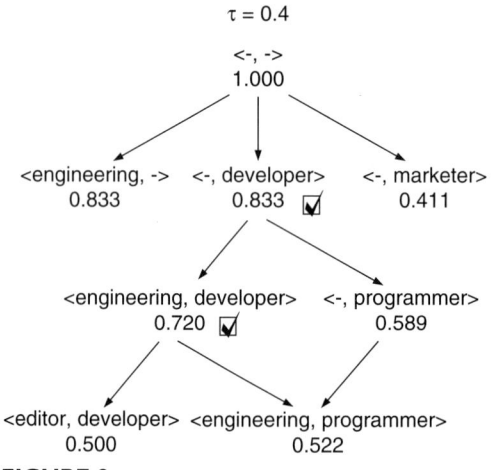

$\tau = 0.4$

```
            <-, ->
            1.000
      ╱       ↓       ╲
<engineering,->  <-, developer>  <-, marketer>
   0.833          0.833 ☑         0.411
              ╱      ╲
   <engineering, developer>  <-, programmer>
         0.720 ☑                  0.589
           ╱        ╲        ╱
  <editor, developer>  <engineering, programmer>
        0.500                  0.522
```

FIGURE 9 The third specialization of the generalized records.

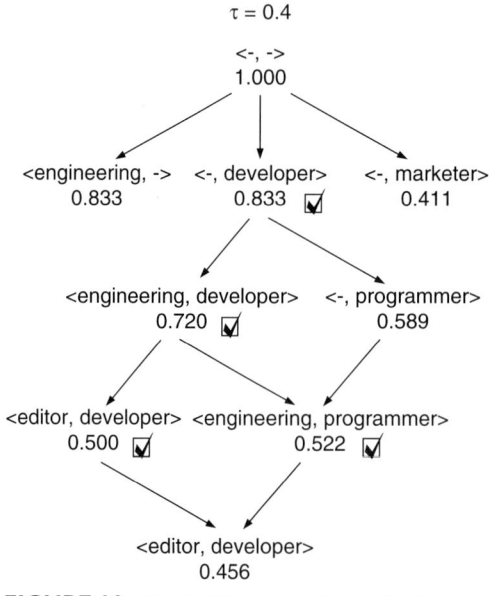

$\tau = 0.4$

```
            <-, ->
            1.000
      ╱       ↓       ╲
<engineering,->  <-, developer>  <-, marketer>
   0.833          0.833 ☑         0.411
              ╱      ╲
   <engineering, developer>  <-, programmer>
         0.720 ☑                  0.589
           ╱        ╲        ╱
  <editor, developer>  <engineering, programmer>
       0.500 ☑                0.522 ☑
             ╲            ╱
            <editor, developer>
                 0.456
```

FIGURE 10 The final hierarchy of generalized records.

Along with the specificity of generalized records, support degrees also affect the information values. For example, ⟨editor, programmer⟩ with the support degree 0.9 could be regarded as more informative than the same generalized record with the support degree 0.3. It is because the former seems to give information about 90% of the original collection of database records, while the latter seems to give information about only 30% of them. Strictly speaking, this argument alone may mislead. Both the specificity and the support degree should be considered simultaneously to obtain more exact information value as detailed in the following sections.

a. The Notion of Shannon's Entropy

In Shannon's information theory, the amount of information carried by a message is measured *as* the amount of uncertainty reduced by the existence or the occurrence of that message [24]. When there are n possible alternatives in the system on hand, Shannon's entropy measures the amount of uncertainty of the system as $\log_2 n$. If a message arrives, the number of alternatives might be reduced to m ($m \leq n$) owing to the information carried by the message. Then the amount of uncertainty is reduced to $\log_2 m$. In this situation, we say that the message reduces uncertainty; in other words, it delivers information as much as $\log_2 n - \log_2 m = \log_2 n/m$. This notion of Shannon's entropy is adopted to analyze how much information content a generalized record delivers.

Let us denote the set of all possible data collections on a given attribute scheme as $\Omega(\bullet)$, and a set of data collections on the same attribute scheme that make it possible for a qualified generalized record g to be discovered as $\Omega(g)$ ($\Omega(g) \subseteq \Omega(\bullet)$).

Then the amount of information that the generalized record g delivers is $\log_2\{|\Omega(\bullet)|/|\Omega(g)|\}$, where $|A|$ denotes the cardinality of a set A.

b. An Informativeness Measure for Generalized Records

Prior to deriving formulae for $\Omega(\bullet)$, $\Omega(g)$, and in turn $\log_2\{|\Omega(\bullet)|/|\Omega(g)|\}$, let us observe some characteristics of database summarization. Firstly, a data collection C for summarization can have *duplicates*. It holds even for relational database systems whose underlying data model represents a data collection as a relation. To justify this argument, let us consider an example. Suppose that a computer log relation has an attribute scheme such as ⟨PROGRAM, USER, TTY, DURATION, START_TIME⟩ as in the /var/adm/pacct file in the UNIX system and users want to obtain summaries on which users have executed which computer programs. They must project the relation onto those two attributes PROGRAM and USER before summarization. If duplicate records are eliminated after projection, unfit results may be obtained since several numbers of executions of a program by the same user look like just one execution in the duplicate eliminated table. Most of current relational database languages such as SQL permit duplicates in data tables [25].

Secondly, we assume that attribute dependencies such as functional dependencies and multivalued dependencies are not known in advance. Finally, we suppose that the cardinality or the range of each attribute domain is known. Note that the *support set* [20] of the fuzzy set ω on an attribute domain is equivalent to the attribute domain itself.

Now, we explain how to obtain $|\Omega(\bullet)|$ and $|\Omega(g)|$ in our context. Suppose that a given data collection C has an attribute scheme $(A_1, \ldots, A_m)$. Let $\Psi[j]$ denote the domain of the jth attribute. Then the set of all possible records that can be composed from the domains, denoted as Ψ, becomes $\Psi[1] \times \ldots \times \Psi[m]$, under the ignorance assumption of attribute dependencies. Consequently,

$$|\Omega(\bullet)| = |\Psi|^{|C|}, \qquad (1)$$

since duplicates in the data collection C are allowed.

With respect to a generalized record g, the given data collection C can be thought to being divided into two parts, denoted as C_g and $C_{g'}$. C_g is a set of database records supporting g, and $C_{g'}$ is its complement. Recall that the support degree implies the fraction of supporting database records to the total data collection, i.e., $|C_g|/|C|$. Thus,

$$|C_g| = |C|SD(g), |C_{g'}| = |C|(1-SD(g)). \qquad (2)$$

Also, Ψ can be thought as being divided into two parts denoted as Ψ_g and $\Psi_{g'}$, with respect to g. Ψ_g is a set of records consistent with a generalized record g, and $\Psi_{g'} = \Psi - \Psi_g$. If we define the coverage degree, CV, of a generalized record g as $|\Psi_g|/|\Psi|$, to measure the fraction of Ψ that is consistent with g, Ψ_g and $\Psi_{g'}$ can be written as

$$|\Psi_g| = |\Psi|CV(g), |\Psi_{g'}| = |\Psi|(1 - CV(g)), \qquad (3)$$

The coverage degree will be precisely defined in the next subsection. At the moment, let us assume that it is given from somewhere. It is obvious that the coverage degree of a generalized record is, by definition, greater than 0. Complete coverage degree, i.e., one, of a generalized record, implies that the generalized record is $\langle \omega, \ldots, \omega \rangle$. By definition, $\Omega(\langle \omega, \ldots, \omega \rangle)$ is the same as $\Omega(\bullet)$.

As depicted in Fig. 11, database records in C_g and $C_{g'}$ are thought to be selected from Ψ_g and $\Psi_{g'}$, respectively. Thus, we can formulate $|\Omega(g)|$ by (2)

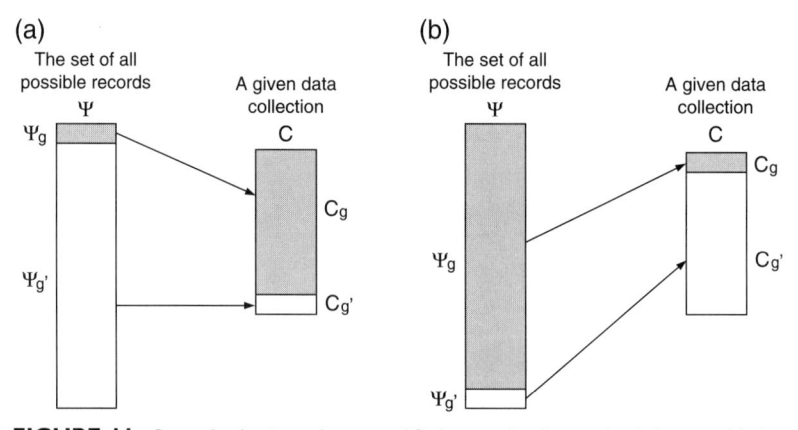

FIGURE 11 Record selection when a qualified generalized record g is known: (a) denotes a case where the coverage degree of g is very low but the support degree is high (low CV and high SD) and (b) denotes the opposite case (i.e., high CV and low SD).

and (3) as

$$|\Omega(g)| = |\Psi_g|^{|Cg|}|\Psi_{g'}|^{|Cg'|}$$
$$= |\Psi|CV(g)^{|C|SD(g)}|\Psi|(1-CV(g))^{|C|(1-SD(g))}, \quad (4)$$

when $0 < CV(g) < 1$. If $CV(g) = 1$ then $|\Omega(g)| = |\Omega(\bullet)|$.

As a result, the information content of a generalized record g is formulated as

$$INFO(g) = \log_2\{|\Omega(\bullet)|/|\Omega(g)|\}$$
$$= \log_2[|\Psi|^{|C|}/\{|\Psi|CV(g)^{|C|SD(g)}|\Psi|(1-CV(g))^{|C|(1-SD(g))}\}]$$

by (1) and (4)

$$= \log_2[1/\{CV(g)^{|C|SD(g)}(1-CV(g))^{|C|(1-SD(g))}\}], \quad (5)$$

when $0 < CV(g) < 1$. If $CV(g) = 1$ then $INFO(g) = \log_2 1 = 0$.

Let us observe the behavior of *INFO*. Figure 12 depicts the values of *INFO* with respect to *SD* and *CV*. There are two areas where informativeness becomes high. One area include cases where *CV* is low and *SD* is high (see the right peak in Fig. 12). It shows that a specific generalized record with a high support degree delivers much information, because low *CV* and high *SD* implies that most records (i.e., $|C|SD(g)$) in the original data collection *C* come from a small number of alternatives covered by the generalized record (i.e., $|\Psi|CV(g)$): see Fig. 11a.

The other area includes cases where *CV* is high and *SD* is low (see the left peak in Fig. 12). It shows that although the support degree is low, a generalized record can deliver much information if it is very nonspecific. As Fig. 11b shows, it is also informative since the fact of high *CV* and low *SD* implies that most records (i.e., $|C|(1-SD(g))$) in the data collection *C* come from a small number of alternatives not covered by the generalized record (i.e., $|\Psi|(1-CV(g))$).

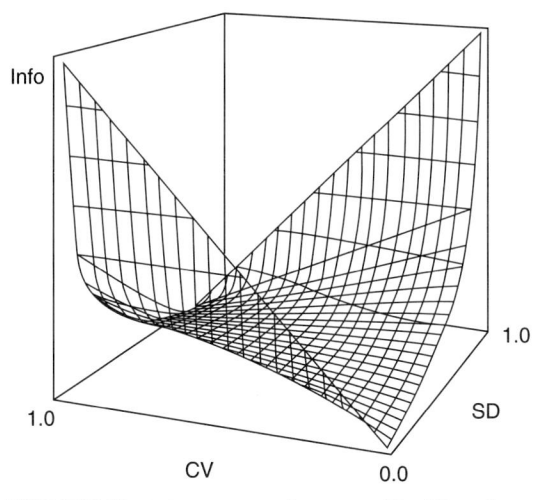

FIGURE 12 Informativeness for various SD–CV combinations.

c. The Coverage Degrees of Generalized Records

So far, we have assumed that the coverage degree of a generalized record is given from somewhere. Now let us consider how to actually obtain the coverage degree of a generalized record g.

Definition 4 (Coverage Degree). The *coverage degree* of a generalized record $g = \langle f_1, \ldots, f_m \rangle$ on an attribute scheme $(A_1, \ldots, A_m)$ is defined as

$$CV(g) = \left\{ \sum_{x_1 \in \Psi_1, \ldots, x_m \in \Psi_m} \otimes [\mu_{f_1}(x_1), \ldots, \mu_{f_m}(x_m)] \right\} \Big/ \{|\Psi_1| \times \ldots \times |\Psi_m|\}.$$

Note that by substituting $\sum$ operations by $\int$ operations, the formula can be adapted to the case where continuous domains of attributes are involved. Let us see an example of the coverage degree computation: Suppose that we are considering two generalized records on an attribute scheme having two attributes, and attribute domains are $\{a, b, c\}$ and $\{\alpha, \beta\}$ for the first and second attributes. Those two generalized records are given as

$g_1 = \langle f_{11}, f_{12} \rangle$, where $f_{11} = \{0.1/a, 1.0/b, 0.5/c\}$, $f_{12} = \{0.4/\alpha, 1.0/\beta\}$,

$g_2 = \langle f_{21}, f_{22} \rangle$, where $f_{21} = \{0.1/a, 1.0/b, 0.0/c\}$, $f_{22} = \{0.1/\alpha, 1.0/\beta\}$.

Then the coverage degrees of those generalized records are computed as follows:

$$|\Psi_1| \times |\Psi_2| = |\{a, b, c\}| \times |\{\alpha, \beta\}| = 3 \times 2 = 6 \tag{6}$$

$$\sum_{x_1 \in \Psi_1, x_2 \in \Psi_2} \otimes [\mu_{f_{11}}(x_1), \mu_{f_{12}}(x_2)]$$

$$= \otimes[\mu_{f_{11}}(a), \mu_{f_{12}}(\alpha)] + \otimes[\mu_{f_{11}}(a), \mu_{f_{12}}(\beta)] + \otimes[\mu_{f_{11}}(b), \mu_{f_{12}}(\alpha)]$$
$$+ \otimes[\mu_{f_{11}}(b), \mu_{f_{12}}(\beta)] + \otimes[\mu_{f_{11}}(c), \mu_{f_{12}}(\alpha)] + \otimes[\mu_{f_{11}}(c), \mu_{f_{12}}(\beta)]$$
$$= \otimes[0.1, 0.4] + \otimes[0.1, 1.0] + \otimes[1.0, 0.4]$$
$$+ \otimes[1.0, 1.0] + \otimes[0.5, 0.4] + \otimes[0.5, 1.0]$$
$$= 0.1 + 0.1 + 0.4 + 1.0 + 0.4 + 0.5$$
$$= 2.5. \tag{7}$$

Similarly,

$$\sum_{x_1 \in \Psi_1, x_2 \in \Psi_2} \otimes [\mu_{f_{21}}(x_1), \mu_{f_{22}}(x_2)] = 1.3. \tag{8}$$

By (6) and (7), $CV(g_1) = 2.5/6 = 0.42$, and by (6) and (8), $CV(g_2) = 1.3/6 = 0.22$. As a result, we can say that g_1 and g_2 cover the Ψ as much as 42 and 22%, respectively. Figure 13 depicts how those generalized records cover Ψ graphically.

B. Bottom-Up Data Characterization

DBLEARN adopts an attribute-oriented induction method to extract database summaries [9]. In its attribute-oriented induction, each attribute value of a

DATA MINING

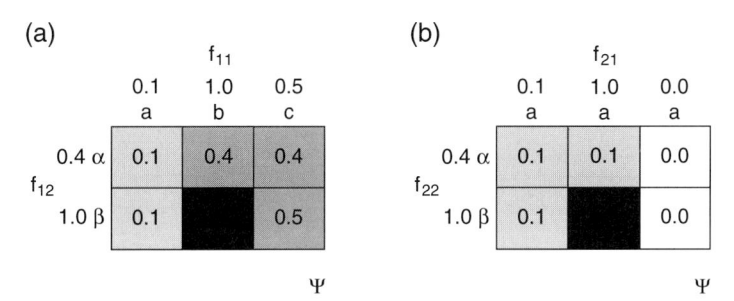

FIGURE 13 Coverage of generalized records: (a) is for $g_1 = \{f_{11}, f_{12}\}$, where $f_{11} = \{0.1/a, 1.0/b, 0.5/c\}$ and $f_{12} = \{0.4/\alpha, 1.0/\beta\}$. (b) is for $g_2 = \{f_{21}, f_{22}\}$, where $f_{21} = \{0.1/a, 1.0/b, 0.0/c\}$ and $f_{22} = \{0.1/\alpha, 1.0/\beta\}$. In each diagram, the whole six-block area represents Ψ_g, and the shaded area represents Ψ_{g1} (or Ψ_{g2}). The density of shade implies how completely the generalized record covers the corresponding area.

record is substituted with a more general concept. After one pass of the substitution, equivalent classes of generalized records are identified and each class is regarded as a candidate summary. This bottom-up procedure is repeated until satisfactory summaries are obtained.

Let us examine the procedure with an example. Suppose that we have a data table as in Table 7. Note that the last attribute, "Vote," is augmented to denote how many records are represented by the record. Initially, it is given as one for each record since only one record is represented by itself. In the process of summarization, the "Vote" value increases.

Also suppose that we have ISA hierarchies on the domains, "Major," "Birth Place," and "GPA" as in Fig. 14. Firstly, we remove the key attributes because it is meaningless to summarize such attributes. In Table 7, the first attribute, "Name," is removed since it is the key of the table. Each attribute value in the remaining table is substituted for its direct generalization in the given ISA hierarchies. This is called attribute-oriented substitution. After the first attribute-oriented substitution, we obtain the results in Table 8.

We can see the first and the fourth records are equivalent to each other. The second record is also the same as the third. Thus, each pair is merged into a single record as in Table 9.

Note that the "Vote" values for the first and second records in Table 9 are increased to 2. They represent that each of them represent two records in

TABLE 7 A Data Table, "STUDENT," To Be Summarized

Name	Major	Birth place	GPA	Vote
Lee	Music	Kwangju	3.4	1
Kim	Physics	Soonchun	3.9	1
Yoon	Math	Mokpo	3.7	1
Park	Painting	Yeosu	3.4	1
Choi	Computing	Taegu	3.8	1
Hong	Statistics	Suwon	3.2	1

Note. Each record represents a brief profile of a student.

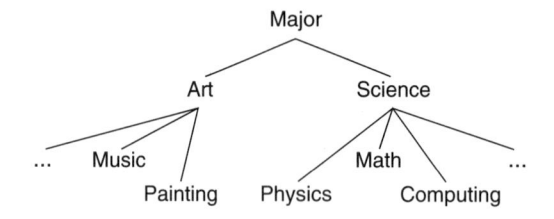

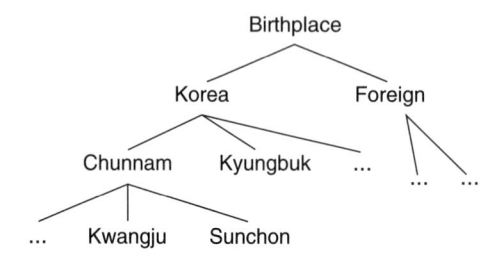

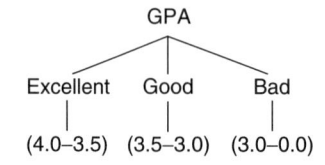

FIGURE 14 ISA hierarchies on the "Major," "Birth Place," and "GPA."

the original table. Commonly, users are interested only in records with high "Vote" values, since they represent the significant portions of the data table. Thus, the user must determine the acceptable minimum for the "Vote" values as the threshold value. If we determine the threshold value as 2 in this small example, the last two records should be removed from the result as in Table 10.

Since the data table contains small number of records and each ISA hierarchy has a few levels for simple illustration, there seldom remain more chances to summarize further. However, this substitution–merge process will be repeated several times in real situations where the data table has a large number of records and each ISA hierarchy has a significant number of levels.

TABLE 8 The Data Table, "STUDENT," after the First Application of Attribute-Oriented Substitution

Major	Birth place	GPA	Vote
Art	Chonnam	Good	1
Science	Chonnam	Excellent	1
Science	Chonnam	Excellent	1
Art	Chonnam	Good	1
Science	Kyungbuk	Excellent	1
Science	Kyunggi	Good	1

TABLE 9 The Data Table, "STUDENT," after Merging Redundant Records

Major	Birth place	GPA	Vote
Art	Chonnam	Good	2
Science	Chonnam	Excellent	2
Science	Kyungbuk	Excellent	1
Science	Kyunggi	Good	1

C. Comparison of Top-Down and Bottom-Up Approaches

This section has been devoted to introduce top-down and bottom-up approaches for data characterization. In the classification of inductive learning paradigms, the top-down approach belongs to the "model-driven generate-and-test" approach. Fuzzy set hierarchies given as the domain knowledge guide the learning process. The process generates hypothetical summaries and tests their validity over the given instance space. In addition, users can easily control the selection of search paths as well as the search depth. In actual database applications, where a great number of possible search paths exists, such kind of path control is quite useful.

Meanwhile, the bottom-up approach also has its own advantages. First of all, the size of data to be scanned is reduced as the characterization proceeds. Initially, the whole data records must be scanned. After each substitution–merge operation, several records are merged into a single reord, and some merged records are removed according to the given threshold value. Even though the size of original data set is very large, the size is reduced significantly after several steps of substitution–merge operations.

IV. CLASSIFICATION TECHNIQUES

Even though classification has been the well-known problem in machine learning, there still remain many areas to investigate in the context of data mining. It is due to the differences that the target database has much more records than the training set for machine learning algorithms, and the database also contains erroneous data and missing values.

Suppose that a marketing manager of a company is planning a direct mailing program to promote the sales of a new product. The company has already

TABLE 10 The Data Table, "STUDENT," after Removing Records with Low "Vote" Values

Major	Birth place	GPA	Vote
Art	Chonnam	Good	2
Science	Chonnam	Excellent	2

constructed the customer database containing the properties of each customer, such as address, gender, age, and job. It has been reported that the response ratio of direct mailing falls below 5% in most cases. It means that less than 5,000 customers purchase the new product in response to the direct mail when the company delivers 100,000 brochures for advertisement. If the expense of direct mailing is $1 per each customer, the total cost becomes $100,000. Thus, the marginal profit of each unit of sale must be over $200 for the direct mailing program to be regarded as beneficial since $100,000 ÷ 5,000 customers = $200/customer. Note that we do not consider extra expenses such as product delivery fee and sales employee salary for the sake of simplicity.

If the marketing manager can distinguish the customers who are likely to respond to the advertisement, the situation becomes quite different. As an extreme, if the manager can exactly identify in advance the 5,000 customers to purchase the product, it is still beneficial as long as the marginal profit of each unit of sale in the previous example is more than only $1. If the manager can identity the customers to purchase the product with 50% precision, he has to deliver only 10,000 brochures for advertisement for 5,000 units of sales. In this case, it is still beneficial as long as the marginal profit of each unit of sale is more than two dollars.

Classification techniques can remedy this situation. It means the activity of finding common properties of a given group of entities that distinguish them from other groups. In the previous example, the manager can determine through classification techniques common properties of those customers likely to purchase the product in terms of their addresses, gender, ages, jobs, and so on. Then he/she can choose the addresses of such customers from the whole customer database and deliver the advertisement brochures to them.

In the context of classification, a record consists of multiple descriptive attributes and its class label. The descriptive attributes represent several properties of each record, while the class label represents the class to which the record belongs. We need to have a training set consisting of preclassified records to build a specific classification facility. By being preclassified, we mean that the class label as well as descriptive attributes are already known. Once a classification facility is constructed, classification implies determining the class label of a new record that has only descriptive attributes. The goal is to devise a classification facility that will allow us effective and efficient classification. Effectiveness means how correctly the method classifies new records, and efficiency means how less classification cost is.

There have been several techniques for classification such as decision tree induction, artificial neural networks, and genetic algorithms. Each has its own relative advantages over and disadvantages against the others. Thus, it is important to understand them, and adopt proper techniques according to the application requirements.

A. Decision Tree Induction

A decision tree is a tree structure representing classification rules. Suppose that a database is given as in Table 11. The attributes A1, A2, and A3 of each record describe certain properties of each entity, and the final attribute C represents

TABLE II An Example Database for Classification

A1	A2	A3	C
a	d	k	1
a	e	r	2
b	f	m	3
b	g	o	3

the class label. From the table, a decision tree can be induced as in Fig. 15. Each node represented as a rectangle is called a decision node. The terminal nodes are called result nodes. The classification process begins from the root node. According to the decision in the decision node, the corresponding edge is followed to the next decision node. When the edge traversal reaches a terminal node, the classification result is obtained. For example, suppose that we have a new record ⟨a, e, k⟩ and that the decision tree classifies it into a class "2."

Note that given a database, there can be several decision trees. Thus, the issue of decision tree induction is how to construct an effective and efficient decision tree. Effectiveness means how correctly the decision tree classifies new records, and efficiency means how less the representation cost of the decision tree is. There are a variety of algorithms for constructing decision trees. Two of the most popular go by the acronyms CART and CHAID, which stand for "classification and regression trees" and "chi-squared automatic interaction detection," respectively. A newer algorithm C4.5 is gaining popularity and is now available in several software packages.

CART constructs a binary tree by splitting the records at each node according to a function of a single input field. The first task, therefore, is to decide which of the descriptive attributes makes the best splitter. The measure used to evaluate a potential splitter is "diversity." There are several ways of calculating the index of diversity for a set of records. With all of them, a high index of diversity indicates that the set contains an even distribution of classes, while a low index means that members of a single class predominate. The best splitter is the one that decreases the diversity of the record sets by the greatest amount.

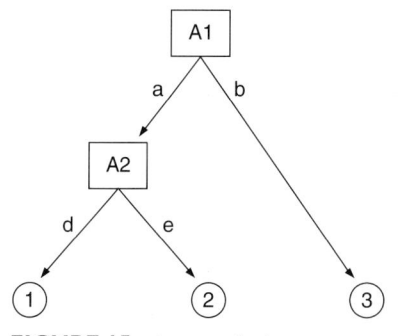

FIGURE 15 An example decision tree.

In other words, we want to maximize the value of the expression

diversity(the original set) − (diversity(the set in the left child)
+ diversity(the set in the right child)).

As the diversity function, several functions combining probability functions, logarithms, minimum operations, and so on have been introduced [4].

C4.5 is a descendent of the well-known classical decision tree induction method, ID3, which stands for "Iterative Dichotomiser 3" proposed by Quinlan and Rivest [10]. The primary difference between C4.5 and CART is that the former constructs m-ary trees rather than binary trees. Especially, when an attribute on a categorical domain is chosen as a splitter, C4.5 makes m-ary branches for them. The advantage of it is highly dependent on the domain of classification.

CHAID is the most widely used since it is distributed as part of popular statistics packages like SPSS and SAS. The largest difference between CHAID and the two decision tree induction algorithms that we have mentioned is that it attempts to stop growing the tree before overfitting occurs, rather than first overfitting the data, then pruning. Another difference is that CHAID is restricted to categorical variables. Continuous variables must be broken into ranges or replaced with classes such as high, low, medim [4].

The attractiveness of tree-based methods for classification is due in large part to the fact that, in contrast to artificial neural networks, decision trees represent rules in human-understandable form [4].

B. Artificial Neural Network-Based Classification

Artificial neural networks are computer programs whose behaviors imitate the human brain. It is known that the human brain consists of a great number of neurons [26, 27]. Transmission of electric signals among neurons causes complex brain activities such as decision and recognition. Artificial neural networks are also composed of artificial neurons that are actually parts of programs. Figure 16 depict a structure of an artificial neuron. Each input has its own weight. The left part of the neuron denoted as "$\sum$" is a combination function, which combines all the inputs into a single value. The weighted summation is commonly used as a combination function. The right part of the neuron denoted as "$\int$" is a transfer function, which calculates the output value from the result of the combination function. The output is exactly one value usually taken from 0 to 1.

Neurons are connected together to construct an artificial neural network. Figure 17 illustrates some types of artificial neural networks. An artificial neural

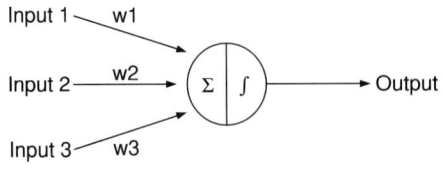

FIGURE 16 Structure of an artificial neuron.

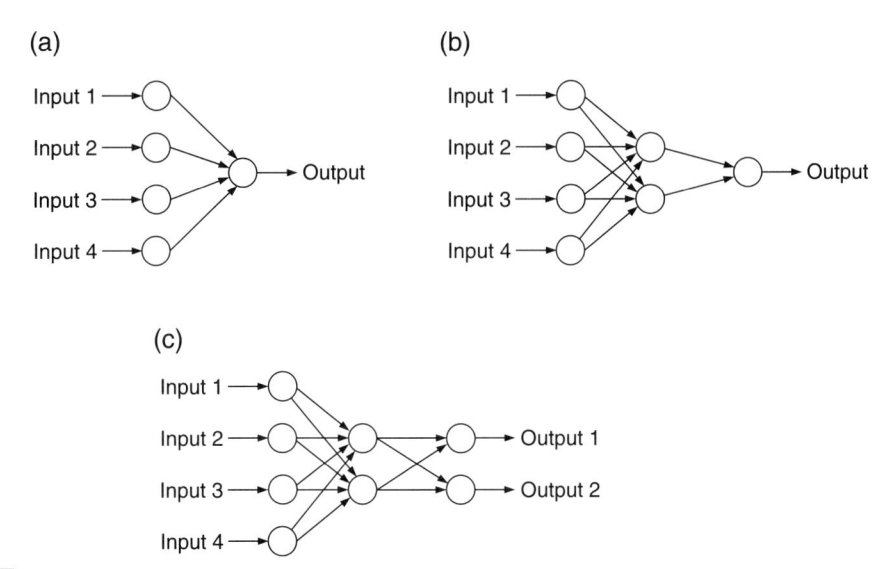

FIGURE 17 Several types of artificial neural networks: (a) a simple network, (b) a network with a hidden layer, and (c) a network with multiple outputs.

network commonly has three layers, input layer, ouput layer, and hidden layer. The first type (a) is a very simple neural network with only input and output layers. The second type (b) also has a hidden layer. The hidden layer makes the network more powerful by enabling it to recognize more patterns. The third type (c) can produce multiple output values.

Classification with artificial neural networks consists of the following steps. Firstly, we must identify the input and output features of records. Even though descriptive attributes become input features and the class label becomes the output feature, we must encode them so their range is between 0 and 1. In the second step, we must set up a network with an appropriate topology. For example, the number of neurons in the hidden layer must be determined. In the third step, it is required to train the network on a representative set of training examples. In the fourth step, it is common to test the performance of the network with a set of test data. Note that the test data must be strictly independent from the previous training data. If the result of the test is not acceptable, we must adjust the network topology and parameters. Lastly, we apply the network to classify new records.

The training step is one of the most important parts of neural network-based classification. Actually, it is the process of setting the best weights on the inputs of each neuron. So far the most common technique is back-propagation originally developed by Hopfield [26]. In back-propagation, after the network calculates the output using the existing weights in the network, it calculates the error, i.e., the difference between the calculated result and the expected. The error is fed back through the network and the weights are adjusted to minimize the error.

As compared to decision tree-based classification, artificial neural networks are reported much more powerfully especially in complicated domains. They incorporate nonlinear combinations of features into their results, not limiting themselves to rectangular regions of the solution space. In addition, it is also an advantage that artificial neural networks are already available in many off-the-shelf software packages.

However, the primary shortcoming of artificial neural networks is that they cannot explain results in a human-understandable way. The internal behavior of a network is regarded as a black box, and human users can examine only input and the corresponding output values. Furthermore, it is also regarded as the limitation that all inputs and outputs must be encoded as numbers between 0 and 1. This requires additional transforms and manipulations of the input data.

V. ASSOCIATION RULE DISCOVERY

An association rule implies the likelihood of co-occurrence of several events. Since it was first introduced [15], there have been many active research efforts in a variety of applications such as supermarket sales analysis, telephone network diagnosis, and Internet browsing pattern analysis [18].

A. Definition of the Association Rule

Given a set of events $I = \{i_1, i_2, \ldots, i_m\}$, an association rule $X => Y$ is defined, where X and Y are subsets of I. It is interpreted as "when events in X occur, events in Y are likely to occur simultaneously." When we have a transaction database, where each record, i.e., transaction, represents a set of events occurring simultaneously, we can evaluate the validity of a certain association rule twofold. Firstly, the support degree of an association rule, $X => Y$, indicates how much portion of the database contains the set of events in $X \cup Y$. In other words, it represents the statistical significance of the rule. Secondly, the confidence of an association rule, $X => Y$, indicates how many records also contain the set of events in Y among the records containing the set of events in X. It implies the strength of the rule. The goal is to determine association rules with high support degree and confidence with respect to a given transaction database.

B. Association Rule Discovery Algorithms

The first algorithm for association rule discovery is called Apriori [15]. Although there have been many variations of the algorithm to reduce the execution time or to enhance the functionality, we introduce Apriori herein since it shows the fundamental issues of association rule discovery effectively. Suppose that we have a transaction database as in Table 12.

The discovery of association rules is composed of two tasks. The first task is to determine the sets of events with high support degrees. We call those event sets with support degrees higher than a given threshold value frequent event sets. Once we have the frequent event sets, it is straightforward to elicit association rules with high confidence from them. Thus, most efforts for association rule discovery have focused on the first step.

DATA MINING

TABLE 12 An Example Transaction Database for Association Rule Discovery

Transaction ID	Events
101	A, C, D
102	B, C, E
103	A, B, C, E
104	B, E

Figure 18 depicts the first task on the database in Table 12 step by step. Suppose that the given threshold value for support degree is 40%. Firstly, by scanning the whole database, we produce event sets, each of which contains a single event. The result becomes C1. The attribute label as "Support" indicates how many transactions in the original database contain the corresponding event. Since the number of transactions in the database is four and the threshold value is 40%, the event set should have a "Support" of value more than 1. Thus, the fourth event set is removed as in L1. By combining event sets in L1, we produce event sets, each of which contains exactly two events. The result becomes C2. We count how many transactions in the database contain each event set by scanning the whole database again. The only event sets with a

C1

Event set	Support
{A}	2
{B}	3
{C}	3
{D}	1
{E}	3

L1

Event set	Support
{A}	2
{B}	3
{C}	3
{E}	3

C2

Event set	Support
{A,B}	1
{A,C}	2
{A,E}	1
{B,C}	2
{B,E}	3
{C,E}	2

L2

Event set	Support
{A,C}	2
{B,C}	2
{B,E}	3
{C,E}	2

C3

Event set	Support
{B,C,E}	2

L3

Event set	Support
{B,C,E}	2

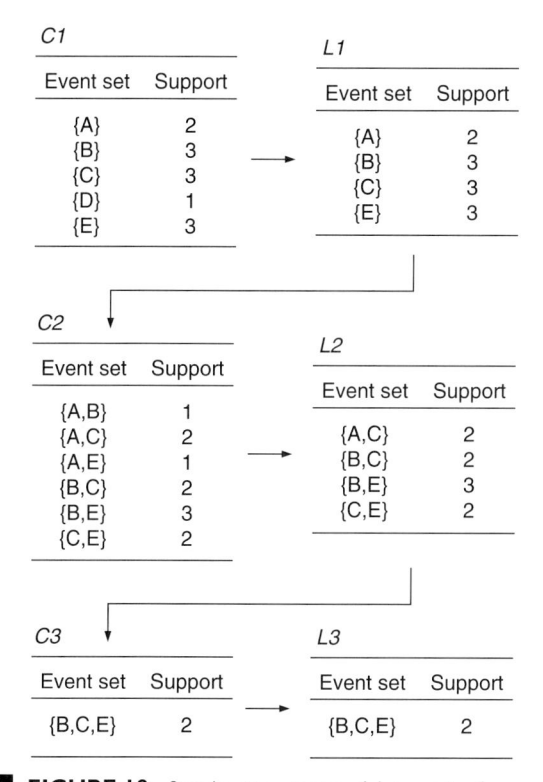

FIGURE 18 Step-by-step process of determining frequent event sets.

"Support" value more than 1 are preserved as in L2. Again, we produce event sets, each of which contains exactly three events by combining event sets in L2. It becomes C3. This process is repeated until no more operations are possible. In this example, we obtain frequent event sets as L1 ∪ L2 ∪ L3.

Let us examine the second task, i.e., eliciting association rules with high confidence in an instance. Since the "Support" values of the event sets {B, C, E} and {B, E} are 2 and 3 respectively, the confidence of the association rule {B, E} => {C} becomes 67%. It means that 67% of event sets also contain the event C among event sets containing B and E.

Several variations of the Apriori algorithm have tried to reduce the execution time by exploiting hashing, database partitioning, and so on [16, 30]. In addition, there are variations for discovering multilevel association rules. For example, it may be unnecessarily detailed to have an association rule such as "if a customer purchases a 160-ml Jones Milk (Product ID: 78-2456), then she is likely to purchase a 200-g Hayes Bread (Product ID: 79-4567)." Instead, it may be more useful just to know that milk customers are apt to also be bread customers. There have been several research efforts to devise effective algorithms to discover such generalized rules as well as detail ones [28–30].

VI. CONCLUDING REMARKS

This chapter has discussed several representative data mining techniques such as data characterization, classification, and association. In addition to the techniques discussed here, there are a lot of useful techniques such as clustering, sequential pattern discovery, and time series search. Likely to the SQL case where application demands lead to the development of new features, it is expected that new techniques will be continuously introduced according to the application requirements.

There have been many research projects and experimental or commercial systems for data mining. The QUEST project at IBM Almaden Research Center has investigated various data mining techniques including association rules [15]. IBM recently announced and began to deliver its data mining system, Intelligent Miner, whose theoretical background is strongly based on the QUEST project. Bell Laboratory has also developed IMACS (Intelligent Market Analysis and Classification System) [31]. The project emphasizes the aspect of human interaction in the data mining process, and suggests the term "data archeology" to express its data mining paradigm. GTE Laboratory has developed KDW (Knowledge Discovery Workbench), which incorporates a variety of data mining techniques in a unified framework [32]. Professor J. Han at Simon Fraser University in Canada has also been devoting active efforts to data mining. Recently, he announced DBMiner, GeoMiner, and WebMiner as a series of data mining systems [33, 34].

Meanwhile, there has come a new wave of information management called "data warehousing" in the information technology recently. Data warehousing is a large-scale project where a large volume of data is extracted from disparate sources of operational databases, and organized in the forms appropriate for enterprise-wide decision making. Figure 19 depicts the architecture of a data

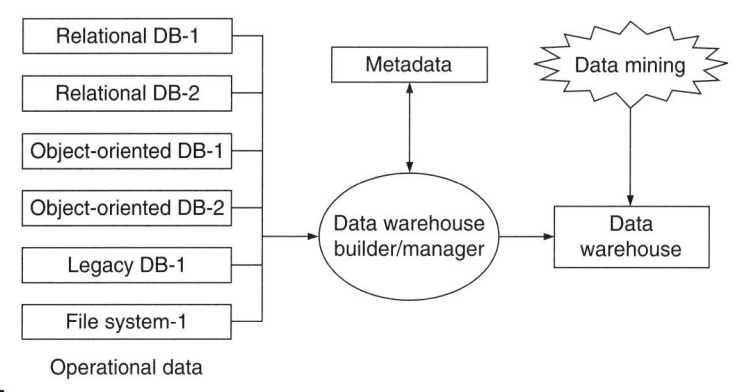

FIGURE 19 Architecture of a data warehousing system.

warehousing system. Since operational databases have been built for their own operational purposes, it is rare that their structures fit together in the enterprise-wide decision making. Furthermore, their schema are quite different to each other and some information is apt to be duplicated. A data warehouse builder must rearrange and adjust all the heterogeneity in the disparate data sources. When the content of a data source changes, it should be propagated to the data warehouse properly. It is under the responsibility of the data warehouse manager. Since Metadata represent the global schema information of the data warehouse, all queries on the data warehouse must refer to Metadata. Additionally, some systems adopt data marts, which are small-scale data warehouses for specific portions of the decision making.

As indicated in Fig. 19, data mining techniques can reveal their strength strongly in data warehousing systems since the data warehouse already contains proper data sources for valuable data mining. Although online analytical processing (OLAP) provides the querying interface for data warehouses currently, the application coverage of it is so limited. Thus, there have been active efforts for integrating data mining techniques and data warehousing systems.

REFERENCES

1. Frawley, W., Piatetsky-Shapiro, G., and Matheus, C. Knowledge discovery in databases: An overview. In *Knowledge Discovery in Databases,* pp. 1–27. AAAI Press, Menlo Park, CA, 1991.
2. Silberschatz, A., Stonebraker, M., and Ullman, J. Database systems: Achievement and opportunities. The Lagunita Report of the NSF Invitational Workshop, TR-90-22, Department of Computer Science, University of Texas at Austin, 1990.
3. Cohen, P., and Feigenbaum, E. *The Handbook of Artificial Intelligence,* Vol. 3, pp. 411–415. Kaufmann, Los Altos, CA, 1982.
4. Berry, M. J. A., and Linoff, G. *Data Mining Techniques: For Marketing, Sales, and Customer Support.* Wiley, New York, 1997.
5. Cabena, P., Hadjinian, P., Stadler, R., Verhees, J., and Zanasi, A. *Discovering Data Mining: From Concept to Implementation.* Prentice-Hall PTR, Englewood Cliffs, NJ, 1998.
6. Lee, D. H., and Kim, M. H. Discovering database summaries through refinements of fuzzy hypotheses. In *Proc. 10th Int'l Conf. on Data Engineering,* pp. 223–230, 1994.

7. Lee, D. H., and Kim, M. H. Database summarization using fuzzy ISA hierarchies. *IEEE Trans. Systems Man Cybernet.* **27**(4): 671–680, 1997.
8. Yager, R. On linguistic summaries of data. In *Knowledge Discovery in Database,* pp. 347–363. AAAI Press, Menlo Park, CA, 1991.
9. Han, J., Cai, Y., and Cercone, N. Knowledge discovery in databases: An attribute-oriented approach. In *Proc. of Int'l Conf. on Very Large Databases,* pp. 547–559, 1992.
10. Quinlan, J., and Rivest, R. Inferring decision trees using the minimum description length principle. *Inform. Comput.* **80**: 227–248, 1989.
11. Yasdi, R. Learning classification rules from database in the context of knowledge acquisition and representation, *IEEE Trans. Knowledge Data Eng.* **3**(3): 293–306, 1991.
12. Agrawal, R., Ghosh, S., Imielinski, T., Iyer, B., and Swami, A. An interval classifier for database mining applications. In *Proc. of Int'l Conf. on Very Large Databases,* Vancouver, Aug. 1992, pp. 207–216.
13. Ng, R., and Han, J. Efficient and effective clustering methods for spatial data mining. In *Proc. of Int'l Conf. on Very Large Databases,* pp. 144–155, 1994.
14. Xu, X., Ester, M., Kriegel, H.-P., and Sander, J. A distribution-based clustering algorithm for mining in large spatial databases. In *Proc. of Int'l Conf. on Data Engineering,* pp. 324–333, 1998.
15. Agrawal, R., Imielinski, T., and Swami, A. Mining associations between sets of items in massive databases. In *Proc. of ACM SIGMOD Conf.,* Washington D.C., May 1993.
16. Agrawal, R., and Srikant, R. Fast algorithms for mining association rules in large databases. In *Proc. of Int'l Conf. on Very Large Databases,* Santiago, Sep. 1994, pp. 487–499.
17. Agrawal, R., and Srikant, R. Mining sequential patterns. In *Proc. of Int'l Conf. on Data Engineering,* Taipei, Mar. 1995, pp. 3–14.
18. Chen, M.-S., Park, J. S., and Yu, P. S. Data mining for path traversal patterns in a web environment. In *Proc. ICDCS,* pp. 385–392, 1997.
19. Zadeh L. Fuzzy Sets. *Inform. Control* **8**: 338–353, 1965.
20. Zimmermann, H. *Fuzzy Set Theory and Its Applications.* Kluwer–Nijhoff, Dordrecht, 1985.
21. Klir, G. J., and Folger, T. A. *Fuzzy Sets, Uncertainty, and Information,* pp. 260–265. Prentice-Hall, Englewood Cliffs, NJ, 1988.
22. Zadeh, L. A fuzzy set theoretic interpretation of linguistic hedgese. *J. Cybernet.* **2**(2): 4–34, 1972.
23. Ullman, J. *Principle of Databases and Knowledge-Base Systems.* Computer Science Press, New York, 1988.
24. Shannon, C. The mathematical theory of communication. *Bell System Tech. J.* **27**: 379–423, 623–656, 1948.
25. ISO 9075: Information Processing Systems–Database Language SQL, 1992.
26. Bigus, J. *Data Mining with Neural Networks.* McGraw-Hill, New York, 1996.
27. Lu, H., Setiono, R., and Liu, H. NeuroRule: A connectionist approach to data mining. In *Proc. of Int'l Conf. on Very Large Databases,* Zurich, Sep. 1995, pp. 478–489.
28. Srikant, R., and Agrawal, R. Mining generalized association rules. In *Proc. of Int'l Conf. on Very Large Databases,* Zurich, Sep. 1995, pp. 407–419.
29. Han, J., and Fu, Y. Discovery of multiple-level association rules from large databases, In *Proc. of Int'l Conf. on Very Large Databases,* Zurich, Sep. 1995, pp. 420–431.
30. Park, J.-S. and Fu, Y. An efficient hash based algorithm for mining association rules In *Proc. of ACM SIGMOD Conf.,* pp. 175–186, 1995.
31. Brachman, R., and Halper, F. Knowledge representation support for data archeology. In *Proc. of Int'l Conference on Information and Knowledge Management,* pp. 457–464, 1992.
32. Piatetsky-Shapiro, G., and Matheus, C. Knowledge discovery workbench for exploring business databases. *Int. J. Intell. Syst.* **7**(7): 675–686, 1992.
33. Han, J., et al., DBMiner: A system for mining knowledge in large relational databases. In *Proc. of Int'l Conf. on Knowledge Discovery in Databases,* 1996.
34. Han, J. et al., GEOMiner: A system prototype for spatial data mining. In *Proc. of ACM SIGMOD Conf,* 1997.

3
OBJECT-ORIENTED DATABASE SYSTEMS

HIROSHI ISHIKAWA

Department of Electronics and Information Engineering, Tokyo Metropolitan University, Tokyo 192-0397, Japan

I. INTRODUCTION   77
II. FUNCTIONALITY   78
   A. Data Model   78
   B. Database Programming Language   81
III. IMPLEMENTATION   87
   A. Data Management Subsystem   88
   B. Object Management Subsystem   94
IV. APPLICATIONS   103
   A. Introduction   103
   B. System Architecture   105
   C. Our Approach to Implementation   109
   D. Conclusion   118
V. CONCLUSION   119
   REFERENCES   120

I. INTRODUCTION

Initially, complex, large-scale database applications such as CAD [15], hypermedia [14], and AI [11, 12] spawned object-oriented databases (OODBs). Moreover, OODBs have gone beyond them toward advanced applications such as networked multimedia applications [24]. In this paper, we describe how we designed and implemented an object-oriented DBMS called Jasmine [13, 15, 16, 18, 23]. (Note that Jasmine throughout this paper is not a product name but a prototype code name of Fujitsu Laboratories Ltd.) We also discuss how we applied Jasmine to advanced multimedia applications to verify its basic validity and how we extended Jasmine for such applications.

This paper has the following contributions. First, we focus on the impact of the design of its object-oriented model and language on database implementation technology. We describe what part of traditional relational database technology we extend to handle object-oriented features such as object identifiers, complex objects, class hierarchies, and methods. We introduce nested relations to efficiently store and access clustered complex objects. We use hash-based methods to efficiently access nonclustered complex objects. We provide user-defined functions directly evaluated on page buffers to efficiently process method invocation. We devise object-oriented optimization of queries including class hierarchies, complex objects, and method invocation. We incorporate dedicated object buffering to allow efficient access to objects through object identifiers. Second, we describe nontrivial applications of Jasmine in detail and discuss the validity of object-oriented databases. We focus on networked multimedia databases, which can be basically implemented by taking advantage of the extensibility of Jasmine. Further, we focus on how we extend Jasmine to implement its advanced facilities such as real time video play.

This paper is organized as follows. Section II describes the object model and the object manipulation language of Jasmine. Section III describes the implementation of Jasmine. Section IV discusses an object-oriented database approach to networked multimedia applications. Section V compares our system with other related work and gives concluding remarks.

II. FUNCTIONALITY

A. Data Model

In this section, we will briefly describe Jasmine's object model. (See [18] for the formal semantics.) Objects are a collection of attributes, which are categorized into properties (enumerated attributes) and methods (procedural attributes). Properties are object structures and methods are operations on objects. Objects are categorized into instances and classes. Instances denote individual data and classes denote types (i.e., structures) and operations applicable to instances of the class. Instances consist of a collection of attribute names and values. Classes consist of attribute names, definitions, and associated information such as demons. Objects are uniquely identified by values of the system-defined attribute object identifier (OID). On the other hand, values such as numbers and character strings have no OIDs but do have classes defined by the system. Objects with OIDs are called reference objects and values with no OIDs are called immediate objects. Objects can include other objects (i.e., OIDs) as attribute values. This enables the user to directly define complex objects (composite objects) [26], which supports aggregation directly.

Classes are organized into a hierarchy (more strictly, a lattice) by generalization relationships. This hierarchy is called a class hierarchy. Classes (i.e., subclasses) can inherit attribute definitions from their superclasses. The user can make instances (i.e., instantiate) from any class in a class hierarchy unlike Smalltalk-80 [9]. Such instances are called intrinsic instances of the class. Classes not only define object types and methods, but they are also interpreted as a set of instances, which supports classification. That is, the instances of a class is the union of all the intrinsic instances of itself and all its subclasses. This differentiates Jasmine from other OODBs such as GemStone [32] where the user must define separate classes both as type and as a set. Objects can have a set of objects as well as a singleton object as an attribute value. The former are called multiple-valued attributes and the latter single-valued attributes.

OBJECT-ORIENTED DATABASE SYSTEMS

Specialized functions called demons can be attached to attributes. Constraint demons are checked before values are inserted into attributes. The values are only inserted if the demon returns true. If-needed, if-added, if-removed, and if-updated demons are invoked when values are referenced, inserted, deleted, and replaced. Before and after demons are invoked before and after the procedural attributes they are attached to are invoked. The user can combine these demons to flexibly implement active databases [19, 33]. Unlike other systems, Jasmine allows the user both to specify system-defined integrity constraints, such as mandatory and multiple, and to specify user-defined integrity constraints as demons.

Consider the class PATIENT as an example (see Fig. 1). The keyword Enumerated is followed by the definition of user-supplied enumerated attributes. The name facet such as Doctor denotes the name of an attribute. The class facet before the attribute name denotes the range class such as FLOAT of Height. The value of the attribute of an instance must be an instance of the range class (see Fig. 2). The domain of the attribute is the class being defined, PATIENT. The multiple facet denotes that the attribute is multiple-valued such

```
PATIENT
    Db              MEDICAL
    Super           PERSON
    Enumerated      DOCTOR    Doctor mandatory
                              STRING Category default  outpatient
                              INTEGER Cardinality common
                              FLOAT Temperature multiple
                                    constraint {(value > 34.0 && value <43.0)}
                              FLOAT Weight mandatory constraint {(value > 0.0)}
                              FLOAT Height constraint {(value > 0.0)}
                    If-needed
                        { int h;
                          h = self.Weight;
                          return h + 100.0;}
    Procedural      MEDICAL_CERTIFICATE make-medical-certificate (date)
        STRING date;
    { MEDICAL_CERTIFICATE  mc;
            mc = <MEDICAL_CERTIFICATE>.instantiate ();
        mc.Patientname = self.Name;
        mc.Doctorname = self.Doctor.Name;
        mc.Diseasename = self.Disease.name;
        mc.Date = date;
        return mc;}
```

FIGURE 1 Example of class definition.

MedicalPatient007

    Sex   male

    Age   36

    Name   James Bond

    Address   Tokyo

    Doctor   MedicalDoctor010

    Category inpatient

    Temperature   37.5 37.3 38.1

    Weight   76.0

    Height   176.0

FIGURE 2 Example of an instance.

as Temperature. The mandatory facet denotes that the attribute allows no null value such as Doctor and Weight. The mandatory attribute must be specified its value at instantiation. The common facet denotes that the attribute value is common to all the instances as the domain objects. The common attribute is not necessarily a constant, such as Cardinality. The default facet contains a default value referenced when the attribute value is not yet specified, such as Category of PATIENT. The if-needed demon, invoked if the referenced attribute has a null value, computes a value such as Height of PATIENT. The keyword Procedural is followed by the definition of procedural attributes. Procedural attributes such as make-medical-certificate also have facets. The class facet such as MEDICAL_CERTIFICATE denotes the range class of the procedural result.

A superclass in a class hierarchy is denoted by the system-defined attribute Super. The superclass, for example, PERSON, includes its subclasses, PATIENT, as a set. The attributes of the superclass are inherited to the subclass, such as Age of PATIENT. An attribute can be newly defined in the subclass such as Doctor of PATIENT. Intrinsic instances of a nonleaf class can represent incomplete knowledge of the domain. For example, PERSON intrinsic instances directly denote a set of persons known to be neither a patient nor a doctor.

A class can be divided into disjoint subclasses (see Fig. 3). Those subclasses are collectively called a partition. Each subclass is called a member of

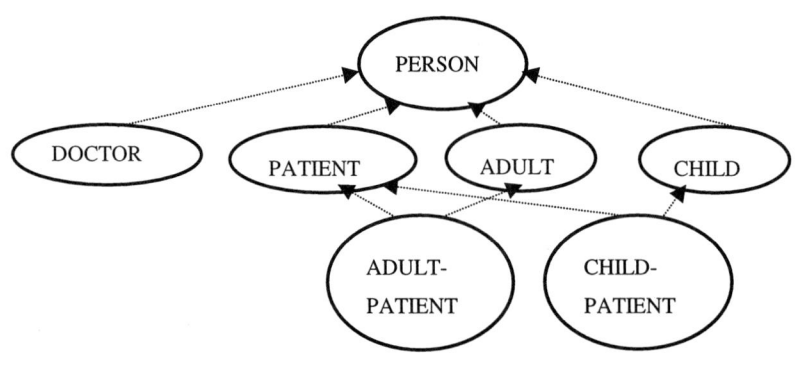

FIGURE 3 Example of a class lattice.

the partition. For example, PERSON has a partition consisting of DOCTOR and PATIENT. A partition denotes a categorization based on one viewpoint. Different viewpoints generate different partitions. PERSON has another partition of ADULT and CHILD. Members of distinctive partitions may not be disjoint, such as PATIENT and ADULT. Categorization conditions can be explicitly specified to make the partition semantics clear such as "Age <18" of CHILD. Then the attribute Age is called a categorization attribute. The categorization conditions are basically specified by a subset of the database programming language described in Section II.B. They can be used by the query optimization described in Section III.

Jasmine allows a class to have multiple superclasses. They must be nondisjoint members of different partitions of a class. For example, ADULT-PATIENT inherits Doctor from PATIENT and Occupation from ADULT (multiple inheritance [35]). Multiple superclasses sometimes have properties of the same name. We must resolve such conflicts. Assuming that the class of a property of a subclass should be either the class of or its subclass of the same property of a superclass, the rules are as follows: (1) A property with the most specific class is chosen if there is only one such property. (2) Otherwise, a property with the most specific class first found by a system-defined search (i.e., depth-first search) is chosen. (3) A property other than that determined by rule (1) or (2) can be chosen by explicitly specifying the superclass in the property definition if necessary.

B. Database Programming Language

This section describes an object manipulation language called Jasmine/C [18] as a database programming language which integrates a general-purpose programming language (C) and a database language in an object-oriented context, and which allows the user to program advanced applications. In Jasmine, the user manipulates objects by sending messages to objects just as in object-oriented programming languages. This type of access is called singleton access or individual access. The user can assign values to attributes and reference attribute values. Jasmine allows set-oriented access in addition to singleton access. Set-oriented access is done by a query on objects. The query language of Jasmine has the following features different from those of SQL [3]. The semantics can be formally defined through query translation by object operators as described in [18].

The basic unit of a query expression consisting of target and condition parts is an object expression, a class name followed by a series of attribute names. The target part is an object expression, or a list of object expressions. The condition part consists of a logical combination of predicates which compare object expressions. A query on a class returns all the instances of the class and its subclasses, so the user can retrieve by a single Jasmine query what would take multiple relational database queries to retrieve. The object expressions denote object joins. The object expressions can also contain methods, so the user can manipulate objects set-theoretically and filter a set of objects procedurally. If a superclass is specified with a method in a query, methods dedicated to instances of the class and its subclasses can be invoked simultaneously. This facilitates polymorphism [35] in a set-oriented manner. The system-defined methods such as put and delete specified in a query can modify a set of objects. A query can invoke demons which implement integrity facilities introduced by QBE [38]. The user can specify multiple-valued attributes in a query. The user can control unnesting of multiple values and apply aggregate functions correctly. Multiple-valued attributes are existentially or universally quantified.

The integration of query and programming facilities is another important feature for advanced applications. First, the user can specify methods in a query as described above. The user can extend the functionality of the query language just by defining and specifying a method in a query, without modifying the query language processor. The user can develop application programs more compactly without specifying details such as iteration variable declaration and control structures. Making this type of iteration implicit can increase physical data independence [3] of application programs by allowing the system to optimize the query expression. Second, the user can also define methods by specifying a query for them. This can define so-called virtual attributes and increase logical data independence [3] of application programs when applications evolve. Third, the fact that the user invokes a query from programs is one of the salient aspects of advanced applications. We introduce set variables to solve the impedance mismatch problem [3] between the query and programming languages. The set variable has a class defined by an object model as its type and can contain a set of objects returned by a query as its value. The user can fetch an object by sending the scan message to the set variable and operate on the object by sending a message to the object in an object-oriented programming manner.

Class objects can also be operated set-theoretically for advanced applications. Basic database functions such as transactions, locking, and logging can be provided through system-defined classes. Multimedia data types and operations are provided by implementing them from system-defined primitive classes in a bootstrap manner.

Now we describe the syntax and semantics of a query through examples. The query has the syntax

"["object_expression(s)"]" [where condition] [groupby object_expression(s)],

where the object expression has the form class_name ["." attribute_name ["." attribute_name]...].

The query expression evaluates to a set of the target objects satisfying the condition. The elements of the constructed set are objects (OIDs), or values belonging to the database, or newly constructed tuple values. The result type is determined by the query. For example, to find the name and address of outpatients, the user forms a query as

(Query 1) [PATIENT.Name, PATIENT.Address]
where PATIENT.Category == "outpatient".

The tuple operator "[ ]" allows the construction of tuple values, corresponding either to the projection or to the join of relations. Like this example, the query corresponds to projection only if the target list has the form

[common_object_expression.attribute1, common_object_expression.attribute2, ...].

OBJECT-ORIENTED DATABASE SYSTEMS

Immediate objects are compared by ==, !=, >, >=, <, and <=, based on values.

In general, joins are categorized into implicit and explicit joins. Jasmine supports implicit joins as

(Query 2) PATIENT.Doctor.Name where PATIENT.Name == "James Bond".

This finds the name of doctors who are in charge of James Bond. The operator "[ ]" can be omitted only if the target list contains only one object expression. Assuming that C is a class and Ai is an attribute and Oi is an object, an implicit join denoted by an object expression $C.A1. \ldots An$ has the following semantics:

{ $On | O0$ belongs to C and for all $i = 1, \ldots, n$, either of the following holds:

(1) Oi is equal to Ai of Oi-1 if Ai is single-valued
(2) Oi belongs to Ai of Oi-1 if Ai is multiple-valued}.

Nested sets generated by multiple-valued attributes are automatically flattened unless the user prohibits that. Jasmine can also support explicit joins as

(Query 3) [PATIENT.Name, DOCTOR.Name] where
PATIENT.Age == DOCTOR.Age.

This retrieves pairs of names of patients and doctors who happen to be of the same age. "[ ]" in this case corresponds to join. Reference objects can also be compared by == and != based on OIDs. For example, assume Disease and Specialty are reference attributes (see Fig. 4):

(Query 4) [PATIENT.Name, DOCTOR.Name] where
PATIENT.Disease == DOCTOR.Specialty.

This query finds the names of patients and doctors who specialize in their disease.

The object expression with multiple-valued attributes evaluates to a set of sets. However, multiple-valued attributes are automatically unnested unless the user specifies the prohibition of unnesting by a special operator described later. Therefore, the following query retrieves a flattened set of temperatures of serious patients:

(Query 5) PATIENT.Temperature where PATIENT.Condition == "serious"

A condition on multiple-valued attributes is interpreted as at least one value satisfying the condition, that is, existentially. Universally quantified multiple

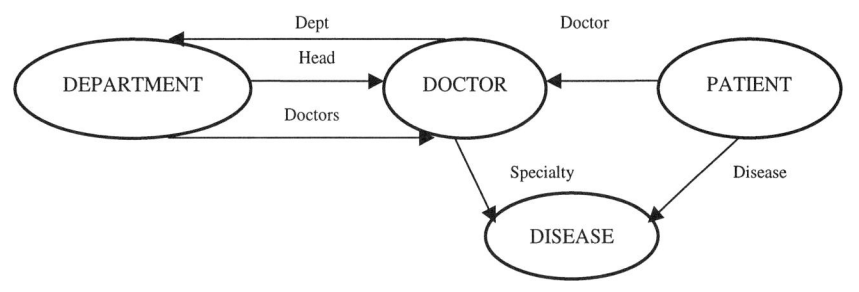

FIGURE 4 Part of a medical database structure.

attributes can also be specified as described later. The following retrieves the names of patients who ran a temperature of higher than 37.5°C at least once:

(Query 6) PATIENT.Name where PATIENT.Temperature >37.5.

Any class, leaf or nonleaf, in a generalization lattice can be specified in a set-oriented query. According to the interpretation of a class, the intrinsic instances of a nonleaf class and the instances of its subclasses can be retrieved at the same time. For example, to find persons who live in Kyoto:

(Query 7) PERSON where PERSON.Address == "Kyoto".

This causes a query be specified compactly because several queries against subclasses such as PATIENT and DOCTOR can be formulated in a single query.

Objects can be retrieved without precise specification since a general class can be specified in a query together with an attribute defined in its subclasses. In general, assuming that C and C' are classes and A is an attribute, C is systematically translated into C' in a query only if the following set is not empty: $\{C'|C'$ is a subclass of C and A is defined or inherited by $C'\}$. The original query usually generates multiple queries. Note that Query 7 is a special case where A (e.g., Address) is defined or inherited by all classes in a class hierarchy with C (e.g., PERSON) as its top. For example, to find the names of persons whose disease is a cancer:

(Query 8) PERSON.Name where PERSON.Disease.Name == "cancer"

The class PERSON is automatically specialized to the subclass PATIENT with the attribute Disease defined. In the extreme case, OBJECT can be used in a query. This mechanism fits with how we defined some concepts by differentiating a general concept by providing specializing attributes. The user can thus formulate a query without knowing specificity like a natural language query.

A condition can be imposed on the categorization attribute of a general class with a partition. If the specified condition matches some of the categorization conditions of the partition, the specified class can be specialized to some of the partition members. In general, assuming that C and C' are classes, C is systematically translated into C' only if the following set is not empty: $\{C'|C'$ is a subclass of C and the condition of a query and the categorization condition of C' are not exclusive $\}$. For example, to find infants (i.e., younger than seven):

(Query 9) PERSON where PERSON.Age <7

The class PERSON is automatically specialized to CHILD with its categorization condition Age <18.

The user can do operations other than retrieval set-theoretically by using procedural attributes, which can be specified in any part of an object expression of a query. The additional parameters of the procedural attribute are given in parentheses. In general, the object expression has the following form: receiver.method (parameter, parameter, ...). A receiver is an object expression and a parameter is an object expression, an object, or a value. The result is also an object, a value, or a set of objects or values. For example, to make and print a copy of serious patients' medical certificates dated February 11, 1999, the user formulates the query

(Query 10) PATIENT.make-medical-certificate("19990211").print()
where PATIENT.Condition == "serious".

If we operate on objects set-theoretically in a setting other than Jasmine, we then must retrieve a set of objects and scan and operate on each object in an iteration construct. In contrast, Jasmine makes this type of iteration implicit and iteration variable declaration unnecessary and allows the user to compactly specify a query without knowing the details.

We can also specify procedural attributes in incomplete knowledge access. If we specify a general class whose subclasses have procedural attributes of the same interface which have different implementations, the different attributes are invoked in a single query at the same time. In general, assuming that C and C' are classes and M is a method, C is systematically translated into C' only if the following set is not empty: $\{C'|C'$ is a subclass of C and M is defined or inherited by $C'\}$. M has a different implementation, depending on C', so this realizes polymorphism in a set-oriented manner. For example, to display all heterogeneous media objects belonging to James Bond, such as X-ray and CT, the user specifies the query

(Query 11) MEDIA.display() where MEDIA.Patient.Name == "James Bond".

Both system-defined and user-defined procedural attributes can be specified in the same way unlike other systems such as [6]. The system-defined procedural attributes include print and object modification operations such as put, replace, delete, and destroy. Of course, they can be invoked in a set-oriented query. In other words, the user can extend the query language without changing the parser or the code generator. For example, the following query adds 38.0°C to James' temperature (multiple-valued attribute):

(Query 12) PATIENT.put("Temperature", 38.0)
where PATIENT.Name == "James Bond".

Attributes taking a set of objects and giving a singleton, called aggregate functions, can be specified in a set-oriented query. They include the system-defined attributes such as count, average, sum, max, and min. Since a set in our context allows duplication of objects, the user can use the aggregate functions naturally. For example, to find the number of outpatients who are under 7 years of age, the user forms a query as

(Query 13) PATIENT.count() where PATIENT.Age <7
and PATIENT.Category =="outpatient".

The following query finds the average of the ages of inpatients:

(Query 14) PATIENT.Age.average() where PATIENT.Category == "inpatient".

In general, the aggregate functions take as input the whole flattened set retrieved just before the function evaluation. This can cause subtle problems when the user applies the aggregate functions to the multiple-valued attribute. Assuming that the attribute Temperature is multiple-valued, consider the following:

(Query 15) PATIENT.Temperature.average() where
PATIENT.Category == "inpatient".

This evaluates to the average of an automatically normalized set of objects as the values of Temperature of more than one inpatient. Therefore, if the user wants to apply the average to Temperature values of each PATIENT object, the user specifies a special operator "{}" to prohibit automatic unnesting of multiple-valued attributes as

(Query 16) PATIENT.{Temperature}.average() where
PATIENT.Category == "inpatient".

Multiple-valued attributes can be universally quantified by specifying "All" before comparison operators. The following query retrieves the names of patients whose temperatures are all over 37.5 in contrast to Query 6.

(Query 17) PATIENT.Name where PATIENT.{Temperature} All > 37.5.

Grouping is allowed. The following calculates average temperatures for each group of inpatients of the same age:

(Query 18) PATIENT.Temperature.Average() where
PATIENT.Category =="inpatient" groupby PATIENT.Age.

Procedural attributes can also be specified in object expressions in the condition part of a query to filter objects procedurally. This is powerful in a variety of applications. A content-based search of multimedia data can be done by defining an attribute such as like. The following finds a patient whose X-ray looks like sample-1 containing some disease although content-based multimedia retrieval will be discussed in Section IV in detail:

(Query 19) X-ray.Patient where X-ray.like(sample-1) == true.

Usually the syntactically same object expressions in a query have the same semantics. However, making aliases of object expressions is possible anywhere in a query by qualifying them if necessary, for example, to do self-join. The following query retrieves pairs of patients who suffer from the same disease. Note that the second condition eliminates duplication:

(Query 20) [P1:PATIENT, P2: PATIENT] where P1: PATIENT.Disease == P2: PATIENT.Disease and P1: PATIENT.Id < P2: PATIENT.Id.

Now we can define the semantics of a query by using the semantics of object expressions defined earlier. First, the condition part is evaluated as follows: If simple conditions comparing object expressions are evaluated to be true, based on the values of the object expressions, the Boolean combination of them is evaluated in the usual way. If the result is true, we then evaluate the target part and we get a tuple of objects or values as a query result.

It is necessary to individually access a set of retrieved objects in application programs. To this end, we introduce a variable that can be bound to a set of objects. The variable is called a set variable. The set variable is usually set to the result of a set-oriented query. The user can access objects one by one by scanning the set variable. The instance variable is also introduced to hold a singleton. The instance variable holds a single object like usual variables in a conventional programming language. The instance variable and set variable constitute the object variable. The object variable integrates set-oriented access of a database system and singleton access of a programming language. The existence of a multiple option at declaration specifies that the object variable is a set variable. For example,

PATIENT *ps* multiple, *p*;

ps and *p* are declared as set variable and instance variable of PATIENT type. In general, the set variable is set to the result set of a set-oriented query at the right-hand side of a statement. The user can access objects individually by using the system-defined procedural attributes as

ps = PATIENT where PATIENT.Diseasee == "cancer";
ps.openscan();
while (*p* = *ps*.next())
    {...}
ps.closescan();

The procedural attribute next returns an object at each invocation, which is set to the instance variable *p* for further use.

Procedural attributes can include set-oriented queries. The following attribute of the class DEPARTMENT defines interns who work in a department:

Procedural DOCTOR intern() multiple
    { self.Doctor where self.Doctor.Status =="internship" }.

This can be specified in a query to retrieve interns in the pediatrics department as

DEPARTMENT.intern() where DEPARTMENT.Name == "pediatrics".

We do not provide a special syntax for nesting queries. Instead, nested queries can be simulated by procedural attributes defined by queries like the above example. Correlated queries can be formulated explicitly by passing object expressions as parameters to the procedural attributes or implicitly through the system-defined variable self.

III. IMPLEMENTATION

Relational databases have already accumulated large amounts of implementation technology. We don't think that it is clever to throw it away and to build object-oriented databases from scratch. Relational technology provides basically applicable techniques such as storage structures, access methods, query optimization, transaction and buffer management, and concurrency control. Therefore, we take a layered architecture consisting of object management and data management and use relational technology as data management (see Fig. 5). However, traditional relational technology has limitations in efficient support for object-oriented concepts including object identifiers, complex objects, class hierarchies, and methods. We extend relational technology to overcome such limitations. In addition to flat relations, we incorporate nested relations to efficiently store and access clustered complex objects. We support

```
                    ┌─────────┐    ┌──────────────┐
                    │  Users  │    │ Applications │
                    └────┬────┘    └──────┬───────┘
                         │                │
                    ┌────┴────────────────┴───┐
                    │    Object Management    │
                    └────────────┬────────────┘
                                 │
                    ┌────────────┴────────────┐
                    │     Data Management     │
                    └────────────┬────────────┘
                                 │
                           ╭───────────╮
                           │ Databases │
                           ╰───────────╯
```

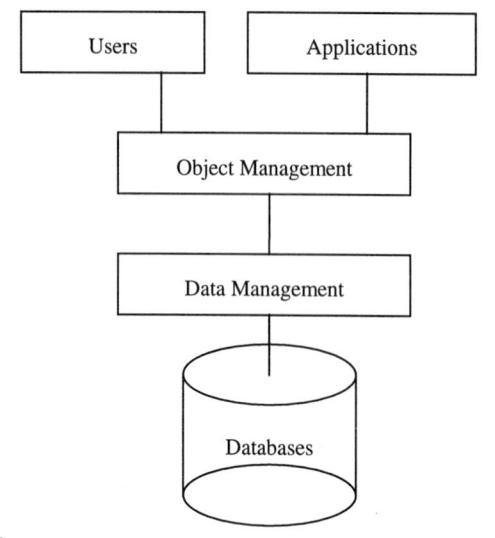

FIGURE 5 System architecture.

both hash and B-tree indexes to efficiently access objects through object identifiers. In addition to a nested-loop join and a sort-merge join, we provide a hash join to efficiently process nonclustered complex objects in queries. We extend query optimization to process object-oriented queries including class hierarchies and method invocation. Note that such optimization is done not by the data management subsystem but by the object management subsystem. We provide user-defined manipulation and predicate functions directly evaluated on page buffers. Methods are compiled into them and efficiently processed. We devise object buffering in addition to page buffering and integrate these two schemes to evaluate queries. In a word, our approach is to provide an object-oriented model and language interface to an extensible database kernel [37], such as GENESIS [1] and EXODUS [2].

Of course, there are alternatives to our extended relational approach to object-oriented database implementation. A pure relational approach such as Iris [31] has drawbacks as described above. Another approach uses WiSS (Wisconsin Storage System) such as O2 [5], which provides record-based, single-relation operators. This makes it difficult for us to focus on query optimizations based on set-oriented relational operators. In the extreme case, monolithic architectures could be considered in contrast to our layered approach. This would be less flexible to further tuning and extension. In this section, we will explain the function and implementation of the data management subsystem, and storage of objects and implementation of the object manipulation language.

A. Data Management Subsystem

1. Data Structures

Advanced applications of OODBs require a variety of indexes such as hash and B-tree indexes, clustered and nonclustered indexes, and extended data dictionaries. Such indexes and data dictionaries are usually implemented as special data structures in relational database systems because of access efficiency. The conventional approach using special data structures makes the system less compact and less flexible to future extension. So the data management subsystem as a database kernel supports only relations (sequential, B-tree, hash, and inner relations) to allow the user of this subsystem to customize data dictionaries and indexes by using relations.

Only fixed-length and variable-length data are supported as field types of tuples by the data management subsystem. The data management subsystem makes no interpretation of field values except for TIDs and inner relations. Any type of data can be stored such as an array, a list, and a relation. Inner relations can be implemented as variable-length fields. Inner relations can have other inner relations as field values, so nested relations can be recursively defined. The length of a tuple must be less than the page size for efficient access and simple implementation. The length and number of fields in a tuple are subject to this limit.

The data management subsystem supports four types of relations as follows:

1. Sequential relations have pages that are sequentially linked. Tuples are stored in the order of insertion. The location of inserted tuples is fixed, so an index can be created on sequential relations.

2. B-tree relations have B-tree structures. Tuples are stored in the leaf pages in the order specified by user-defined order functions. This allows new access methods to be assimilated by supplying dedicated comparison and range functions. B-tree relations consist of key fields and nonkey fields. B-tree relations used as an index on sequential relations consist of several key fields and one TID field. This corresponds to a nonclustered index. B-tree relations that contain the whole data can be viewed as relations with a clustered index.

3. Hash relations use a dynamic hashing scheme called linear hashing with partial expansion [30], an extension to linear hashing. We choose this scheme because the space required to store data is proportional to the amount of data and the space utilization ratio is adjustable and high. Hash relations also consist of key fields and nonkey fields. The hash function is supplied by the user.

4. Inner relations for realizing nested relations are stored in variable-length fields of tuples. Tuples of inner relations are sequentially inserted. Nested relations can be recursively implemented by storing inner relations into fields of another inner relation. We provide nest and unnest operations for nested relations in addition to retrieval, insertion, deletion, and update. Retrieved inner relations can be operated as sequential relations. Update of inner relations can be done by retrieving inner relations, updating them as sequential relations, and replacing old ones by new ones. We provide the functions interpreting the variable-length fields according to the nested relation schemes to operate on inner relations. Note that a theoretical basis for the nested relational model was provided by Kitagawa and Kunii [27].

Tuple structures are uniform independently of relation types (see Fig. 6). The first two bytes of a tuple contains the tuple length. The tuple consists of fixed and variable parts. Fixed-length fields are stored in the fixed part.

| 49 | 007 | | male | | 36 | 10 | James Bond | | 5 | Tokyo |

Tuple length | Fixed part | Variable part

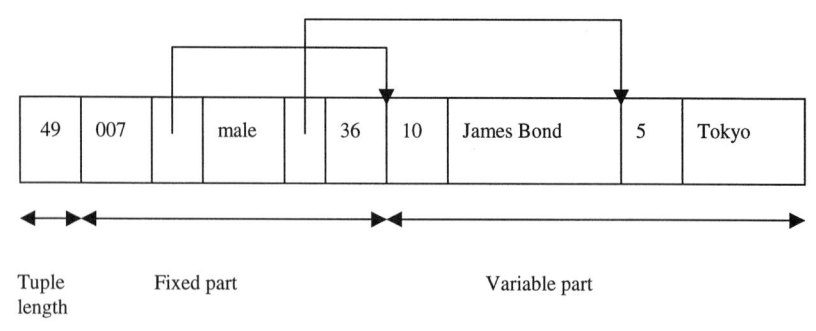

FIGURE 6 Tuple structure.

Variable-length fields are stored in the variable part. The offsets of the variable-length fields from the top of the tuple are stored in the fixed part. Any data can be accessed in a constant time, although this tuple structure does not allow null-value compression. Modification of the variable-length data can be done without affecting the fixed-length data.

TIDs, which can be stored in fixed-length fields, act as pointers to tuples. A variety of data structures can be implemented by using TIDs. For example, a nonclustered index can be implemented by defining an index key field and a TID field in B-tree or hash relations (see Fig. 7).

Access to fields must be efficiently processed since it is a frequent operation. We provide pointer arrays for field access (see Fig. 8). Each pointer points to the corresponding field in a tuple on page buffers. Simple tuple structures allow efficient construction of pointer arrays. One alternative is to copy field values to different areas. The alternative is good for data protection, but is rather time-consuming. Field pointer arrays are passed to user-defined functions such as manipulation and predicate functions for field access.

To efficiently access data, we move as few data as possible and fix tuples in buffers if possible. Internal sorting uses pointer arrays for tuples to be sorted (see Fig. 9). Such pointers are moved instead of tuples. Similarly, when a hash table is created for internal hashing, pointers to tuples are linked instead of tuples.

INDEX

Name	TID
James Bond	
Tom Jones	

PATIENT

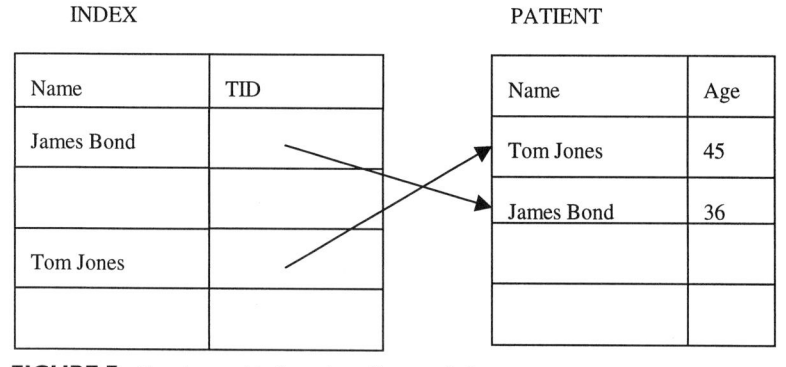

Name	Age
Tom Jones	45
James Bond	36

FIGURE 7 Nonclustered index using a B-tree relation.

OBJECT-ORIENTED DATABASE SYSTEMS

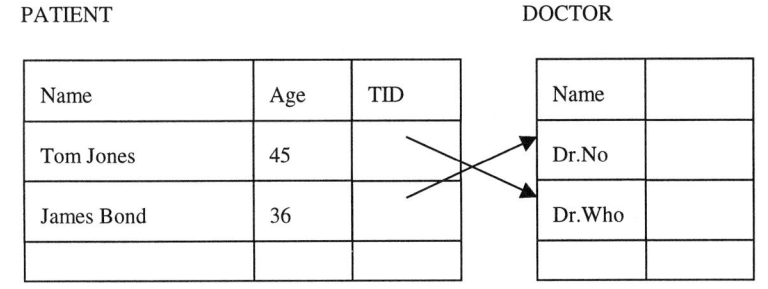

FIGURE 8 Precomputed join.

2. Hash-Based Processing

Set operations such as set-difference and duplicate elimination require OID-based access. Object-oriented queries usually equi-joins based on OIDs. If either of two joined relations can be loaded into main memory, we can use the hash join method [36]. Even if neither of them can be loaded into main memory, the hash join method generally requires less CPU time and I/O times than the sort-based method. We adopted the hash-based method for equi-joins and set operations. Unlike Jasmine, other object-oriented systems such as ORION use nested-loop and sort-merge joins.

The internal hash join is used when either of two input relations for joins can be loaded into main memory. Recursion is not used in the internal hash join. Only one relation is partitioned into subrelations. The other relation is only scanned tuple by tuple. It is not necessary to load both of the relations entirely. We describe the outline of the algorithm. Only main memory is used during processing.

(1) Determine which input relation is to be partitioned. Let the partitioned input relation be A.
(2) Determine a partition number p and a hash function h.

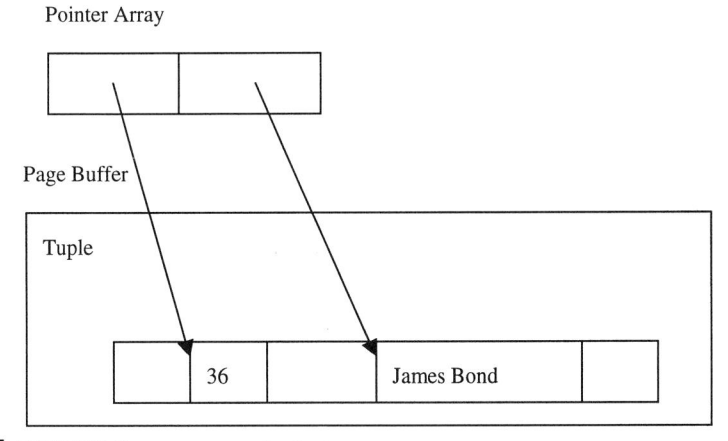

FIGURE 9 Pointer array for field access.

(3) Partition the relation A into p subrelations $Ai = \{a$ belongs to $A|h$ (key of $a) = i\}$ $(i = 0, \ldots, p\text{-}1)$.
(4) For each tuple b of the other relation B, compute $k = h$ (key of b) and compare each tuple of Ak with b on the join key. When they match, make a new tuple from them and output it to the output relation C.

The external hash join is used when neither of two input relations can be loaded into main memory. The essential difference between the external hash join and the internal hash join is the use of recursion and the partitioning of both of the input relations. The outline of the algorithm is as follows:

(1) Determine a partition number p and a hash function h.
(2) Partition the relation A into p subrelations $Ai = \{a$ belongs to $A|h$ (key of $a) = i\}$ $(i = 0, \ldots, p\text{-}1)$, and partition B into p subrelations $Bi = \{b$ belongs to $B|h$ (key of $b) = i\}$ $(i = 0, \ldots, p\text{-}1)$. Each subrelation is stored in secondary memory.
(3) For each $i = 0, \ldots, p\text{-}1$, if either Ai or Bi can be entirely loaded into main memory, Ai and Bi are joined using the internal hash join. Otherwise, steps (1) through (3) are executed recursively.

3. User-Defined Functions

Methods are often specified in target and condition parts of object-oriented queries. Conventionally, applications retrieve all data and filter and manipulate them. This approach is rather inefficient because it requires extra data transfer and conversion between buffers and applications. System-defined comparators are also inefficient because they interpret any data according to data types. So we implement application-specific parts such as methods as user-defined functions and embed them into the the data management subsystem. The user can specify application-specific parts as follows.

(1) A predicate function specifies a retrieval condition of selection or join operators.
(2) A manipulation function specifies operators on each tuple satisfying the predicate in selection or join.
(3) An order function specifies the order used by sorting or B-tree relations.
(4) A range function specifies a search condition of B-tree relations such as $a< = x < b$ or $c < x$.
(5) A static hash function is used by hash-based relational operators such as join, union, and difference.
(6) A dynamic hash function is used by hash relations.

To separate application-specific parts by providing user-defined functions allows both flexible customization by the user and efficient execution by compiling. For example, the following predicate function filters tuples by using a simple condition with the system-defined comparison operator <:

```
predicate 1 (flag, OID, condition, age)
{if (flag == MAIN)
    {if (age < 13) return true
        else return false}}
```

Whether this predicate is invoked for PREprocessing, MAINprocessing, or POSTprocessing depends on the variable flag. Preprocessing and postprocessing are done only once while the main processing is done tuple-wise. Control is transferred to manipulation functions which manipulate filtered data only if the predicate function returns true. The predicate functions are compiled into operations on tuples in the buffer and are efficiently processed because no type is dynamically checked and no data are interpreted. The user-defined complex condition is also defined as a predicate function. If no predicate is explicitly supplied, control is always passed to manipulation functions.

Manipulation functions are compiled to operate directly on tuples in the buffer and are invoked only if predicate functions return true. For example, the following function operates on tuples of a relation by using a make-medical-certificate program and inserts the result into another relation tmp3:

```
manipulate3 (flag, OID, doctor, name, disease)
{if (flag == PRE) openinsert(tmp3);
   else if (flag == MAIN)
      {result = make-medical-certificate("19990211");
         insert(tmp3, result);}
   else if (flag == POST) closeinsert(tmp3);}
```

In general, selection and join operators described below require predicate and manipulation functions. Data are thus efficiently filtered by predicate functions and operated on by manipulation functions.

4. Architecture

The data management subsystem has a layered architecture consisting of relational, tuple, and storage layers (see Fig. 10). All of these are open to the user. The data management provides neither a query parser nor an optimizer because they are rather high-level and application-dependent. It is just an executer of operators provided by the three layers.

The relational layer provides functions that execute set operations as an extended relational algebra. For example, (1) select (rb, pb, mb) extends

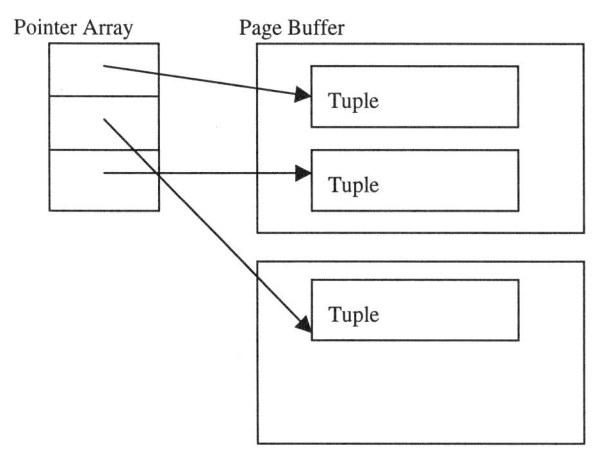

FIGURE 10 Pointer array for internal sorting.

selection of relational algebra. It has three parameters rb, pb, and mb. rb is the data block that specifies the source relation. pb and mb specify user-defined predicate and manipulation functions, respectively. (2) hjoin(rb1, rb2, mb, hb) performs an equi-join of relations specifying rb1 and rb2. mb is performed on each pair of tuples which match on join fields. This operation is based on a hash function specified by hb. (3) join(rb1, rb2, pb, mb) performs a general join of relations rb1 and rb2. (4) tjoin(rb1, rb2, TID, mb) joins each tuple of rb1 with a tuple of rb2 pointed by its TID field and performs mb on such a pair of tuples. (5) sort(rb1, rb2, ob) sorts rb1 and stores the results into rb2. The order function is specified by ob. (6) unique(rb1, rb2, hb) eliminates duplicates of rb1 and stores the result into rb2. This operation is hash-based. (7) nest(rb1, rb2, fid, hb) generates a nested relation rb2 from a flat relation rb1 with fields specified by fid. This operation is also hash-based. (8) unnest(rb1, rb2, fid) generates a flat relation rb2 from a nested relation rb1.

Functions of the tuple layer operate on four types of relations. The operators are as follows: (1) Scan scans a relation sequentially and finds a tuple satisfying the specified predicate. (2) Raster scans a relation sequentially fixing scanned pages on buffers. It is used in internal sorting or making internal hash tables. (3) Access directly accesses a tuple satisfying the specified predicate. (4) Fetch, (5) delete, and (6) update directly accesses, deletes, and updates a tuple specified by a given TID, respectively. (7) Insert inserts a tuple or a group of fields. (8) Clear deletes all tuples. (9) Flac constructs a field pointer array for the specified fields.

The functions of the storage layer include disk I/O, page buffers, transactions, concurrency control, and recovery. Disk I/O management includes allocation and deallocation of subdatabases (segments) and pages. A database consists of two types of subdatabases. One is a subdatabase that is permanent and recoverable. The other is a subdatabase which is used as a workspace for keeping temporary relations, and is only effective in a transaction. This is not recoverable. Subdatabases are composed of a number of pages.

The storage layer supports variable-length pages sized $2i$ KB ($i = 2, \ldots, 8$), consisting of several 4 KB physical pages, which form a virtually continuous page on buffers. We use the buddy system for buffer space allocation. The page length can be specified for each relation because multimedia data and inner relations may exceed 4 KB.

We use concurrency control based on granularity and two-phase locking. Deadlock detection is done by examining a cycle in the Wait-For-Graph. One of the deadlocked transactions in the cycle in the graph is chosen as the victim for rollback. ORION uses deadlock detection based on timeouts. Our transaction recovery is based on shadow-paging for simplicity.

B. Object Management Subsystem

1. Object Storage

We efficiently store nested structures of objects by use of nested relations supported by the data management subsystem unlike other systems. Storage structures differ from instance to class. Translation of objects to relations is automatically done by the system. Information about the translation is held by classes.

```
┌──────────────────┐
│ Relational Layer │
└────────┬─────────┘
         │
┌────────┴─────────┐
│   Tuple Layer    │
└────────┬─────────┘
         │
┌────────┴─────────┐
│  Storage Layer   │
└──────────────────┘
```

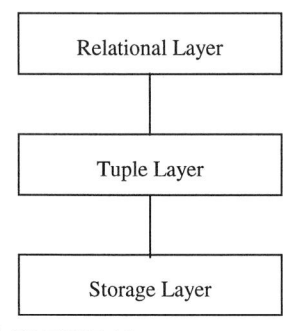

FIGURE 11 Architecture.

All intrinsic instances of a class are stored in a relation, corresponding an instance to a tuple and an attribute to a field (see Fig. 11). Instances of different classes are stored in separate relations. Multiple-valued attributes such as Temperature are stored as a multiple-valued field, the simplest form of nested relations. We resolve attribute inheritance before storing instances. We treat inherited attributes such as Age and newly defined attributes such as Weight uniformly. We store intrinsic instances of a superclass and those of a subclass in separate relations. If we instantiate or destroy intrinsic instances of a class, we do not have to propagate any modification to its superclass or subclass.

We store fixed-length strings and numbers in fixed-length fields and variable-length strings in variable-length fields. As for reference attributes such as Doctor we store only OIDs in fixed-length fields. This implements nonclustered complex objects. Nonclustered complex objects are needed by CAD applications where complex objects are created bottom-up; that is, component objects are reused. Of course, the user can enforce complex object integrity on nonclustered complex objects by attaching demons to methods of whole objects such as instantiate [14]. We correspond relation objects in attributes to inner relations of nested relations and their attributes to fields of the inner relations. Inherently, component objects of relation objects cannot exist without their whole objects. Clustered complex objects, implemented by relation objects, can be managed as a unit both logically and physically. Nested relations naturally realize clustering of complex objects, although component objects must be hierarchically accessed from root objects.

The OID attribute also corresponds to a field. An OID consists of a database id-number, a class id-number, and an instance id-number, so an OID alone can inform us of its database and class information directly (see Fig. 12). Unlike the OID of O2 [5], the OID of Jasmine is logical in that it contains no physical addresses in secondary memory. No OIDs need to be changed even at data reorganization, although OIDs need to be changed if objects are migrated to another class. The user can choose among sequential, B-tree, and hash relations as instance storage. The user can attach indexes to attributes.

As classes are instances of the system-defined CLASS in Jasmine, we store all classes in one nested relation and facilitate efficient associative access of class objects. Basically we correspond one class object to one tuple. Since attribute categorization, such as enumerated and procedural, is common to all

PATIENT (Instance Table)

Oid	Sex	Age	Name	Doctor
MedicalPatient007	male	36	James Bond	MedicalDoctor000

Category	Temperature	Weight	Height
inpatient	36.5 37.3 38.1	76.0	181.0

CLASS (Class Table)

Name	Db	Super	Property		
			name	Class	if-needed
PATIENT	MEDICAL	PERSON	Doctor	DOCTOR	
			Weight	FLOAT	
			Height	FLOAT	DEMON030

Method		
name	Class	Main
Make-medical-certificate	Medical-certificate	METHOD001

FIGURE 12 Examples of an instance table and a class table.

classes and attributes have a fixed set of facets, we store enumerated and procedural attributes in different inner relations and facets in the fields of the inner relations. Procedural attribute (method) definitions are also stored in relations and are retrieved and utilized during query optimization. The system-defined attributes such as Super are stored in separate fields (see also Fig. 12). To store heterogeneous classes in one relation makes set-oriented access to them efficient.

2. Set-Oriented Access Support

We compile both set-oriented access and singleton access to do early binding and reduce run-time overhead. The Jasmine compiler is implemented using a C compiler. The application programs written in Jasmine/C are precompiled to C programs, which are compiled and linked with the run-time support library. Preprocessing is used to take maximum advantage of portability and code optimization of the C compiler. An interactive query needed by application development is processed by the interpreter, not by the compiler.

Application programs are translated into C in three phases: query graph generation, access plan generation, and code generation. The query graph generation phase makes a query graph corresponding to the user query by referencing the object model. The query graph is a subgraph of the object model annotated with the target and condition information. For example, consider the query

$$PATIENT.make\text{-}medical\text{-}certificate(\text{``}19990211\text{''}),$$

where PATIENT.Age < 13 and PATIENT.Doctor.Name == "Dr. No".

This makes the following query graph:

$$CHILD\text{-}PATIENT\ (make\text{-}medical\text{-}certificate(\text{``}19990211\text{''}),$$
$$Age < 13, DOCTOR\ (Name == \text{``}Dr.\ No\text{''})).$$

Note that the user query containing incomplete knowledge access is transformed into a more efficient one during this phase. In Jasmine, the user can form a query by specifying a general class such as PATIENT instead of the specific class CHILD-PATIENT. Then it is necessary to restrict the general class to its appropriate subclass.

Then the access plan generation phase translates the query graph into an optimal plan of a series of extended relational operators using the object model information such as statistics, access methods, and mapping from class to relation. This phase uses rule-based optimization. Rules are grouped into sets of rules called rulesets [12] according to patterns of queries. This increases the modularity of rules. Rulesets can be more efficiently processed than flat rules because of this modularity. They are also easier to maintain and extend. Object-oriented query optimization is fully described later. Here we just illustrate the overall flow of query processing. Object-oriented features such as complex objects, class hierarchies, and methods (procedural attributes) constitute patterns of rulesets. Their occurrences in queries invoke associated rulesets. For example, the object expression is processed by different rulesets depending on whether it contains a procedural attribute.

First, the case where object expressions contain no procedural attributes is considered. In general, the object expression generates equi-joins between instance relations corresponding to a functional join. In addition, the conditions generate selections and explicit joins. For equi-join, a predicate function which joins two instance relations by an attribute field of one relation and an OID field of the other is generated. For selection, a condition concerning one instance relation is generated as a predicate function of a select operator. For an explicit join, a join predicate function which may contain a non-equi-join is generated. Manipulation functions are generated to project fields for later operation.

The query results in a set of OIDs, values, or tuples. A query against a nonleaf class evaluates to a relation containing OIDs of instances of several classes. As OIDs have the same structure for all objects, they can be stored in one relation. Each scan returns an object, by scanning the result relation and then selecting the base instance relation by the OID. At that time, if an object is already on core, it is used.

Usually, if a selection predicate of the sequential relation can use an index, selection by index, which selects a B-tree relation for the index by the key condition, sorts the result relation containing TIDs, and then joins the result relation and the original sequential relation by using TIDs, is chosen. The rest of the selection condition is evaluated at the same time. For B-tree and hash relations, if a predicate concerns the key fields, key-based searching is done. Note that if a whole relation of any type is small enough to be contained within one page, sequential access is chosen.

If one of two relations being joined is small enough to be contained within a page and the join key is indexed by the other relation, tuple substitution is chosen. If one of two relations is contained within a page and no index is provided, nested loop is chosen. Otherwise, hash join is chosen. For B-tree and hash relations, the join is similarly processed. In case of a join of several relations, the order of join is dynamically determined by the size of the intermediate result relations. First, we choose the smallest relation and the second smallest one among relations to be joined. Then we join them to obtain an expectedly small relation as a result. We add the result to relations to be joined and repeat this process. This dynamic scheme based on exact relation sizes is expected to be more efficient than static schemes based on database statistics.

Next, consider the case where object expressions contain procedural attributes. User procedural attributes appearing in the target part are translated into manipulation functions. Procedural attributes in conditions are translated into predicate functions. For example, the above query graph generates the relational operator sequence and the predicate and manipulation functions as follows:

```
select(DOCTOR, predicate1, manipulate 1);
select(CHILD-PATIENT, predicate 2, manipulate 2);
if (within-page(tmp1)||within-page(tmp2)) join(tmp1, tmp2, predicate3,
   manipulate3);
else hjoin(tmp1, tmp2, predicate3, manipulate3, hashfunc);

predicate 1 (flag, OID, name)
  {if (flag == MAIN)
     {if (name == "Dr. No") return true
        else return false }}

manipulate1 (flag, OID)
  {if (flag == PRE) openinsert (tmp1);
     else if (flag == MAIN) insert(tmp1, OID);
     else if (flag == POST) closeinsert(tmp1);}
predicate2 (flag, OID, condition, age)
  { if (flag == MAIN)
     {if (age < 13) return true
      else return false}}
```

```
manipulate2 (flag, OID, doctor, name, disease)
   {if (flag == PRE) openinsert(tmp2);
      else if (flag == MAIN)
         {Acertificate = make-medical-certificate ("19990211");
          insert(tmp2, doctor, Acertificate);}
      else if (flag == POST) closeinsert(tmp2);}

predicate3 (flag, OID, doctor)
   {if (flag == MAIN)
      {if (OID == doctor) return true
         else return false }}

manipulate3 (flag, Acertificate)
   {if (flag == PRE) openinsert(tmp3);
      else if (flag == MAIN) insert(tmp3, Acertificate);
      else if (flag == POST) closeinsert(tmp3);}
```

If an index on Name of DOCTOR is available, the first select will be replaced by the sequence select–sort–tjoin (selection by index). The system-defined procedural attributes such as aggregate functions and update functions are also translated into manipulation functions. In particular, the update functions are translated into relational update operators. If demons are defined and the option is specified, they are integrated into manipulation and predicate functions. Lastly, the C codes for the given query are generated to feed the C compiler.

3. Object-Oriented Query Optimization

The features of query optimization in an object-oriented database are different from those of query optimization in a relational database because multiple-valued attributes, implicit joins, procedural attributes (methods), and nonleaf classes in a class hierarchy are specified in a query. First, we describe processing of multiple-valued attributes. As for non-clustered complex objects, reference attributes contain only OIDs and multiple-valued attributes contain only elements of a set. Then multiple-valued attributes contain a set of OIDs or values. Since only sequential access is supported for inner relations of nested relations, multiple-valued attributes are unnested into flat relations and are optimized conventionally except for application of aggregate functions. As for clustered complex objects implemented by nested relations, predicate and manipulation functions of inner relations of nested relations are nested into those of outer relations of the nested relations. They are recursively evaluated from outer relations to inner relations.

Next, we describe implicit joins of relations generated by object expressions such as DOCTOR.Patient.Age. If there is no available index on the OID field of the relation for the class of the attribute (e.g., PATIENT), the join is processed by hash joins. The order of more than one join is dynamically determined by the size of the intermediate result relations. If there is an index available on the OID, the join is processed by TID joins. In case of several joins, they are processed from left to right in the object expression. Section predicates, if any, are evaluated during join processing. Note that there are methods for precomputing joins. For example, to process the query (DOCTOR.Patient.Age where DOCTOR.Patient.Age > 30), an index with Age as a key value and the OID of DOCTOR as a pointer value is created. Other systems such as ORION use this approach. However, it is rather difficult to maintain such an index properly.

We describe how to process queries containing nonleaf classes in a class hierarchy. We assume that PATIENT has ADULT-PATIENT and CHILD-PATIENT as subclasses. Consider the following examples,

(Query 21) PATIENT.Name where PATIENT Age > 12
 and PATIENT.Age < 20
(Query 22) DEPARTMENT.Doctor.Patient.Name where
 DEPARTMENT.Name == "pediatrics".

For Query 21, the system generates two subqueries:

result = ADULT-PATIENT.Name where ADULT-PATIENT.Age < 20
result = result + CHILD-PATIENT.Name where CHILD-PATIENT.Age > 12.

The two query results are inserted into the same output relation.

For Query 22, the join of DEPARTMENT and DOCTOR is processed first. During the join processing, the intermediate output relations are switched according to the class of the OID for DEPARTMENT.Doctor.Patient. The class can be determined just by looking at the OID. The pseudo queries are

adult-intermediate = DEPARTMENT.Doctor.Patient
 where DEPARTMENT.Name == "pediatrics" and
 DEPARTMENT.Doctor.Patient.Class == <ADULT-PATIENT>
child-intermediate = DEPARTMENT.Doctor.Patient where
 DEPARTMENT.Name == "pediatrics" and
 DEPARTMENT.Doctor.Patient.Class == <CHILD-PATIENT>.

The switching is done during a single-join operation. The code for the switching is translated into the manipulation function of the join operator. Then a pair of adult-intermediate and ADULT-PATIENT and a pair of child-intermediate and CHILD-PATIENT are joined, and the results are merged. As described above, the intermediate result of selection or join operations is switched to separate relations containing only OIDs relevant to successive joins. This can establish optimal preconditions for the joins by avoiding unnecessary search.

Classes (e.g., PERSON, DOCTOR, and PATIENT) in a class hierarchy share inherited attributes such as Age. Basically there are two methods for creating indexes on classes in a class hierarchy. One method is to create only one index on a whole class hierarchy, called a class-hierarchy index. The other is to create a separate index, called a single-class index, on each class. Jasmine uses single-class indexes. Other systems such as ORION and O2 use class-hierarchy indexes. The class-hierarchy index has an advantage that the total size of index pages and the total number of accessed index pages are smaller than those of the single-class index. However, it is not always optimal when a class hierarchy is partially specified in a query. Moreover, it is rather difficult to maintain such class-hierarchy indexes.

In some cases, semantic information such as categorization can be used to specialize nonleaf classes to specific ones. When a condition on the categorization attribute such as (Age < 7) is specified in a query containing a nonleaf class PATIENT, if the condition matches one of the categorization conditions of partition classes (Age < 18 for CHILD-PATIENT), the nonleaf class (PATIENT) is specialized into the subclass (CHILD-PATIENT) with the matched categorization condition. This can reduce the size of the search space for the query.

The system translates methods such as make-medical-certificate of PATIENT specified in a query into the manipulation and predicate functions of selection or join operators, and processes them on page buffers, which avoids unnecessary data transfer between page buffers and application programs. Methods defined by a query such as intern of DEPARTMENT is expanded into the outer query. To this end, the source codes and compiled codes for methods and demons are stored as program objects in databases. They are retrieved and compiled during query optimization. To store programs in databases makes the integration of query and programming facilities more elegant than to store them in ordinary program files. Polymorphic methods are translated into their corresponding implementation functions.

4. Object Buffering

Singleton access is also compiled into C programs, which are compiled and linked with the run-time support library. First, run-time support will be described. The first access of an object fetches the object from secondary memory to the page buffer. Then the object is cached in the active object table (AOT), a dedicated internal hash table for object buffering (see Fig. 13).

The primary role of AOT is to efficiently look up objects. When an instance is referenced through its OID for the first time, the instance is hashed by its OID as a hash key. A hash entry (an object descriptor) and an in-memory instance data structure is created. The hash entry points to the instance data structure. If the instance is referenced through its OID by other instances resident in AOT, the OID is mapped to the pointer to the hash entry through the AOT. The pointer can be cashed into the attribute of the referencing instance since

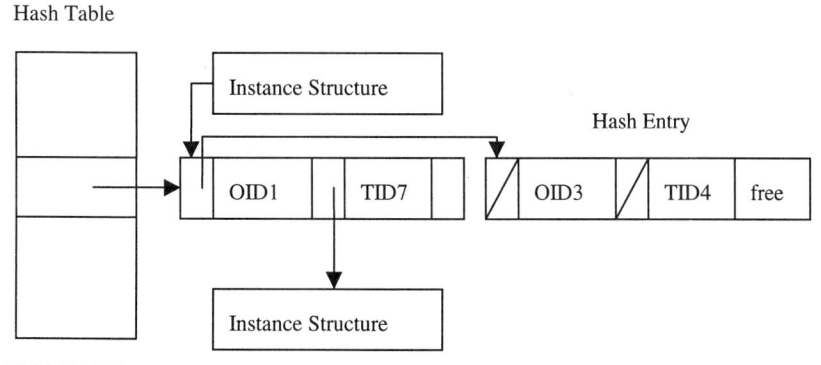

FIGURE 13 AOT structure.

an OID is longer than a physical pointer. Later, the instance can be directly accessed by the pointer without hashing.

Another important role is to maintain the status flags for update of objects. When an object is newly created or updated, the status flag in the hash entry for the object is set to create or update. When a transaction is committed, the object with the status create or update is modified or added into the page buffers. When an object is destroyed, the corresponding in-memory data structure is deallocated and the status flag is changed to destroy. Later, if the destroyed object is referenced, the validity of reference is checked and an exception handler is invoked. This can support referential integrity. When a transaction is committed, the object is destroyed in databases.

When objects fill up AOT, extraneous objects are swapped out. Such an object is flushed to the page buffers and the in-memory instance data structure is deallocated and the status flag in the hash entry is set to free. When the object is referenced again, the object is directly fetched from databases to AOT through its TID cashed in the hash entry.

The object management subsystem requires AOT, that is, object buffers in addition to page buffers of the data management subsystem for the following reason. In general, buffers are directly associated with patterns of access of objects. Page buffers have structures suitable for access of different instances of the same class. AOT have structures suitable for access of correlated instances of different classes. Advanced applications such as CAD have combinations of two such patterns. This necessitates a dual buffer scheme consisting of page buffers and object buffers, not a single-buffer scheme, which would contain unnecessary objects and decrease memory utilization.

The dual buffer approach, however, makes the same object appear in different formats in different buffers at the same time, so we must maintain internal consistency between two objects denoting the same entity. Currently, we first write back updated or newly created instances from AOT to page buffers in query evaluation. Then we evaluate a query against page buffers. An alternative is to devise different search mechanisms for different buffers and evaluate the same query on different buffers and integrate the results, which would make the system less compact.

Basically there are two methods for query evaluation using object buffers and page buffers as follows.

Single-buffer evaluation method: (1) The instances newly created or updated associated with the classes specified by the query are searched in the object buffers. (2) They are flushed from the object buffers to the page buffers. (3) The query is evaluated against the page buffers.

Dual-buffer evaluation method: (1) The query is evaluated against the object buffers. (2) The same query is evaluated against the page buffers. (3) The two results are merged into one.

Jasmine adopts the single-buffer evaluation method while ORION adopts a more sophisticated version of the dual-buffer evaluation method. The single-buffer evaluation method needs to transfer objects from the object buffers to the page buffers. However, the single-buffer evaluation method eliminates the need for dual evaluation programs and makes the system small and processing simple in contrast to the dual-buffer evaluation method. Anyway, the combinational use of object buffers and page buffers can support the integration of programming and query facilities at an architecture level.

IV. APPLICATIONS

A. Introduction

New multimedia applications emerging on top of information infrastructures include digital libraries [34] and document warehousing for document management and analysis, which are supposed to be most promising as such networked multimedia applications. We need next-generation database systems which enable users to efficiently and flexibly develop and execute networked multimedia applications.

First, we analyze the characteristics of these networked multimedia applications and discuss the requirements for a multimedia information system consisting of database, operating system (OS), and network layers and the issues for a multimedia database system. Then we describe our approach based on OODB and extended with agents, focusing on a general architecture of a multimedia database system and its implementation.

1. Requirements for a Multimedia Information System

First, we discuss the requirements for a multimedia information system in general.

1. Multimedia applications must be interactive. So each layer of the system must allow control of *quality of service* (QOS) parameters, such as latency, bit and frame rates, to interactively process multimedia data in real-time.

2. A huge amount of data in forms such as text, video, and images are required for multimedia services which every layer of the system must efficiently process. In the database layer, database techniques for efficiently storing and accessing a large volume of data, which include access methods and clustering, are required. In the OS layer, techniques such as hierarchical storage systems, and thread mechanisms are required. In the network layer, network protocols suitable for multimedia along with the ability to efficiently process such protocols are required.

3. There is heterogeneity in media data such as text and video, and temporal and spatial dependency between them. Users must be able to uniformly manipulate heterogeneous media data. Users must also be able to structure heterogeneous media data explicitly by defining links among them, that is, *hypermedia links*. Users must also be able to define temporal and spatial relationships among various media data. Such functionality must be provided by the database layer as *multimedia data models*. Heterogeneous physical media, such as magnetic optical disks, and CD-ROMs, must also be uniformly accessed. Stream media data, such as audio and video, must be temporally synchronized and processed in real-time essentially by the OS layer. The network

layer must efficiently process multimedia network protocols based on ATM, to accommodate various types of media traffic.

4. Advanced multimedia applications must allow for distributed processing. In particular, site autonomy must be guaranteed for developing distributed multimedia applications. Users should be able to use distributed, object-oriented computing techniques, known as *active objects* or *agents*. Heterogeneity in data models, database systems, and database schemas must also be resolved, so the database layer must provide multidatabase management [21, 29]. The OS layer must perform distributed resource management.

2. Issues for a Multimedia Database System

Now we address the issues for a multimedia database system for networked multimedia applications, which are not comprehensive but mandatory.

1. We must distinguish between logical media data and physical media data. For example, in networked multimedia applications, multimedia contents are updated or deleted, or even moved from one server to another. We must allow users to access such contents independently of physical details such as locations. We must also allow users to access contents in a uniform fashion independent of data formats such as MPEG and Motion JPEG. Thus, we must allow users to flexibly define multimedia views by specifying mappings between logical and physical data.

2. We must provide a query facility based on keywords, which is a prerequisite for database systems, needless to say. Browsing alone is insufficient because a large amount of media data take a long time to play.

3. We must also provide a content-based retrieval facility [7]. In networked multimedia applications, keywords are not always attached to a large amount of data in advance. Moreover, users should sometimes express a query over multimedia data by using features, such as colors and motion directions, which are different from conceptual keywords. So we need content-based retrieval, which allows an inexact match in contrast to an exact match facilitated by the keyword-based retrieval facility.

4. We must provide a navigational search facility in addition to the query facility. Of course, the navigational search can be done through user-specified hyperlinks among data [14]. However, in large-scale networked applications, explicit specification of links requires a considerable amount of work. So we must logically cluster multimedia data based on similarity of keywords and characteristic data, such as colors, for navigation.

5. We must allow users to select physical storage appropriate for applications and physical clustering if necessary.

6. We must provide parallel, distributed processing in networked multimedia applications. For example, several streams are sometimes required to be played in parallel. Distributing process burdens, such as special effects of video streams, among servers is required. Federating a query to several distributed servers is also required.

7. We must handle program components as first-class objects. Program components are used to control access to databases and to make database application development more efficient.

8. We must control QOS in networked multimedia applications. For example, when a single or multiple users require multiple streams to play in parallel, we cannot guarantee QOS required by users unless we manage resources such as CPU and network.

B. System Architecture

1. Our Data Model

a. Multimedia

We think that multimedia data are not just static data, but rather compositions of several media data and operations on them. So we provide structural, temporal, spatial, and control operations as media composition operators, as described later. In other words, our model has multiple facets and subsumes existing models, such as object, temporal, spatial, and agent models. Individual operations are orthogonal to one another. Our model is integrated seamlessly with existing technologies.

Multimedia systems consist of multimedia databases and applications. Multimedia databases consist of a set of media data. Media types include texts, graphics, images, and streams. Stream types include audio, video, and streamed texts, graphics, and images as well. Multimedia applications consist of a set of scripts. Basically, a script has an identifier (ID) and temporal and spatial operations on a set of streams with QOS options. A stream has an ID and temporal and spatial operations on a set of frames. A frame has an ID and temporal and spatial operations on frame data.

QOS options are parameters given to a QOS controller. QOS types include latency, jitter, various bit rates and frame rates, resolution, colors, and fonts. QOS is controlled either by executing specified QOS functions or by retrieving stored QOS data. The QOS function takes a stream and a time and gives frame IDs. The QOS data consisting of time and a frame ID are stored in advance by obtaining them from rehearsal.

In order to concretely explain the features of our data model, we consider the following multimedia application or script, called Script1, assuming that there exist multimedia databases containing multiple video streams that have filmed the same object.

Script1:

(a) Retrieves all video streams which filmed the Prime Minister on January 17th, 1995.
(b) selects only parts of the retrieved video streams temporally overlapping each other.
(c) Arranges the selected parts on the same presentation space (i.e., window).
(d) Plays the parts in temporal synchronization.

b. Structural Operations

Jasmine models structures of multimedia objects and provides structural operations on them. For example, media objects such as streams and frames are defined (see Fig. 14).

STREAM		MPEG		FRAME	
Super	MEDIA	Super	STREAM	Super MEDIA-Data	
Property		Property		Property	
TIME	Internal Time	Set MPEG-Frame Frame		TIME	Time
TIME	Real Time	Method		FRAME-Data	Data
SPACE	Internal Space	MPEG	AddFrame ()		
SPACE	Real Space	MPEG	RemoveFrame()		
Set FRAME	Frame	VOID	Forward()		
STRING	Topic	VOID	Backward()		

FIGURE 14 Definition of media objects.

For example, the following query retrieves streams that filmed the Prime Minister on January 17th, 1995, which realizes Script1 (a):

STREAM.Frame from STREAM where STREAM.RealTime = "01171995" and STREAM.Topic = "the Prime Minister".

c. Temporal and Spatial Operations

Temporal and spatial data are viewed as universal keys common to any stream media data. Such temporal and spatial relationships structure multimedia data implicitly in contrast to explicit links. We define set-oriented temporal and spatial operators specifying such relationships, which are analogous to relational algebra [3].

Although time is one-dimensional and space is three-dimensional, they have similar characteristics. Real-time is elapsed time taken for recording streams in the real world. Internal time is time required for a usual play of streams. External time is time taken for real play of streams by scripts. Usually, real time is equal to internal time. In the case of high-speed video, real time is shorter than internal time. External time is specified by providing a magnification level of internal time. Default magnification is one; that is, external time is equal to internal time by default. In the case of slow play of streams, external time is longer than internal time; in the case of fast play, external time is shorter than internal time. Assuming that S1 and S2 are streams and that P is a predicate on frames of a stream, temporal composition of streams is achieved by temporal operators as follows:

(a) Tintersection (S1, S2) returns parts of S1 and S2 which temporally intersect.
(b) Tdifference (S1, S2) returns a part of S1 that does not temporally intersect with S2.
(c) Tunion (S1, S2) returns S1 and S2 ordered in time with possible overlaps.
(d) Tselect(S1, P) returns a part of S1 which satisfies P.
(e) Tjoin (S1, S2, P) = Tselect(Tunion(S1, S2), P).
(f) Tproject(S1, Func) returns the result of Func on S1,

where Func is an operation on frames that may include the spatial operators described below.

Note that internal time of a composite stream is the union of external time of its component streams. Real time of a composite stream is the union of real time of its component streams. For example, we assume that the query result of

OBJECT-ORIENTED DATABASE SYSTEMS

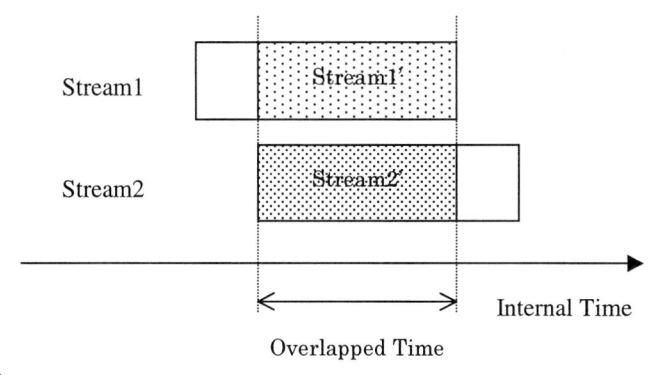

FIGURE 15 Schematic explanation of an expression Tintersection (Stream1, Stream2).

Script1(a) is scanned and is individually set to streams Stream1 and Stream2. To select only parts of Stream1 and Stream2 which temporally overlap one another, which realizes Script1 (b), we have only to execute an expression Tintersection (Stream1, Stream2) based on the internal time. Here we name the selected parts Stream1' and Stream2' for Stream1 and Stream2, respectively. The schematic explanation of the effect of the expression is presented in Fig. 15.

Similarly, space is divided into real space, internal space, and external space. Real space is space occupied by streams in the real world. Internal space is space typically occupied by streams in presentation. External space is space occupied by streams during the actual presentation of scripts, is specified by providing a magnification of internal space, and is equal to internal space by default. Assuming that F1 and F2 are frames and that P is a predicate on pixels of a frame, spatial composition of streams is accomplished by spatial operators as follows:

(a) Sintersection (F1, F2) returns parts of F1 and F2 that intersect in space.
(b) Sdifference (F1, F2) returns a part of F1 that does not intersect in space with F2.
(c) Sunion (F1, F2) returns F1 and F2 merged in space.
(d) Sselect(F1, p) returns a part of F1 that satisfies P.
(e) Sjoin (F1, F2, P) = Sselect (Sunion (F1, F2), P).
(f) Sproject(F1, Func) returns the result of Func on F1,

where Func is an operation on pixels.

Note that the internal space of a composite stream is the union of the external space of its component streams. The real space of a composite stream is the union of the real space of its component streams. For example, to arrange two frames Frame1 of Stream1' and Frame2 of Stream2' on the same window, which realizes Script1 (c), we evaluate an expression Sunion (Frame1, Frame2) based on the external space, whose effect is schematically explained in Fig. 16.

d. Control Operators

Processes, called agents, represent control structures. Processes consist of events, conditions, and actions. Event specification allows for serial, parallel,

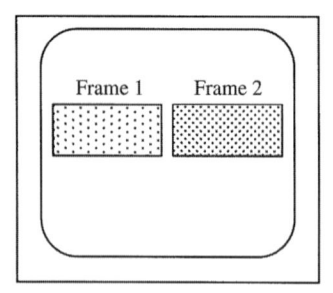

FIGURE 16 Schematic explanation of an expression Sunion (Frame1, Frame2).

and alternative occurrences of component events. Time is specifiable in events with keywords such as "before," "after," "between," "at," and "periodically." Events are invoked by actions within other processes. Conditions can monitor database states, process states, and QOS states. Actions specify control of processes, such as parallel, serial, and alternative, and other model operators, such as structural, temporal, and spatial. Concurrency is represented as annotation together with QOS options, which reduces to other model operators in the case of serial compilers. Serial specification is nothing but object-oriented programming and query languages. The merging of processes is specified by the conjunction of events. QOS is given as parameters to the process construct.

For example, two streams Stream1' and Stream2' executing in parallel, taking two QOS parameters latency and bit rate into consideration, is specified as follows based on the external time, which realizes Script1 (d):

>QOS (Latency, Bit Rate);
>Set1 = (Stream1', Stream2');
>Set1.parallel.play;

The effect is schematically shown in Fig. 17. We describe how to satisfy QOS parameters later.

2. Overall Architecture

Now we describe the overall architecture of a multimedia database system. As shown in Fig. 18, the system architecture consists of agent management,

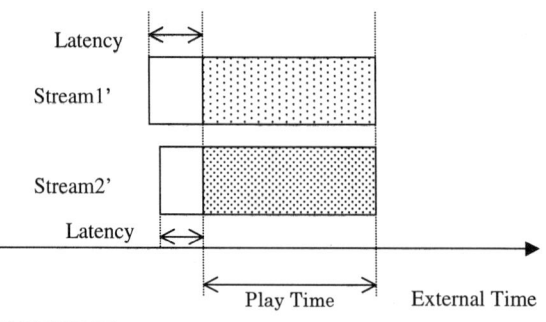

FIGURE 17 Schematic explanation of QOS-constrained concurrent playback of two streams.

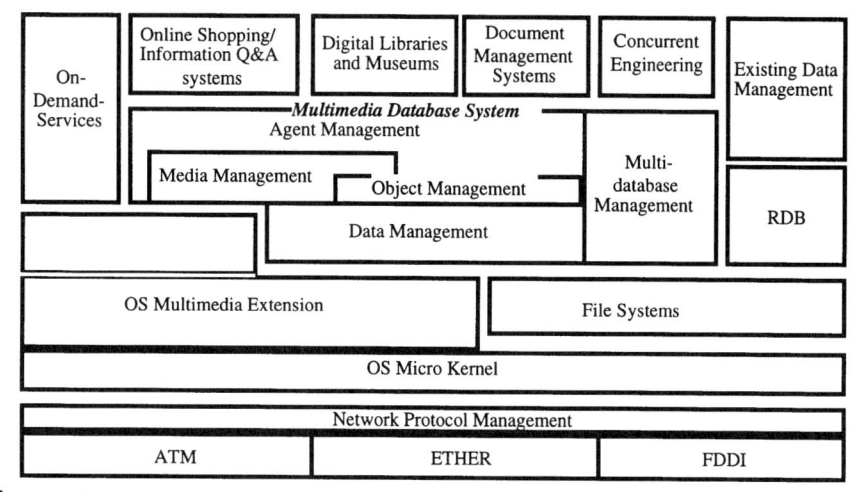

FIGURE 18 System architecture.

media management, object management, data management, and multidatabase management layers on top of OS and network protocol management layers. The agent management layer enables users to flexibly describe multimedia applications, as described in detail later. The media management layer provides interfaces to individual media data. The object and data management layers which provide basic database management facilities are based on Jasmine OODB. The multidatabase management layer provides integrated access to traditional media, such as numbers and character strings, in RDB and new media, such as audio and video streams, in OODB.

C. Our Approach to Implementation

1. Agents and Related Work

Before we describe our extended object-oriented approach based on agents to the implementation of a multimedia database system, we define our agents by extending object definitions described in Section II. In this paper, agents are defined as follows:

(1) Agents are basically objects in the context of OODB.
(2) Agents have at least one of the following characteristics:
   (2.1) Agents can be executed in a parallel or distributed fashion like processes. Conventionally, methods of objects are restricted to serial execution like subroutine calls.
   (2.2) Agents are mobile. Thus, agents move from one server to another like migrated processes. Agents may come back to the originating server or move further to a third server.
   (2.3) Agents can respond to events. Agents change behaviors in response to events incurred by the system, applications, or users.

Note that definitions of agents differ, depending on researchers. To clarify our approach, we strictly confine our definition of agents to the above definition. In the following subsections, we describe agent-based approaches to the database issues discussed previously, focusing on multimedia data, that is, videos, texts, and program components, which are related to one another by explicit links or implicit links, such as keyword associations, similarity of contents, and temporal and spatial synchronization.

To solve all the database issues, we focus on the development of a database system that enables flexible and efficient acquisition, storage, access and retrieval, and distribution and presentation of large amounts of heterogeneous media data [22]. We take a realistic approach based on an OODB Jasmine [18, 20, 23], which is more suitable for the description of media structures and operations than a traditional RDB.

We propose a basic multimedia data model as an integration of structural, temporal, spatial, and control functionality. Our extended data model based on agents provides uniform interfaces to heterogeneous media in addition to defining structures and operations specific to such media. The model allows the representation of temporal and spatial relationships and of temporal synchronization and QOS control, through extending a *scripting language* suitable for multimedia application development. That is, we take an object-oriented database approach suitable for description of media structures and operations and extend the object-oriented approach by providing temporal and spatial operators, and control of distributed computing based on agents and QOS (quality of service). In particular, we adopt and *Event–Condition–Action* paradigm of active databases [19] to allow users to flexibly specify agent processes.

There are models that support temporal descriptions such as those of [8, 10]. Almost all of them focus only on temporal functionality and pay little attention to the other functionalities, such as spatial functionality. Our model provides set-oriented operators for associative (or partial) access to an ordered set of internal frames constituting streams, which are analogous to relational algebra [3] for associative access to an unordered set of records constituting tables. In general, control structures that support features such as concurrency are needed for the development of distributed multimedia applications. In our model, control is described as annotations to other functionality, i.e., structural, temporal, and spatial. In addition to concurrency control, QOS parameters such as latency and bit rates are specifiable in concurrency annotations for allowing real-time execution of stream media. We extend the annotated approach to concurrency to allow for QOS control options. QOS is controlled either by executing methods or by retrieving stored data. An Event–Condition–Action (ECA) paradigm of active databases [19] is applicable. However, it needs to be extended for real-time use. We use techniques such as prefetching and caching. In general, event specification facilitates relative invocation of synchronization or serialization of media objects. In particular, time events enable absolute invocation of media objects at specified times. Temporal relationships such as "before" and "after" are directly described by structural operators of the OODB. In summary, our multimedia data model is unique in that it allows concurrent object-oriented computing (i.e., agents) and QOS control for the development of distributed and real-time multimedia applications in addition to set-oriented temporal and spatial operators for associative access to media data unlike other data models.

2. Approach to Videos

Logical video contents need a semantic description of contents, that is, what are recorded. Moreover, logical contents are recorded in several ways, that is, in CODEC such as MPEG and Motion JPEG, and in quality such as frame sizes and rates. Long-duration play of whole video streams is not always required. Users should rather have partial access to video streams to jump to only their necessary portions. We allow users to access video streams with uniform interfaces independent of CODEC by using polymorphism of objects.

To facilitate interactive retrieval of multimedia, we enable users to flexibly and efficiently access partial data such as substreams of videos by temporal information (e.g., temporal intervals), keywords, and other related information. This technique of subsetting a large amount of media data is analogous to RDB views. Note that efficient processing of partial accesses is fully facilitated by combining software techniques such as access methods, clustering, and taking advantage of available hardware such as parallel servers. For example, Fig. 19 illustrates relationships among views, logical contents, and physical streams. A stream view selects a subset of logical contents by specifying a time interval. Keywords are attached to views for keyword-based retrieval. Characteristic data, such as figures, colors, and motion directions, are attached to frames of streams corresponding to views for content-based retrieval. Logical contents have several physical streams of different quality, which are chosen for appropriate QOS control in playback.

Unlike other approaches, we use a lightweight technique to segment scenes and recognize moving objects for content-based retrieval of stream data. First, the system detects scene cuts by using differences in successive frames, such as motion vectors of macro blocks of MPEG and colors. In MPEG coding, we abstract motion vectors of macro blocks by taking advantage of similarity between successive frames and make motion compensation by using such motion vectors. Motion compensation, however, becomes difficult at the point between successive different scenes. At that point, macro blocks with no motion compensation become dominant. So we detect cuts by checking such macro blocks. To enhance the precision of cut detection, we use the difference of colors between successive frames.

Then the user can define views of streams (i.e., substreams) by attaching keywords to such cut scenes. Keywords of stream views enable association between video data and other media data such as texts. Further, the user can

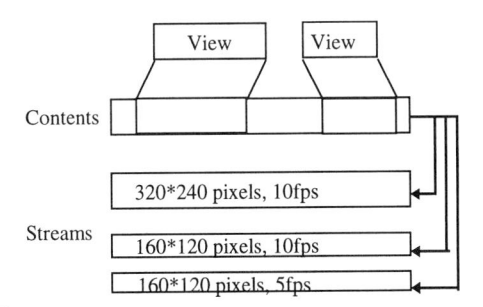

FIGURE 19 Views, contents, and streams.

define new views recursively by combining existing stream views. The system also chooses representative frames within a scene and abstracts characteristic data and stores them into databases. Please note here that matching with representative frames can reduce the recall ratio of a content-based query since characteristic data, such as colors and layouts, change even within a single scene.

The system also detects moving objects by using motion vectors of MPEG. The system decreases the number of colors to more accurately recognize moving objects. The system stores motion directions in addition to figures and colors associated with moving objects. Of course, the user can retrieve substreams corresponding to views with specified keywords. The user can further retrieve substreams containing samples of user-specified colors, figures, and motion directions. The system allows the users to retrieve video substreams containing user-specified moving objects without any interference from the background information because the system distinguishes between the moving objects and the backgrounds unlike other approaches such as QBIC [7]. Content-based retrieval is used by both end users and content providers.

Now we illustrate a scenario for content-based query by using scripts. Scripts allow specification of playback control such as parallel or serial and of layout of played streams. For example, a script for content-based retrieval is specified as follows:

> Script2:
> Set1 = VIEW from VIEW where VIEW.like (Sample1);
> On Event Selection by User;
> Set2 = Set1 from Set1 selected by User;
> Set2.parallel.play;

Here the user specifies a sample, such as Sample1, through a GUI as shown in Fig. 20. A sample figure consists of several parts like a human body. The system abstracts characteristics data from the user-specified sample. The system uses the largest part, such as a human trunk, as a search key to a

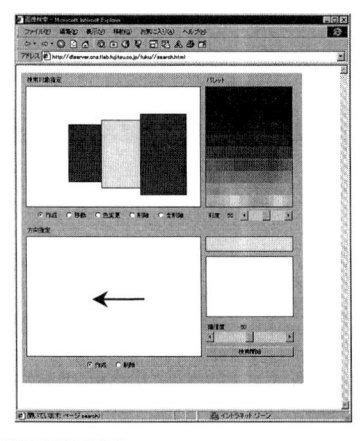

FIGURE 20 A GUI for content-based retrieval.

multidimensional index associated with characteristic data, such as R-tree and its variations [7]. In reality, we use eight indices for eight motion directions (up, down, left, right, and their middles). Each index has three dimensions corresponding to the three primary colors of objects moving in the same direction. The system selects an appropriate index for the user-specified direction and searches the primary key part against the index. The system evaluates the other parts, such as a head and legs, as additional conditions of a query by using the selected index. Of course, the user may explicitly specify favorite key parts other than the largest one. A content-based query evaluates to a set of views, such as Set1. Then the user chooses several views, such as Set2, among the resultant set for simultaneous playback.

We provide means for flexible distribution and presentation of retrieved multimedia data over distributed networks by executing QOS control and scripts. To this end, we use techniques, such as prefetching, caching, synchronization, and distributed processing.

In particular, our script scheduler [25] detects overlaps of intervals of view streams appearing in users' scripts and selects appropriate physical streams by using views to enforce QOS control, unlike other approaches. For example, if the user chooses three streams for parallel playback in Script1, the total playback time is divided into three intervals as shown in Fig. 21. The scheduler chooses physical streams of appropriate quality that can be played with available CPU resources within each interval. In other words, physical streams of different quality may be chosen for the same view such as a stream for View3. We first choose larger frame sizes and then larger frame rates. The system stores load factors obtained by rehearsal play of physical streams and GOP (group Of pictures) numbers and addresses for partial play.

Streams, such as videos, sounds, "streamfield" texts, and combinations of all, can be temporally synchronized with each other. Thus, all streams are guaranteed to be played without losing any frames if there no change occurs in the available CPU resources. Otherwise, the system skips frames which have missed deadlines.

We summarize an agent-based implementation of video data. We represent video streams as agents. As a result, video streams can be executed in parallel. As it takes much CPU load to transform video streams for special effects in general,

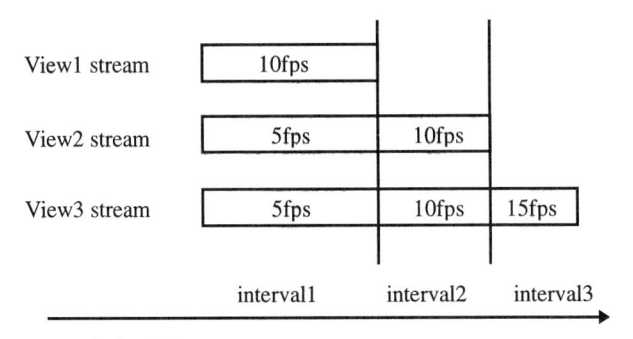

FIGURE 21 A script schedule example.

a stream to transform can be migrated to a different server for processing and only a result stream can be fed back the the originating client. Playback of streams is invoked by events such as the termination of other streams and user interactions.

We logically cluster video streams by using a multidimensional index on characteristic data. So we can allow users to do a similarity-based navigational search through the logically clustered video data. We allow users to store video data either in files, databases, or dedicated servers. We use databases to store logical data, such as keywords, time intervals, and physical data such as load factors, quality, GOP numbers. Bulk data are stored by either files or dedicated stream processors like VOD servers. We sequentially cluster streams in files. However, we decluster streams in dedicated stream servers for striping to provide wider IO bandwidth. We consider networked video applications such as digital libraries, VOD, NOD (news On-demand), and content management by providers.

3. Approach to Texts

Our database system allows users to acquire newly produced media data via distributed networks including ATM LANs and the Internet. Moreover, multidatabase functionality is provided to manage metadata (e.g., a directory) of existing data files or databases and to establish interoperable access to such files and databases. Our technology includes schema translation between OODB and RDB [7, 21, 29], uniform WWW gateways to databases, directory management by databases, and HTML (hypertext markup language) page management by databases. We consider digital libraries and on-line publishing as promising networked text applications.

Now we discuss an approach to text data management, focusing on HTML page management. First, mapping between text contents and formats such as HTML, SGML, and ODA is necessary. We resolve such heterogeneity by using polymorphism, too. Moreover, we need to allow users to acquire texts and reorganize them for further distribution. To this end, we provide HTML page management by databases including storage and retrieval. The system abstracts keywords from texts of collected HTML pages automatically and stores keywords and URL associated with texts into databases. Either HTML texts themselves, or only their file names and URL are stored in databases. In-line images as components of HTML texts are also stored by databases. The system adds URL, file names, titles, anchor character strings (i.e., links), and data types (e.g., GIF, JPEG) as default keywords. The user can delete or add favorite keywords. We prefer the recall ratio to the precision ration of keyword-based retrieval. Relatively addressed links (i.e., URL) are transformed to absolutely addressed links. The users can retrieve pages or components by a wide variety of keywords and drag and drop retrieved pages and components into work pages to create new home pages is a WYSIWYG fashion (see Fig. 22). Content-based retrieval of texts is facilitated by using a full text search engine.

Ease of data acquisition through WWW, however, makes the size of collected data unmanageable for the user. Keyword-based retrieval alone is not sufficient. So we logically cluster texts for similarity-based navigation. The system automatically abstracts keywords from collected HTML or SGML

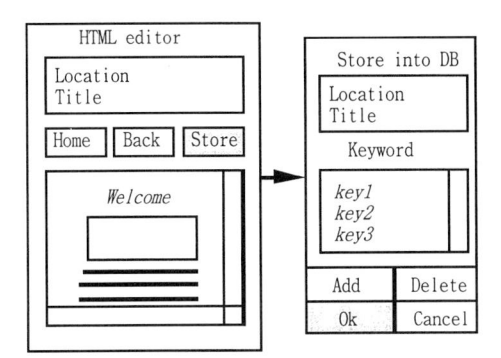

FIGURE 22 An HTML editor session.

texts. Then the system chooses the most frequent 100 keywords contained by a set of texts and places each text in the information space of 100 axes ranging from having the corresponding keyword to not having it. The system uses a *Self-Organizing Map* (SOM) [28] technique to logically cluster a set of collected texts into the given number of groups in the retrieval space. The system displays the structured map by using 2-D or 3-D graphics such as VRML. The user can retrieve texts by navigating a 2-D or 3-D user interface. Ti and Ki in Fig. 23 denote texts and keywords, respectively. The point is that the users cluster collected texts for their own use. Of course, content providers can use this technique when they cluster their own texts in advance.

We briefly describe how we have applied the SOM technique to logical text clustering. Input patterns to the information space, that is, texts have normalized characteristic vectors Vi [$vi1, \ldots, viM$] $i = 1, \ldots, N$. We choose 100 for M, that is, the most 100 frequent keywords. N denotes the total number of texts and is 100 for the moment. If a value of vij is 1, an input text i has a keyword

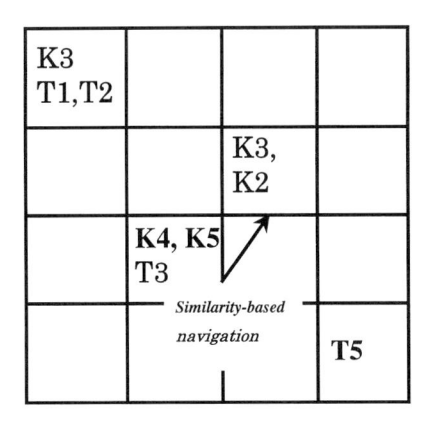

FIGURE 23 An SOM retrieval map.

key j; if the value is 0, then the text has no such keyword. On the other hand, grid patterns in the two-dimensional retrieval space Pij are assigned appropriate characteristic vectors as initial values $Vpij$ in the information space. For example, we use 10-by-10 grid patterns with a torus nature. Here we define similarity SIM between characteristic vectors Vi and Vj, distance DIS between them, length of a vector LEN, and vector operations PLUS, MINUS, DIV as follows:

SIM (Vi, Vj): sum ($vik * vjk$) $k = 1, \ldots, M$.
DIS (Vi, Vj): square-root (sum (square($vik - vjk$)) $k = 1, \ldots, M$).
LEN (Vi): square-root (sum (square(vik)) $k = 1, \ldots, M$).
PLUS (Vi, Vj): [($vik + vjk$)] $k = 1, \ldots, M$.
MINUS (Vi, Vj): [($vik - vjk$)] $k = 1, \ldots, M$.
DIV (Vi, C): [(vjk/C)] $k = 1, \ldots, M$.

Procedure (1). First, we select an input pattern Vi which has the maximum similarity with a grid pattern Pij and we move Pij, that is, its characteristic vector $Vpij$, closer to Vi in the information space. New $V'pij$ is calculated as

V' = PLUS ($Vpij$, DIV (MINUS (Vi, $Vpij$), exp ($A*R*R$)))
$V'pij$ = DIV (V', LEN (V')); normalization,

where $A < 1$ and R = DIS (Vi, $Vpij$).

Next we move grid patterns in the neighborhood of Pij (i.e., $Pij+1$, $Pij-1$, $Pi+1j$, $Pi-1j$, $Pi+1j+1$, $Pi+1j-1$, $Pi-1j+1$, $Pi-1j-1$) closer to Vi at that time.

We repeat PROCEDURE (1) until the maximum similarity between grid patterns and input patterns exceeds a limit. For the moment, we choose A such that repetition times is less than 10. After the termination of PROCEDURE (1), each input pattern is mapped to its nearest grid patterns in the retrieval space. We also apply PROCEDURE (1) to keywords, which are represented as characteristic vectors having only one nonzero element. Thus, we can map input patterns and keywords to the retrieval space with holding their topological relationships in the information space.

Once the clustering by SOM is completed, we map new input patterns to grid patterns whose vectors are most similar to those of new input patterns unless the total number of input patterns exceeds a limit. If the total number exceeds the limit, we recluster all the input patterns. We can avoid too frequent clustering by implementing the clustering as an agent. The clustering agent responds to the event that the total number of input patterns exceeds a limit ($N*n, n = 1, 2, \ldots$).

We can apply the SOM technique to cluster videos and components programs, too. If we apply the SOM to a mixture of videos, texts, and program components, we get hypermedia links among heterogeneous media data, based on similarity of contents.

Generally, we provide media data management mechanisms which enable efficient storage and access of large amounts of media data. They enable users to customize media-specific storage in aspects such as indexing, clustering, and buffering. We take an object-oriented approach to resolving heterogeneity in data formats, CODEC, and physical media, used for implementation of logical media.

Here we describe our physical clustering facility by taking structured texts or compound documents consisting of simple texts, graphics, images, and videos. Structured texts such as SGML texts are often accessed according to component links. The system clusters relevant texts in the same or neighborhood pages to allow efficient retrieval of them. We assume that the user chooses to cluster texts. Thus, the user specifies how data are clustered. Then the system actually clusters data according to the user's specification. In future, we plan to provide a facility to monitor hot spots of access patterns. Either the system or the user clusters data based on the result of monitored accesses. We allow the user to recluster data after heavy updates. In addition to heterogeneous clustering, we allow homogeneous clustering such as all instances of the same class. We allow subtrees of a whole component tree to be flexibly clustered according to the user's specification by combining homogeneous and heterogeneous clustering.

To implement physical clustering, we introduce two types of pages. We usually use a single page to store instances of the same class, that is, for homogeneous clustering. We devise a multiple page to store instances of heterogeneous classes, that is, heterogeneous clustering. A multiple page consists of single pages. Each of them has its own size and contains instances of its own class. Multiple pages as a whole are mapped to contiguous space.

4. Approach to Program Components

To allow for access control of digital libraries, we must maintain integrity of programs for database access. Further, we must maintain program components for software reuse such as digital library application development. We must divide processing between clients and servers. The retrieved result is rather large, so we must adopt protocols sufficient for transfer of bulk data different from HTTP.

To this end, we allow users to execute or download programs on-line such as database access and to download program components for application development. So we manage component programs such as Java Applets and ActiveX Controls by maintaining integrity of programs, that is, consistent combinations of component programs. Programs can be executed on-line and visually.

Program components are managed by database servers. The system maintains information such as consistent combination or configuration of programs. When the user requires programs, the system compares the user's configuration and the server's current configuration and then sends only differences by looking up the configuration version and the user level stored by databases.

Programs are updated and further moved from one server to another. Programs have physical aspects such as program names, program files (or OID), and versions. Programs have logical aspects such as interfaces (i.e., signatures). So we provide program views as mapping between physical and logical aspects of programs. We can conceal changes of physical aspects from users by using such program views. Integrity maintenance is done either by eager propagation of updates using an ECA paradigm or by deferred propagation of updates using a time stamp.

The system processes programs by distributing processes between clients and servers specified by scripts. For example, client processes take care of a graphical user interface and server processes take care of database access. The query result is sent back to the client by the database system's protocols.

In addition to direct access of program components, a query over components by keywords is allowed. If a user's query for program components is not satisfied by one server, the query is federated to other servers. We take an agent-based approach to such a federation. The search agent also uses the SOM technique to construct a map for navigating the query through relevant servers, which is a new approach. The query retrieval is sent to the mail box specified by the client, from which the client obtains program components.

The system automatically abstracts keywords for program components from their signatures and explanatory texts and logically clusters program components based on such keywords using the SOM technique. As a result, we obtain an *intraserver map* for similarity-based search, which is more useful in a program query than the simple keyword-based query facility.

A map for guide in the navigation of servers is constructed from the results of application of the SOM technique to a set of component servers. Thus, keywords selected for an intraserver map when the SOM is applied to cluster program components within local servers are considered as characteristic data of local servers. Then we cluster servers by again using the SOM to get a *interserver map*. The interserver map associates keywords and servers, instead of texts. The system can find most relevant servers using the interserver map. Please note that the interserver map by the SOM can be constructed for videos and texts, too. Moreover, physical clustering applied to structured texts can also be applied to component programs through caller–callee relationships between program components like parent–child relationships between structured texts.

We summarize an agent-based implementation of program component management. Selected programs can be executed *in situ* using distributed object management such as CORBA, although they can be downloaded to client sites like Java Applets. So component programs are agents executable in a distributed manner. The search process moves from server to server via the interserver map for federating a query. Thus, the search process has agent characteristics. Integration maintenance by ECA responds to the event of updates as an agent process.

D. Conclusion

In this section, we have proposed a multimedia database system for networked multimedia applications such as digital libraries and document warehousing, based on an OODB model extended with concepts of agents. We have implemented an early prototype multimedia database system to verify the proposed approach. This prototype supports multimedia scripting, keyword-based and content-based multimedia view retrieval with QOS control, SOM-based logical data clustering, heterogeneous physical data clustering, and WWW/database integration. It has been applied to in-house digital libraries and has proved to be effective. We plan to enhance the functionality and performance of our system in order to make the system applicable to industrial applications.

V. CONCLUSION

First, in this paper we described a prototype object-oriented DBMS called Jasmine, focusing on the implementation of its object-oriented features. Jasmine shares a lot of functionality with other object-oriented database systems. However, Jasmine has the following features that differentiate it from other systems. Jasmine provides a powerful query language that allows users to specify complex objects, class hierarchies, and methods in queries. Jasmine optimizes such object-oriented queries by using hash joins, B-tree and hash indexes, and semantic information. Individual object access is evaluated on object buffers. Jasmine extends relational database technology. Jasmine provides nested relations to efficiently manage complex objects and provides user-defined functions evaluated on page buffers to efficiently process method invocation in queries. Jasmine provides a view facility for schema integration and a constraint management facility including integrity constraints, triggers, and rules. We compare Jasmine with current commercial object-oriented database systems and research prototypes as follows.

GemStone [32] originates from the attempt to make Smalltalk-80 programs databases. The GemStone data model is based on Smalltalk-80 and supports only single inheritance while Jasmine supports multiple inheritance. In addition to C, C++, and Smalltalk-80 interfaces, GemStone provides a programming interface called OPAL. GemStone distinguishes between a class and a collection of objects. A query expressed by OPAL is formulated against a single collection of objects. A Jasmine query is formulated against classes, allowing explicit joins.

ORION [26] supports a variety of functions, such as multiple inheritance, composite objects, versions, queries, and schema evolution. ORION is built in Lisp on a secondary storage system that provides facilities for segment and page management. ORION provides a programming interface to an object-oriented extension of Lisp. A query returns a collection of instances of a single class while a Jasmine query can generate instances combining more than one class. Mapping object identifiers to pointers is done by extensible hashing. A query with attributes of nonleaf classes is processed by use of a class-hierarchy index unlike Jasmine. ORION evaluates a query against the object and page buffers and merges the results while Jasmine uses the single-evaluation scheme. ORION uses sort-merge joins while Jasmine uses hash joins.

In O2 [5], an object contains a value, a list, a set, and a tuple as an attribute value. O2 is used through an object-oriented extension of C called CO2. The query language is defined rather formally. The query retrieves and composes a list, a set, and a tuple. O2 is implemented on top of WiSS (Wisconsin Storage System) in C. WiSS provides persistency, disk management, and concurrency control for flat records. Unlike Jasmine, O2 uses physical identifiers of WiSS records as object identifiers. Like ORION, O2 adopts a dual buffer management scheme. Like Jasmine, O2 uses a hash table to manage in-memory objects, but unlike Jasmine, O2 uses a class-hierarchy index to process queries against nonleaf classes.

In IRIS [31], based on the DAPLEX functional model, properties or methods defined by a class are represented as functions on the class. Functions are stored or derived from other functions. IRIS supports multiple inheritance, versions, schema evolution, and queries. Query optimization is done by rule bases. Unlike Jasmine, IRIS is implemented on a relational storage system that supports only flat relations. IRIS has C and Lisp interfaces, but supports no integration with object-oriented programming languages while Jasmine does.

Next we discussed an object-oriented database approach to engineering as an advanced application. Then we described schema translation by view as an extension to Jasmine. OODBs have just been developed, so there are very few reports of real applications. We would like to apply our OODB Jasmine to various real-world problems, not only to verify the validity of our approach but to also give feedback to Jasmine from the experiences.

Our future plans include research on technical issues associated with exploratory aspects of advanced applications such as design: The incorporation of version management, constraint management, and view management in a heterogeneous environment. Version management is mandatory for exploratory applications, but concepts of versions differ from application to application. It is important to propose generic concepts of versions from which specific versions can be derived and to include both instance and class versioning. To explore design alternatives and propagate updates, we must incorporate generalized constraint management including constraint satisfaction rules and composite events [19]. To support cooperative exploration in a heterogeneous environment consisting of relational and object-oriented systems, we must provide more advanced view support that allows the user to look at schemas defined by other users in other systems (e.g., relational systems) differently from the original ones as if they were object-oriented.

REFERENCES

1. Batory, D. S., Leung, T. Y., and Wise, T. E. Implementation concept for an extensible data model and data language, *ACM Trans. Database Syst.* 13(3): 231–262, 1988.
2. Carey, M. J., Dewitt, D. J., and Vandenberg, S. L. A data model and query language for EXODUS. In *Proc. of the 1988 ACM SIGMOD Conference*, Chicago, IL, June 1988, pp. 413–423. ACM, New York, 1988.
3. Date, C. J. *An Introduction to Database Systems*, Vol. 1. Addison-Wesley, Reading, MA, 1990.
4. Debloch, S. *et al.* KRISYS: KBMS support for better CAD systems. In *Proc. of the 2nd International Conference on Data and Knowledge Systems for Manufacturing and Engineering*, Gaithersburg, MD, Oct. 1989, pp. 172–182. IEEE, Los Alamitos, CA, 1989.
5. Duex, O. *et al.* The story of O2. *IEEE Trans. Knowledge Data Eng.* 2(1): 91–108, 1990.
6. Fishman, D. H. *et al.* IRIS: An object-oriented database management system. *ACM Trans. Office Inform. Systems* 5(1): 48–69, 1987.
7. Flickner, M. *et al.* Query by image and video content: The QBIC system. *IEEE Computer* 28(9): 23–32, 1995.
8. Gibbs, S., Breiteneder, C., and Tsichritzis, D. Data modeling of time-based media. In *Proc. of ACM Sigmod Conference*, May 1994, pp. 91–101.
9. Goldberg, A., and Robson, D. *Smalltalk-80: The Language and Its Implementation*. Addison-Wesley, Reading, MA, 1983.
10. Hamakawa, R., and Rekimoto, J. Object composition and playback models for handling multimedia data. *ACM Multimedia Systems* 2: 26–35, 1994.
11. Ishikawa, H., Izumida, Y., Yoshino, T., Hoshiai, T., and Makinouchi, A. A knowledge-based

approach to design a portable natural language interface to database systems. In *Proc. of the IEEE Data Engineering Conference*, pp. 134–143. IEEE, Los Alamitos, CA, 1986.

12. Ishikawa, H., Izumida, Y., Yoshino, T., Hoshiai, T., and Makinouchi, A. KID: Designing a knowledge-based natural language interface. *IEEE Expert* 2(2): 57–71, 1987.

13. Ishikawa, H., Suzuki, F., and Makinouchi, A. Object-oriented multimedia knowledge base management system: Design and implementation. In *Proc. of the 2nd International Symposium on Interoperable Information Systems*, Tokyo, Japan, Nov. 1988, pp. 195–202. INTAP, Japan, 1988.

14. Ishikawa, H. An object-oriented knowledge base approach to a next generation of hypermedia system. In *Proc. of the 35th IEEE COMPCON Conference*, San Francisco, CA, pp. 520–527, IEEE, Los Alamitos, CA, 1990.

15. Ishikawa, H., Izumida, Y., and Kawato, N. An Object-oriented database: System and applications. In *Proc. of the IEEE Pacific Rim Conf. Communications, Computers, and Signal Processing*, Victoria, B.C., Canada, pp. 288–291. IEEE, Los Alamitos, CA, 1991.

16. Ishikawa, H. *The Design and Implementation of an Object-Oriented Database System for Advanced Applications*. Ph.D. Thesis., University of Tokyo, 1992.

17. Ishikawa, H. *et al.* An object-oriented database system and its view mechanism for schema integration. In *Proc. of the Second Far-East Workshop on Future Database Systems*, Kyoto, Japan, April 1992, pp. 194–200.

18. Ishikawa, H. *et al.* The design and implementation of an object-oriented multimedia knowledge base management system. *ACM Trans. Database Systems* 18(1): 1–50, 1993.

19. Ishikawa, H., and Kubota, K. An active object-oriented database: A multi-paradigm approach to constraint management. In *Proc. of the 19th VLDB Conference (Dublin, Ireland)*, Aug. 1993, pp. 467–478. VLDB endowment.

20. Ishikawa, H. *Object-Oriented Database System*. Springer-Verlag, Berlin, 1993.

21. Ishikawa, H. *et al.* A script-based approach to relational and object-oriented database interoperability. In *Proc. of Intl. Symposium on Advanced Database Technologies and Their Integration*, Oct. 1994.

22. Ishikawa, H. *et al.* A next-generation industry multimedia database system. In *Proc. of IEEE 12th Intl. Conference on Data Engineering*, pp. 364–371, 1996.

23. Ishikawa, H. *et al.* An object-oriented database system Jasmine: Implementation, application, and extension. *IEEE Trans. Knowledge Data Eng.* 8(2): 285–304, 1996.

24. Ishikawa, H. *et al.* An extended object-oriented database approach to networked multimedia applications. In *Proc. of IEEE 14th Intl. Conference on Data Engineering*, pp. 259–266, 1998.

25. Kato, K., Kondo, A., and Ishikawa, H. Multimedia database infoServer—Script and video playback. In *Proc. of the 7th Data engineering Workshop*, pp. 109–114, 1996. [In Japanese.]

26. Kim, W. *et al.* Architecture of the ORION next-generation database system. *IEEE Trans. Knowledge Data Eng.* 2(1): 109–124, 1990.

27. Kitagawa, H., and Kunii, T. L. *The Unnormalized Relational Data Model for Office Form Processor Design*. Springer-Verlag, Tokyo, 1989.

28. Kohonen, T. *Self-Organizing Maps*. Springer-Verlag, Berlin, 1995.

29. Kubota, K., and Ishikawa, H. Structural schema translation in multidatabase system: Jasmine/M. In *Proc. of IPSJ Advanced Database Symposium*, 1994. [In Japanese.]

30. Larson, P.-A. Linear hashing with partial expansions. In *Proc. of the 6th VLDB Conference*, Montreal, Canada, 1980, pp. 224–232. ACM, New York, 1980.

31. Lyngbaek, P., and Vianu, V. Mapping a semantic database model to the relational model. In *Proc. of the 1987 ACM SIGMOD Conference*, San Francisco, CA, 1987, pp. 132–142. ACM, New York, 1987.

32. Maier, D. *et al.* Development of an object-oriented DBMS. In *Proc. of the 1st OOPSLA Conference*, Portland, OR, 1986, pp. 472–482. ACM, New York, 1986.

33. Morgenstern, M. Active databases as a paradigm for enhanced computing environments. In *Proc. of the 9th VLDB Conference*, Florence, Italy, Oct. 1983, pp. 34–42. VLDB endowment, 1983.

34. Special Issue: Digital Libraries, *CACM* 38(4): 1995.

35. Stefik, M., and Bobrow, D. G. Object-oriented programming: Themes and variations. *AI Magazine* 6(4): pp. 40–62, 1986.

36. Yamane, Y. A hash join technique for relational database systems. In *Proc. of the Foundation of Data Organization Conference,* Kyoto, Japan, May 1985, pp. 388–398.
37. Yamane, Y. *et al.* Design and evaluation of a high-speed extended relational database engine, XRDB. In *Proc. of International Symposium on Database Systems for Advanced Applications,* Seoul, Korea, April 1989, pp. 52–60.
38. Zloof, M. Security and integrity within the query-by-example data base management language. IBM Research Report RC6982, Feb. 1978.

4
QUERY OPTIMIZATION CONCEPTS AND METHODOLOGIES IN MULTIDATABASE SYSTEMS[1]

CHIANG LEE

Institute of Information Engineering, National Cheng-Kung University, Tainan, Taiwan, Republic of China

I. INTRODUCTION   124
II. SEMANTIC DISCREPANCY AND SCHEMA CONFLICTS   126
   A. Semantic Discrepancy   126
   B. Schema Conflicts   127
III. OPTIMIZATION AT THE ALGEBRA LEVEL   130
   A. Fundamentals and the Concepts of Lub   131
   B. The Structure of a Hyperrelation (R^H)   133
   C. Schema Conformation: R^H Schema and the Mapping   134
   D. The Hyperrelational Algebra   139
   E. A Comparison with Related Works   149
IV. OPTIMIZATION AT THE EXECUTION STRATEGY LEVEL   151
   A. Assumptions   154
   B. Where Should an Intersite Operation Be Performed?   154
   C. Different from the Issues in Traditional Database Systems   156
   D. Two Scheduling Strategies Not Involving PDBS   157
   E. PDBS Sharing Workload with the MDBS   159
   F. The Maximum Merge Scheduling (MMS) Strategy   161
   G. Performance Study   165
V. CONCLUSIONS   170
   REFERENCES   171

In a multidatabase system (MDBS), the participating databases are autonomous. The schemas of these databases may be different in various manner even though the same information is represented. The execution of a global query in this environment involves levels of translations. Query optimization can be partially achieved in each of these levels. We first discuss in this chapter the past research at these optimization levels. A problem with translation is that it lacks a convenient representation of the integrated

[1]This work was supported by the National Science Council under Grant NSC85-2213-E-006-018.

schema at the system level and a sound mathematical basis for data manipulation in a multidatabase system. To resolve this problem, we present the concept of hyperrelation and use it as a powerful and succinct model for the global level representation of heterogeneous database schemas. A hyperrelation has the structure of a relation, but its contents are the schemas of the semantically equivalent local relations in the databases. With this representation, the metadata of the global database and local databases and the data of these databases are all representable by using the structure of a relation. The impact of such a representation is that all the elegant features of relational systems can be easily extended to multidatabase systems. A hyperrelational algebra is designed accordingly. This algebra is performed at the MDBS level such that query transformation and optimization is supported on a sound mathematical basis.

Another most critical level of optimization is at the execution strategy level. Difficulties of optimization at this level is that each participating database system does not own the information (data) and the mechanism (software) required for converting data of one database to another to resolve the data-type conflict problems. More importantly, this confines the processing of an intersite operation (such as a join over two relations of different databases) to within the MDBS only. The participating database systems are not able to share the workload of the MDBS in this environment. Hence, how to minimize the consumption of MDBS resources is an urgent problem. In the second part of this chapter, we present three scheduling algorithms that are used in an MDBS to reduce the processing cost of a multidatabase query. A major difference between our strategies and the past methods is that ours does not require the regeneration of the cost models of the participating databases. Hence, it also minimizes the indeterminacy existing in multidatabase query optimizations.

I. INTRODUCTION

A multidatabase system is a system that manages databases as a repository resource and allows application programs to access this resource in a heterogeneous distributed environment [1, 3, 13, 39, 40, 69, 74, 79]. In such an environment, query processing is very time-consuming as multiple levels of conversions (of data as well as the query) among heterogeneous systems are required. Query optimization becomes an especially important task in order to reduce the query processing time. This issue, however, has attracted far less attention from researchers than it deserves. Looking into those approaches proposed, we see that the multidatabase query optimization issues were studied from different levels of a multidatabase system. They include:

Schema level. This is the highest level of optimization and the least-studied level in multidatabase systems. A query may be expressible in completely different forms in different databases, as schemas of different databases are often represented in different manners. As a result, selecting a proper site will facilitate the execution of a query. This allows us to achieve query optimization at the multidatabase schema level. Studying the effect of different schemas (i.e., representations of data) on the cost of query execution is the focus of research at this level. References [46, 49] are the only works found in the literature proposing solutions for issues in this category. More research in this area is needed.

Semantic query optimization level. It intends to reduce query execution cost through the elimination/reduction of operations or reduce query search space by utilizing the semantic knowledge of databases (e.g., the sum of a person's salaries in all databases is the person's total salary). Reference [64] gives an example of research in this category. However, only aggregate operations (such as *sum, avg, max, min*) have been discussed so far in current research.

Algebra level. There are also approaches utilizing algebraic transformation for query optimization. Similar to centralized databases, a query is expressed in an algebraic expression. By using transformation rules, the expression is representable as a set of equivalent expressions. Optimization is achieved by choosing one of the expressions that incurs the least processing cost. The algebra, however, is an extension of the relational algebra. These researches include a multirelational algebra [33] for loosely coupled multidatabase systems (those without an integrated schema) and a hyperrelational algebra [48] for tightly coupled multidatabase systems (those with an integrated schema).

Execution strategy level. The goal of this level of optimization is to estimate the processing time for relational operations (mainly join) by figuring out the *cost model* of a given DBMS [24, 61, 83, 86]. Whether the join is performed by a hash, a sort-merge, or a nested loop algorithm, and whether a relation is indexed/clustered are the key factors considered in their research. Based on the estimated cost models of the participating databases in a multidatabases environment, the multidatabase management system (MDBS) is able to determine the most suitable database(s) to process the query. Du *et al.* [25] later proposed strategies for reducing the response time of query processing in multidatabase systems. Although an autonomy of systems is considered in these approaches, representation discrepency of data in different systems are not taken into account. Reference [50] relaxes this assumption and proposes solutions for query optimization considering data heterogeneity.

Operation level. Outerjoin and outerunion are frequently used operations in multidatabase systems. Reference [11] studies the optimization of an outerjoin operation. An outerjoin of R and S can be expressed as the union of three components: (1) the join of R and S, (2) the dangling tuples of R padded with null values, and (3) the dangling tuples of S padded with null values. Reference [11] identifies the situations when an outerjoin can be reduced to a one-sided (i.e., left or right) outerjoin or even a regular join operation when there is no data inconsistency. Reference [63] extends the result to situations when data inconsistency exists.

In this chapter, we discuss the optimization issue at the two most important levels: the algebra level and the execution strategy level. They are the two levels easiest to implement and most influential in terms of improving the performance. The algebra level optimization is important because by applying algebraic transformation to a query, we can derive the equivalent expressions of the query. They all lead to the same query result but incur different exeuction costs. Hence, optimization at the algebra level is a key step in every database management system. Optimization at the execution strategy level is crucial due to a very similar reason: it is a necessary component in a query optimizer. By

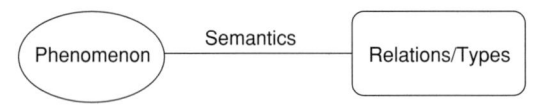

```
┌─────────────┐   Semantics   ┌──────────────┐
│  Phenomenon │───────────────│ Relations/Types│
└─────────────┘               └──────────────┘
```

FIGURE 1 Semantics.

generating and evaluating various execution strategies, a system is able to find an optimal plan for a query execution. The content of this presentation is based on our previous work published in [48] and [50].

The rest of this chapter is organized as follows. In Section II, we depicts the concepts of semantic discrepancy and the various types of schema conflicts. In Section III, we present the optimization at the algebra level. A hyperrelational algebra is presented accordingly. The algebraic transformation rules are also discussed in detail, and a comparison of this algebra with another multirelational algebra is given in this section. In Section IV, we discuss the optimization at the execution strategy level. A few strategies are presented and their cost models and performance analysis are discussed. Finally, the conclusion of this chapter is given in Section V.

II. SEMANTIC DISCREPANCY AND SCHEMA CONFLICTS

A. Semantic Discrepancy

Most of the information systems provide a set of constructs to model data of the real world. Each of these constructs is considered as a type, which may be a complex type (usually defined by the user) or a primitive type (normally provided by a system). The connection between the type and the data represented by that type is called the semantics. According to *The Oxford English Dictionary*[2] semantic (semasiology) is "the relationships between linguistic symbols and their meanings, or the interpretation of signs in general." In addition, the *Webster's Third New International Dictionary*[3] says that semantics is "the study dealing with the relations between signs and what they refer to, or the study of the relations of a sign to its referent and to other signs within a system."

In relational database systems, relations are the only user-defined types used to model the real world phenomena, and the relationships between the types and the referents decide the semantics of the relations, as shown in Fig. 1.

Two relations are said to be semantically equivalent if the relationships between the types and their corresponding referents are the same. For example, Fig. 2 shows two relations *Student* and *Stud* used in distinct databases to model students of two universities. They are considered semantically equivalent because they both model the information about students (i.e., the types and their corresponding referents are the same), no matter whether the sets of students are the same.

On the other hand, even if the sets of referents of two relations are the same, it does not necessarily imply that the two relations are semantically equivalent. For example, in Fig. 3, two databases model the same set of persons from

---

[2] Second Edition, Volume XIV, Clarendon Press, Oxford.
[3] Merriam-Webster, Incorporated, 1976.

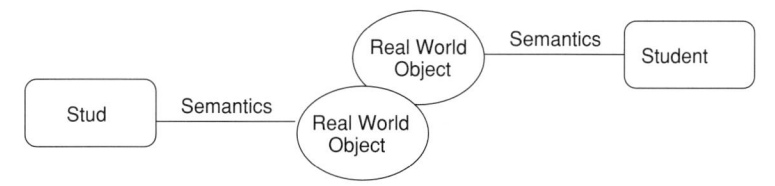

FIGURE 2 Two semantically equivalent relations.

different viewpoints. One models them as *Student*, while the other models them as *Employee*. They are not semantically equivalent because the relationships between the types and their referents (*Student* and *Employee*) are different.

Semantically equivalent relations need not have the same set of attributes. For example, in Fig. 4 the two relations *Student* and *Stud* are semantically equivalent, but their sets of attributes are not equivalent. The address information in *Student* is represented as *street, city, state*, but represented as *address* in *Stud*. Also, *Student* has *birthday*, whereas *Stud* has *gender*.

B. Schema Conflicts

Various types of conflicts can exist between schemas of relations in different databases. Since *value, attribute,* and *table* are the three major components of a database, the conflicts can be roughly classified into six types: *value-versus-table, value-versus-attribute, value-versus-value, attribute-versus-table, attribute-versus-attribute,* and *table-versus-table* conflicts [49]. An X-versus-Y conflict means that an X in one database is represented as a Y in another database. A multidatabase UNIV-DATABASE will be used as an example for illustration. The database consists of component databases of four universities and colleges as shown in Fig. 5.

1. Value-versus-Value Conflict

The value-versus-value conflict arises when different types of values are used in the same type of attributes. This type of conflict includes *expression conflicts, data unit conflicts,* and *precision conflicts*. Suppose that one database use {Excellent, Good, Fair, Poor, Bad} to represent the score of a student, while {1, 2, 3, 4, 5} is used in another database. We say that there exist expression conflicts between these two databases. A unit conflict exists if in one database the height of a student is measured in centimeters and in another it is in feet. A precision conflict exists if the scores of students fall in the range {0--100} in one database and {0.0--100.0} in another database.

In the literature, these problems are also referred to as the domain mismatch problems. Many works have been proposed to resolve these problems [20, 45, 55, 56, 75, 78].

FIGURE 3 Two semantically different relations.

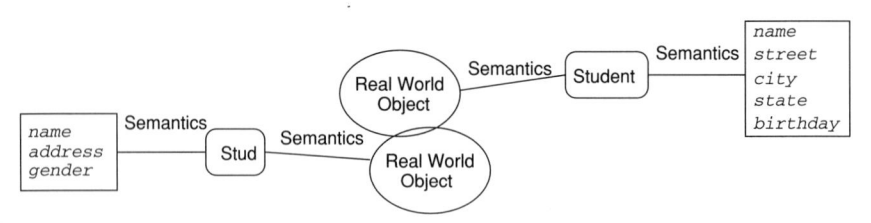

FIGURE 4 Information provided by databases.

2. Attribute-versus-Attribute Conflict

This type of conflict occurs when the relations in component databases use different numbers of attributes to represent the same information. For example, in CDB1 the addresses of the students are stored in one attribute **Addr**, while in CDB2 and CDB3 the same information is stored in three attributes (No, Str, State) and (Str, City, State), respectively. This type of conflict can be further classified into the following subtypes: *one-to-zero, one-to-one, one-to-many*, and *many-to-many* conflicts. A one-to-zero conflict is a *missing attribute* conflict, meaning that some attributes in a table do not appear in any form in the corresponding semantically equivalent table(s) of another database. For example, both the tables **Stud** of CDB1 and **CS_Stud** of CDB2 store data about students. However, the attribute **Gender** is missing from the table **CS_Stud**. A many-to-many attribute conflict means that two different sets of attributes are

University Database	Relation Name	Attributes
CDB1 (Uni. A)	Stud	(S#, Name, Addr, Tel#, Gender, Class)
	Course	(C#, Name, Credit, Type)
	Take	(S#, C#, Grade)
	Faculty	(SSN, Name, Addr, SpouseName)
CDB2 (College. B)	CS_Stud	(SN, FN, LN, No, Str, State, Tel#, Grade)
	Math_Stud	(SN, FN, LN, No, Str, State, Tel#, Grade)
	EE_Stud	(SN, FN, LN, No, Str, State, Tel#, Grade)
	Fndmntl_Crs	(CN, Name, Credits)
	Advncd_Crs	(CN, Name, Credits, Prereq-C#)
	Participate	(SN, CN, Score)
	Faculty	(F-SSN, Name, Addr, S-SSN)
	Spouse	(S-SSN, Name)
CDB3 (Uni. C)	Studs	(SSN, SNo, Name, Str, City, State, Gender, Class)
	Lecture	(CNo, Name, Credit)
	Tutorial	(CNo, Name, Credit)
	Seminar	(CNo, Name)
	Indvl_stdy	(CNo, Name)
	Takes	(SSN, CNo, Grade)
CDB4 (College. D)	ST1	(S#, Name, Addr, Tel#, Sex)
	ST2	(S#, Name, Addr, Tel#, Sex)
	ST3	(S#, Name, Addr, Tel#, Sex)
	ST4	(S#, Name, Addr, Tel#, Sex)
	Courses	(C#, Name, Credit, Hours, Fndmntl, Advncd)
	Enroll	(S#, C#, Score)

FIGURE 5 Component database schemas of four universities.

used to model the same information in two databases. Actually, the one-to-one and the one-to-many attribute conflicts are only special cases of the many-to-many conflict.

3. Attribute-versus-Table Conflict

This type of conflict occurs when an attribute in a relation of one database is represented as a table in another database. For example, in Fig. 5 the attribute SpouseName in relation Faculty of CDB1 stores the names of the spouses of the faculties, while in CDB2 the same information is modeled as a relation Spouse. As relevant information is stored in separate relations (e.g., Faculty and Spouse of CDB2), a foreign key is used in the Faculty of CDB2 to link to the associated Spouse information.

4. Value-versus-Attribute Conflict

In the multidatabase example, Course in CDB1 and Courses in CDB4 are two tables storing the data about the courses provided in the universities. They include the course number, the course name, the credits, and the type of courses. Suppose that the domain of Type of the courses in CDB1 is {fundamental, advanced}, and in CDB4 fundamental courses are further separated into lectures and tutorials, and advanced courses are also divided into seminars and individual studies. Then the value of attribute Type is expressed as attributes Fndmntl and Advncd in CDB4. This conflict is called the value-versus-attribute conflict, since the values in one database are treated as attributes in another database.

5. Value-versus-Table Conflict

In CDB1, student information is kept in one relation Stud, while in CDB2 they are distributed into three relations CS_Stud, Math_Stud, and EE_Stud, and in CDB4 the data are distributed into four relations ST1, ST2, ST3, and ST4. The three relations CS_Stud, Math_Stud, and EE_Stud store data about students majoring in "Computer Science," "Mathematics," and "Electronic Engineering," respectively. Also the four relations ST1, ST2, ST3, and ST4 store data about freshman, sophomore, junior, and senior students, respectively. These conflicts are considered as value-versus-table conflicts, as the values of an attribute in one database (e.g., Stud.Class of CDB1) are represented as the names of tables in another database, or equivalently, the data in one table are the metadata of another table. This type of conflict together with the value-versus-attribute conflict are often referred to as the types of conflicts between data and metadata.

6. Table-versus-Table Conflict

The table-versus-table conflict can be explored via two dimensions—*difference in number of tables* and *difference in the set of attributes*. The first dimension indicates that different numbers of tables are employed to model the same real world semantics in the databases. As the semantic information is the same, the difference must be caused by either the value-versus-table conflicts or the attribute-versus-table conflicts. (Other types of conflicts will not result in different numbers of tables when the same information is modeled.) Note that both of these two types are covered already. As for issues on the second dimension in this type of conflict, i.e., the sets of attributes are different (but the numbers of involved tables in the two databases are the same), they are exactly what the attribute-versus-attribute type of conflict is talking about. Hence, all scenarios of table-versus-table conflicts are not new; they have been fully covered in the previous cases.

III. OPTIMIZATION AT THE ALGEBRA LEVEL

Schema conformation primarily emphasizes the task of homogenizing the *semantically equivalent*, but *structurally different* (i.e., schema conflicting) classes of data [43, 49]. For instance, height is an attribute of student relations of two databases. It may be measured in feet in one database, while in meters in another database. However, the semantics of "height" in the two databases are the same. For another example, the address information of employees in one database is described by one attribute, while in another database it is modeled as a relation separate from the employee relation. An explicit mapping for these schemas to a global schema needs to be defined and the mapping between the schemas also must be maintained in such multidatabase systems for future query translation.

It is the second (the schema conformation) issue on which this section is focused. In the past, although there have been various proposals for MDBS data modeling and even database languages [5, 7, 17, 20, 56, 58], these proposals are based on fairly high-level and intuitive understanding rather than formal and systematic mapping mechanisms. The hyperrelation concepts presented in the following provides a uniform representation of the global schema and the local schemas (both in relational form) such that the mapping between these two levels of schemas can be clearly defined. In our design, the global schema of a multidatabase system is composed of a set of *hyperrelations*. A hyperrelation is itself a relation containing a set of tuples and each tuple represents the schema of a relation of a component database. The semantics of a hyperrelation is the *least upper bound* (**lub**) of the semantics of the relations mapped onto the hyperrelations (to be detailed). We will demonstrate that by using such a structure; all types of schema-conflicting relations can be mapped to hyperrelations.

Because of this uniform representation of global and local schemas, the relational algebra can be easily extended to an algebra at the multidatabase level. This algebra, termed a hyperrelational algebra, is designed for query transformation and query optimization at the global level.

The major issues answered in this section include:

- How to determine the schema of a hyperrelation such that it properly conveys the semantics of local relations?
- How to map all the local relations onto hyperrelations? (This mapping is important for translating a global query to local subqueries.)
- How to define an algebra based on the designed hyperrelation structure so as to facilitate query transformation and optimization?

For the purposes of this work it is assumed that all other types of heterogeneities such as hardware, operating systems, networks, as well as semantic heterogeneity (as discussed) and value inconsistencies (caused by different units, different precisions, etc.) have been resolved via a homogenizing veneer on each individual database.

A. Fundamentals and the Concepts of Lub

1. Ordering on Information Capacity

In relational databases, attributes are used to describe real world objects. We say that the *capacity* of the information conveyed by a relation is confined by the set of attributes of the relation. For semantically equivalent relations, as their attributes describe objects of the same semantics, the relations' information capacities are comparable. We can envision that a relation with attributes conveying more detailed information should have a greater information capacity than a relation whose attributes express less information. In order to compare the information capacities of two relations, we have the following definition.

DEFINITION 1 (ORDERING ON INFORMATION CAPACITY). Let $A(a_1, a_2, \ldots, a_n)$ and $B(b_1, b_2, \ldots, b_m)$ be two semantically equivalent relations, where a_i $(i = 1, \ldots, n)$ and b_j $(j = 1, \ldots, m)$ are attributes. We say that A is greater in information capacity than B, denoted by $A \sqsupseteq B$, if $\forall b \in \{b_1, b_2, \ldots, b_m\}$, $\exists \alpha \subseteq \{a_1, a_2, \ldots, a_n\}$, such that α and b are corresponding attributes.

Consider the following example. Let Stud(Name, Address, Gender, Age) and Student(Name, Street, City, State, Country, Gender, Birthday) be two (semantically equivalent) relations. The information capacity of Student is greater than that of Stud, since the information that Stud can provide is also provided by Student (i.e., each attribute Stud has a corresponding attribute in Student), but not vice versa. For semantically inequivalent relations, their information capacities are uncomparable (as they describe data of different types).

Note that the statement "$\exists \alpha \subseteq \{a_1, a_2, \ldots, a_n\}$" shows that α can be a subset of attributes in $\{a_1, a_2, \ldots, a_n\}$. Its corresponding attribute b, however, is only an attribute in $\{b_1, b_2, \ldots, b_m\}$. According to this definition, the information capacity of an attribute, such as {Address}, is not equivalent to that of {Street, City, State}, but {Address} $\sqsubseteq$ {Street, City, State} (assuming that all information in Address, such as country name, is also contained in the representation {Street, City, State}). This is the information capacity between *one-to-many* type corresponding attributes. As for *many-to-many* type corresponding attributes, their ordering of information capacity depends on the relationship between attributes. Suppose that $\{r_1, r_2\}$ and $\{s_1, s_2, s_3\}$ are corresponding attributes.

Case 1. The correspondence between attributes of these two sets can be decomposed to one-to-one and one-to-many types of correspondence. For example, r_1 corresponds to s_1 and s_2, and r_2 corresponds to s_3. According to our discussion on corresponding attributes of one-to-many type, we know that $\{r_1, r_2\} \sqsubseteq \{s_1, s_2, s_3\}$.

Case 2. There do not exist one-to-one/one-to-many correspondences between attributes. For instance, r_1 and r_2 represent a semantics that can be further divided into (t,u) and (v,w), respectively, and s_1, s_2, and s_3 are divisible into (t), (u,v), and (w), respectively. In this case, the information capacities of these two sets of attributes are uncomparable. This leads to the definition of the concept of *least upper bound* to be given shortly.

The task of integrating a set of semantically equivalent relations can be viewed as defining another relation such that (1) it is semantically equivalent to the set of relations to be integrated, (2) its information capacity is greater than the set of relations, and (3) it should not contain any information not provided by the set of relations. In other words, the integrated relation schema should be the *least upper bound* of the schemas in component databases. Based on these concepts, we define the least upper bound of relations.

DEFINITION 2 (LEAST UPPER BOUND). Let $\mathcal{U}$ be the universal set of relations, and **A**, **B**, and **C** $\in \mathcal{U}$. **A** and **B** are semantically equivalent relations. We say that **C** is the least upper bound of **A** and **B**, denoted by **C**=**lub**(**A**, **B**), if

1. **C** $\sqsupseteq$ **A** and **C** $\sqsupseteq$ **B**, and
2. $\forall$ **W** $\in \mathcal{U}$, if **W** $\sqsupseteq$ **A** and **W** $\sqsupseteq$ **B**, then **W** $\sqsupseteq$ **C**.

From the definition, we find some obvious properties as follows.

PROPERTY 1 (MINIMAL INCLUSION). *Let $\mathcal{U}$ be the universal set of relations, and **A**, **B**, and **C** $\in \mathcal{U}$. **A** and **B** are semantically equivalent relations. If **C**= **lub**(**A**, **B**), then we have*

1. *Covering: **C** is semantically equivalent to **A** and to **B**.*
2. *Fineness: The information capacity of **C** is greater than those of **A** and **B**.*
3. *Minimality: **C** does not arbitrarily contain the information not provided either by **A** or by **B**.*

PROPERTY 2 (IDEMPOTENCE). *For any relation **A**, the **lub** of **A** is **A** itself.*

PROPERTY 3 (UNIQUENESS). *For each set of semantically equivalent relations, their **lub** is unique.*

Proof. Let **C** and **C**′ be two **lubs** of a given set of relations {**A**, **B**}. According to the definition of **lub**, we have **C** $\sqsupseteq$ **A** and **C** $\sqsupseteq$ **B**, and **C**′ $\sqsupseteq$ **A** and **C**′ $\sqsupseteq$ **B**. As **C** is the **lub** of **A** and **B**, any relation (such as **C**′) satisfying **C**′ $\sqsupseteq$ **A** and **C**′ $\sqsupseteq$ **B** must also satisfy **C**′ $\sqsupseteq$ **C**. Similarly, we can derive that **C** $\sqsupseteq$ **C**′ must be true. Therefore, **C** and **C**′ are equivalent in information capacity, meaning that the **lub** of **A** and **B** is unique. ∎

The concepts of **lub** and the properties *covering, fineness,* and *minimality* can be used as a general guideline in the schema integration process in determining the attributes of an entity (relationship) type. In our approach, the local relations are divided into groups of relations. Within each group the relations are semantically equivalent. One hyperrelation that is in semantics the **lub** of the local relations is used to represent the schemas of the local relations. In this way, the representation of the schemas of the local relations is in a uniform manner—the schemas of relations are still relations. Also, because a hyperrelation is the **lub** of its underlying relations, there will not be any unnecessary information added as attributes to the hyperrelation. Hence, a global query issued against the hyperrelations can always be translated into (local) queries specified on the underlying (local) relations. In the next section, we define the structure of a hyperrelation.

B. The Structure of a Hyperrelation (R^H)

In relational databases, a relation represents a class of tuples of the same type, and each tuple describes the characteristics (type) of a real world entity as shown in Fig. 6a. We extend this concept to define the structure of a hyperrelation. We consider that a hyperrelation represents a class of relations having the same semantics. Each entity in a hyperrelation is the schema of an existing relation in a component database. This concept is exemplified in Fig. 6b.

Formally, we define the structure of a hyperrelation as follows.

DEFINITION 3 (THE HYPERRELATION). *A hyperrelation R^H is composed of a set of tuples, each having the schema of a relation in a component database as its data. The relations corresponding to the tuples in a R^H are all semantically equivalent relations, and R^H has the schema R^H* (**Database, Relation,** $A_1, \ldots, A_n$), *where R^H ($A_1 \ldots, A_n$) = $\text{lub}(t_1, \ldots, t_m)$, $t_1, \ldots, t_m$ are the tuples of R^H, and $A_1, \ldots, A_n$ are the attributes mapped from $t_1, \ldots, t_m$.* **Database** *and* **Relation** *are two system-defined attributes. The domain of* **Relation** *is the set of names of the local relations mapping onto R^H, and the domain of* **Database** *is the set of names of the databases to which these local relations belong.*

According to the definition, the structure of a hyperrelation is similar to that of an ordinary relation. Each hyperrelation also has a *hyperrelation name* and consists of a number of attributes, each having an *attribute name*. However,

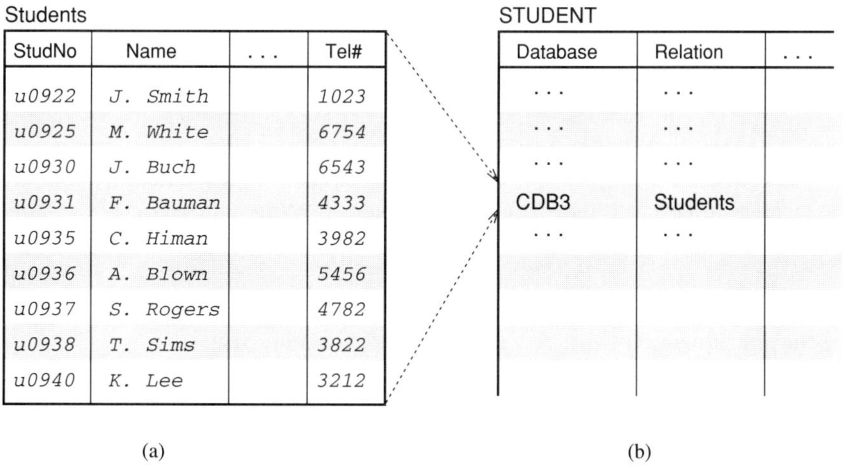

Students

StudNo	Name	...	Tel#
u0922	J. Smith		1023
u0925	M. White		6754
u0930	J. Buch		6543
u0931	F. Bauman		4333
u0935	C. Himan		3982
u0936	A. Blown		5456
u0937	S. Rogers		4782
u0938	T. Sims		3822
u0940	K. Lee		3212

STUDENT

Database	Relation	...
...	...	
...	...	
...	...	
CDB3	Students	
...	...	

(a)   (b)

FIGURE 6 A hyperrelation structure analogous to a relation structure.

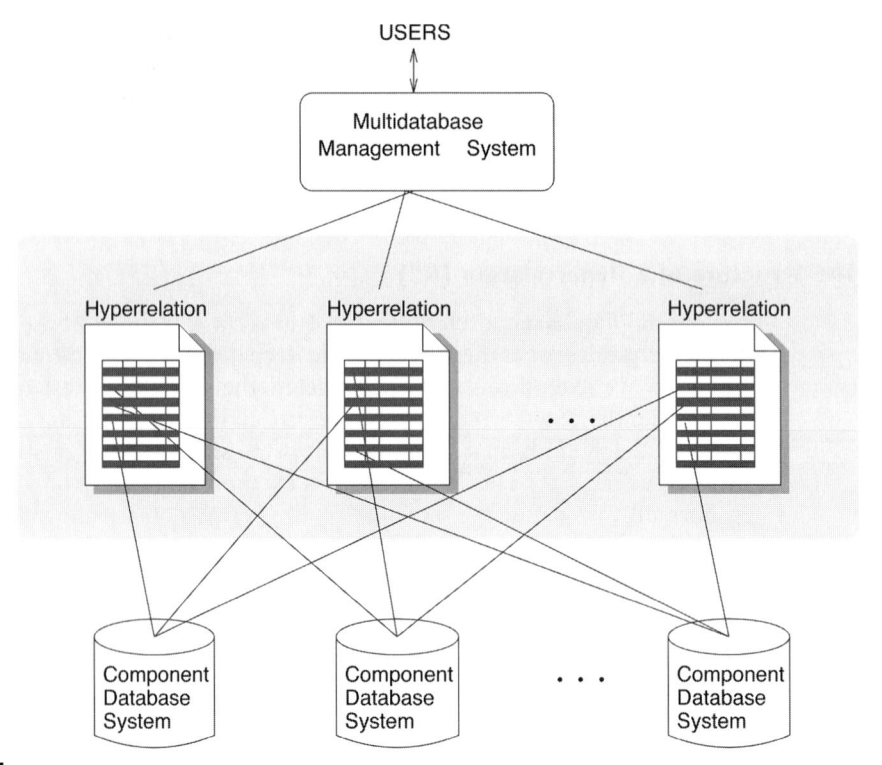

FIGURE 7 The environment of multidatabase systems.

instead of corresponding to a real-world entity, each *tuple* in a hyperrelation corresponds to a local relation that is semantically equivalent to the hyperrelation. The design of such a structure is for a representation of the local relations at the global level so as to facilitate query transformation and processing based on an algebra (to be presented). The user of a MDBS is allowed to inquire the hyperrelation schemas in order to issue a global query. The environment of such a multidatabase system is illustrated in Fig. 7, in which the hyperrelations in the middle represent the global schema of the component databases. Each global query is issued against the schemas of the hyperrelations.

Note that the hyperrelation is not just a directory or catalog as those in homogeneous distributed databases that keeps track of the attribute information of local relations. A hyperrelation needs also to reflect the conflicts between relations in a uniform manner, and more importantly, it allows a global query that accesses data in different expressions to be translated and executed locally in component databases. We discuss these issues in the following section.

C. Schema Conformation: R^H Schema and the Mapping

We discuss here how to determine the hyperrelation schema from (semantically equivalent) relations of conflicting schemas and how to map them onto a hyperrelation. A combination of more than one type of conflict can be decomposed into the above basic types and mapped to hyperrelations by following their corresponding mapping mechanisms. We start our description from simpler (more intuitive) types of conflict to allow the reader to easier comprehend the whole mapping scheme.

1. Value-versus-Value Conflict

As data conflicts can normally be resolved by using conversion functions to convert the data, schema conformation techniques are not needed for this type of conflict.

2. Attribute-versus-Attribute Conflict

For ease of understanding, we first describe the conformation of schemas with missing attribute conflicts. Then we discuss the one-to-many attribute conflict before we discuss the most general many-to-many conflict. The one-to-one conflict case is covered in the discussion of the other two cases.

Missing Attribute Conflict

Let $R_1(a_{11},\ldots,a_{1r_1}), R_2(a_{21},\ldots,a_{2r_2}),\ldots, R_m(a_{m1},\ldots,a_{mr_m})$ be a set of relations of different databases and among them there exists a missing attribute conflict. According to the requirements of **lub**, the set of attributes of their corresponding hyperrelation must be the union of all attributes of the relations, i.e., $\{a_{11},\ldots,a_{1r_1}\} \cup \{a_{21},\ldots,a_{2r_2}\}, \cup \ldots \cup \{a_{m1},\ldots,a_{mr_m}\}$. In the union, $\{a_p\} \cup \{a_q\}$ = either $\{a_p\}$ or $\{a_q\}$, but not both, if they are the corresponding attributes. The mapping of R_i to this hyperrelation is straightforward: $R_i.a_{ij}$ is the value of the corresponding attribute in R^H (for $1 \le i \le m, 1 \le j \le r_i$) and is a **NULL** if R_i does not have such an attribute.

One-to-Many Conflict

Let $R(r_1,\ldots,r_m)$ ($\in DB_1$) and $S(s_1,\ldots,s_n)$ ($\in DB_2$) be two semantically equivalent relations, where $m < n$ and r_i is a same attribute as s_i, for $1 \le i \le m-1$, and r_m corresponds to $s_m,\ldots,s_n$ (i.e., a one-to-many attribute conflict). As a hyperrelation should be in the finest structure to convey the most detailed information (according to the definition of the **lub**), the structure $(s_1,\ldots, s_m,\ldots, s_n)$ should be chosen as the schema of R^H (in addition to the attributes **Database** and **Relation**). The attribute names $s_1,\ldots,s_{m-1}$ of R^H can be $r_1,\ldots,r_{m-1}$ too because there is no mismatch between them. To map the relation onto R^H, R is mapped to a tuple as

$$\langle DB_1, R, r_1,\ldots,r_{m-1}, \overbrace{r_m,\ldots,r_m}^{n-m+1} \rangle.$$

The values of $R.s_i$ in R^H is r_i, for $1 \le i \le m-1$, and the values of $R.s_i$, for $m \le i \le n$, are defined as r_m. S is mapped to

$$\langle DB_2, S, s_1,\ldots,s_m,\ldots,s_n \rangle$$

in R^H. Both of the mappings strictly follow the attribute correspondence rule mentioned in Section II.

For an example, the student relations of CDB1, CDB2, and CDB3 are mapped to **STUDENT** as shown in Fig. 8. The **Stud** of CDB1 in **STUDENT** has Name as the values for FN and LN because of the one-to-many conflict with the corresponding attributes in CDB2. The address information of these

STUDENT

Database	Relation	StudNo	FN	LN	No.	Street	City	State	Tel#	Gender	Grade
CDB1	Stud	S#^{K}	Name	Name	Addr	Addr	Addr	Addr	Tel#	Gender	Class
CDB2	CS-Stud	S#^{K}	FN	LN	No	Str	Str	State	Tel#	NULL	Grade
CDB2	Math-Stud	S#^{K}	FN	LN	No	Str	Str	State	Tel#	NULL	Grade
CDB2	EE-Stud	S#^{K}	FN	LN	No	Str	Str	State	Tel#	NULL	Grade
CDB3	Studs	S#^{K}	Name	Name	Str	Str	City	State	NULL	Gender	Class

FIGURE 8 The schema of the hyperrelation STUDENT.

relations are mapped to STUDENT based on the same principle. This mapping is also important for query transformation based on algebra. We will get to that in a later section.

Many-to-Many Conflict

As for the many-to-many conflict, the basic idea is the same. We illustrate the mapping by using a conflict example involving two attributes in one relation and three attributes in another relation. A general case will simply be an extension of the case presented here. Let r_1 and r_2 be attributes of R and s_1, s_2, s_3 be attributes of S, and $\{r_1, r_2\}$ are the corresponding attributes of $\{s_1, s_2, s_3\}$. Assume that r_1 and r_2 represent a semantics that can be further divided into (a, b) and (c, d), respectively; i.e., a, b, c, and d are subsemantics of r_1 and r_2. In S, the same semantics (a), (b, c), and (d) are modeled in s_1, s_2, and s_3, respectively. Then the hyperrelation should choose a, b, c, and d as its attributes since this representation is semantically richer than the other two representations. In other words, R^H has the schema $R^H(\ldots, a, b, c, d, \ldots)$ (irrelevant attributes are denoted by dots). Based on the mapping principle presented above, r_1 and r_2 are mapped to $\langle \ldots, r_1, r_1, r_2, r_2, \ldots \rangle$ in R^H and s_1, s_2, and s_3 are mapped to $\langle \ldots, s_1, s_2, s_2, s_3, \ldots \rangle$ in R^H.

3. Attribute-versus-Table Conflict

Consider the Faculty relation of CDB1 and the Faculty and Spouse relations of CDB2. As the Spouse relation is semantically different from the Faculty relation, there should be two hyperrelations FACULTY and SPOUSE in the global database.

Formally, let us assume that $R(a_1, \ldots, a_p, a_{p+1})$ is a local relation of DB_1 that semantically corresponds to $R_1(a_1, \ldots, a_p, f)$ and $R_2(f, b_1, \ldots, b_q)$ of DB_2, where $R.a_i$ corresponds to (i.e., the corresponding attribute of) $R_1.a_i$, for $1 \leq i \leq p$, $R.a_{p+1}$ corresponds to $R_2.b_1$, and f is the foreign key (key) attribute of R_1 (R_2). R and R_1 are semantically equivalent relations. In this circumstance, the hyperrelations will have the schemas R_1^H (*Database, Relation*, $A_1, \ldots, A_p, F$) and R_2^H (*Database, Relation, F*, $B_1, \ldots, B_q$), where R_1^H is obtained from the schemas of R and R_1, and R_2^H from that of R_2. F is a key or a foreign key of these hyperrelations to express the referencing information. We define that R_1 and R_2 are mapped to the tuples

$$\langle DB_2, R_1, a_1, \ldots, a_p, f \rangle$$

and

$$\langle DB_2, R_2, f, b_1, \ldots, b_q \rangle$$

in hyperrelations R_1^H and R_2^H, respectively. The relation R is mapped to two tuples

$$\langle DB_1, R, a_1, \ldots, a_p, \rangle$$

and

$$\langle DB_1, R, \mathcal{L}, \overbrace{a_{p+1}, \text{Null}, \ldots, \text{Null}}^{q} \rangle$$

in R_1^H and R_2^H, respectively, because a_{p+1} corresponds to b_1 and R does not have the other (i.e., $B_2, \ldots, B_q$) attributes. $\mathcal{L}$ is a special character to indicate that relation R does not have such an attribute and can be grouped back to one relation schema through this link (i.e., $\mathcal{L}$). In this manner, a global query issued based on the hyperrelation schema can be correctly translated to local queries expressed in local schemas.

4. Value-versus-Attribute Conflict

Let $R_1(a_1, a_2, \ldots, a_p)$ and $R_2(a_{11}, a_{12}, \ldots, a_{1k}, a_2, \ldots, a_p)$ be the relations of databases DB_1 and DB_2, respectively, where a value-versus-attribute conflict exists between the values of $R_1.a_1$ and the attributes $a_{11}, a_{12}, \ldots, a_{1k}$ of R_2, and $R_1.a_i$ corresponds to $R_2.a_i$ (no schema conflict between them) for $2 \le i \le p$. As $\{a_{11}, a_{12}, \ldots, a_{1k}\}$ has a finer structure than a_1, the schema of their corresponding hyperrelation should be $R^H(Database, Relation, A_{11}, A_{12}, \ldots, A_{1k}, A_2, \ldots, A_p)$, where a_{1j} corresponds to A_{1j} (for $1 \le j \le k$) and a_i to A_i (for $2 \le i \le p$). Mapped to R^H, the schema of R_1 becomes the tuple

$$\langle DB_1, R, \overbrace{a_1, a_1, \ldots, a_1}^{k}, a_2, \ldots, a_p \rangle.$$

Since R_2 has no conflict with R^H, the mapping result is simply R_2's schema.

For example, the attribute **Type** of **Course** in **CDB1** is mapped onto the hyperrelation **COURSE** as shown in Fig. 9, in which the attributes **Fundamental** and **Advanced** of the **CDB1** tuple have the value "Type."

5. Value-versus-Table Conflict

Let $R(r, a_1, \ldots, a_p)$ be a relation in the database DB_1 that has a value-versus-table conflict with the set of relations $R_1(a_1, \ldots, a_p), \ldots, R_m(a_1, \ldots, a_p)$ in database DB_2. Formally, we say that the domain of the attribute r of R is an index set $\{r_1, \ldots, r_m\}$ on R_i ($i = 1, \ldots, m$), where r_i refers to the domain

COURSE

Database	Relation	CNo	CName	Credits	Hours	Fundamental	Advanced	Prereq
CDB1	Course	C#^{K}	Name	Credit	NULL	Type	Type	NULL

FIGURE 9 The schema of the hyperrelation COURSE.

STUDENT

Database	Relation	SSN	StudNo	FN	LN	No.	Street	City	State	Tel#	Gender	Grade
CDB4	ST1	Null	S#^{k}	Name	Name	Addr	Addr	Addr	Addr	Tel#	Sex	CDB4.ST1.Grade*
CDB4	ST2	Null	S#^{k}	Name	Name	Addr	Addr	Addr	Addr	Tel#	Sex	CDB4.ST2.Grade*
CDB4	ST3	Null	S#^{k}	Name	Name	Addr	Addr	Addr	Addr	Tel#	Sex	CDB4.ST3.Grade*
CDB4	ST4	Null	S#^{k}	Name	Name	Addr	Addr	Addr	Addr	Tel#	Sex	CDB4.ST4.Grade*

CDB4.ST1.Grade -> {freshman},   CDB4.ST2.Grade -> {sophomore}
CDB4.ST3.Grade -> {junior},   CDB4.ST4.Grade -> {senior}

FIGURE 10 The hyperrelation STUDENT.

of relation R_i.[4] It is the global database designer's responsibility to define the domains of relations (analogous to defining the domain of an attribute) in the database design process. As a hyperrelation, not counting the attributes **Database** and **Relation**, is the **lub** of the underlying relations, R^H have the schema R^H (*Database, Relation, r, $A_1, \ldots, A_p$*), where $A_1, \ldots, A_p$ correspond to $a_1, \ldots, a_p$, respectively, and $R^H.r$ to $R.r$. The relation R of DB_1 is mapped to a tuple in R^H as

$$\langle DB_1, R, r, a_1, \ldots, a_p \rangle.$$

As for R_i of DB_2, it is mapped to a tuple as

$$\langle DB_2, R_i, r_i^\star, a_1, \ldots, a_p \rangle$$

in which the value of the attribute r is not null but $r_i^\star$ (where r_i is an index to the domain of R_i). In the example discussed above, the relations **ST1**, **ST2**, **ST3**, and **ST4** of **CDB4** given in Fig. 5 are mapped to tuples of a hyperrelation **STUDENT** shown in Fig. 10. The values of the added attribute **Grade** are set to {**CDB4.ST1.Grade***, **CDB4.ST2.Grade***, **CDB4.ST3.Grade***, **CDB4.ST4.Grade***} for the relations. The ⋆-tagged values indicate (to the global user) that the local relation does not have the corresponding attributes, but each index ($r_i^\star$) refers to the domain of a local relation, as indicated in Fig. 10. The k-tagged values in the hyperrelation stand for the key attributes of the local relations.

Note that in a previous attribute-versus-table conflict the relations $R_1(a_1, \ldots, a_p, f)$ and $R_2(f, b_1, \ldots, b_q)$ of DB_2 are mapped to different hyperrelations, while the $R_1(a_1, \ldots, a_p), \ldots, R_m(a_1, \ldots, a_p)$ of this value-versus-table conflict are mapped onto the same hyperrelation. The reason is that the relations $R_1(a_1, \ldots, a_p), \ldots, R_m(a_1, \ldots, a_p)$ in the latter type of conflict are semantically equivalent, whereas the semantics of R_1 and R_2 in the former case are distinct. The solutions of these two cases are therefore different.

6. Table-versus-Table Conflict

Thus far, we have classified the schema conflicts and discussed the mappings of each type of conflicts to hyperrelations. Based on the principles discussed

---

[4]For simplicity, we have assumed here that there exists a one-to-one and onto mapping from the values in the domain of the attribute r, i.e., $\{r_1, \ldots, r_m\}$, to the domains of the set of relations $\{R_1, \ldots, R_m\}$ in DB_2. We have found that this is indeed the case most of the time.

QUERY OPTIMIZATION CONCEPTS AND METHODOLOGIES 139

STUDENT

Database	Relation	SSN	StudNo	FN	LN	No.	Street	City	State	Tel#	Gender	Grade
CDB1	Stud	Null	S#^{K}	Name	Name	Addr	Addr	Addr	Addr	Tel#	Gender	Class
CDB2	CS_Stud	Null	SN^K	FN	LN	No	Str	Str	State	Tel#	NULL	Grade
CDB2	Math_Stud	Null	SN^K	FN	LN	No	Str	Str	State	Tel#	NULL	Grade
CDB2	EE_Stud	Null	SN^K	FN	LN	No	Str	Str	State	Tel#	NULL	Grade
CDB3	Studs	SSN^K	SNo	Name	Name	Str	Str	City	State	NULL	Gender	Class
CDB4	ST1	Null	S#^{K}	Name	Name	Addr	Addr	Addr	Addr	Tel#	Sex	CDB4.ST1.Grade*
CDB4	ST2	Null	S#^{K}	Name	Name	Addr	Addr	Addr	Addr	Tel#	Sex	CDB4.ST2.Grade*
CDB4	ST3	Null	S#^{K}	Name	Name	Addr	Addr	Addr	Addr	Tel#	Sex	CDB4.ST3.Grade*
CDB4	ST4	Null	S#^{K}	Name	Name	Addr	Addr	Addr	Addr	Tel#	Sex	CDB4.ST4.Grade*

CDB4.ST1.Grade -> {freshman}, CDB4.ST2.Grade -> {sophomore}
CDB4.ST3.Grade -> {junior}, CDB4.ST4.Grade -> {senior}

FIGURE 11 The hyperrelation STUDENT.

above, multidatabase relations can be mapped onto their corresponding hyperrelations. Some of the hyperrelations mapped from the relations given in Fig. 5 are shown in Figs. 11, 12, and 13.

D. The Hyperrelational Algebra

In this section, we introduce how the relational operations are extended to hyperrelational operations and how these operations are performed on a hyperrelation. Analogous to the relational algebra in the relational model, the hyperrelational algebra provides a mathematical foundation for expressing global queries and the transformation and optimization of the queries.

1. The Hyperrelational Operations

The hyperrelational operations are a direct extension of the relational operations. They are performed on hyperrelations. These operations include H-SELECTION (σ^H), H-PROJECTION (π^H), H-JOIN ($\bowtie^H$), H-INTERSECTION ($\cap^H$), H-UNION ($\cup^H$), H-DIFFERENCE ($-^H$), and

COURSE

Database	Relation	CNo	CName	Credits	Hours	Fundamental	Advanced	Prereq
CDB1	Course	C#^{K}	Name	Credit	NULL	Type	Type	NULL
CDB2	Fndmntl_Crs	CN^K	Name	Credits	NULL	α	NULL	NULL
CDB2	Advncd_Crs	CN^K	Name	Credits	NULL	NULL	γ	Prereq-C#
CDB3	Lecture	CNo^K	Name	Credit	NULL	β	NULL	NULL
CDB3	Tutorial	CNo^K	Name	Credit	NULL	δ	NULL	NULL
CDB3	Seminar	CNo^K	Name	NULL	NULL	NULL	λ	NULL
CDB3	Indvl_Stdy	CNo^K	Name	NULL	NULL	NULL	ω	NULL
CDB4	Courses	C#^{K}	Name	Credit	Hours	Fndmntl	Advncd	NULL

α = CDB2.Fndmntl_Crs.Fundamental* β = CDB3.Lecture.Fundamental*
δ = CDB3.Tutorial.Fundamental* γ = CDB2.Advncd_Crs.Advanced*
λ = CDB3.Seminar.Advanced* ω = CDB3.Indvl_stdy.Advanced*

FIGURE 12 The hyperrelation COURSE.

TAKE

Database	Relation	SSN	SNo	CNo	Score
CDB1	Take	Null	S#^{K}	C#^{K}	Grade
CDB2	Participate	Null	SN^K	CN^K	Score
CDB3	Takes	SSN^K	Null	CN^K	Grade
CDB4	ENROLL	Null	S#^{K}	C#^{K}	Score

FIGURE 13 The hyperrelation TAKE.

H-PRODUCT ($\times^H$). They are defined based on the relational operations, the relational algebra, and the set theory. The relational set operations, including union, intersection, and difference operations, are in their broader sense in the transformation; that is, the set operations are *outer-union, outer-intersection*, and *"generalized-difference"* operations (in which the generalized-difference operation is a new operation to be introduced). Each global query is expressible in a hyperrelational algebraic expression by using these operations. During execution, a hyperrelational operation is used to select qualifying tuples, which represent some local relations, and is then converted to corresponding relational operations. The result of the operation is obtained by performing the corresponding relational operations on the selected local relations. The result is still a relation.

Before giving definitions of the operations, we first introduce an operation that is used in all the hyperrelational operation acting as a conflict conformation operator. This operator is called the ⋆-*expansion* (read *star expansion*) operator. It is applied to the tuples of a hyperrelation when a hyperrelational operation is being performed.

DEFINITION 4 (⋆-EXPANSION). Let $r(v_1, \ldots, v_m)$ be the schema of r and $\langle db, r, c_1^\star, \ldots, c_n^\star, v_1, \ldots, v_m \rangle$ be the tuple of r in R^H, where c_i are ⋆-tagged values. The ⋆-expansion of $c_1^\star, \ldots, c_n^\star$ on r, or simply the ⋆-expansion of r, is defined as

$$\star_{\{c_1,\ldots,c_n\}} db.r = \star(\langle db, r, c_1^\star, \ldots c_n^\star, v_1, \ldots, v_m \rangle)$$
$$= \{\langle c_1 \rangle\} \times \ldots \times \{\langle c_n \rangle\} \times r(v_1, \ldots, v_m).$$

This definition implies that the result of the ⋆-expansion operation is a relation that has the attributes $c_1, \ldots, c_n$ (i.e., ⋆-tagged values) in addition to the attributes $v_1, \ldots, v_m$ contained in $db.r$ (i.e., the relation r of database db). The values of these new attributes are set to be the same as their attribute names. In our multidatabase example, for instance, the relation ST1 in CDB4 stores the data about the freshmen in College D. The ⋆-expansion of ST1 is $\{\langle \text{freshman} \rangle\} \times $ ST1; that is, the original information about the grade of a student is added as an attribute to the relation and all its values of the tuples in the student relation are "freshman." The ⋆-expansion is performed on all $c_i^\star$ (if more than one), but not any subset of them. Since all $c_i^\star$ will be applied, the operation $\star_{\{c_1,\ldots,c_n\}} db.r$ can also be expressed as $\star db.r$ for an abbreviation. The purpose of this operation is to mediate the conflict between data and metadata. It is automatically applied whenever a hyperrelation operation is performed on the hyperrelation (to be shown shortly).

PROPERTY 4 (IDEMPOTENCE). $\star(\star \cdots \star(\langle c_i^\star, \ldots, c_n^\star, v_1, \ldots, v_m \rangle)\ldots) = \star(\langle c_1^\star, \ldots, c_n^\star, v_1, \ldots, v_m \rangle)$.

The proof of this property is quite straightforward and is therefore omitted. This property guarantees that multiple applications of the $\star$ operation on a hyperrelation do not incur an erroneous result.

The H-SELECTION Operation

The H-SELECTION operation is to perform selections on a hyperrelation and then to perform transformed selection operations on the selected local relations. Formally, the operation is defined as follows.

DEFINITION 5 (H-SELECTION). Given a hyperrelation R^H having the set of tuples $\{t_1, \ldots, t_n\}$, the H-SELECTION (σ^H) on R^H under the selection condition SC is defined as

$$\sigma_{SC}^H(R^H) = \sigma_{SC_1}(\star t_1) \cup \cdots \cup \sigma_{SC_n}(\star t_n),$$

where σ and $\cup$ are the relational operator SELECTION and the set operator UNION,[5] respectively. Assume that the SC is a minterm[6] and expressed as $SC = (a_{i_1} \theta_1 \omega_1) \wedge (a_{i_2} \theta_2 \omega_2) \ldots \wedge (a_{i_j} \theta_j \omega_j)$, where a_{i_k} is an attribute of R^H, $\theta_k \in \{>, \geq, =, \neq, <, \leq\}$, and ω_k is a constant value, for all $k = 1, \ldots, j$. If the values of the attributes $a_{i_1}, \ldots, a_{i_j}$ of the tuple $\star t_p (p = 1, \ldots, n)$ are $v_{i_1}, \ldots, v_{i_j}$, respectively, and none of them is a NULL, then $SC_p = (v_{i_1} \theta_1 \omega_1) \wedge (v_{i_2} \theta_2 \omega_2) \ldots \wedge (v_{i_j} \theta_j \omega_j)$, If any of the attribute values is a NULL, then $\sigma_{SC_p}(\star t_p) = \phi$.

The H-SELECTION operation is composed of a number of relational SELECTIONs and UNIONs. A H-SELECTION on a hyperrelation is carried out by applying SELECTIONs on the tuples of the hyperrelation, i.e., the underlying relations from component databases, and UNIONs of the results from each component databases. For instance, given a hyperrelation STUDENT as shown in Fig. 11, the hyperrelational query

$$\sigma^H{}_{\text{Grade=freshman}}(\text{STUDENT})$$

is equal to the following query expressed in relational algebra:

$$\sigma_{\text{Class=freshman}}(\text{CDB1.Stud}) \cup \sigma_{\text{Grade=freshman}}(\text{CDB2.CS\_Stud}) \cup$$

$$\sigma_{\text{Grade=freshman}}(\text{CDB2.MATH\_Stud}) \cup$$

$$\sigma_{\text{Grade=freshman}}(\text{CDB2.EE\_Stud}) \cup \sigma_{\text{Class=freshman}}(\text{CDB3.Studs}) \cup$$

$$\sigma_{\text{freshman=freshman}}(\star_{\{\text{freshman}\}}\text{CDB4.ST1}) \cup$$

$$\sigma_{\text{sophomore=freshman}}(\star_{\{\text{sophomore}\}}\text{CDB4.ST2}) \cup$$

$$\sigma_{\text{junior=freshman}}(\star_{\{\text{junior}\}}\text{CDB4.ST3}) \cup$$

$$\sigma_{\text{senior=freshman}}(\star_{\{\text{senior}\}}\text{CDB4.ST4})$$

---

[5] It is actually an outer-union operator. We will have a detailed explanation in a moment.
[6] Two OR-ed minterms such as $(A \wedge B) \wedge (C \wedge D)$ can be viewed as two queries and treated separately.

For the selection conditions of the CDB4 relations, as the condition freshman=freshman is always true, all tuples of the local relation ST1 are selected. On the other hand, no tuples will be selected from ST2, ST3, and ST4 because their selection conditions are always false.

Also, if a tuple r of R^H has a NULL value for an attribute that is involved in the SC, we define that the $\sigma_{SC}(r) = \phi$: The reason for not processing such a relation is to avoid uncertain (maybe) results. Let R^H (DB, Rel, Studno, Name, Address, Gender) be the schema of a hyperrelation and ⟨db$_1$, r$_1$, S#, SName, Addr, NULL⟩ and ⟨db$_2$, r$_2$, S#, SName, Addr, Sex⟩ be two tuples of the hyperrelation. If a selection query is to find the information of students whose gender is female, then none of the data of relation r$_1$ should be considered, as the gender of those students is unknown. Only the relation corresponding to the second tuple (db$_2$.r$_2$) should be processed. However, if maybe values are welcome in a particular environment, the hyperrelational algebra will still work by changing the definition of H-selection to allow selection on uncertain information.

An interesting aspect of this algebra is that as some relations corresponding to a R^H may not have all the attributes defined in R^H, the issue of *union compatibility* [28] is involved in the UNION operation in σ^H (refer to the definition). There are two choices in dealing with this problem:

1. Strictly confine that all relations to be unioned must have the same set of attributes. If any relation does not meet this condition, it is removed from the σ^H expression.
2. Take the *outer-union* approach, which releases the union compatibility constraint by allowing relations of different sets of attributes to be unioned and the resulting relation contains all attributes from the unioned relations.

We take the second approach for the hyperrelational algebra, because it allows the user to obtain the largest set of information as the result. If the first choice is taken, then following the last example a relation in R^H (DB, Rel, Studno, Name, Address, Gender) that has the schema ⟨db$_3$, r$_3$, S#, SName, NULL, Sex⟩ will not be processed (because the relations are union incompatible), even though the sexuality of students is known. To the user, the resultant female students not including those in r$_3$ are an incomplete set of students. The answer of a multidatabase query is by default to inquire all existing qualifying tuples. Hence, the second choice above is considered. A formal definition of the outer-union operation can be found in [28]. The column of Address for r$_3$ tuples can simply be filled with NULLs to indicate nonavailability of the information.

There may be a concern that the result of an outer-union of two partially compatible relations having schemas such as Student(SSN, Name, Address, Class) and Teacher(SSN, Name, Address, Rank) will have the schema R(SSN, Name, Address, Rank, Class) (i.e., all attributes of Student and Teacher are included). Hence, an outer-union of multiple relations without a guidance will likely make the semantics of the result relation too complex to be clear and precise. In our definition of the hyperrelational algebra, however, this situation will not occur because the union is confined to those relations (tuples) within the same R^H. These relations are semantically equivalent; the relations in the above example (**Student** and **Teacher**) will never be outer-unioned in our case. Also, as the semantics of the relations mapped to a R^H are equivalent to that of the R^H, the result of the outer-union of any of the relations still has the same semantics as R^H. In the following operations, all the "∪" symbols (not including $\cup^H$) denote an outer-union, unless specified otherwise.

The H-PROJECTION Operation

The H-PROJECTION operation is to perform projections on the tuples of a hyperrelation. The H-PROJECTION operation is defined as follows.

DEFINITION 6 (H-PROJECTION). Given a hyperrelation R^H having the set of tuples $\{t_1, \ldots, t_n\}$, the H-PROJECTION (π^H) of R^H on a set of attributes $\{PA\}$ is defined as

$$\pi^H_{\{PA\}}(R^H) = \pi_{\{PA_1\}}(\star t_1) \cup \cdots \cup \pi_{\{PA_n\}}(\star t_n),$$

where π is the relational operator PROJECTION and $\{PA_i\}$ is the set of attributes of t_i corresponding to the attributes $\{PA\}$.

Let us take the hyperrelation **STUDENT** shown in Fig. 11 as an example. The H-PROJECTION operation on **STUDENT**

$$\pi^H_{\{FN,LN,Tel\#\}}(\text{STUDENT})$$

is equal to the operations

$\pi_{\{Name,Name,Tel\#\}}(\text{CDB1.Stud}) \cup \pi_{\{FN,LN,Tel\#\}}(\text{CDB2.CS\_Stud}) \cup$

$\pi_{\{FN,LN,Tel\#\}}(\text{CDB2.MATH\_Stud}) \cup \pi_{\{FN,LN,Tel\#\}}(\text{CDB2.EE\_Stud}) \cup$

$\pi_{\{Name,Name,NULL\}}(\text{CDB3.Studs}) \cup \pi_{\{Name,Name,Tel\#\}}$

$(\star_{\{freshman\}}\text{CDB4.ST1}) \cup \pi_{\{Name,Name,Tel\#\}}(\star_{\{sophomore\}}\text{CDB4.ST2}) \cup$

$\pi_{\{Name,Name,Tel\#\}}(\star_{\{junior\}}\text{CDB4.ST3}) \cup$

$\pi_{\{Name,Name,Tel\#\}}(\star_{\{senior\}}\text{CDB4.ST4}).$

The projection operation $\pi_{\{Name,Name,Tel\#\}}(\text{Stud})$ is equal to $\pi_{\{Name, Tel\#\}}(\text{Stud})$, as according to the set theory $\{A, A, B\}$ is equal to $\{A, B\}$. Note that although the relation **CDB3.Studs** does not have the **Tel#** attribute, its data are still included in the result. The consideration here about a **NULL** value is somewhat different from that in the H-SELECTION operation. In the H-SELECTION operation, if a local relation does not have the attribute specified in the condition of a global selection query, the entire local relation is excluded from the result. The intention is to avoid creating uncertain tuples in the final result. In the H-PROJECTION, however, tuples having a missing attribute are still included in the result. This is because projection on a missing attribute does not cause an uncertainty problem. All the tuples in such a relation are still true tuples (instead of maybe tuples as in the H-SELECTION case). It is similar to the case in relational databases in which an employee tuple in an employee relation, for instance, with unknown Tel# is still considered a legal and valid tuple in the relation.

The H-JOIN Operation

The H-JOIN operation is used to select related tuples from two hyperrelations and then performs joins on each pair of the selected tuples. We defined the H-JOIN operation as follows.

DEFINITION 7 (H-JOIN). Given two hyperrelation R^H and S^H having the set of tuples $\{t_1, \ldots, t_n\}$ and $\{u_1, \ldots, u_m\}$, respectively. The H-JOIN ($\bowtie^H$) on R^H and S^H under the join condition JC is defined as

$$(R^H) \bowtie^H_{JC} (S^H) = ((\star t_1) \bowtie_{JC_{11}} (\star u_1)) \cup \cdots \cup ((\star t_1) \bowtie_{JC_{1m}} (\star u_m)) \cup \cdots$$
$$\cup ((\star t_n) \bowtie_{JC_{nm}} (\star u_m)),$$

where $\bowtie$ is the relational JOIN operation. The join condition JC is a Boolean expression and is specified on attributes from the two hyperrelations R^H and S^H. JC_{ij} is the transformation of JC by substituting the attributes of the hyperrelations with the values of the attributes. $(\star t_i) \bowtie_{JC_{ij}} (\star u_j) (i = 1, \ldots, n$ and $j = 1, \ldots, m)$ is an empty set if any of the values of the attributes of t_i and u_j involved in JC_{ij} is a NULL.

For example, the following H-JOIN

$$\text{STUDENT} \bowtie^M_{\text{StuNo=SNo}} \text{TAKE}$$

is equal to

$$\left(\text{Stud} \bowtie_{\text{S\#=S\#}} \text{Take}\right) \cup \left(\text{Stud} \bowtie_{\text{S\#=SN}} \text{Participate}\right) \cup \left(\text{Stud} \bowtie_{\text{S\#=Null}} \text{Takes}\right) \cup$$

$$\left(\text{Stud} \bowtie_{\text{S\#=S\#}} \text{Enroll}\right) \cup \left(\text{CS\_Stud} \bowtie_{\text{SN=S\#}} \text{Take}\right) \cup \left(\text{CS\_Stud} \bowtie_{\text{SN=SN}} \text{Participate}\right) \cup$$

$$\left(\text{CS\_Stud} \bowtie_{\text{SN=Null}} \text{Takes}\right) \cup \left(\text{CS\_Stud} \bowtie_{\text{SN=S\#}} \text{Enroll}\right) \cup \cdots \cup \left(\text{Studs} \bowtie_{\text{SNo=S\#}} \text{Take}\right) \cup$$

$$\left(\text{Studs} \bowtie_{\text{SNo=SN}} \text{Participate}\right) \cup \left(\text{Studs} \bowtie_{\text{SNo=Null}} \text{Takes}\right) \cup \left(\text{Studs} \bowtie_{\text{SNo=S\#}} \text{Enroll}\right) \cup$$

$$\left(\text{ST1} \bowtie_{\text{S\#=S\#}} \text{Take}\right) \cup \left(\text{ST1} \bowtie_{\text{S\#=SN}} \text{Participate}\right) \cup \left(\text{ST1} \bowtie_{\text{S\#=Null}} \text{Takes}\right) \cup$$

$$\left(\text{ST1} \bowtie_{\text{S\#=S\#}} \text{Enroll}\right) \cup \cdots \cup \left(\text{ST4} \bowtie_{\text{S\#=S\#}} \text{Take}\right) \cup \cdots \cup \left(\text{ST4} \bowtie_{\text{S\#=S\#}} \text{Enroll}\right).$$

The database names in this case need not be given since all local relations happen to have distinct names. Note that the H-JOIN performs a relational join on *every pair* of the relations from the two operand hyperrelations. This definition gives the general formula for a hyperrelational join operation. Note that two students in different universities (databases) having the same student number do not necessarily mean the same person (and most likely they are not). To identify whether two records in different databases refer to the same real-world entity is termed the *entity identification* problem in the literature [11, 16, 20, 81]. As this problem is beyond the focus of this paper, we simply assume that the entity identification process is done before or after the algebraic transformation. In an environment in which entity identification is not supported, the joins between relations of different databases become unnecessary and a hyperrelational join such as

$$\text{STUDENT} \bowtie^H_{\text{StuNo=SNo}} \text{TAKE}$$

is reduced to

$$(\text{Stud} \bowtie_{\text{S\#=S\#}} \text{Take}) \cup (\text{CS\_Stud} \bowtie_{\text{SN=SN}} \text{Participate}) \cup$$
$$(\text{Math\_Stud} \bowtie_{\text{SN=SN}} \text{Participate}) \cup (\text{EE\_Stud} \bowtie_{\text{SN=SN}} \text{Participate}) \cup$$
$$(\text{Studs} \bowtie_{\text{SNo=Null}} \text{Takes}) \cup (\text{ST1} \bowtie_{\text{S\#=S\#}} \text{Enroll}) \cup \cdots \cup (\text{ST4} \bowtie_{\text{S\#=S\#}} \text{Enroll}).$$

The next group of hyperrelational data manipulation operations are the mathematical set operations. These operations include H-UNION, H-DIFFERENCE, H-INTERSECTION, and H-PRODUCT. Note that although they are all based on the relational outer-union operations, they require that *the operand hyperrelations be union-compatible*, analogous to the requirements of their counterpart in relational algebra. Details are given as follows.

The H-UNION Operation

The H-UNION operation ($\cup^H$) is used to merge tuples by first applying unions to two sets of relations and then applying a union again to the unioned relations.

DEFINITION 8 (H-UNION). Given two union-compatible hyperrelations R^H and S^H having the sets of tuples $\{t_1, \ldots, t_n\}$ and $\{u_1, \ldots, u_m\}$, respectively, the H-UNION ($\cup^H$) on R^H and S^H is defined as

$$(R^H) \cup^H (S^H) = ((\star t_1) \cup \cdots \cup (\star t_n)) \cup ((\star u_1) \cup \cdots \cup (\star u_m)).$$

The condition union-compatible in this defintion requires that the schemas of R^H and S^H be the same. This condition is enforced in hyperrelational algebra to avoid producing semantically uninterpretable hyperrelations during query processing. The results are from multiple databases the tuples owned by the relations that are mapped to R^H and S^H.

The H-DIFFERENCE Operation

The H-DIFFERENCE operation is used to select those tuples that are in one hyperrelation but not in another.

DEFINITION 9 (H-DIFFERENCE). Given two union-compatible hyperrelations R^M and S^M having the sets of tuples $\{t_1, \ldots, t_n\}$ and $\{u_1, \ldots, u_m\}$, respectively, the H-DIFFERENCE ($-^H$) on R^H and S^H is defined as

$$(R^H) -^H (S^H) = ((\star t_1) \cup \cdots \cup (\star t_n)) - ((\star u_1) \cup \cdots \cup (\star u_m)),$$
$$= ((\star t_1 - \star u_1) \cup \cdots \cup (\star t_n - \star u_1)) \cap \cdots \cap ((\star t_1 - \star u_m) \cup \cdots \cup (\star t_n - \star u_m)),$$

where $-$ is the relational DIFFERENCE operation.

Similar to the H-UNION operation, the H-DIFFERENCE operation can be performed only on union-compatible hyperrelations. Also similar to $\cup$, $\cap$

is an **OUTER-INTERSECTION** operation [28]. That is, $R \cap S$ (R and S are relations) will have all the attributes from R and S. Tuples of the relations having the same key values will be retained. For the same purpose, $R - S$ does not require that R and S be union compatible. We generalize the concept of the relational difference operation and define a new operation named G-difference (Generalized-difference, $-^G$) operation as follows.

DEFINITION 10 (G-DIFFERENCE). Given two semantically equivalent relations R and S having the schemas $R(r_1, r_2, \ldots, r_n)$ and $S(s_1, s_2, \ldots, s_m)$, respectively, the *G-DIFFERENCE* on R and S is defined as

$$R -^G S = \{v \mid v \in R \text{ and } v \notin S, \text{ and } \forall v \text{ has the same schema as } R(r_1, r_2, \ldots, r_n)\}.$$

As we can see, this operation relaxes the union compatibility restriction of the relational difference operations and requires only that two relations be semantically equivalent. Hence, their schemas need not be exactly the same. The result of $R - S$ will have the same schema as relation R. Beyond this distinction, the **G-difference** is the same as the relational difference operation. Note that the operation "$-$" in Definition 3.9 as well as in the rest part of the paper is actually the difference operation in the generalized sense. By generalizing the $\cap$, $\cup$, and $-$ operations to **OUTER-UNION**, **OUTER-INTERSECTION**, and **G-DIFFERENCE** operations, the hyperrelational algebra can provide a multidatabase system with the greatest flexibility on processing local relations to obtain the maximal set of data without sacrificing the semantic integrity of the data.

The H-INTERSECTION Operation

DEFINITION 11 (H-INTERSECTION). Given two union-compatible hyperrelations R^H and S^H having the sets of tuples $\{t_1, \ldots, t_n\}$ and $\{u_1, \ldots, u_m\}$, the H-INTERSECTION ($\cap^H$) on R^H and S^H is defined as

$$(R^H) \cap^H (S^H) = ((\star t_1) \cup \cdots \cup (\star t_n)) \cap ((\star u_1) \cup \cdots \cup (\star u_m))$$
$$= (\star t_1 \cap \star u_1) \cup \cdots \cup (\star t_1 \cap \star u_m) \cup (\star t_2 \cap \star u_1) \cup \cdots \cup (\star t_n \cap \star u_m).$$

The results of this operation are those tuples from multiple databases that belong to every pair of relations mapped to R^H and S^H.

The H-PRODUCT Operation

The H-PRODUCT ($\times^H$) operation is to perform **CARTESIAN PRODUCT**s ($\times$) on every pair of relations mapped to the two operand hyperrelations, and then to perform outer-unions on the results of the **CARTESIAN PRODUCT** operations to form the final result.

DEFINITION 12 (H-PRODUCT). Given two hyperrelations R^H and S^H having the sets of tuples $\{t_1, \ldots, t_n\}$ and $\{u_1, \ldots, u_m\}$, the H-PRODUCT ($\times^H$) of R^H and S^H is defined as

$$(R^H) \times^H (S^H) = ((\star t_1) \times (\star u_1)) \cup \cdots \cup ((\star t_1) \times (\star u_m)) \cup \cdots \cup ((\star t_n) \times (\star u_m)),$$

where $\times$ is the relational operator **CARTESIAN PRODUCT**.

In the following, we will explore the properties of operations in the hyperrelational algebra. As we have stated in the Introduction, the properties will serve as a mathematical basis for global query optimization at the algebraic level.

2. Transformation of Hyperrelational Operations

Based on the above definitions, the hyperrelational operations can be transformed from one form to another. Interestingly, even though the hyperrelations stores the schemas of local relations, all the transformation rules in relational algebra are still applicable to the hyperrelational operations. In the following, we give the main theorems on the transformation rules for hyperrelational operations. The proofs of these properties are a direct extension of those given in [28], and hence are omitted here. Note that in the following $attr(X)$ denotes the set of attributes involved in the Boolean expression X, if X is a selection or join condition, and it can also mean the set of attributes of X, if X is a hyperrelation.

PROPERTY 5 (IDEMPOTANCE OF σ^H, π^H).

$$\sigma_C^H R^H \Rightarrow \sigma_{C_1}^H(\sigma_{C_2}^H R^H), \qquad if\ C = C_1 \wedge C_2$$

$$\pi_A^H R^H \Rightarrow \pi_A^H(\pi_{A_1}^H R^H), \qquad if\ A \subseteq A_1.$$

PROPERTY 6 (COMMUTATIVITY OF σ^H, π^H).

$$\sigma_{C_1}^H \sigma_{C_2}^H R^H \Rightarrow \sigma_{C_2}^H \sigma_{C_1}^H R^H$$

$$\sigma_{C_1}^H \pi_{A_2}^H R^H \Rightarrow \pi_{A_2}^H \sigma_{C_1}^H R^H$$

$$\pi_{A_1}^H \sigma_{C_2}^H R^H \Rightarrow \sigma_{C_2}^H \pi_{A_1}^H R^H, \qquad if\ attr(C_2) \subseteq A_1$$

$$\pi_{A_1}^H \pi_{A_2}^H R^H \Rightarrow \pi_{A_1}^H R^H, \qquad if\ A_1 \subseteq A_2.$$

PROPERTY 7 (COMMUTATIVITY AND ASSOCIATIVITY OF $\bowtie^H, \times^H, \cup^H, \cap^H$).

$$R^H\ \theta\ S^H \Rightarrow S^H\ \theta\ R^H, \qquad \theta \in \{\bowtie^H, \times^H, \cup^H, \cap^H\}$$

$$R^H\ \theta\ S^H\ \theta\ T^T \Rightarrow (R^H\ \theta\ S^H)\ \theta\ T^H, \qquad \theta \in \{\bowtie^H, \times^H, \cup^H, \cap^H\}$$

$$\Rightarrow R^H\ \theta\ (S^H\ \theta\ T^H).$$

PROPERTY 8 (DISTRIBUTIVITY OF σ^H AND π^H OVER $\bowtie^H, \times^H, \cup^H, \cap^H$).

$$\sigma_C^H(R^H \bowtie^H S^H) \qquad\qquad if\ C = C_{R^H} \wedge C_{S^H}$$
$$\Rightarrow \sigma_{C_{R^H}}^H(R^H) \bowtie^H \sigma_{C_{S^H}}^H(S^H)$$

$$\sigma_C^H(R^H \times^H S^H) \qquad\qquad if\ C = C_{R^H} \wedge C_{S^H}$$
$$\Rightarrow \sigma_{C_{R^H}}^H(R^H) \times^H \sigma_{C_{S^H}}^H(S^H)$$

$$\pi_A^H(R^H \bowtie_C^H S^H) \qquad\qquad attr\ (C) \subseteq A$$
$$\Rightarrow \pi_{A_{R^H}}^H(R^H) \bowtie_C^H \pi_{A_{S^H}}^H(S^H),$$

$$\pi_A^H(R^H \times^H S^H)$$
$$\Rightarrow \pi_{A_{R^H}}^H(R^H) \times^H \pi_{A_{S^H}}^H(S^H)$$
$$\sigma_C^H(R^H \theta S^H) \qquad \theta \in \{\cup^H, \cap^H\}$$
$$\Rightarrow \sigma_{C_{R^H}}^H(R^H) \theta \sigma_{C_{S^H}}^H(S^H),$$
$$\pi_A^H(R^H \theta S^H) \qquad \theta \in \{\cup^H, \cap^H\}$$
$$\Rightarrow \pi_{A_{R^H}}^H(R^H) \theta \pi_{A_{S^H}}^H(S^H),$$

where in this property C_{R^H} and C_{S^H} are the selection conditions involving only R^H and S^H, respectively, and A_{R^H} and A_{S^H} are the projected attributes belonging to only R^H and S^H, respectively.

PROPERTY 9 (TRANSFORMATION RULE BETWEEN $\cup^H$, $-^H$, AND $\cap^H$).

$$X \cap^H Y \equiv (X \cup^H Y) -^H ((X -^H Y) \cup^H (Y -^H X)),$$

where X and Y are two hyperrelations.

In the relational algebra the set of operations $\{\sigma, \pi, \cup, -, \times\}$ is a *complete* set, i.e., any other relational operations can be expressed as a composition of operations in this set. Similarly, the complete set of the hyperrelational algebraic operations is $\{\sigma^H, \pi^H, \cup^H, -^H, \times^H\}$. The proof is also similar to that of the relational case.

3. Examples

We give a few examples to show how hyperrelational algebra works for expressing global queries in a multidatabase environment. The databases used in these examples are those given in Fig. 5, and the hyperrelations are shown in Fig. 11 through Fig. 13. SQL will be the query language used in the examples.

Query 1. Find the names of the students who take the database course. The SQL of this query is as follows:

> Select FN, LN
> From STUDENT, COURSE, TAKE
> Where STUDENT.StudNo=TAKE.SNo
> and COURSE.CNo=TAKE.CNo
> and COURSE.CName='Database'

In this query, the relations **STUDENT**, **COURSE**, and **TAKE** are the hyperrelations. This global query can also be expressed in hyperrelational algebra as

$$\pi_{FN,LN}^H \{\sigma_{COURSE.CName='Database'}[(STUDENT \bowtie_{StudNo=SNo}^H TAKE)$$
$$\bowtie_{CNo=CNo}^H COURSE]\}.$$

Query 2. Find the names of the courses taken by only female students or by only male students.

The SQL of this global query can be written as follows:

    Select   CName
    From   COURSE C
    Where   Not Exists
        (Select *
          From   TAKE T, STUDENT S
          Where C.CNo=T.CNo
          and   T.SNo= S.StudNo
          and   S.Gender='Female')
    Union   Not Exists
        (Select *
          From   TAKE T, STUDENT S
          Where C.CNo=T.CNo
          and   T.SNo= S.StudNo
          and   S.Gender='Male')

The algebraic expression of this global query is

$$\{[\pi_{CNo}\ COURSE - \pi_{CNo}(\sigma_{Gender='Female'}\ STUDENT \bowtie_{StudNo=SNo} TAKE)]$$
$$\cap \pi_{CNo} TAKE\}$$
$$\cup \{[\pi_{CNo}\ COURSE - \pi_{CNo}(\sigma_{Gender='Male'}\ STUDENT$$
$$\bowtie_{StudNo=SNo} TAKE)] \cap \pi_{CNo}\ TAKE\}.$$

Using the hyperrelational algebra, a global query can be expressed precisely based on the hyperrelations. The expansion of the hyperrelational operations (to relational operations), not shown in the examples as the details have been given in the previous subsections, will allow the local databases to process these queries and return the correct results. Based on the transformation rules given above, a global query can be equivalently converted to different forms. Optimization of a global query can be realized at the multidatabase systems level by choosing from the equivalent algebraic expressions the one that incurs the least execution cost.

E. A Comparison with Related Works

Not much work has been proposed in this category. As we mentioned earlier, although schema integration in the context of semantic conformation has been studied for a long time, it has a different goal than what we are trying to achieve in multiple autonomous databases environments. Recently, Agarwal et al. [2] proposed a *flexible relation* approach to the integration of multiple relational databases. This model extended the classical relational model by providing support for inconsistent data. Inconsistent data in their paper refers to those attribute values of an entity, such as a person's age, that in different databases are not the same. For example, a database says that a person is 19 years old, while another says that the same person is 20 years old. Flexible mechanisms were provided to resolve the data inconsistency problems. An algebra was also proposed for this flexible relation model. Their focus, however, using our terminology, was only on the "value-versus-value conflict" issues discussed in this paper. Reference [20] is an earlier example trying to resolve the same problems (termed *domain mismatch* problems in the latter). Although an algebra was provided in both works, they cannot be applied to resolving the schema integration issues, nor can it resolve the global query optimization issues at the schema level, because the scope of their algebra is limited to value inconsistency problems. Schema conflict issues, the key part of our work, were not dealt with in their papers.

Zhao *et al.* [85] proposed a universal relation approach to manage the schemas of federated databases. They extended the notion of *universal relation* to a heterogeneous multiple database environment by keeping all federated attributes in a single table. The main purpose was to facilitate the translation of a global query to local queries. The resolution of structural conflicts of local schemas, however, was not a concern of the paper. Also, no algebra based on their approach was proposed. Hence, optimization of a global query at the multidatabase system level could not be supported easily in this approach.

We consider the *multirelational approach* proposed by Grant *et al.* in [33], a work most similar and comparable to ours. Their approach, however, was designed for multidatabase systems without the need of an integrated global schema. All kinds of representational conflicts were specified in a query issued by the global user. Hence, the user must be knowledgeable enough to define clearly the differences between schemas of data. The major advantage of their work was that the schema integration issues were avoided. An algebra, named the *multirelational algebra*, associated with their model was proposed. This algebra played a role very similar to that of hyperrelational algebra. (For more details of the work, the reader is directed to [55, 56, 58].) As this work is very similar to the hyperrelational algebra (except that the application domains are different), an in-depth comparison of the two works is given in the following.

- Both algebras are based on the relational algebra and both are an extension of the relational algebra.
- Operations in both algebras are convertible to relational operations.
- All transformation properties in relational algebra remain valid in both algebras.
- Both algebras function as a mathematical basis for query transformation and optimization.

The differences:

- Supporting environments are different. The multirelational algebra is designed to support an environment that does not need a global schema (i.e., the multidatabase language approach as mentioned earlier). The hyperrelational algebra, however, is dedicated to those tightly integrated systems in which a global schema exists. It is based on this schema that a user query is issued.
- Definitions of "multirelation" and "hyperrelation" are different. In the multirelational algebra, a multirelation is a set of local relations that are involved in a user query. In other words, it is dependent on the query and, hence, there is not a fixed structure for a multirelation. In the hyperrelational algebra, however, both the structure and the contents of a hyperrelation are explicitly defined. They are completely determined by the integrated global schema. Each hyperrelation has a clearly defined semantics. Structurally, a hyperrelation is the

same as a relation; contentwise, it has the schemas of all semantically equivalent relations in the multidatabase system.

• Outputs of an algebraic expression in two cases are different. The result of a multirelational algebraic expression is still a set of relations, dissimilar to the relational algebra. The schemas of the relations in the result may not even be the same. For instance, $M Join(\{R_{11}, R_{12}, \ldots, R_{1n}\}, \{R_{21}, R_{22}, \ldots, R_{2m}\} : C)$ is a multirelational join operation on two sets of relations based on the join condition C. The result of this operation is $\{Join(R_{11}, R_{21} : C), \ldots, Join(R_{11}, R_{2m} : C), \ldots, Join(R_{1n}, R_{2m} : C)\}$. The schemas of these relations may not be the same. Hence, the result relations may have very different schemas. The user needs to interpret the semantics of the result, just like being responsible for specifying all necessary schema/data conflicts in a query. In the hyperrelational algebra, the result of an algebraic expression is still a relation. Hence, the semantics of the result relation is very clear. The user need not refer to any local relations to understand the semantics of the result.

• Requirements on union compatibility are different. In multirelational algebra, the operand multirelations need not be union compatible in executing a set operation. For example, the result of executing MUnion($\{R\}, \{S\}$) (where MUnion is a multirelational union operator) is $\{R, S\}$ if the local relations R and S are not union compatible. The union compatibility is enforced, however, when a multirelational operation is converted to relational operations. In contrast to their work, the operand hyperrelations must be union compatible if a set operation is executed. This difference is caused by the fact that the hyperrelational operations are performed on hyperrelations, each of them having a well-defined schema. This in a sense is the same as the relational algebra in which each relation has a well-defined schema. Union compatibility is enforced in these cases, as mentioned in the discussion of the H-SELECTION operation, to avoid performing set operations on semantically completely different relations. When a hyperrelation is converted to relational operations, the union compatibility requirement is relaxed because all operand relations are semantically equivalent.

IV. OPTIMIZATION AT THE EXECUTION STRATEGY LEVEL

In this section, we discuss multidatabase query optimization at another key level, the execution strategy level. The optimization at the algebra level focuses on the optimization that can possibly be achieved during the transformation of a global query to local queries. The execution strategy level optimization follows the task at the algebra level by finding an optimal execution strategy for the global query. Several important considerations at this level will be discussed in this section. A few optimization strategies and a performance study of them will also be presented.

In an MDBS, autonomous and heterogeneous database systems are integrated to serve for users who want to retrieve data from the component databases, i.e., the participating databases. Execution of a global query often involves the systems of these participating databases. For convenience in presentation, we will refer to these systems as the participating database systems and easier to implement than those complex cost model regeneration methods proposed in the past.

Finally, we note that the reason for not considering the other two well-known join algorithms, i.e., the nested-loop algorithm and the hash-based algorithm, in our method is because they are either impossible or inefficient to be implemented in a MDBS environment. We will clarify this point further also in a later section.

A. Assumptions

From the information exchange point of view, we can classify the participating database systems into three categories [24]:

- *Proprietary DBMSs.* The PDBSs can provide all the relevant information on cost functions and database statistics to the MDBS.
- *Conforming DBMSs.* The PDBSs provide database statistics but are incapable of divulging the cost functions.
- *Nonconforming DBMSs.* The PDBSs are incapable of divulging either the database statistics or the cost functions.

Our discussion in the following is dedicated to the *nonconforming DBMSs* environment. The reasons are, first, it is the least studied environment up to now. All past query optimization methods have not been designed for this environment [24, 25, 27, 29, 61, 68, 86]. Second, it is the most realistic environment considering the fact that almost all DBMSs today either have had or will be supplied with an accessing interface to the World Wide Web. There are also vendors utilizing *data warehousing* and *digital library* techniques to provide users with various data sources. All these sources are basically heterogeneous, same as in the nonconforming DBMSs environment. Both of the other two environments discussed in [24] require a major modification/enhancement to the core modules of the existing DBMSs.

B. Where Should an Intersite Operation Be Performed?

One difficulty of processing a multidatabase query is that data conflicts may exist. While performing an intersite operation (such as join, union), the conflicts of data must first be resolved. This is normally achieved by converting local data to a certain globally recognized format, such as that specified by the global schema. The mapping functions (or mapping tables) of heterogeneous data and the mapping mechanisms (software) all reside in the MDBS. Can the mapping tables for resolving data discrepancy can be sent to a PDBS to let the PDBS perform the tasks that are otherwise performed in the MDBS? The answer is no because not only the mapping tables but also the mechanisms (software) are needed to execute those conversions. Without the mechanisms, a PDBS is still unable to convert data of different types. All past research mentioned earlier ignored this issue in the design of an intersite join optimization strategy.

However, is it feasible to let the MDBS convert the data and the PDBS perform the intersite joins after data discrepancy is resolved? This issue should be examined in more detail. Basically, only two query execution schemes are feasible: (1) PDBSs perform the operations, and the MDBS converts the data, and (2) the MDBS performs the operations and data conversion. Let us use an example to illustrate these two schemes. Assume that $R \bowtie_1 S \bowtie_2 T$ is a multidatabase query, where R, S, and T belong to distinct databases.

1. *PDBSs perform the operations.* Assume that the databases containing R, S, and T are $PDBS_R$, $PDBS_S$, and $PDBS_T$, respectively. A strategy of this category contains the following steps:

   (a) $PDBS_R$ sends R to MDBS for data conversion.
   (b) MDBS converts R to a format understandable to $PDBS_S$.
   (c) MDBS sends R to $PDBS_S$.
   (d) $PDBS_S$ performs $R \bowtie_1 S$.
   (e) $PDBS_S$ sends the result, letting it be RS, to MDBS for another conversion.
   (f) MDBS converts RS to a format understandable to $PDBS_T$.
   (g) MDBS sends RS to $PDBS_T$.
   (h) $PDBS_T$ performs $RS \bowtie_2 T$.
   (i) $PDBS_T$ sends the result, letting it be RST, to MDBS for conversion.
   (j) MDBS converts the result and sends it back to the user.

Certainly, we can also send S to $PDBS_R$ to perform the join, or even perform $\bowtie_2$ before $\bowtie_1$. However, as long as joins are performed in PDBSs, the required communications between PDBSs and the MDBS as well as the data conversion to be performed in the MDBS are basically the same.

2. *MDBS performs the operations.* The same query will be executed in the following steps:

   (a) $PDBS_R$, $PDBS_S$, and $PDBS_T$ send R, S, and T, respectively, to MDBS simultaneously.
   (b) MDBS performs conversion on these relations.
   (c) MDBS performs $\bowtie_1$ and $\bowtie_2$.
   (d) MDBS sends the result to the user.

Obviously, the first scheme involves too much communication between each PDBS and the MDBS, causing serious overhead on query processing. It can be aggravated in today's applications that are accessed through the World Wide Web (WWW), a key feature desired by the users and implemented by most DBMS vendors in their current/next generation DBMSs. On the other hand, the second scheme does not require as much communication. In addition, many joins performed in MDBS can be reduced to simply a merge operation if the relations (subquery results) sent out from PDBSs are sorted. Hence, the second scheme is a preferred option. However, the MDBS's workload is heavy in this strategy. How to reduce query cost becomes crucial to the performance of a MDBS.

As the MDBS is heavily involved in global query execution, a major concern of optimization is to minimize the consumption of MDBS system resources so that it will not be easily overloaded during query processing. In other words, the optimization goal at this level should be to minimize the query execution cost so that the MDBS can serve a maximum number of concurrent users.

Other assumptions made are, first, the autonomy of a PDBS should not be violated or compromised for any reasons. The MDBS can only interact with a PDBS and utilize a PDBS's processing power under this restriction. Through this assumption, a running database system is ensured to be able to participate in a multidatabase without the need of modifying any part of its system code for the query optimization purpose. The second assumption is that all local operations (i.e., involving relations of a single database) of a query must be performed locally. A multidatabase (global) query after compilation is decomposed into subqueries, each being processible in a PDBS. For instance, a selection operation on a local relation should be performed before the local relation is sent to the MDBS (to participate in an operation involving relations of multiple databases). The processed result is then transmitted to the MDBS. Certainly, it is possible that the result size of a local operation (such as a join) becomes larger than its input size such that it seems to be better to send its input relations, instead of its result, to the MDBS and let the MDBS perform the (join) operation so as to reduce communication overhead. We do not consider this approach because our major concern here is that the MDBS could easily be overloaded if all locally processible tasks are sent to the MDBS. Since our optimization goal is to minimize the query execution cost in the MDBS, processing local operations locally becomes a natural choice.

C. Different from the Issues in Traditional Database Systems

As each PDBS is like a processor in a parallel as well as in a distributed database system, it is natural to ask whether our problem is the same as query optimization in parallel database systems, or in homogeneous distributed database systems? Also as all received relations are processed solely in the MDBS (as the second scheme in the previous section), how this part is different from a query optimization in a centralized database system is another question that needs explanations. We answer these questions in the following.

- *Different from query optimization in parallel database systems.* In a parallel database system, each task (such as sort and join) can be assigned to multiple processors [12, 37, 62]. There is apparent parallelism between consecutive tasks or even within a single task. In the MDBS environment under discussion, local tasks are processed locally and intersite operations are all processed in the MDBS. Therefore, a two-level data processing mechanism, one in PDBSs and the other in the MDBS, is employed in our design. Compared to a parallel database system where tasks can be assigned freely to any processors, the environment under study is much more restrictive on the collaboration of PDBSs for task assignment.

- *Different from query optimization in distributed database systems.* Similar to a parallel database system, a local system of a homogeneous distributed database system can process data sent from any other database freely, except that communication cost due to data transmission through communication network needs to be taken into account. No restrictions (due to heterogeneity) on task assignment to processors need to be considered. Hence, it is very different from the issue discussed in our environment.

QUERY OPTIMIZATION CONCEPTS AND METHODOLOGIES   157

- *Different from query optimization in centralized databases.* A key difference is that in a centralized database hash-based join methods are normally considered more efficient than sort–merge join methods [12, 22]. This is because the sorting process has a complexity of $O(n \log n)$ for n records, which is much higher than the linear hash process when n is large. Even if sort–merge join is sometimes used when the distribution of data is highly skewed where hash join becomes less efficient, we do not sort all the base relations before joining them. In a multidatabase environment under study, however, since sorting the subquery results is performed in each PDBS rather than in the MDBS, it is desired to have them all sorted (on an attribute on which the next join is performed) before they are sent to the MDBS to alleviate the burden of and facilitate the global joins in the MDBS. The focus becomes to design an optimization algorithm which is able to utilize as many sorted results from PDBSs as possible—a still different problem from that in traditional database systems.

From the above discussion, we see that the past query optimization methods cannot be directly applied to the new environment. New methods must be designed.

D. Two Scheduling Strategies Not Involving PDBS

Figure 14 is a "reduced" join graph of a multidatabase query in a MDBS. By reduced graph, we mean that operations and relations of a local query (subquery) are represented by simply one node, which is in fact the result of a local query. Hence, each node is a result relation from a PDBS. In this particular example, the number of PDBSs involved in this multidatabase query is 11. Each edge between two nodes stands for a join on the two corresponding relations. Each node is labeled by the name of the relation and each edge labeled by the join attribute. Formally, let us refer to such a graph as $G(V, E)$, where V and E are the sets of nodes and edges, respectively. Let the number of nodes (relations) and edges (joins) be $|V|$ and $|E|$, respectively.

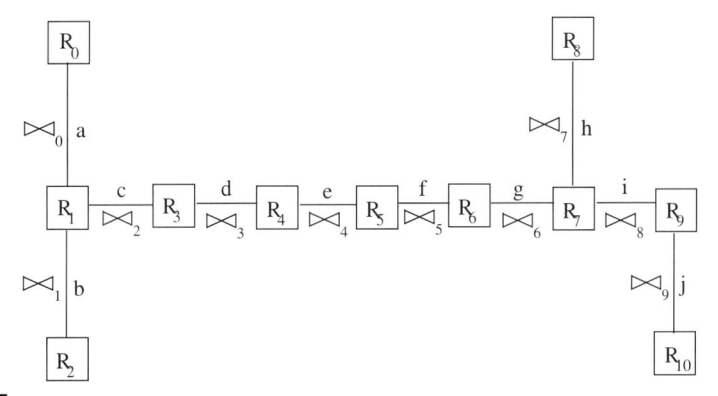

FIGURE 14   A join graph.

1. The First-Come-First-Serve (FCFS) Strategy

A straightforward method of joining the incoming relations in the MDBS is to use a first-come-first-serve (FCFS) strategy, meaning whichever relations that are received first by the MDBS are joined first in the MDBS. For instance, two joins $R_1 \bowtie R_2$ and $R_3 \bowtie R_4$ are involved in a query. If R_1 and R_2 are received in the MDBS earlier than R_3 and R_4, MDBS will perform $R_1 \bowtie R_2$ before $R_3 \bowtie R_4$. This strategy represents a case that we do not have any knowldge at all about the possible execution order of joins. MDBS will perform a join on whichever relations that have arrived at the MDBS. Intuitively, this is a good strategy because we normally have no control over the traffic of a network. A predetermined sequence of joins may not give a good performance if a relation that is scheduled to be joined early is blocked by the traffic of a network. We studied the performance of this strategy and the results will be presented in a later section. In Fig. 15 we give a formal presentation of the FCFS strategy. The complexity of this strategy is $O(|E|)$, where $|E|$ is the number of edges of a query graph $G(V, E)$, because each edge (i.e., join) need only be visited once in the algorithm.

2. The Greedy Scheduling (GRS) Strategy

The GRS strategy is an iterative algorithm that selects in each iteration the join that has the lowest join selectivity factor at the current stage. This algorithm is named so because it produces the least amount of data at every join stage. The details of this strategy is listed in Fig. 16.

A number of criteria could be used to select a join [12, 60] in a greedy multijoin algorithm. Three frequently seen criteria include:

1. **min(JS)**: select a join with the minimum join selectivity factor (producing *relatively* the least amount of data, or $|R_i \bowtie R_j|/(|R_i| * |R_j|)$ being minimum).
2. **min($|R_i| + |R_j|$)**: select a join whose total amount of input data is minimum.
3. **min($|R_i| * |R_j| * JS$)**: select a join that produces the least amount of data, i.e., $|R_i \bowtie R_j|$ being minimum.

```
FCFS strategy :
  Input : a join graph G(V, E);
  Output : a join sequence Q;

  Repeat until |V| = 1 ;
    Begin
      Choose R_i ⋈ R_j such that R_iR_j ∈ E and R_i and R_j have been arrived MDBS
        (if more than one joins can be performed (their operands are ready),
         an arbitrary one is selected);
      Add R_i ⋈ R_j into Q ;
      Update graph G by merging nodes R_i and R_j into R_min(i,j) ;
    End Begin
  End Repeat
```

FIGURE 15 The First-Come-First-Serve (FCFS) strategy.

GRS strategy :

Input : a join graph $G(V, E)$;
Output : a join sequence Q;

Repeat until $|V| = 1$;
  Begin
    Choose $R_i \bowtie R_j$ such that $\overline{R_i R_j} \in E$ and it has the lowest join selectivity factor
      at the current stage;
      (if more than one such joins are available, an arbitrary one is selected;)
    Add $R_i \bowtie R_j$ into Q;
    Update graph G by merging nodes R_i and R_j into $R_{min(i,j)}$;
  End Begin
End Repeat

FIGURE 16 The Greedy Scheduling (GRS) strategy.

These criteria aim at minimizing the intermediate relation sizes so as to achieve a lower total execution cost. Each of them has its strength and weakness. The third criterion may look attractive at the first sight. However, the smallest join result (i.e., $|R_i \bowtie R_j|$) may simply be incurred by the join of two small relations. The relative gain $|R_i \bowtie R_j|/(|R_i| * |R_j|)$ may be much less than that of the first criterion. A performance study of these criteria has been conducted in [60] and the result shows that none of them outperforms the others in all circumstances. In this paper, we simply adopt the first criterion, min(JS), in the GRS strategy.

The complexity of the GRS strategy is $O(|E|^2)$, where $|E|$ is the number of edges, because it needs $|E|$ iterations and each iteration checks on at most $|E|$ edges.

E. PDBS Sharing Workload with the MDBS

1. Utilizing PDBS Processing Power?

The hash, the sort–merge, and the nested-loop join algorithms are the most frequently used algorithms in traditional database systems. Especially, the hybrid hash join algorithm has been considered the fastest join algorithm among all [22]. Now the question is in a nonconforming DBMS environment can these algorithms be similarly implemented and still be as efficient as in a centralized database environment? We briefly discuss this issue in the following.

Assume that R_A (A1, A2, A3) and R_B (B1, B2, B3) are relations of different databases, and a multidatabase query is to join these two relations on A1 and B1 (i.e., $R_A.A1 = R_B.B1$). To implement a hash join algorithm is this environment, both R_A and R_B should be hashed in their own database systems before the hashed data buckets are sent to the MDBS to proceed on the probing phase.[7] However, as each PDBS is an autonomous system, the MDBS has no control over the hash function used in the PDBSs. The two hash functions used in the two databases are likely different. If the MDBS simply lets each PDBS hash its data in its own way, there may not exist any matching data buckets between the two relations. Besides, there is not a database language for the MDBS to

---

[7] A hash join can be split into two phases: hash and probe.

instruct a PDBS to perform simply a hash operation. In order to utilize PDBSs' processing power, hash join must be implemented by sending a set of queries to each PDBS to partition tuples of a local relation into buckets of different value ranges. Then corresponding buckets of the relations can be formed and joined in the MDBS. In the above query, for instance, the MDBS sends the following set of queries to database A (the one containing R_A):

select *	From R_A	Where $R_A.A1 \leq 20$
Select *	From R_A	Where $20 \leq R_A.A1 \leq 40$
Select *	From R_A	Where $40 \leq R_A.A1 \leq 40$
Select *	From R_A	Where $60 \leq R_A.A1 \leq 80$
Select *	From R_A	Where $80 \leq R_A.A1$

In this example we have assumed that the data type of attribute A1 is an integer. The relation is hashed into five buckets containing tuples having values in the ranges $(-\infty, 20], (20, 40], (40, 60], (60, 80], (80, +\infty]$, respectively. Similarly, the MDBS sends the same set of queries to database B (the one containing R_B) except that R_A in the queries is changed to R_B and A1 is changed to B1. Assume that $R_A^1, R_A^2, R_A^3, R_A^4$, and R_A^5 are the results of the five SQL queries on R_A and $R_B^1, R_B^2, R_B^3, R_B^4, R_B^5$ are those on R_B. Then R_A^i and R_B^i (for $1 \leq i \leq 5$) are the corresponding hashed buckets of the two relations and the probing phase can be executed in the MDBS. This way of hashing, however, requires that each PDBS executes as many queries as the number of hashed buckets. When hundreds or even thousands of hashed buckets are required, it will lead to a significant overhead for compiling and processing this large set of queries. This shortcoming prohibits PDBSs from sharing the workload with the MDBS in implementing a hash join method.

To implement a sort–merge algorithm in the same environment, only one query is needed to send to each PDBS. The query requires that the resulting relation be sorted in order on the join attribute. In the above example, a query sent to database A will be like this:

Select *
From R_A
Order By $R_A.A1$

The same query but asking for a sorted order on attribute B1 will be sent to database B. The results obtained from these two databases can then be easily merged by the MDBS to obtain the join result. This sort–merge approach is much simpler and more efficient than the hash join approach. As merge is a simple and linear process, the workload added onto the MDBS is extremely light.

The nested-loop join algorithm is the easiest to implement since it only requires the MDBS to send the following query to each PDBS to access the data:

Select *
From R_A

The PDBS need not process the relation in any manner. Since it does not fully utilize the PDBS's processing power, we do not consider it as a viable approach.

QUERY OPTIMIZATION CONCEPTS AND METHODOLOGIES **161**

One may wonder whether it is possible for database A and database B to send one block of data at a time to the MDBS such that the MDBS simply join these two blocks of data in memory. In this manner, the MDBS need not save the entire relations R_A and R_B to disk in order to run the nested-loop join algorithm, hence helping to reduce the workload of the MDBS. This scheme however is infeasible because the required low-level handshaking mechanism violates the autonomy of a PDBS. Thus, it is not implementable in a nonconforming DBMSs environment.

The following table summarizes the features of the three join algorithms implemented in a nonconforming DBMS environment. It is apparent that the sort–merge join is the most suitable algorithm for joins in a multidatabase environment, and therefore it is adopted as the global join algorithm in this research.

Algorithms	Consumed PDBS processing power	Consumed MDBS processing power
Hash join	Very high	Medium
Sort-merge join	Medium	Low
Nested-loop join	Low	Very high

F. The Maximum Merge Scheduling (MMS) Strategy

In order to reduce the burden of a MDBS, the best we can do is to ask the PDBSs to sort their local results before they send the results to the MDBS. When the MDBS receives the sorted relations, it only needs to merge them rather than starting from the very beginning to hash or sort the received relations to perform the join. In this way, the workload of a MDBS is highly minimized. So the MDBS's task is to determine the maximum number of pairs of sorted relations that can be merged (i.e., join) and instruct the corresponding PDBSs to sort their results. If we take the join graph in Fig. 14 as an example, the maximum number of pairs would be five, as shown in Fig. 17. Certainly, there may be other choices on the pairs of relations, such as choosing R_1 and R_2 as a pair rather than the pair R_0 and R_1. Based on the matching, the MDBS asks the PDBSs to sort their results on the given join attributes. For instance, the MDBS will ask the PDBS having R_0 to sort it on attribute a and the same to the PDBS having R_1. In this way, there will be five joins simplified to a simple "merge" process in the MDBS, greatly reducing the burden of the MDBS. In our algorithm (to be presented shortly), we group those larger relations as a pair when we have multiple choices because by sorting larger relations, the PDBSs share more workload of the MDBS.

An existing algorithm, named the *maximum matching algorithm* [10], can be used to find the maximum number of matching pairs of a given graph. In this maximum matching algorithm, a graph G is called **1-regular** if every vertex of G has degree 1, where the **degree** of a vertex is the number of vertices adjacent to this vertex. Let adjacent edges be those having the same terminal vertex. A **matching** of a graph G is a 1-regular subgraph of G, that is, *a subgraph*

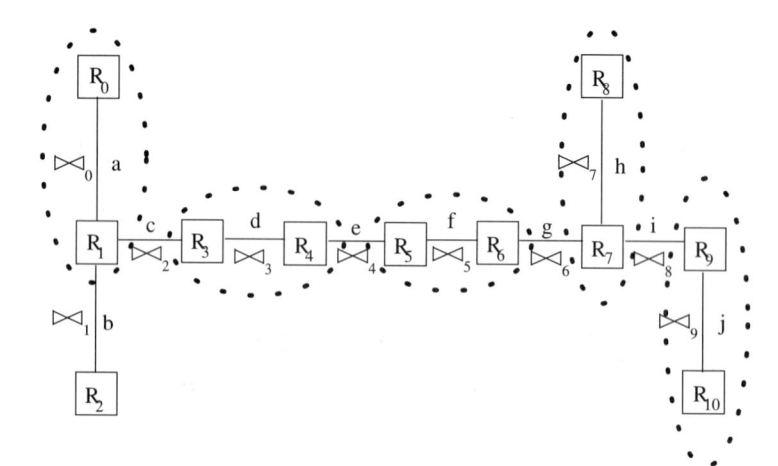

FIGURE 17 One of the maximum matchings found using the maximum matching algorithm.

containing a collection of nonadjacent edges. The **cardinality** of a matching represents the number of nonadjacent edges within the matching. A matching of the maximum cardinality of graph *G* is called a **maximum matching** of *G*. For an example, Fig. 17 shows a maximum matching of the join graph. The pairs of nodes that are circled by dotted ovals are the matching pairs. As this maximum matching algorithm is not difficult to infer based on the above description, we do not list here the details of the algorithm. Readers may refer to [10] for details.

This existing algorithm, however, does not work while there is more than one join on the same attributes. Figure 18 gives another example in which the relations are the same but the join attributes are different from those of Fig. 14. Obviously the maximum matching for our purpose should be the two groups as shown in the graph, because it allows seven joins to be implemented by a sort–merge join rather than five by using the maximum matching algorithm.

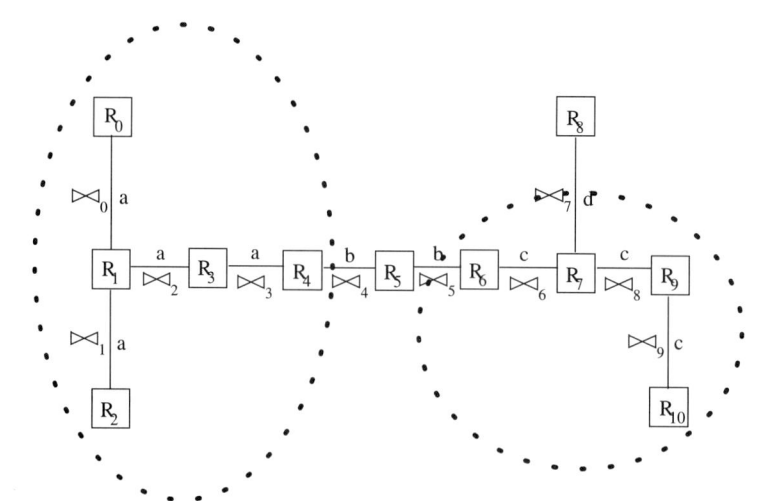

FIGURE 18 The same join graph with a different set of join attributes.

QUERY OPTIMIZATION CONCEPTS AND METHODOLOGIES 163

Our maximum merging strategy (MMS) is designed to work for such general query graphs.

We take a simple and yet effective approach to maximize the number of matching pairs in order to reduce the complexity of our algorithm. The basic idea is that we first use the existing maximum matching algorithm to find the maximum number of relation pairs, and let this graph be G. Then we identify the relations connected through the same join attribute, such as a dotted oval in Fig. 18. For each set, say C, of these relations, we check whether benefit (more matching pairs) is gained if the part of G corresponding to C is replaced by C. If it is beneficial, then they are replaced by C. If the number of matching pairs does not change by replacing them with C, then we check whether the total intermediate result size after the replacement will decrease. If it decreases in size, then the replacement is still adopted because it helps to reduce the workload of the MDBS. The same process continues until all such sets are examined. In order not to miss a large set (i.e., with more nodes), this process should start from the largest set and proceed in a descending order of the set size (number of nodes in a set) because selecting one set of matching relations might affect the selection of a set that is considered later.

Let us illustrate our idea by using the example in Fig. 18. Assume that the maximum matching pairs found by using the maximum matching algorithm is that shown in Fig. 17, but note that their join attributes should be the same as those in Fig. 18. There are three sets of relations, each set of relations being connected through the same attribute. In descending order of the size, they are the set $A = \{R_0, R_1, R_2, R_3, R_4\}$, the set $C = \{R_6, R_7, R_9, R_{10}\}$, and the set $B = \{R_4, R_5, R_6\}$ in which set B is not circled because eventually it is not selected in our result. For convenience, let us denote the set of relations $\{R_i, R_j, \ldots, R_k\}$ that are connected through the same attribute as $\overline{R_i R_j \ldots R_k}$. We start from set A, replace the matching pairs $\overline{R_0 R_1}$ and $\overline{R_3 R_4}$ by the set of matching relations $\overline{R_0 R_1 R_2 R_3 R_4}$, and check whether the number of matching relations in the entire graph increases. Since in this case the number is increased from five to seven, we adopt the new set. Next, we consider the set C. If the matching pairs $\overline{R_5 R_6}$, $\overline{R_7 R_8}$, and $\overline{R_9 R_{10}}$ are replaced by the set $\overline{R_6 R_7 R_9 R_{10}}$, the number of edges is still three. So whether they will be replaced by the new set is determined by the intermediate result size. That is, assuming that the result relation of $R_i \bowtie R_j \bowtie \ldots \bowtie R_k$ is denoted as $R_{ij\ldots k}$, and the size of realtion R is denoted as $|R|$, then the total size of the intermediate result relations (for only the part of involved relations $R_5, R_6, R_7, R_8, R_9, R_{10}$) before the replacement is $|R_{56}| + |R_{78}| + |R_{910}|$, and that after the replacement is $|R_5| + |R_{67910}| + |R_8|$. If the size become smaller, then the replacement is adopted. Otherwise, it is rejected. If C is adopted, then B need not be checked because only one node, R_5, is left for B. Otherwise, the set B is examined similarly. We list our algorithm details in the following.

Maximum Merging Strategy

Input: join graph $G(V, E)$;
Output: join strategy Q;
Let $|V|$ be the number of vertices of G, and $|E|$ be the number of edges of G;
We denote the join result of $R_1 \bowtie R_2 \cdots R_k$ as $R_{12\ldots k}$, and the size of R as $|R|$;

Use the maximum matching algorithm to find for G a set of matching pairs S_G with the number of matching pairs $= M$;

Assume that there are I sets of connected vertices. The edges of each set have the same label (i.e., join attribute) and the number of vertices in each set ≥ 3, where $0 \leq I \leq [|V|/3]$;

Each of these sets of vertices is a subgraph of G, and we denote such a subgraph as $G_i(V_i, E_i)$, where $0 \leq i \leq I$;

Let $V_i = \{R_{i1}, R_{i2}, \ldots, R_{i|V_i|}\}$;

Sort G_i's in descending order (i.e., G_1 is the largest set);

Let $Q = \phi$;

For $i = 1$ to I Do
    Begin
    $G'(V', E') = G(V, E) - G_i(V_i, E_i)$;
    Find maximum matching pairs for G' using the maximum matching algorithm; let the number of matching pairs be M';
    CASE
    • $M < M' + |E_i|$
    Begin
    $G(V, E) = G'(V', E')$;
    $M = M' + |E_i|$;
    $Q = Q + \{\overline{R_{i_1} R_{i_2} \cdots R_{i_{|V_i|}}}\}$; /* $R_{i_j} \in V_i$ */
    End
    • $M = M' + |E_i|$
    Begin
    If $\sum_{\forall h,k} |R_{hk}| + \sum_{\forall f,g} |R_{f,g}| > \sum_{\forall h} |R_h| + |R_{i_1 i_2 \cdots i |V_i|}|$, where $\overline{R_h R_k}$, $\overline{R_f R_g} \in S_G$ and $R_h \in V'$, and $R_k, R_f, R_g \in V_i$
    /* $\overline{R_H R_k}$ is a matching pair of G that is broken by the selection of $G_{ij} \overline{R_f R_g}$ is a matching pair of G residing in G_i. */
    then /* accept G_i */
        $G(V, E) = G'(V', E')$;
        $M = M' + |E_i|$;
        $Q = Q + \{\overline{R_{i1} R_{i2} \ldots R_{i_{|V_i|}}}\}$;
    End
    • $M > M' + |E_i|$
    Begin
    Do nothing;
    End
    End-of-For

Find matching pairs of $G(V, E)$ using the maximum matching algorithm and let $S_G = \{\overline{R_{11} R_{12}}, \overline{R_{21} R_{22}}, \cdots, \overline{R_{m1} R_{m2}}\}$ be the set of matching paris;
/* $G(V, E)$ might have been update so that a recalculation is still needed. */
$Q = Q + S_G$;
/* End of algorithm */

At the end of this algorithm, the relations that will be merge joined are determined. The results of these merge joins, however, could be unsorted on the attribute to be joined next. In general, these later stages of joins could have either one or two of the input relations being unsorted on the join attribute.

QUERY OPTIMIZATION CONCEPTS AND METHODOLOGIES

We process these joins based on two simple rules:

1. if one of the input relations is sorted on the join attribute, then perform an *order-preserving hash sort* on the unsorted relation and then do the merge join. We term this join a *semi-merge join to* distinguish it from a merge join.
2. if both of the relations are unsorted, then perform a hybrid hash join.

The reason why we employ an order-preserving hash sort in rule 1 is as follows. In order to minimize the number of disk accesses in the MDBS, when one of the input relations is already sorted, the second relation is only sorted at the block (bucket) level. This means that after the order-preserving hash sort, if $B_0, B_1, \ldots, B_n$ are the produced blocks, then records $b_0, \in B_0, b_1 \in B_1, \ldots, b_n \in B_n$ are in order, but records within each block are not necessarily in order. Then, joining records of two corresponding blocks can be performed in memory. This is especially efficient for today's systems in which a large memory is usually provided. By sorting only at the block level, the sorting process is accomplished in one scan of the relation, which significantly reduces the number of disk accesses. Since one of the input relations needs to be scanned and order-preserving-hash-sorted, the cost of a semi-merge join is higher than that of a merge join, i.e., *cost*(merge join) < *cost*(semi-merge join). A hash join on both unsorted relations, on the other hand, requires a scan and hash on both relations and then joins them. Hence, it is the most costly operation. Overall, the relationship of the costs of these three operations are *cost*(merge join) < *cost*(semi-merge join) < *cost*(hash join).

As all results sent from PDBSs are sorted, there can be maximally $\lceil N/2 \rceil$ joins reduced to a simple merge process (i.e., merge join) for a global query of N joins, if all join attributes are distinct attributes. If there are multiple joins on the same attribute, then this number can be even higher. Figure 19 shows an example of a query execution tree for Fig. 18, in which each circle is a join and each leaf node is a relation from a PDBS. The number in each circle is simply used to number the joins. In this query tree, seven of the joins (1 to 7) are reduced to a merge process. Join number 8 is a semi-merge join because R_8 can be sorted by its owner PDBS and the MDBS hash-sorts the result of join number 6. The remaining two joins (9 and 10) will be executed in the form of a hash join. Since a maximum number of merge joins is desired, a *bushy query tree* is in general better than a *left* or *right-deep tree* [12, 62]. In the performance study, we generate a set of queries to compare the performance of using different processing strategies. For the MMS, we always build for each query a bushy query tree such that a maximum number of merge joins can be employed.

G. Performance Study

1. Query Model

In order to compare the performance of the proposed strategies, we design a model that generates queries in a random manner. Each query in our model is a graph where a node is a relation and an edge is a join. Local operations are processed locally in the PDBSs. Hence, each node of a generated query graph represents a result relation output from a PDBS. The query can be either

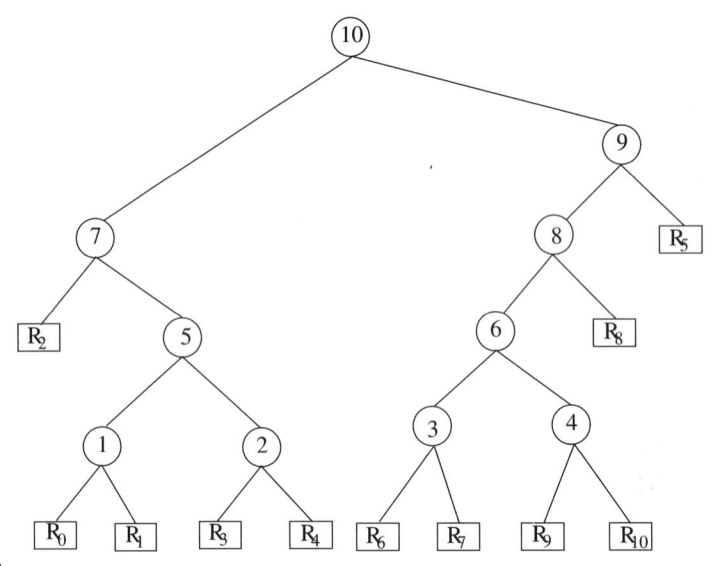

FIGURE 19 A query execution tree.

noncyclic or cyclic (i.e., loops may be formed in a query). A thousand queries will be generated for the experiments. There are two key tasks in generating such graphs. One is to model the joins on pairs of relations and another to model the join attributes. Let the number of relations involved in a query be N_r.

The Steps for Modeling Pairs of Relations

1. Create a node as the initial node.
2. Denote the initial node as R_i.
3. R_i may connect to 1 ~ 4 new nodes according to the following probabilities.
   - 1 node: 1/2
   - 2 nodes: 1/4
   - 3 nodes: 1/8
   - 4 nodes: 1/8.

The nodes that R_i has been connected to are included in the generated number. That is, if p is the generated number (which may be 1, 2, 3, or 4 nodes) and if R_i has been connected to p' nodes before this step, then the actual number of new nodes added to connect to R_i is $p - p'$ if $p > p'$, or 0 if $p \leq p'$. However, the number of nodes of each query should not be more than N_r. When this step is done, mark R_i.

4. If the number of nodes of a query is equal to N_r, go to Step 5.
If all nodes of this join graph are marked but the number of nodes is smaller than N_r, select a new node from this join graph as the initial node and go to Step 2. Otherwise, select an arbitrary unmarked node and denote it as R_i. Go to Step 3.

5. For each pair of nonadjacent nodes in this join graph, an edge is generated to connect them based on a probability of 1/10.

From Step 1 to Step 4 this model creates tree queries. Step 5 is to generate cyclic queries based on a certain probability.

The Steps for Modeling Join Attributes

We say that two edges are adjacent if they have a same terminal node.

1. Assign different join attributes to all edges. Let all edges be unmarked.
2. Randomly select an edge as an initial edge and denote it as E_i.
3. The join attribute of an unmarked edge, say E_j, that is adjacent to E_i may be changed to the same join attribute as E_i based on a probability of 1/4. If $E'_j s$ join attribute is changed to be the same as $E'_i s$ join attribute, then mark E_j. After all unmarked edges adjacent to E_i have been gone through this process, marks E_i.
4. If all edges of a join graph are marked, Protocol stops. Otherwise, arbitrarily select an unmarked edge and let it be E_i. Go to Step 3.

Through these steps, we generate 1000 join queries (for a given N_r) to test the performance of the proposed strategies.

2. Parameter Setting

Parameters used in our study and their default values are summarized in Fig. 20. These values are standard values and have been used in many other works [37, 62]. Also similar to other research, we assume that the memory size is large enough to contain at least a pair of corresponding blocks of the two relations to be joined so as to simplify our simulation task. The execution cost is measured in the number of disk accesses. CPU cost is ignored since it is normally much smaller than disk I/O cost.

3. Results and Discussion

In our experiments, the size of each relation received by the MDBS is assumed to be 10^6. Hence, if JS is equal to 10^{-6}, the result of a join will have a same size as the source relations, i.e., $|R \bowtie S| = |R| = |S|$. In order to examine the effect of join selectivity factor on the performance of the strategies, we divide JS into three ranges.

1. 2×10^{-7}–8×10^{-7}: represents a **low** join selectivity factor. A join in this case will produce a result of only 20–80% of its input size.
2. $8 \times 10^{-7} - 1.2 \times 10^{-6}$: stands for a **medium** join selectivity factor. The result size of such a join falls between 80 and 120% of the input size.

Symbol	Meaning	value
N_r	The number of relations	$5 \sim 30$
$|R|$	The number of tuples of relation R	10^6
T_s	The size of each tuple	200 bytes
P_s	The size of each page	4 Kbytes
JS	The join selectivity factor	$2*10^{-7} \sim 2*10^{-6}$

FIGURE 20 Symbols and their meanings.

3. $1.2 \times 10^{-6} - 1.8 \times 10^{-6}$: stands for a **high** join selectivity factor. The result size of such a join is increased by more than 20% (i.e., 120%) of the input size up to 180%.

Low Join Selectivity

We first examine the result when JS is low. Figure 21 shows the performance ratio of all strategies under a low JS. The performance ratio is obtained by dividing the average execution cost of the generated queries of a proposed strategy by that of the FCFS strategy. "X" in the label of the vertical axis of the figure means one of the three strategies. Hence, the curve for FCFS is always 100%, and X's curve below FCFS's curve means that X is better than FCFS and above FCFS's curve means X is worse.

As we expected, FCFS is the worst because it does not utilize any knowledge about the join selectivity factors in scheduling the join operations. GRS is better than FCFS by only about 10%. MMS is the best and outperforms the other two consistently by about 50%. In other words, it consumes only about half of the computing power that is required by the other two strategies. This is mainly because of the use of reduction of a join to simply a merge process in that strategy. GRS is only slightly better than FCFS because the greedy scheduling scheme provides somewhat benefit. However, this advantage is overshadowed by the large cost for performing joins. The consistent benefit margin of MMS over the others indicates that it is independent of N_r, the number of relations.

Medium Join Selectivity

Figure 22 presents the result of medium join selectivity. In this experiment, we found that GRS performs much better than FCFS at large N_r. This is because the join selectivity factor is larger in this experiment. The greedy strategy becomes more effective when the number of relations to be joined increases. The MMS does not show such a phenomenon. This is because at least half of the joins of each query are simply a merge process. Some of the rest of the joins require only an (order-preserving) hash on one relation followed by a block-level merge of two relations. The number of "true" joins is not many in the

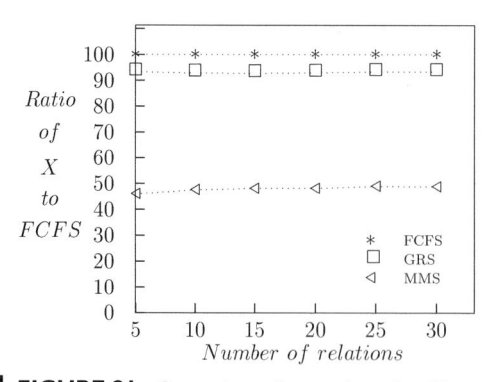

FIGURE 21 Comparison of strategies at low JS.

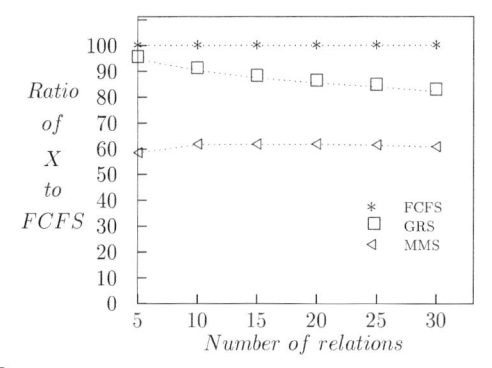

QUERY OPTIMIZATION CONCEPTS AND METHODOLOGIES

FIGURE 22 Comparison of strategies at medium JS.

range of the given number of relations in this experiment. Its saving will become more apparent when the number of relations (N_r) increases outside the range in this experiment.

High Join Selectivity

Figure 23 gives the result of high JS. In this case, both GRS and MMS outperform FCFS by a great margin, especially when N_r is large. This is because the JS is high such that the output size keeps increasing during the joins. Hence, if the number of joins increases, the benefit over FCFS increases too, enlarging the difference between FCFS and the other two strategies. Also we note that the performance of GRS approaches that of MMS at large N_r. This indicates that GRS is actually a good choice too under the condition that JS is high because this algorithm is simple, easy to implement, and does not require the PDBSs to sort their output relations. The only limitation is that it is confined to a high JS.

In summary, the MMS strategy is the best and outperforms the other two by a significant margin in all circumstances. GRS can be a second choice, in an environment where implementation complexity is a consideration and the join selectivity factor is known to be large. We have also conducted other sets of experiments by varying different parameters. Because of size limitation, we will present them in our future report.

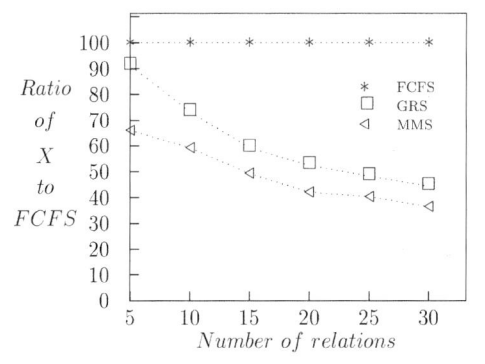

FIGURE 23 Comparison of strategies at high JS.

V. CONCLUSIONS

In a multidatabases environment, query processing is a time-consuming task as multiple levels of conversions (of data as well as the query) are involved. Query optimization in such an environment becomes especially involved. This issue, however, has not attracted much attention from researchers in the past.

In this chapter, we first classify the possible approaches to optimization from different levels. Among these approaching levels, our focus is solely on the algebra level and the execution strategy level. The reasons are that they are the key and necessary tasks of multidatabase query optimization, and optimization at these two levels is more practical and implementable.

For optimization at the algebra level, the task is to first find a uniform representation of conflicting relation schemas for multidatabase query translation. Although there has been plenty of research discussing the semantic conformation issues as cited earlier, there is still a lack of a thorough investigation on the representation and manipulation of data of conflicting schemas. The hyperrelational approach presented here provides support for dealing with these problems. Key concepts discussed for this algebra are as follows:

1. The notion of the least upper bound for a set of semantically equivalent relations is defined. Based on this definition, a hyperrelation can be found for each set of such relations. Instead of being a record keeping attribute values of an entity, a tuple in a hyperrelation keeps the schema information of a local relation. We presented in detail how schemas of each type of conflict are mapped to their corresponding hyperrelation.

2. Extending the notion of relational algebra, we developed a hyperrelational algebra that is performed on hyperrelations. Provided with algebraic transformation rules, the hyperrelational algebra serves as a sound basis for multidatabase query translation and optimization.

Having a clear and succinct tabular representation of conflicting local schemas, we believe that the SQL can be used as a multidatabase DDL/DML with minimum changes (to the SQL), because the tabular structure of a hyperrelation is not much different than that of a relation. This allows a global user to handle a multidatabase system easily, and it also reduces great effort in implementing a multidatabase system. View mechanism, a direct application of the query language, can therefore be easily dealt with in the hyperrelational approach.

For optimization at the execution strategy level, we discussed that conflict resolution on values of relations from different databases is often required in performing intersite database operations because of the heterogeneity of data between autonomous databases. Previous researches ignored this heterogeneity in their query optimization algorithms. In this chapter, we discussed this problem and argued that the MDBS, rather than an arbitrary PDBS, must perform intersite operations because only the MDBS has the required conflict resolution information and mechanisms. The transformed (and optimized) algebraic expression of a global query (obtained from the previous level of optimization) is used to find an optimal execution strategy. As MDBS is the site for executing intersite operations, it can easily become a bottleneck while serving for multidatabase users/applications. We presented algorithms that minimize the consumption of system resources such that the MDBS bottleneck problem can be alleviated. The advantages of our methods are (1) the knowledge of cost models of the PDBSs is no needed such that there is not need to regenerate all PDBSs' cost models in the MDBS (this is however required in all previous works), (2) our methods reduce the load of the MDBS and even distribute part of the task (sort) to the PDBSs, and (3) our methods are much simpler and easier to implement than those complex cost model regeneration methods proposed before.

Overall, query optimization in a multidatabase system can be achieved from multiple levels. Optimization techniques at these levels can be combined into a complete query compilation/transformation/optimization framework and implemented as modules in a multidatabase query optimizer. This integration framework is especially crucial for new applications such as data warehouses, web-based data sources, and mobile information systems, because these applications involve a large number of information sources. We expect that the presented techniques can soon be realized in the next generation information systems.

REFERENCES

1. A Special Issue on Heterogeneous Database (March, S. Ed.), *ACM Comput. Surveys* 22(3): 1990.
2. Agarwal, S., Keller, A. M., Wiederhold, G., and Saraswat, K. Flexible relation: An approach for integrating data from multiple, possibly inconsistent databases. In *International Conference on Data Engineering*, March 1995.
3. Ahmed, R., Smedt, P. D., Du, W., Kent, W., Ketbchi, M. A., Litwin, W. A., Rafii, A., and Shan, M. C. The Pegasus heterogeneous multidatabase system. *IEEE Computer* 24(12): 19–27, 1991.
4. Batini, C., and Lenzerini, M. A methodology for data schema integration in the entity relationship model. *IEEE Trans. Software Engrg.* 10(6): 650–664, 1984.
5. Batini, C., Lenzerini, M., and Navathe, S. A comparative analysis of methodologies for database schema integration. *ACM Comput. Surveys* 18(4): 1986.
6. Bregolin, M. Implementation of multidatabase SQL, technical report. University of Houston, May 1993.
7. Breitbart, R., Olson, P. L., and Thompson, G. R. Database integration in a distributed heterogeneous database system. In *Proc. IEEE Data Engineering Conference*, pp. 301–310, 1986.
8. Bright, M. W., Hurson, A. R., and Pakzad, S., Automated resolution of semantic heterogeneity in multidatabases. *ACM Trans. Database Systems* 19(2):212–253, 1994.
9. Chatterjee, A., and Segev, A. Data manipulation in heterogeneous databases. *SIGMOD Record* 20(4):1991.
10. Chartrand, G., and Oellermann, O. R. *Applied and Algorithmic Graph Theory*. McGraw-Hill, New York, 1993.
11. Chen, A. L. P. Outerjoin optimization in multidatabase systems. In *International Symposium on Databases in Parallel and Distributed Systems*, 1990.
12. Chen, M.-S., Yu, P. S., and Wu, K.-L. Optimization of parallel execution for multi-join queries. *IEEE Trans. Knowledge Data Engrg.* 8(3):416–428, 1996.
13. A Special Issue on Heterogeneous Distributed Database Systems (Ram, S. Ed.), *IEEE Computer* 24(12):1991.
14. Czejdo, B., Rusinkiewicz, M., and Embley, D. W. An approach to schema integration and query formulation in federated database systems. In *Proceedings of Third International Conference on Data Engineering*, 477–484, 1987.
16. Czejdo, B. and Taylor, M. Integration of database systems using an object-oriented approach. In *International Workshop on Interoperability in Multidatabase Systems*, Kyoto, Japan, 1991, pp. 30–37.

17. Dayal, U. Query processing in a multidatabase system. In *Query Processing in Database Systems* (Kim, W., Reiner, D. S., and Batory, D. S. Eds.), pp. 81–108. Springer-Verlag, Berlin, 1984.
18. Dayal, U., and Hwang, H. View definition and generalization for database integration in multidatabase: A system for heterogeneous distributed database. *IEEE Trans. Software Engrg.* 10(6):628–644, 1984.
19. DeMichiel, L. G. *Performing Operations over Mismatched Domain.* In *IEEE Proceedings of the Fifth International Conference on Data Engineering*, 1989.
20. DeMichiel, L. G. Resolving database incompatibility. *IEEE Trans. Knowledge Data Engrg.* 1(4):1989.
21. DeMichiel, L. G. Resolving database incompatibility: An approach to performing relational operations over mismatched domains. *IEEE Trans. Knowledge Data Engrg.* 1(4):485–493, 1989.
22. DeWitt, D. J. et al. Implementation techniques for main memory database systems. In *Proc. ACM SIGMOD Int. Conf. on Management of Data*, June 1984, pp. 1–8.
23. DeWitt, D. J. et al. The gamma database machine project. *IEEE Trans. Knowledge Data Engrg.* 2(1):44–62, 1990.
24. Du, W., Krishnamurthy, R., and Shan, M. Query optimization in heterogeneous DBMS. In *Proc. of the 18th VLDB Conference*, pp. 277–291, 1992.
25. Du, W., Shan, M., and Dayal, U. Reducing multidatabase query response time by tree balancing. In *Proc. of the ACM SIGMOD Conference*, pp. 293–303, 1995.
26. Dwyer, P. A., and Larson, J. A. Some experiences with a distributed database tested system. *Proc. IEEE* 75(5):1987.
27. Egyhazy, C. J., Triantis, K. P., and Bhasker, B. A query processing algorithm for a system of heterogeneous distributed databases. *Distrib. Parallel Databases.* 4(1):49–79, 1996.
28. Elmasri, R., and Navathe, S. B. *Fundamentals of Database Systems.* Benjamin/Cummings, Reduced City, CA, 1994.
29. Evrendilek, C., Dogac, A., Nural, S., and Ozcan, F. Multidatabase query optimization. *Distrib. Parallel Databases.* 5(1):77–114, 1997.
30. Gangopadhyay, D., and Barsalou, T. On the semantic equivalence of heterogeneous representations in multimodel multidatabase systems. *SIGMOD Record* 20(4):1991.
31. Geller, J., Perl, Y., and Neuhold, E. J. Structural schema integration in heterogeneous multidatabase systems using the dual model. In *Proc. the 1st RIDE-IMS Workshop*, Kyoto, Japan, 1991.
32. Graefe, G. Query evaluation techniques for large databases. *ACM Comput. Surveys* 25(2):1993.
33. Grant, J., Litwin, W., Roussopoulos, N., and Sellis, T. Query languages for relational multidatabases. *VLDB Journal* 2(2):1993.
34. Heimbigner, D., and McLeod, D. A federated architecture for information management. *ACM Trans. Office Inform. Systems* 253–278, 1985.
35. Hsiao, D. K., and Kamel, M. N. Heterogeneous database: Proliferations, issues, and solutions. *IEEE Trans. Knowledge Data Engrg.* 1(1):1989.
36. Hua, K. A., Lee, C., and Young, H. Data partitioning for multicomputer database systems: A cell-based approach. *Inform. Systems* 18(5):329–342, 1993.
37. Hua, K. A., Lee, C., and Hua, C. M. Dynamic load balancing in multicomputer database system using partition tuning. *IEEE Trans. Knowledge Data Engrg.* 7(6):968–983, 1995.
38. Hwang, H. Y., Dayal, U., and Gouda, M. Using semiouterjoin to process queries in multidatabase systems. In *ACM SIGMOD Conference on Management of Data*, 1984.
39. Kambayashi, Y., Rusinkiewicz, M., and Sheth, A., (Eds.) *Proceedings of the First International Workshop on Interoperability in Multidatabase Systems*, Kyoto, Japan, 1991.
40. Schek, H-J., Sheth, A., and Czejdo, B., (Eds.). *Proceedings of the International Workshop on Interoperability in Multidatabase Systems*, Vienna, Austria, 1993.
41. Kamel, M. N., and Kamel, N. N. Federated database management system: Requirements, issues and solutions. *Comput. Commun.* 15(4):1992.
42. Kent, W. Solving domain mismatch and schema mismatch problems with an object-oriented database programming language. In *Proceedings of the International Conference on Very Large Data Base*, 1991.
43. Kim, W., and Seo, J. Classify schematic and data heterogeneity in multidatabase systems. *IEEE Computer* 24(12):12–17, 1991.

44. Krishnamurthy, R., Litwin, W., and Kent, W. Language features for interoperability of databases with schematic discrepancies. In *Proc. of the SIGMOD Conference*, pp. 40–49, 1991.
45. Lee, C., and Tsai, C. L. Strategies for selection from heterogeneous databases. In *Proceedings of the Third International Symposium on Database Systems for Advanced Applications*, Taejon, Korea, April 1993.
46. Lee, C., Chen, C.-J., and Lu, H. An aspect of query optimization in multidatabase systems. *ACM SIGMOD Record*, 24(3):28–33, 1995.
47. Lee, C., and Chang, Z.-A. Utilizing page-level join index for optimization in parallel join execution. *IEEE Trans. Knowledge Data Engrg.* 7(6):1995.
48. Lee, C., and Wu, M.-C. A hyperrelational approach to integration and manipulation of data in multidatabase systems. *Int. J. Intell. Cooperative Inform. Systems* 5(4):395–429, 1996.
49. Lee, C., and Chen, J. R. Reduction of access sites for query optimization in multidatabase systems. *IEEE Trans. Knowledge Data Engrg.* 9(6):941–955, 1997.
50. Lee, C., Ke, C.-H., and Chen, Y.-H. Minimization of query execution in multidatabase systems *Int. J. Cooperative Inform. Systems,* 2002.
51. Lim, E.-P., Srivstav, J., Prabhakar, S., and Richardson, J. Entity identification in database integration. In *Proc. of the International Conference on Data Engineering*, pp. 294–301, 1993.
52. Litwin, W. MALPHA: A relational multidatabase manipulation language. In *Proceedings of the International Conference on Data Engineering*, April 1984.
53. Litwin, W., and Abdellatif, A. Multidatabase interoperability. *IEEE Computer* 1986.
54. Litwin, W., and Vigier, P. Dynamic attributes on the multidatabase system MRDSM. In *Proc. of the International Conference on Data Engineering*, 1986.
56. Litwin, W., and Abdellatif, A. An overview of the multi-database manipulation language mDSL. *Proc. IEEE* 75(5):1987.
57. Litwin, W., Mark, Leo., and Roussopoulos, N. Interoperability of multiple autonomous databases. *ACM Comput. Surveys*, 22(3):267–293, 1990.
58. Litwin, W. MSQL: A multidatabase language. *Inform. Sci.* 1990.
59. Litwin, W., Ketabchi, M., and Krishnamurthy, R. First order normal form for relational databases and multidatabases. *ACM SIGMOD Record* 20(4):1991.
60. Lu, H., Shan, M.-C., and Tan, K.-L. Optimization of multi-way join queries. In *Proceedings of the 17th International Conference on VLDB*, Barcelona, September pp. 549–560, 1991.
61. Lu, H., Ooi, B.-C., and Goh, C.-H. Multidatabase query optimization: Issues and solutions. In *Proc. of the Workshop on Interoperability in Multidatabase Systems*, pp. 137–143, 1993.
62. Lu, H., Ooi, B.-C., and Tan, K.-L. (Eds.). *Query Processing in Parallel Relational Database Systems*. IEEE Computer Society Press, Los Alamitos, CA, 1994.
63. Meng, W., Yu, C., Guh, K. C., and Dao, S. Processing multidatabase queries using the fragment and replicate strategy, Technical Report CS-TR-93-16. Department of Computer Science, SUNY at Binghamton, 1993.
64. Meng, W., and Yu, C. Query processing in multidatabase systems. In *Modern Database Systems: the Object Model, Interoperability, and Beyond* (Kim, W. Ed.), Chap. 27. Addison-Wesley, Reading, MA, 1995.
65. Missier, P., and Rusinkiewicz, M. Extending a multidatabase manipulation language to resolve schema and data conflicts, Technical Repost UH-CS-93-10. University of Houston, November 1993.
66. Motro, A. Superviews: Virtual integration of multiple databases. *IEEE Trans. Software Engrg.* 13(7):785–798, 1987.
67. Navathe, S., Elmasri, R., and Larson, J. Integrating user views in database design. *IEEE Computer* 1986.
68. Ngu, A. H. H., Yan, L. L., and Wong, L. S. Heterogeneous query optimization using maximal sub-queries. In *International Conference on Database Systems For Advanced Applications (DASFAA'93)*, Taejon, Korea, April pp. 413–420, 1993.
69. A Special Issue on Semantic Issues in Multidatabase Systems, *ACM SIGMOD Record* 20(4):1991.
70. Rusinkiewicz, M., Elmasri, R., Czejdo, B., Georgakopoulos, D., Karabatis, G., Jamoussi, A., Loa, K., and Li, Y. Query processing in OMNIBASE—A loosely coupled multi-database system, Technical Report UH-CS-88-05. University of Houston, February 1988.

71. Salza, S., Barone, G., and Morzy, T. Distributed query optimization in loosely coupled multidatabase systems. In *International Conference on Database Theory*, 1994.
72. Savasere, A., Sheth, A., Gala, S. K., Navathe, S. B., and Marcus, H. On applying classification to schema integration. In *Proc. First International Workshop on Interoperability in Multidatabase Systems*, Kyoto, Japan, April 1991.
73. Sciore, E., Siegel, M., and Rosenthal, A. Using semantic values to facilitate interoperability among heterogeneous information systems. *ACM Trans. Database Systems* 19(2):254–290, 1994.
74. Sheth, A. P., and Larson, J. A. Federated database systems for managing distributed, heterogeneous, and autonomous databases. *ACM Comput. Surveys* 22(3):1990.
75. Siegel, M., and Madnick, S. E. A metadata approach to resolving semantic conflicts. In *Proc. of the 17th International Conf. on VLDB*, September 1991.
76. Spaccapietra, S., and Parent, C. Conflicts and correspondence assertions in interoperable databases. *SIGMOD Record* 20(4):1991.
77. Spaccapietra, S., Parent, C., and Dupont, Y. Model independent assertions for integration of heterogeneous schemas. *VLDB Journal* 1, 1992.
78. Suardi, L., Rusinkiewicz, M., and Litwin, W. Execution of extended multidatabase SQL. In *IEEE Proceedings of the International Conference on Data Engineering*, 1993.
79. Templeton, M., Brill, D., Dao, S. K., Lund, E., Ward, P., Chen, A. L. P., and Macgregor, R. Mermaid—A front-end to distributed heterogeneous databases. *Proc. IEEE* 75(5):1987.
80. Tresch, M., and Scholl, M. H. Schema transformation processors for federated object-bases. In *DASFAA 1993*.
81. Wang, Y. R., and Madnick, S. E. The inter-database instance identification problem in integrating autonomous systems. In *Proc. of the International Conference on Data Engineering*, 1989.
82. Whang, W. K., Chakravarthy, S., and Navathe, S. B. Heterogeneous database: Inferring relationships for merging component schemas, and a query language, Technical Report UF-CIS-TR-92-048. Department of Computer and Information Sciences, University of Florida, 1992.
83. Yang, J., and Papazoglou, M. P. Determining schema interdependencies in object-oriented multidatabase systems. In *International DASFAA Symposium*, Korea, 1993.
84. Yu, C., Sun, W., Dao, S., and Keirsey, D. Determining relationships among attributes for interoperability of multi-database systems. In *Proc. of the Workshop on Interoperability in Multidatabase Systems*, 1991.
85. Leon Zhao, J., Segev, A., and Chatterjee, A. A univerisal relation approach to federated database management. In *International Conference on Data Engineering*, March, 1995.
86. Zhu, Q., and Larson, P. A. A query sampling method for estimating local cost parameters in a multidatabase system. In *Proc. of the Int'l Conf. on Data Engineering*, pp. 144–153, 1994.

5

DEVELOPMENT OF MULTILEVEL SECURE DATABASE SYSTEMS

ELISA BERTINO

Dipartimento di Scienze dell'Informazione, Università di Milano, 20135 Milano, Italy

ELENA FERRARI

Dipartimento di Chimica, Fisica e Matematica, Università dell'Insubria-Como, Italy

    I. INTRODUCTION 175
   II. ACCESS CONTROL: BASIC CONCEPTS 178
      A. Authorization Objects 179
      B. Authorization Subjects 179
      C. Authorization Privileges 180
  III. MANDATORY ACCESS CONTROL 180
      A. The Bell and LaPadula Model 180
      B. Denning Model 183
  IV. MULTILEVEL SECURITY IN RELATIONAL DBMSs 183
      A. Multilevel Relational Data Model 184
      B. Sea View 185
      C. LDV 186
      D. Jajodia and Sandhu Model 187
      E. The MLR Data Model 187
   V. MULTILEVEL SECURITY IN OBJECT DBMSs 188
      A. Object Data Model 188
      B. SODA Model 189
      C. SORION Model 189
      D. Millen–Lunt Model 190
      E. Jajodia–Kogan Model 190
      F. Modeling Multilevel Entities 193
  VI. SECURE CONCURRENCY CONTROL 194
      A. Architectures 196
      B. Secure Concurrency Control Protocols 197
 VII. CONCLUSIONS 199
     REFERENCES 200

I. INTRODUCTION

Data protection from unauthorized accesses is becoming more and more crucial as an increasing number of organizations entrust their data to database systems [10,33].

An important functionality that every *database management system* (DBMS) must support is the ability to protect data and system resources from intrusions, modifications, theft, and unauthorized disclosures. Since data in a database are related by semantic relationships, a damage in a database environment does not only affect a single user or application, but the entire information system.

Security breaches are typically categorized into the following categories: *unauthorized data observation, incorrect data modification,* and *data unavailability*. Unauthorized data observation results in the disclosure of information to subjects not entitled to gain access to such information. All organizations we may think of, ranging from commercial organizations to social or military organizations, may suffer heavy losses from both financial and human point of views upon unauthorized data observation. Incorrect modifications of data, either intentional or unintentional, result in an inconsistent database state. As a result, the database is no longer correct. Any use of incorrect data may again result in heavy losses for the organization. When data are unavailable, information that is crucial for the proper functioning of the organization may not be readily accessible when needed. Therefore, a complete solution to the data security problem entails addressing three main issues: *secrecy* or *confidentiality, integrity,* and *availability*.

Ensuring secrecy means preventing improper disclosure of information. Ensuring integrity means protecting data from unauthorized or improper modifications or deletions. Finally, ensuring availability means ensuring prevention and recovery from hardware and software errors and from malicious data denials making the database system not available.

The importance assigned to the above aspects greatly depends on the considered environment. For example, secrecy is the most relevant aspect of military environments, whereas in commercial environments most attention is devoted to integrity.

In many environments, such as public institutions, secrecy and integrity are often needed in combination. This is the case, for instance, of hospitals, airline companies or credit institutions, in which, besides privacy constraints, also data correctness is vital.

Data protection is ensured by different components of a DBMS. In particular, the *access control mechanism* ensures data secrecy. Whenever a subject tries to access an object, the access control mechanism checks the right of the subject against a set of authorizations, stated usually by some security administrator. An *authorization* states which subject can perform which action on which object. Authorizations are granted according to the security policies of the organization.

Data integrity is jointly ensured by the access control mechanism and by semantic integrity constraints. Whenever a subject tries to modify some data, the access control mechanism verifies that the subject has the right to modify the data, whereas the semantic integrity subsystem verifies that the updated data are semantically correct. Finally, the recovery subsystem and the concurrency control mechanism ensure that data are available and correct despite hardware and software failures and despite data accesses from concurrent application programs.

Authorization mechanisms provided as part of commercial DBMSs and research prototypes can be classified into two main categories: *discretionary* and *mandatory* authorization mechanisms. Discretionary access control mechanisms are characterized by a high degree of flexibility that makes them suitable for a large variety of application domains. They govern the access of subjects to data on the basis of subjects' identity and authorization rules. Under discretionary policy whenever a subject wishes to authorize another subject to exercise a privilege on a given object, it must insert into the system an authorization rule explicitly stating this right. When an access request is submitted, the access control mechanism checks if there exists a rule authorizing such access. In this case, the access is authorized; otherwise, it is denied. Such mechanisms are discretionary in that they allow subjects to grant other subjects authorization to access the data at their discretion. The main drawback of discretionary access control models is their vulnerability to malicious attacks, such as Trojan Horses, embedded in application programs. The reason is that discretionary authorization models do not impose any control on how information is propagated and used once it has been accessed by properly authorized subjects. The following example clarifies the discussion.

EXAMPLE 1. Consider a relational DBMS and suppose that *John* creates a table *Salary* containing information on the salary of each employee in his department. Suppose moreover that there exists an employee, say *Matt*, who is not authorized to know how much the employees of the department are paid. Suppose that *Matt* wants to get the sensitive information on the employee salary. *Matt* creates a table *Stolen* and gives *John* the write privilege on it. Then *Matt* modifies a worksheet application to include two hidden operations: a read operation on table *Salary* and a write operation on table *Stolen* (see Fig. 1a). Then he gives this application to *John*. When *John* executes the application, all the accesses performed by the application are checked against *John*'s authorizations. As a result, the sensitive information on the employees salaries are transferred into table *Stolen* and thus they are made accessible to *Matt* (see Fig. 1b).

By contrast, mandatory policies ensure a high degree of protection in that they prevent any illegal flow of information. They are therefore suitable for contexts, like the military one, which require a high degree of protection. Mandatory policies require a strict classification of subjects and objects into security levels. Access control is based on a set of axioms stating the relations that must occur between the security level of an object and that of a subject because the subject is granted access to the object. This type of security has also been referred to as *multilevel* security.

In this chapter, we focus on multilevel security. In particular, we deal with multilevel access control mechanisms and on secure concurrency control for DBMSs adopting a mandatory access control policy. We refer the reader to [4] for details on discretionary access control mechanisms. Moreover, a detailed description of transaction models and recovery mechanisms can be found in [5], whereas details on semantic integrity control can be found in any database textbook (see for instance [41]).

FIGURE 1 An example of Trojan Horse.

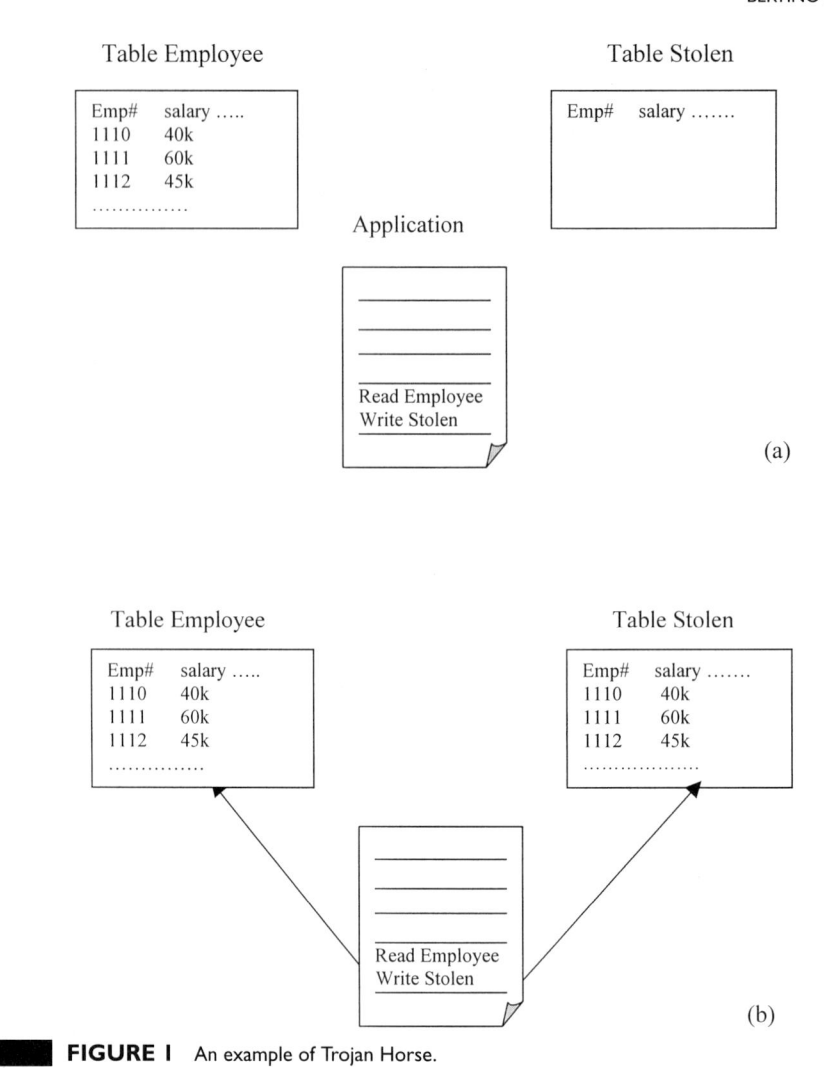

The remainder of this chapter is organized as follows. Section II surveys the basic concepts of access control. Section III illustrates mandatory access control policies and related access control models. Sections IV and V deal with multilevel access control in relational and object-oriented DBMSs, respectively, whereas Section VI deals with secure concurrency control. Finally, Section VII concludes the chapter and discusses future research directions.

II. ACCESS CONTROL: BASIC CONCEPTS

Access control regulates the *privileges subjects* can exercise on the *objects* in the system. The following is a discussion on objects, subjects, and privileges.

A. Authorization Objects

Authorization objects are the passive components of a system to which protection from unauthorized accesses should be given. Objects to be considered depend on the underlying data model. For instance, files and directories are examples of objects of an operating system, whereas if we consider a relational DBMS, resources to be protected are relations, views, and attributes. With respect to the object dimension we can classify access control mechanisms according to the granularity of access control, that is, according to whether it is possible to authorize a subject to access only selected components within an object.

Access control models can be further classified according to whether the set of objects to be protected represents a flat domain or whether the objects are organized into a hierarchy. In the latter case, the semantics assigned to the hierarchy greatly depends on the object nature. For instance, consider an object-oriented context. If objects to be protected are classes, the hierarchy represents the inheritance relations among classes. If objects represent class instances, the hierarchy reflects the way objects are organized in terms of other objects.

B. Authorization Subjects

Authorization subjects are the entities in the system to which authorizations are granted. Subjects can be classified into the following categories:

- **Users**, that is, single individuals connecting to the system.
- **Groups**, that is, sets of users.
- **Roles**, that is, named collection of privileges needed to perform specific activities within the system.
- **Processes**, that is, programs executed on behalf of users.

Note that the above categories are not mutually exclusive. For instance, a model can support both roles and groups, or both users and processes as authorization subjects.

Often, both roles and groups are hierarchically organized. The hierarchy imposed on groups usually reflects the membership of a group to another group. A nested group inherits the privileges of the groups preceding it in the nesting. By contrast, the role hierarchy usually reflects the relative position of roles within an organization. The higher is the level of a role in the hierarchy, the higher is its position in the organization. Thus, a role has all the privileges of the roles in a lower position in the hierarchy.

Processes need system resources to carry on their activities. Generally, processes refer to memory addresses, use the CPU, call other processes, and operate on data. All these resources must be protected from unauthorized accesses. Usually, a process is granted accesses only to essential resources, that is, those necessary to the completion of its tasks. This limits possible damage deriving from faults of the protection mechanism.

As far as users are concerned, sometimes it would be useful to specify access policies based on user qualifications and characteristics, rather than user identity (for example, a user can be given access to an R rated video, only if he/she is older than 18 years). This is the case, for instance, of digital library environments. In access control models supporting these possibilities [1,39] users must provide information, typically about themselves, allowing the access control mechanism to decide whether the access must be authorized.

As a final remark, note that authorization subjects can be further classified into *active* and *passive* subjects. Active subjects can directly require accesses to the objects, whereas passive subjects can only appear as subjects in an authorization but they cannot perform accesses to the objects. Groups are examples of passive subjects, whereas users are examples of active subjects.

C. Authorization Privileges

Authorization privileges state the types of operations that a subject can exercise on the objects in the system. The set of privileges a subject can exercise depends on the resources to be protected. For instance, read, write, and execute privileges are typical of an operating system environment, whereas in a relational DBMS typical privileges are select, insert, update, and delete. Moreover, new environments, such as the digital library environment, are characterized by new access modes, such as the usage or copying of access rights.

Often, privileges are hierarchically organized and the hierarchy represents a subsumption relation among privileges. Privileges toward the bottom of the hierarchy are subsumed by privileges toward the top (for instance, the write privilege is at a higher level in the hierarchy with respect to the read privilege, since write subsumes read operations). Thus, an authorization for a given privilege p implies an analogous authorization for all the privileges following p in the hierarchy.

III. MANDATORY ACCESS CONTROL

Mandatory (or multilevel) access control policies specify the access that subjects have to objects. According to mandatory policies both objects and subjects are given a classification level. Access control is then regulated by a set of axioms that establish the relations that must exist between the classification level of a subject s and an object o, to allow s to access o. In general, such relations depend on the considered privilege. Database systems that satisfy multilevel security properties are called *multilevel secure database management systems* (MLS/DBMSs) or *trusted database management systems* (TDBMSs). Many of the MLS/DBMSs have been designed based on the Bell and LaPadula policy [3] specified for operating systems. In the following subsections we first review the basic concepts of the Bell and LaPadula model [3], then we illustrate another milestone in multilevel access control, that is, the model proposed by Denning [13].

A. The Bell and LaPadula Model

In the Bell and LaPadula model, five different types of privileges are considered, with the following meaning:

1. **read**: a subject having the read privilege on an object can read the information in the object without modifying its content;

2. **append**: the append privilege allows a subject to modify the content of an object, but it does not allow the subject to extract information from the object (i.e., it does not subsume the read privilege);
3. **write**: the write privilege subsumes both the read and the append privilege in that it allows a subject to read information in an object and to modify the object content;
4. **execute**: this privilege allows a subject to execute an object. It applies to objects that contain a program or a routine. The execute privilege does not imply read, append, or write privileges;
5. **control**: it allows the delegation of privileges to other subjects. If a subject has the control privilege on an object, then he/she can extend to another subject the privileges he/she posses on the object.

In the Bell and LaPadula model, both subjects and objects are assigned an *access class*.

An access class consists of two components: a *security level* and a *set of categories*. The set of security levels forms a totally ordered lattice. The lattice usually considered consists of the following levels: Unclassified (U), Confidential (C), Secret (S), and TopSecret (TS), with Unclassified < Confidential < Secret < TopSecret. The security level associated with an object reflects the sensitivity of the information contained in the object; that is, it is a measure of the potential damage that could result from unauthorized disclosure of the information. By contrast, the security level associated with a subject (usually called *clearance*) is a measure of the subject's trustworthiness not to disclose sensitive information to other subjects not cleared to access it. The set of categories is an unordered set. Categories depend on the considered domain. Examples of categories in a military context are NATO, Nuclear, Navy, and Army.

Access classes are partially ordered according to a *dominance relation* (written $\geq$) defined as follows: given two access classes $ac_1 = (L_1, C_1)$ and $ac_2 = (L_2, C_2)$, we say that ac_1 *dominates* ac_2 (written $ac_1 \geq ac_2$) if and only if both the following conditions hold:

1. The security level of ac_1 is greater than or equal to the security level of ac_2 : $L_1 \geq L_2$
2. The set of categories of ac_1 includes the set of categories of ac_2 : $C_2 \subseteq C_1$.

If both the above conditions strictly hold (that is, $L_1 > L_2$ and $C_2 \subset C_1$), we say that the access class ac_1 *strictly dominates* the access class ac_2. Finally, if neither $ac_1 \geq ac_2$ nor $ac_2 \geq ac_1$ holds, ac_1 and ac_2 are said to be *incomparable*.

EXAMPLE 2. Consider the following access classes:

$$ac_1 = (TS, \{Nuclear, Army\})$$
$$ac_2 = (TS, \{Nuclear\})$$
$$ac_3 = (C, \{Army\})$$

$ac_1 \geq ac_2$, since $\{Nuclear\} \subseteq \{Nuclear, Army\}$; $ac_1 > ac_3$, since TS > C and $\{Army\} \subset \{Nuclear, Army\}$. Finally, ac_2 and ac_3 are incomparable with respect to the dominance relation. Indeed, ac_2 does not dominate ac_3, since $\{Army\}$ is not contained in $\{Nuclear\}$, and ac_3 does not dominate ac_2 since TS > C.

In the Bell and LaPadula model, the state of the system is described by a 4-tuple (A,M,L,G), where:

- A is the set of current accesses. Elements of A are triples (s,o,p). If (s,o,p) belongs to A, it means that subject s is currently exercising privilege p on object o;
- M is the access matrix; that is, it is a matrix containing for each object and subject in the system the privileges the subject can exercise on the object;
- L is a function that given an object or a subject returns its access class;
- G is the current hierarchy of objects; that is, it is a hierarchy denoting the objects that are currently accessible in the system.

Modifications to the state of the system are caused by *requests*. Requests can be of four different types:

1. a request by a subject to exercise a particular privilege on an object;
2. a request by a subject to grant another subject an access authorization;
3. a request by a subject to create an object;
4. a request by a subject to delete an object.

In the following, we consider only access requests, that is, request of the first type (these are requests for the read, append, write, and execute privilege). We refer the reader to [3] for the other types of requests.

The answer to a given request is called *decision*. Given a state of the system and a request, the result of the request is decided based on a set of *security axioms*. A system is *safe* if the requests are processed based on these axioms.

As far as access requests are concerned, the Bell and LaPadula model is governed by the following two axioms:

Simple Security Property. A state (A,M,L,G) satisfies the simple security property if for each element $a = (s,o,p)$ in A one of the following conditions is verified:

1. $p =$ execute or $p =$ append;
2. $p =$ read or $p =$ write and $L(s) \geq L(o)$.

*-Property (Read Star Property). A state (A,M,L,G) satisfies the *-property if for each element $a = (s,o,p)$ in A one of the following conditions is verified:

1. $p =$ execute;
2. $p =$ append and $L(s) \leq L(o)$;
3. $p =$ write and $L(s) = L(o)$.

For example, a subject with access class (C,{Army}) cannot read objects with access classes (C,{Navy,NATO}) or (U,{Nato}), since these read operations would violate the simple security property. Moreover, a subject with access class (C,{Army,Nuclear}) cannot write an object with access class (U,{Army}), since this write operation would violate the *-property.

For the sake of simplicity, in the remainder of this chapter we assume an empty set of categories. This allows us to consider only security levels.

B. Denning Model

The model by Denning [13] is an extension of the Bell and LaPadula model presented in the previous section. The main difference between the two models is that in [13] the concept of *security class* is introduced, which unifies the concepts of category and security level of the Bell and LaPadula model. The Denning model consists of five basic components:

1. a set of objects O, representing the resources to be protected;
2. a set of processes P, which are the active entities of the system, requiring accesses to the objects;
3. a set of security classes SC;
4. a flow relation, denoted as $\rightarrow$;
5. a binary operator $\Theta: SC \times SC \rightarrow SC$.

The operator Θ receives as input two security classes sc_1 and sc_2, and returns the security class that should be assigned to the result of any operation that combines information contained into objects whose security class is sc_1 and sc_2, respectively. The flow relation specifies the legal information flow. For example, $sc_1 \rightarrow sc_2$ specifies that a flow of information may take place from objects with security class sc_1 to objects with security class sc_2. Denning proved that the triple $(SC, \rightarrow, \Theta)$ is a finite lattice under the following hypothesis:

1. SC is a finite set;
2. $\rightarrow$ is a partial order relation over SC;
3. Θ is a total function with a least upper bound.

EXAMPLE 3. Consider a database with the following characteristics:

- the database contains three different types of records: medical records (m); financial records (f), and criminal records (c);
- the set of security classes consists of all the subsets of {m,f,c};
- flow of information from a class sc_1 to a class sc_2 is permitted if and only if $sc_1 \subseteq sc_2$;
- Θ is the union operator.

In this case, the triple $(SC, \rightarrow, \Theta)$ is a finite lattice, since all the hypotheses stated above are verified (see Fig. 2).

IV. MULTILEVEL SECURITY IN RELATIONAL DBMSs

This section discusses multilevel security models for relational database systems. Object DBMSs will be considered in the next section. Note that there are several other significant issues concerning multilevel security for database systems. These include inference problems, transaction management, and multilevel

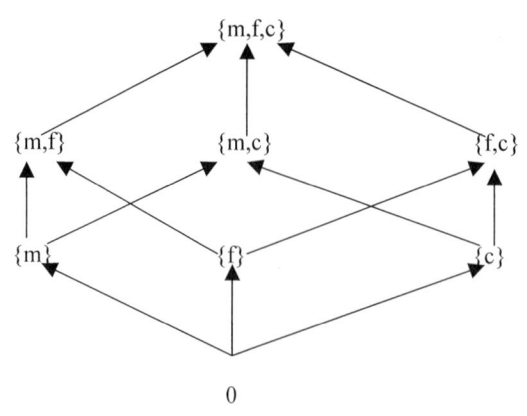

FIGURE 2 Lattice for Example 3.

security for distributed, heterogeneous, and federated database systems. We do not discuss such issues in this chapter, except for concurrency control protocols which are described in Section VI. For details on inference problems we refer the reader to [28]; for information on secure distributed and heterogeneous databases as well as secure federated databases we refer the reader to [38]. In the following, we first review the basic concepts of the multilevel relational data model, we then present some of the most relevant access control models for multilevel relational DBMSs.

A. Multilevel Relational Data Model

In a multilevel database not all of the data are assigned the same security level. If such a database is based on the relational model, the objects of classification may be the entire database, relations, tuples, or attributes. Access to these objects is governed by the mandatory policy discussed in Section II. A multilevel DBMS should protect the multilevel database from unauthorized access or modification by subjects cleared to different security levels. A multilevel relational database consists of a set of relations. The corresponding model is called a *multilevel relational data model*.

A goal of a multilevel relational database designer is to represent multiple versions of the same entity, action, or event at different security levels without violating the integrity or security rules. One of the mechanisms being proposed to represent multiple versions of an entity at different security levels is *polyinstantiation*; that is, the same object can have different interpretations and values at different levels. For example, at the unclassified level an employee's salary may be 30 K and at the Secret level the salary may be 70 K. With multilevel relational models one can have both entries but with their security levels as an additional attribute. One of the main motivations toward handling polyinstantiation is to avoid what is called *covert channels*. For example, if there is an entry at the Secret level that John's salary is 70 K and if an Unclassified subject wants to enter that John's salary is 30 K, and if the update is not permitted there could be a signalling channel from a higher level to a lower level. Over time this could become a covert channel. Polyinstantiation enables two tuples with the same primary key to exist in a relational database at different security levels. However, having two tuples with the same primary key violates the entity integrity property of the standard relational data model.

Several discussions and debates took place on polyinstantiation in the early 1990s. No consensus was reached. Some argued that polyinstantiation is necessary if we are to design multilevel database systems with higher levels of assurance (see, for example, [14]). Some argued that it is important to maintain the integrity of the database and that polyinstantiation violates the integrity (see, for example, [9]). Some used partial polyinstantiation together with security constraint enforcement in their design (see, for example, [32]). An interesting operational example showing the disastrous effects of polyinstantiation is given in the paper by Wiseman [40]. Even among those who support polyinstantiation, there has been much discussion on the correct update semantics to use. A logic for formalizing concepts in multilevel relations and which supports polyinstantiation is given in [36].

B. Sea View

SeaView is a multilevel relational data model, developed in the context of the SeaView project [14]. The SeaView project is a joint project by SRI International and Gemini Computers, Inc. The project also defined MSQL, an extension of SQL to handle multilevel data.

The SeaView security model consists of two components; the MAC (Mandatory Access Control) model and the TCB (Trusted Computing Base) model. The MAC model defines the mandatory security policy. Each subject is assigned a *readclass* and a *writeclass*. A subject can read an object if the subject's readclass dominates the access class of the object. A subject can write into an object if the object's access class dominates the writeclass of the subject.

The TCB model defines discretionary security and supporting policies for multilevel relations, views, and integrity constraints, among others. The data model on which SeaView is based is a multilevel relational data model. Multilevel relations are implemented as views over single level relations, that is, over relations having a single access class associated with them. Implementing multilevel relations as virtual relations (or views) allows subjects to issue insert, delete, and update requests on these views. Appropriate algorithms are then used to map updates on views onto updates on the base relations which are single level. An advantage of the SeaView approach is that the labels of the data elements need not be stored.

Each database operation is executed by a single level subject. When a subject at level L issues a request, a database system subject operating at level L will process the subject's request. This subject then cannot have read access to objects not classified at or below the level L.

Polyinstantiation is the mechanism introduced by SeaView to handle cover stories as well as signaling channels. For example, in a multilevel world, it is possible to have multiple views of the same entity at different security levels.

In the SeaView model, the two views may be represented, say, by two tuples with the same primary key, but at different security levels. The primary key constraint is not violated since in the multilevel relational data model proposed by SeaView a modified entity integrity property is defined. Additional integrity properties such as referential integrity property and polyinstantiation integrity property are also defined in the SeaView model.

C. LDV

In LDV [32], the relational query language SQL is enhanced with constructs for formulating security assertions. These security assertions serve to imply sensitivity labels for all atomic values, contexts, and aggregations in a database. The labeled data are partitioned across security levels, assigned to containers with dominating security markings or levels, and may only flow upward in level unless authorized otherwise.

LDV is based on the LOCK security policy, which consists of both a discretionary and a mandatory security policy. The discretionary security policy regulates the sharing of objects among the various subjects. The mandatory security policy controls the potential interferences among subjects and consists of a mandatory access control policy and a type enforcement policy. The mandatory access control policy is based on the Bell and LaPadula policy. The type enforcement policy restricts accesses of subjects to objects based on the domain of the subject and the type of the object.

Moreover, LDV addresses the problem of updating and querying a multilevel database. The update classification policy addresses the problem of proper classification of the database data. When the database is updated, the classification level of the data is determined. The data are then inserted into an object whose level dominates the level of the data. The response classification policy addresses the problem of proper classification of response to queries. This is a problem because the response may be built based on the data in many base relations. In the process of manipulating and combining the data, it is possible that the data will be used in a manner that reveals higher level information. The problem becomes more acute when one realizes that the response will be released into an environment in which many responses may be visible. Thus, the problem becomes one of aggregation and inference over time as well as across relations. In the LDV model, a response can only be released if it is placed in an object whose level dominates the derived level of the response, where the derived level is the maximum level of any information that can be deduced from the response by a subject reading this response.

Subjects interact with LDV through a request importer and a request exporter. Access to data as well as metadata is controlled by LOCK. Information in the database as well as the meta-database is stored in single-level files, i.e., LOCK objects. LOCK ensures that these database files may be manipulated only by subjects executing at the appropriate levels, and in the appropriate database domains. The three major operations performed by LDV are query, update, and metadata management. Each of these operations is an interaction between a non-LDV subject representing a user, and the LDV subjects that manipulate the database.

D. Jajodia and Sandhu Model

Jajodia and Sandhu [21] proposed a reference model for multilevel relational DBMSs and addressed on a formal basis entity integrity and update operations in the context of multilevel databases.

In the model by Jajodia and Sandhu a multilevel relation scheme is denoted as $R(A_1,C_1,\ldots,A_n,C_n,TC)$, where A_i is an attribute over a domain D_i, and C_i is a classification attribute for A_i, $i = 1,\ldots,n$. The domain of C_i is the set of access classes that can be associated with attribute A_i. TC is the classification attribute of the tuples. Furthermore, for each access class c, a relational instance R_c is defined. Elements of R_c are of the form $R(a_1,c_1,\ldots a_n,c_n,tc)$, where a_i is a value in the domain D_i, c_i is a classification attribute for a_i, $i = 1,\ldots,n$, and tc is the classification attribute of the tuples; tc is determined by computing the least upper bound of each c_i in the tuple. The relational instance R_c represents a view of the multilevel relation for subjects having access class c. The instance at level c is obtained from the multilevel relation by masking all attribute values whose classification is higher than or incomparable with c. This is obtained by substituting them with null values. Thus, subjects with different access classes have different views of the same multilevel relation. The entity integrity property of the standard relational data model is restated as follows: a multilevel relation R satisfies the entity integrity property if, for all instances R_c of R, and for each tuple t of R_c, the following conditions are satisfied:

1. the attributes of the primary key must be not null in t;
2. the attributes of the primary key must have the same access class in t;
3. the access class associated with a nonkey attribute must dominate the access classes associated with the attributes in the primary key.

The model by Jajodia and Sandhu supports both attribute and tuple polyinstantiation. Similar to the SeaView model, the key of a multilevel relation is defined as a combination of attributes, their classifications, and the classification of all the other attributes in the relation.

E. The MLR Data Model

The Multilevel Relational (MLR) data model proposed by Chen and Sandhu in [11] is an extension of the model proposed by Jajodia and Sandhu [21]. The data model is basically the one presented in the previous subsection, the main difference being that in the MLR data model the constraint that there can be at most one tuple in each access class for a given entity is imposed. The MLR model tries to overcome some of the ambiguities contained in the Jajodia and Sandhu model. To illustrate the problem consider a multilevel relation Employee with attributes SS#, NAME, SALARY, and DEPT#. Let SS# be the primary key. Suppose that Employee consists of the following tuples: (Sm101,U,Smith,U,10K,U,100,U,U) and (Sm101,U,Smith,U,20K,S,100,U,U). According to the Jajodia and Sandhu model, a TS subject sees a null value for attribute salary, even if there are two values for salary classified at lower levels. The alternative can be to return to the TS subject the highest value, among those available at lower levels (that is, those classified at level S).

However, there can be situation in which the TS subject would prefer the value at the lowest level, instead of that at the highest level. Thus, in the MLR model a new semantics for data classified at different levels is proposed, based on the following principles:

1. The data accepted by a subject at a given security level consist of two parts: (i) the data classified at his/her level; and (ii) the data borrowed from lower levels;
2. The data a subject can view are those accepted by subjects at his/her level and by subjects at lower levels;
3. A tuple with classification attribute c contains all the data accepted by subjects of level c.

V. MULTILEVEL SECURITY IN OBJECT DBMSs

Applying the Bell and LaPadula paradigm to object-oriented data models is not straightforward. Objects combine the properties of passive information repositories, represented by attributes and their values, with the properties of active entities, represented by methods and their invocations. Moreover, notions such as complex objects and inheritance hierarchies, make the object-oriented data model intrinsically complex. However, despite this complexity, the use of an object approach offers several advantages from the security perspective. The notion of encapsulation, which was originally introduced in object-oriented systems to facilitate modular design, can be used to express security requirements in a way that is comprehensible to the users. Moreover, messages are the only means by which objects exchange information. Due to these characteristics information flow in object systems has a very concrete and natural embodiment in terms of messages and their replies. Thus, information flows in object systems can be controlled by mediating message exchanges among objects.

In this section we present some of the major multilevel object-oriented access control models described in the literature. We start by reviewing the basic concepts of the object data model [7].

A. Object Data Model

According to the object-oriented paradigm, each real-word entity is modeled as an object. An object is associated with a unique object identifier (*oid*), which is fixed for the whole life of the object, a set of instance attributes, also called *instance variables*, and a set of procedures, called *methods*. Attributes represent relevant features of the entity being modeled (for instance, name, age, nationality, address, and ssn are examples of attributes of an object modeling a person). The value of an attribute can be an object or a set of objects. Each attribute is defined by specifying its *name* and its *domain*. Each method is defined by specifying a *signature* and a *body*. The signature specifies the name of the method and the input and output parameters. The body provides the implementation of the method. Input parameters are defined by specifying their name and their domain. Output parameters are defined by specifying their domain. Similar to attributes, the value of each parameter of a method can be either an object or a set of objects. The methods of an object can be invoked by sending a message to the object. Upon receipt of the message, the corresponding method is executed, and a reply is returned to the object sender of the message. The reply can be an oid, a primitive value, or a special null value that denotes that no value is returned. Read, write, and create operations are enforced by means of primitive messages invoking the corresponding system-defined primitive methods. Primitive methods are elementary in the sense that they cannot invoke other methods, that is, they cannot send any messages. Primitive messages can only be sent by an object to itself. If the need arises of invoking them from other objects, they must be properly encapsulated in nonprimitive methods.

The values of the attributes of an object represent the object *state*, whereas the set of methods of an object represents the object *behavior*. Objects sharing the same set of attributes and methods are grouped together into a class. Each object belongs to (is an instance of) a class. Classes are hierarchically organized into an inheritance hierarchy. Such hierarchy represents which classes are subclasses of (inherit from) other classes. Each class inherits all the attributes and methods of its superclasses. Additionally, it can have its own methods and attributes, and it can refine the inherited ones. Each class is defined by specifying its name, the names of its superclasses, and the attributes and methods of its instances.

B. SODA Model

The SODA model [22], proposed by Keefe *et al.*, was the first to incorporate multilevel security in object-oriented data models. SODA has been designed to enforce the Bell and LaPadula principles described in Section III. A. The rules governing the model are the following:

1. Any method activation can read a value within an object only if the access class of the object is dominated by the access class of the method. If the access class of the object dominates the current access class of the method, then the method's classification is raised to the level of the object being read.

2. A method activation may modify or create a new object of a particular classification if the method's current classification equals that of the object in question, the method's current classification is dominated by the upper bound of the classification range (as specified by the constraint), and the lower bound of the classification range specified by the constraint is dominated by the subject's clearance.

If the above rules are not satisfied, then a write/create operation fails.

C. SORION Model

Thuraisingham investigated security issues for the ORION object-oriented data model [35]. The secure model was called SORION.

In SORION, subjects and objects are assigned security levels. The following rules constitute the policy:

1. A subject has read access to an object if the subject's access class dominates that of the object.

2. A subject has write access to an object if the subject's access class is equal to that of the object.
3. A subject can execute a method if the subject's access class dominates the access class of the method and that of the class with which the method is associated.
4. A method executes at the level of the subject who initiated the execution.
5. During the execution of a method m_1, if another method m_2 must be executed, then m_2 can execute only if the execution level of m_1 dominates the level of m_2 and the class with which m_2 is associated.
6. Reading and writing of objects during method execution are governed by rules 1 and 2.

D. Millen–Lunt Model

Millen and Lunt have proposed a secure object model for knowledge-based applications [26]. The security properties enforced by the model are the following:

1. The *hierarchy property* states that the level of an object dominates that of its class.
2. The *subject-level property* states that the level of a subject created to handle a message dominates both the level of the subject that originated the message and the level of the object receiving the message.
3. The *object locality property* states that a subject can execute methods or read variables only in the object where it is located, or any superclass of that object. It can write variables only in that object.
4. The **-property* states that a subject may write into an object only if its security level is equal to that of the object.
5. The *return value property* states that an invoking subject can receive a return value from a message, only if the message handler subject is at the same security level as the invoking subject.
6. The *object creation property* states that the security level of a newly created object must dominate the level of the subject that requested its creation.

E. Jajodia–Kogan Model

Information flow in object systems can be checked by mediating message exchanges among objects. This is the idea underlying the *message filtering* approach proposed by Jajodia and Kogan in [19] to prevent illegal information flows during message exchange among objects. Under this approach, every message and every reply is intercepted by a trusted component of the object system (i.e., the *message filter*) in charge of preventing illegal information flow. In particular, information can legally flow from an object o_i to an object o_j if and only if the security level of o_i is lesser than the security level of o_j. All the other flows are illegal.

Upon the receipt of a message or a reply, the message filter decides appropriate actions to be taken, based on the message (or reply) and on the classifications

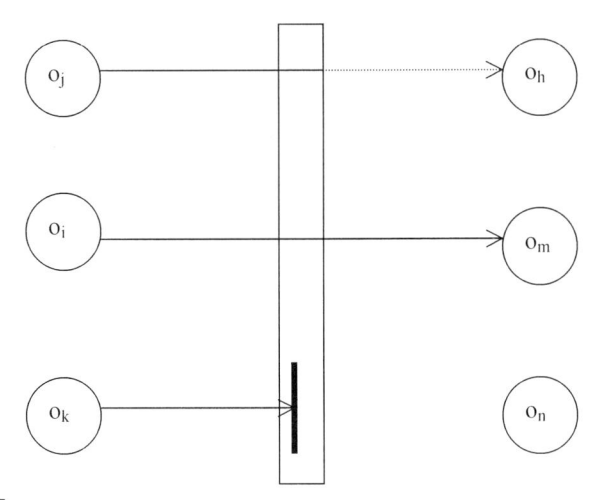

FIGURE 3 The message filter model.

of the sender and receiver object. Several actions are possible. For instance, the message can be sent unaltered to the receiver object, or it may be rejected. The latter action is taken when a low-classified object sends a message to a higher-classified object requesting to read some attributes of the latter.

A third possible action is to send the message to the receiver with the constraint that the invoked method is executed in *restricted* mode. This means that, even though the receiver can see the message, the execution of the corresponding method on the receiver should leave the state of the receiver (as well as of any other object at a level not dominated by the level of the receiver) as it was before the execution. Thus, the attributes of the receiver (and of any other object at a level not dominated by the level of the receiver) should not be modified by the method invoked upon receipt of the message.

Figure 3 exemplifies the message filter model. In the graphical representation, objects are denoted by nodes, and messages by oriented arcs from the sender object to the receiver. Each arc is intercepted by the message filter. An arc that does not pass through the message filter denotes a rejected message; an example is the message from object o_k in Fig. 3. An arc that after passing through the message filter becomes a dashed arc denotes a message to be executed by the receiver in restricted mode; an example is the message from object o_j in Fig. 3. Finally, an arc that passes through the message filter without any change denotes a message sent to the receiver, without requiring execution in restricted mode. An example is the message from object o_i in Fig. 3.

Note that information does not necessarily flow every time a message is sent between objects in that an object acquires information only by modifying its internal state, that is, by changing the values of some of its attributes. Thus, no information flow is enacted if the attribute values of an object have not been modified as part of the method executed in answer to the message. In such cases, the forward flow is said to be ineffective. Similarly, whenever a null reply is sent back as reply to a message, the backward information flow is ineffective.

In an object-oriented system, information flow can take place either (i) when a message is sent from an object to another or (ii) when an object is created. In case (i), information flow can be from the sender to the receiver, or vice versa. The forward flow is from the message sender to the receiver and is carried through the message arguments. The backward flow is from the message receiver to the sender and is carried through the message reply. In case (ii), information flow is only in the forward direction through the attribute values with which the newly created object is to be initialized. Those flows are called direct flows.

Information flow can also be indirect in that a message from an object to another may result in a method execution as part of which a message to a third object is sent. Consider for instance the case of an object o_i sending a message g_i to another object o_j. Suppose that o_j does not change its internal state as a result of receiving g_i, but instead sends a message g_j to a third object o_k. Moreover, suppose that the arguments of g_j contain information derived from the arguments of g_i (e.g., by copying some arguments of g_i to g_j). If the corresponding method execution in o_k results in updating the state of o_k, a transfer of information has taken place from o_i to o_k. Note that the flow from o_i to o_k has been enacted, even though no message exchange has been performed between o_i and o_k. Note, moreover, that a flow from o_i to o_k does not necessarily imply a flow from o_i to o_j.

The message filter intercepts every message and reply exchanged among objects to prevent both direct and indirect illegal flows of information. For an object system to be secure, all flows must be from lower level objects to higher level objects. To prevent all the illegal flows of information, the message filter makes use of a special indicator. Such an indicator, denoted in the following as *rlevel*, keeps track, for each method invocation t, of the least upper bound of the levels of all objects encountered in the sequence of method invocations starting from the object that began the computation and ending with t.

The message filter works as follows. Let o_1 and o_2 be the sender and receiver object, respectively. Moreover, let t_1 denote the method invocation on o_1 as part of which the message g_1 is sent to o_2; t_2 denotes the method invocation on o_2 performed upon receiving message g_1. Two major cases arise depending on whether g_1 is a primitive message. Let us first consider the case of nonprimitive messages. The following cases arise:

1. the sender and receiver are at the same level: the message and the reply are allowed to pass;
2. the levels of the sender and receiver are incomparable: the message is blocked and a null reply is returned to method t_1;
3. the receiver has a higher level than the sender: the message is passed through; however, the actual reply from t_2 is discarded and a null reply is returned to t_1. To prevent timing channels the null value is returned before executing t_2;
4. the receiver has a lower level than the sender: the message and reply are allowed to pass. t_2 is executed in restricted mode; that is, it is restricted from modifying the state of the receiver or creating a new object (i.e., the method invocation is memoryless). Moreover, this restriction is propagated along with further messages sent out by t_2 to other objects.

The security mediation of primitive messages is performed according to the following principles: (1) read operations are always secure because read-up operations are never allowed. Indeed, read operations are confined to an object's methods, and cannot be directly invoked by methods of other objects. The results of a read operation can thus only be exported by messages or replies, which are filtered by the message filter; (2) write operations succeed only if the status of the method invoking the operations is unrestricted. Finally, (3) create operations succeed only if the *rlevel* of the method invoking the operation is dominated by the level of the created object.

F. Modeling Multilevel Entities

An aspect common to all the proposals illustrated so far is the requirement that objects be single-level; i.e., all attributes of an object must have the same access class. The main advantage of a single-level object model, as opposed to a multilevel object model, is its simplicity and its compatibility with a security kernel. The main drawback of single-level models is that they do not reflect the real world, in which applications often need to represent multilevel entities. The solution is to use a single-level object system and map the multilevel entities onto several single-level objects. This approach has two main variants, depending on whether inheritance or aggregation is used to support the multilevel view.

For instance, Thuraisingham in [35] and Jajodia and Kogan in [19] propose an approach based on the use of inheritance hierarchies. In their proposals, each entity is mapped onto several objects, one for each access class appearing in the entity. An inheritance hierarchy is then defined over the objects onto which an entity has been mapped. The use of the inheritance hierarchy, however, has several drawbacks. First, it leads to a replication of information: since a multilevel entity is modeled as several single-level objects in a class inheritance hierarchy, some attributes of high-level objects are replicas of attributes of low-level objects (because of inheritance). Second, if not carefully monitored, updates may lead to mutual inconsistency of replicated data. In particular, changes to low-level copies of the information must be propagated to the corresponding high-level copies. Changes to high-level copies of the data should not be allowed because they cannot be propagated to low-level copies and would therefore introduce inconsistencies. Finally, this approach overloads the notion of inheritance, which is used both for conceptual specialization and for supporting multilevel entities.

The approach proposed by Millen and Lunt in [27] to store values at different classifications is based on the use of back references going from higher to lower objects. This choice is motivated by the requirement that an object cannot store references to objects at higher levels. In this approach, however, values classified at higher levels are not directly reachable by accessing the object representing the entity. Since no multilevel entity interface is provided, the burden of collecting all attributes and values referring to the same entity remains with the subject.

The approach by Boulahia-Cuppens *et al.* [8] is based on the use of reference links. In this approach, each multilevel entity is mapped onto (possibly several) single-level objects, one for each security level in the entity. Each object contains all the attributes of the multilevel entity. Values at a level lower than the level of the object are reachable through reference links. The approach is based on the assumption that the database schema is not protected; i.e., all attribute definitions are visible to every subject (even if the subject cannot see attribute values).

Finally, Bertino *et al.* [6] have recently proposed an approach to model multilevel entities by using composite objects and delegation [17]. The approach basically consists in mapping each multilevel entity type onto a corresponding set of single-level classes, which are stored in the underlying object DBMS. Those classes are related by appropriate composite references. Moreover, each class is equipped with a set of accessor methods, which allow the retrieval of information from component objects. One important feature of the approach presented in [6] is that an attribute of a multilevel entity type may take on values at different security levels. For each level, the application designer may specify the desired policy with respect to polyinstantiated attribute values. For example, the designer may specify that a low value is a cover story, and thus it should not be considered at higher levels, or that it should be considered at a higher level only if no other value is specified for that level. The generation of such class schema can be however quite difficult. Thus, in [6] a methodology that takes as input the specification of a set of multilevel entity types organized into aggregation and inheritance hierarchies and returns a set of corresponding single-level classes is defined. Each class is equipped with the proper composite references and methods to read and write the attributes of their instances. Algorithms implementing this methodology are also presented in [6]. The single-level object representation is thus transparent to the users in that the generated single-level objects provide the same interfaces, i.e., respond to the same messages, as if multilevel objects were directly supported. The methodology proposed in [6], called Class Schema Generation (CSG), methodology consists of four steps to be sequentially executed. These steps are illustrated in Fig. 4. The first phase of the methodology, called schema completion phase, modifies the input entity-type schema to make easier the execution of the subsequent phases. The second phase is the class generation phase, which generates the single-level classes corresponding to the multilevel entity types received as input. During this phase only the class names and the inheritance relationships are defined. Attributes and methods are defined by the two subsequent phases, called attribute generation and method generation phase, respectively.

VI. SECURE CONCURRENCY CONTROL

Concurrency control in MLS/DBMSs must address two main issues: (1) ensure the correct execution of concurrent transactions; and (2) ensure multilevel security [2]. However, ensuring that transaction executions do not violate the Bell and LaPadula principles is not enough to prevent all possible leakages of information. In particular, those principles do not prevent *signaling channels*. A signaling channel may arise when two transactions access the same data. For example, a higher-level transaction, by reading lower level data, may cause a delay in the execution of a lower level transaction by attempting to write these data. In such a way, a higher level transaction may transmit sensitive

MULTILEVEL SECURE DATABASE SYSTEMS

Entity schema

↓

(Schema completion)

↓

Completed entity schema

↓

(Class generation)

↓

Partial class schema

↓

(Attribute generation)

↓

Partial class schema

↓

(Method generation)

↓

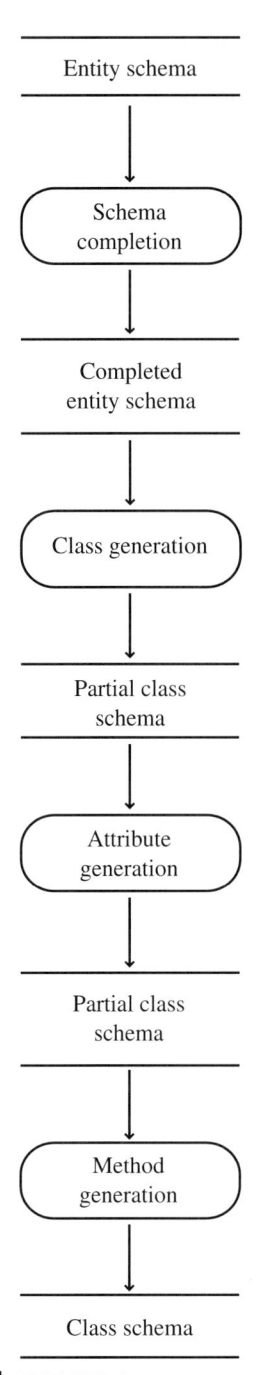

Class schema

FIGURE 4 The CSG methodology.

information to lower level subjects. Thus, in addition to verify the Bell and LaPadula principles, a concurrency control protocol for MLS/DBMSs must be free of signaling channels.

In the remainder of this section we first survey the most important architectures on which secure concurrency control relies; we then illustrate some of the most relevant secure concurrency control protocols for MLS/DBMSs.

A. Architectures

Most of the research on secure transaction processing in MLS/DBMSs can be categorized into two broad categories: one based on a *kernelized architecture* and the other based on a *replicated architecture*. Both architectures rely on the notion of trusted front end (TFE), which cannot be bypassed. In the kernelized architecture (illustrated in Fig. 5) a multilevel database is partitioned into a set of single-level databases, each of which stores data at one particular level. The TFE component ensures that when a subject submits a query to the system, this query is submitted to the DBMS with the same security level as the subject. By contrast, the trusted back end makes sure that the Bell and LaPadula principles are satisfied. The main drawback of the kernelized architecture is that the query execution performance greatly degrades when queries access data from multiple security levels, since data at different levels are stored separately. In contrast, the main advantage of the kernelized architecture is that the transaction scheduler can be decomposed into several untrusted schedulers, one for each security level.

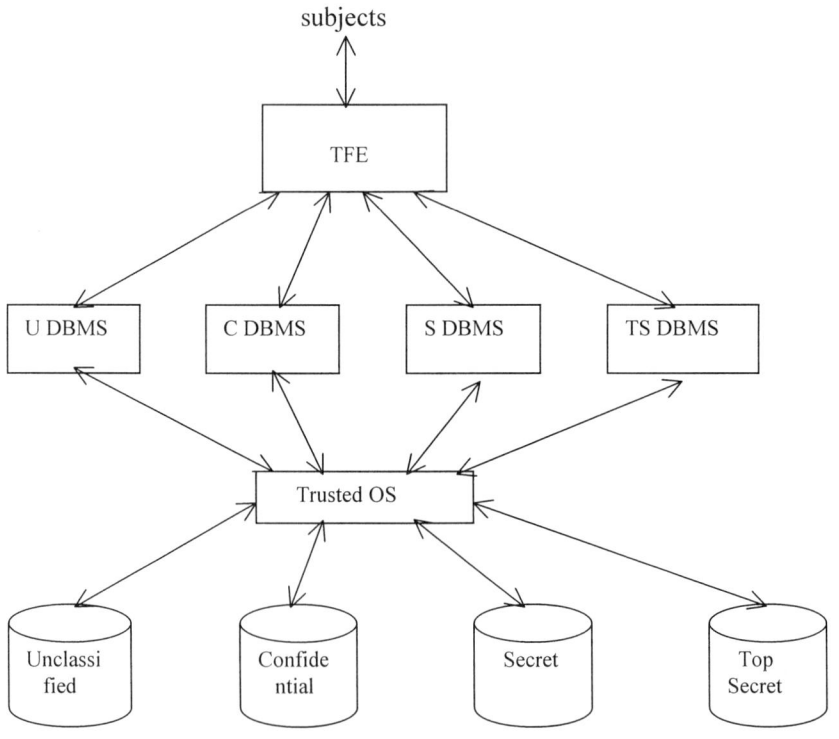

FIGURE 5 The kernelized architecture.

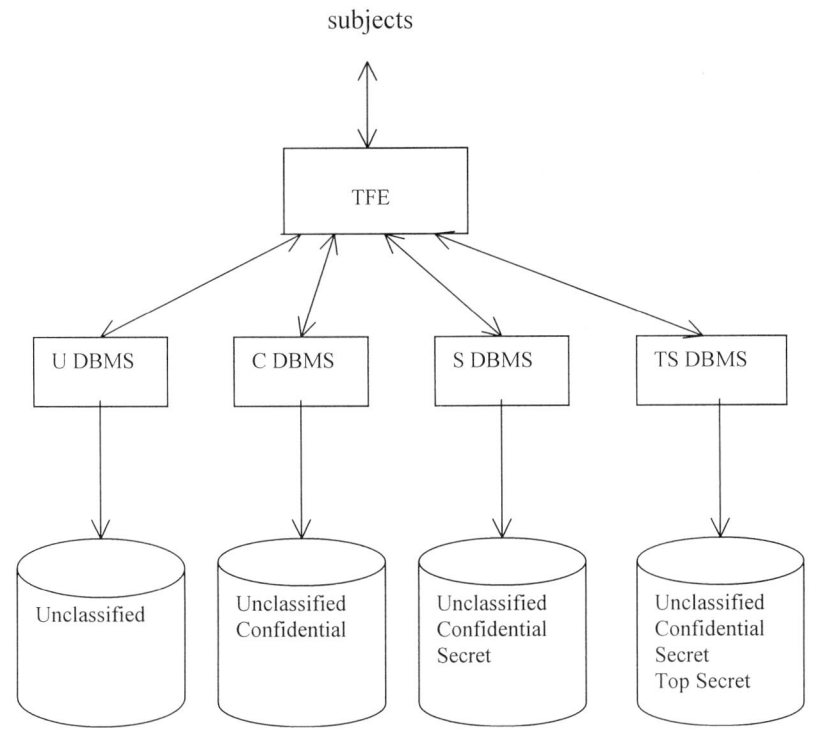

FIGURE 6 The replicated architecture.

The replicated architecture, like the kernelized architecture, uses different databases to store data at different levels. For each security level, a different database exists. However, unlike the case of the kernelized architecture, the database at a security level L contains all the data which are classified either at level L or at a level lesser than L.

The replicated architecture is illustrated in Fig. 6. In this architecture, when a transaction at a given level wishes to read data at lower levels, it will be given the replica of the lower level data stored in the database at its own security level.

Although, the replicated architecture makes query execution more efficient with respect to the kernelized architecture, it suffers from several drawbacks. First, this architectures is not practical for a large number of security levels. The propagation of updates from lower to higher levels is also a critical issue. For these reasons, in the following we consider the kernelized architecture only. We refer the interested reader to [12,16,20] for secure update propagation protocols in replicated architectures.

B. Secure Concurrency Control Protocols

The problem of secure concurrency control in MLS/DBMSs has been extensively investigated and several proposals can be found in the literature [18,23–25,31]. Algorithms for concurrency control can be divided into two main categories: *two-phase locking algorithms* and *timestamp-ordering algorithms*.

In two-phase locking algorithms, transactions should acquire locks on data before performing any actions on them. A read lock should be obtained before reading data, whereas a write lock should be obtained before writing data. With respect to locks, a transaction execution must be divided into two phases: a *growing phase*, in which the transaction should acquire all the locks it needs for its execution, and a *shrinking phase*, during which the transaction unlocks the data it has accessed. The constraint is imposed that once a transaction releases a lock, it cannot acquire any more lock.

In timestamp-ordering algorithms a unique timestamp is assigned to each transaction. Moreover, for each data, two distinct timestamps are maintained: a read timestamp and a write timestamp. A transaction is allowed to read a data only if the timestamp of the data is not greater than the timestamp of the transaction. The same constraint is applied to write operations. Upon a read or write operation the timestamp of the data is updated by setting it equal to the timestamp of the transaction.

The main problem of both the two-phase locking and the timestamp-ordering algorithms is that they are not free from signaling channels. The following example clarifies this problem.

EXAMPLE 4. Consider a database storing data at two different security levels and suppose that a two-phase locking algorithm is adopted for concurrency control. According to the multilevel security principles, a low transaction can only read and write low-level data, whereas a high transaction can read and write high data and, in addition, can also read (but not modify) low data. Consider the concurrent execution of two transactions T_1 and T_2 of level low and high, respectively. Suppose that T_2 wishes to read a data x, classified at level low. According to the two-phase locking protocol, it thus requires a read lock on x. Suppose that next T_1 wishes to modify data x. It thus requires a write lock on x, but, since x has been already locked by T_2, transaction T_1 is forced to wait until T_2 releases the lock. Thus, by selectively issuing requests to read low data, transaction T_2 could modulate the delay experienced by transaction T_1, and thus transmitting to transaction T_1 high-level information that the transaction is not authorized to access. Note that the same problem happens also in the case of timestamp-ordering algorithms.

To avoid signaling channels several approaches that apply to both the two-phase locking and the timestamp-ordering protocols have been proposed. In the following, we illustrate the most relevant proposals for both these protocols.

A method for avoiding the problem of signaling channel when a two-phase locking protocol is used is to abort a higher-level transaction having a lock on lower-level data, whenever a lower-level transaction requires the access to these data. Clearly, this approach avoids the problem of signaling channels; however, its main drawback is that it can cause transaction *starvation*, that is, it may cause a transaction to always be aborted and never complete its execution.

McDermott and Jajodia proposed a method for reducing transaction starvation [25]. The idea is that whenever a high transaction must release a lock because of a write request of a lower-level transaction, it does not abort. Rather, it enters a queue containing all the high-level transactions waiting for reading that data. The main drawback of this approach is, however, that it does not always produce serializable schedules.

As far as timestamp-ordering protocols are concerned, the main problem with this approach is that when a high transaction reads lower-level data, it cannot modify the read timestamp of such data since this will result in a write-down operation (that violates the Bell and LaPadula principles). Several approaches to eliminate this problem and to avoid the problem of transaction starvation have been proposed. One of the solutions is to maintain multiple versions of the same data. When multiple copies of the same data are maintained, the notion of correctness for concurrent transaction executions is restated as follows. The concurrent execution of transactions is said to be correct when its effect is equivalent to that of a serial execution of the transactions on a one-copy database (this property is called *one-copy serializability*). In the following, we briefly describe two of the most relevant proposals of timestamp-ordering protocols for secure concurrency controls [18,23]. More details on this topic can be found in [2].

The approach proposed by Keefe and Tsai [23] uses a variation of the timestamp-ordering protocol, which differs from the conventional one, in the way of assigning timestamps to transactions. To avoid the problem of signaling channels a transaction is assigned a timestamp that is smaller than the timestamps of all the other transactions with a lower security level. The Keefe and Tsai method ensures secure concurrent execution of transactions, guarantees one-copy serializability, and avoids the problem of starvation. However, it uses a multilevel scheduler which, therefore, needs to be trusted.

The approach proposed by Jajodia and Atluri [18] assigns timestamps to transactions based on their arrival order. Whenever a transaction reads data from lower levels, it must postpone its committing until all the transactions from these lower levels with smaller timestamps have committed. The protocol uses a single-level scheduler that does not need to be trusted. Moreover, it guarantees secure concurrency control as well as one-copy serializability, and it avoids the problem of starvation.

VII. CONCLUSIONS

This chapter has provided a fairly comprehensive overview of the developments in secure multilevel database systems. We have first reviewed the basic concepts of access control. Then we have discussed the basic principles of mandatory access control, and we have presented two milestones in the development of access control models for multilevel DBMSs: the model by Bell and LaPadula and the model by Denning. Furthermore, we have provided an overview of the proposals for multilevel access control both in relational and in object database systems. Next, we have provided details on secure concurrency control in multilevel database systems by illustrating the architectures that can be used and the protocols that have been proposed.

Directions in secure database systems will be driven by the developments in system architectures. Database systems are no longer stand-alone systems. They are being integrated into various applications such as multimedia, electronic commerce, mobile computing systems, digital libraries, and collaboration systems. Therefore, security issues for all these new generation systems will be very important. Furthermore, there are many developments on various object technologies such as distributed object systems and components and frameworks. Security for such systems is being investigated. Eventually, the security policies of the various subsystems and components must be integrated into policies for the entire systems. There will be many challenges in formulating policies for such systems. New technologies such as data mining will help solve security problems such as intrusion detection and auditing. However, these technologies can also violate the privacy of individuals. This is because adversaries can now use the mining tools and extract unauthorized information about various individuals. Migrating legacy databases and applications will continually be a challenge. Security issues for such operations cannot be overlooked. These new developments in data, information, and knowledge management will involve numerous opportunities and challenges for research in database security.

REFERENCES

1. Atluri V., Adam, N., Bertino E., and Ferrari, E. A content-based authorization model for digital libraries, *IEEE Trans. Knowledge Data Eng., in press.*
2. Atluri, V., Jajodia, S., and Bertino, E. Transaction processing in multilevel secure databases with kernelized architectures. *IEEE Trans. Knowledge Data Eng.* 9(5):697–708, 1997.
3. Bell, D., and LaPadula. L. Secure computer systems: Unified exposition and multics interpretation. Technical Report ESD-TR-75-306, Hanscom Air Force Base, Bedford, MA, 1975.
4. Bertino. E. Data security. *Data Knowledge Eng.* 25(1–2):199–216, 1998.
5. Bertino, E., Catania, B., and Vinai A. Transaction modeling and architectures. In *Encyclopedia of Computer Science and Technology.* Marcel Dekker, New York, 2000.
6. Bertino, E., Ferrari, E., and Samarati, P. Mandatory security and object-oriented systems: A multilevel entity model and its mapping onto a single-level object model. *Theory Practice Object Systems* 4(4):1–22, 1998.
7. Bertino, E., and Martino, L. *Object-Oriented Database Systems: Concepts and Architectures.* Addison-Wesley, Reading, MA, 1993.
8. Boulahia-Cuppens, N., Cuppens, F., Gabillon, A., and Yazdanian, K. Decomposition of multilevel objects in an object-oriented database. In *Computer Security—ESORICS 94* (D. Gollmann, Ed.), Lecture Notes on Computer Science 875, Springer-Verlag, Berlin, 1994.
9. Burns, R. Referential secrecy. In *Proc. of the IEEE Symposium on Security and Privacy*, Oakland, CA, May 1990.
10. Castano, S., Fugini, M. G., Martella, G., and Samarati, P. *Database Security.* Addison-Wesley, Reading, MA, 1995.
11. Chen F., and Sandhu, R. S. The semantics and expressive power of the MLR data model. In *Proc. of the IEEE Symposium on Security and Privacy,* Oakland, CA, May 1995.
12. Costich, O. Transaction processing using an untrusted scheduler in a multilevel database with replicated architecture. *Database Security V: Status and Prospects.* North-Holland, Amsterdam, 1992.
13. Denning. D. E. *Cryptography and Data Security.* Addison-Wesley, Reading, MA, 1982.
14. Denning, D. E., and Lunt, T. A multilevel relational data model. In *Proc. of the IEEE Symposium on Security and Privacy*, Oakland, CA, April 1987.
15. Goguen, J., and Messeguer, J., Noninterference security policy. In *Proc. of the IEEE Symposim on Security and Privacy*, Oakland, CA, April 1982.
16. Kang, I. E., and Keefe, T. F. On transaction processing for multilevel secure replicated databases. In *Proc. European Symposyum In Research in Computer Security (ESORICS 92)*, 1992.
17. Kim, W., Bertino, E., and Garza, J. F. Composite object revisited. In *Proc. ACM Sigmod International Conference on Management of Data*, Portland, OR, 1991.

18. Jajodia, S., and Atluri, V., Alternative correctness criteria for concurrent execution of transactions in multilevel secure databases. In *Proc. of the IEEE Symposium on Security and Privacy*, Oakland, CA, 1992.
19. Jajodia, S., and Kogan, B. Integrating an object-oriented data model with multilevel security. In *Proc. of the IEEE Symposium on Security and Privacy*, Oakland, CA, 1990.
20. Jajodia, S., and Kogan, B. Transaction processing in multilevel-secure databases using replicated architeture. In *Proc. of the IEEE Symposium on Security and Privacy*, Oakland, CA, 1990.
21. Jajodia, S., and Sandhu, R. S. Toward a multilevel secure relational data model. In *Proc. ACM Sigmod International Conference on Management of Data*, Denver, CO, May 1991.
22. Keefe, T., Tsai, T. W., and Thuraisingham, B. SODA—A secure object-oriented database system. *Comput. Security* 8(6):1989.
23. Keefe, T., and Tsai, T. W. Multiversion concurrency control for multilevel secure database systems. In *Proc. of the IEEE Symposium on Security and Privacy*, Oakland, CA, 1990.
24. Lamport, L. Concurrent reading and writing. *Commun. ACM* 20(11):806–811, 1977.
25. McDermott, J., and Jajodia, S. Orange locking: Channel free database concurrency control via locking. In *Database Security VI: Status and Prospects*. North-Holland, Amsterdam, 1993.
26. Millen, J., and Lunt, T. Security for knowledge-based systems. In *Proc. of the IEEE Symposium on Security and Privacy,* Oakland, CA, 1992.
27. Millen, J., and Lunt, T. Security for object-oriented database systems. In *Proc. of the IEEE Symposium on Security and Privacy,* Oakland, CA, 1992.
28. Morgenstern, M. Security and inference in multilevel database and knowledge base systems. In *Proc. of the ACM Sigmod International Conference on Management of Data*, San Francisco, CA, 1987.
29. Morgenstern, M. A security model for multilevel objects with bidirectional relationships. In *Proc. of the 4th IFIP 11.3 Working Conference in Database Security*, Halifax, England, 1990.
30. Rosenthal, A., Herndon, W., Graubart, R., Thuraisingham, B. Security for object-oriented systems. In *Proc. of the IFIP 11.3 Working Conf. on Database Security*, Hildesheim, August 1994.
31. Reed, D. P., and Kanodia, R. K. Synchronization with event counts and sequencers. *Commun. ACM* 22(5):115–123, 1979.
32. Stachour, P., and Thuraisingham, M. B. Design of LDV—A multilevel secure database management system. *IEEE Trans. Knowledge Data Eng.* 2(2):1990.
33. Summers, R. C. *Secure Computing: Threats and Safeguard*. McGraw-Hill, New York, 1997.
34. TDI, Trusted database interpretation. Department of Defense Document, 1991.
35. Thuraisingham, B. Mandatory security in object-oriented database management systems. In *Proc. of the ACM Conference on Object-oriented Programming Systems, Languages and Applications (OOPSLA)*, New Orleans, LA, 1989.
36. Thuraisingham, B., NTML. A nonmonotonic types multilevel logic for secure databases. In *Proc. of the Computer Security Foundations Workshop*, Franconia, NH, June 1991.
37. Thuraisingham, B. A tutorial in secure database systems, MITRE Technical Report, June 1992.
38. Thuraisingham, B. Multilevel security for distributed heterogeneous and federated databases. *Comput. Security* 14, 1994.
39. Winslett, M., Ching, N., Jones, V., and Slepchin, I. Using digital credentials on the World-Wide Web. *J. Comput. Security* 5, 1997.
40. Wiseman, S. On the problem of security in databases. In *Proc of the IFIP 11.3 Conference on Database Security,* Monterey, CA, September 1989.
41. Ullman, J. *Principles of Database and Knowledge-Base Systems*, Vol. 1. Computer Science Press, Rockville, MD, 1988.

6

FUZZY QUERY PROCESSING IN THE DISTRIBUTED RELATIONAL DATABASES ENVIRONMENT

SHYI-MING CHEN

Department of Computer Science and Information Engineering, National Taiwan University of Science and Technology, Taipei 106, Taiwan, Republic of China

HSIN-HORNG CHEN

Department of Computer and Information Science, National Chiao Tung University, Hsinchu, Taiwan, Republic of China

I. INTRODUCTION 203
II. FUZZY SET THEORY 205
III. FUZZY QUERY TRANSLATION BASED ON THE α-CUTS
   OPERATIONS OF FUZZY NUMBERS 207
IV. FUZZY QUERY TRANSLATION IN THE DISTRIBUTED
   RELATIONAL DATABASES ENVIRONMENT 214
V. DATA ESTIMATION IN THE DISTRIBUTED RELATIONAL
   DATABASES ENVIRONMENT 217
VI. CONCLUSIONS 231
   REFERENCES 231

This chapter presents a fuzzy query translation method based on the α-cuts operations of fuzzy numbers to translate fuzzy queries into precise queries in the distributed relational databases environment. We also present a method for estimating incomplete data when the relations stored in a failed server failed to access in the distributed relational databases environment. We have implemented a system to translate fuzzy SQL queries to precise queries in the distributed relational databases environment. The proposed methods allow the users to deal with fuzzy information retrieval in a more flexible manner in the distributed relational databases environment.

I. INTRODUCTION

Data processing is an important activity in business processing. There is a lot of information generated when business is running. A database system keeps that information for the enterprise. There are many types of database systems on the commercial market. Relational database systems are most widely used in the enterprise. Existing relational database systems only provide precise query operations. They cannot deal with imprecise queries. For example, if a user would only like to know whose salaries are high in his company, he cannot get the answer from the existing database systems because the query condition "high" for salary is unknown for the traditional relational database systems. Moreover, users cannot actually know what data they need. If they submit queries in current relational database systems, sometimes they cannot get the right answers. Thus, how to provide a user-friendly query mechanism or relaxed query condition to let the user get the required answer is more and more important.

Sometimes a company is distributed logically into divisions. Thus, a distributed system enables the structure of the database to mirror the structure of the company, where local data can be kept locally and the remote data can be accessed when necessary by means of computer networks. It may happen that one of the distributed databases stored in a failed server fails to access when queries are submitted from the end users. In this case, we need a mechanism for deriving the incomplete information which is nearly equal to the failed data before the failed server has recovered to the normal state.

Since Zadeh proposed the theory of fuzzy sets in 1965 [33], some researchers have investigated the application of fuzzy set theory for query translations for relational databases systems. In [9], Chen *et al.* present techniques of fuzzy query translation for relational database systems. In [31], Yeh and Chen present a method for fuzzy query processing using automatic clustering techniques. In [4], Chang and Ke present a database skeleton and introduce its application to fuzzy query translation. In [5], Chang and Ke present a method for translation of fuzzy queries for relational database systems. In [1], Bosc *et al.* propose an extension of DBMS querying capabilities in order to allow fuzzy queries against a usual database. In [14], Hou and Chen apply the fuzzy set theory to the structural query language of relational database systems. In [23], Nakajima and Senoh investigate the operations of fuzzy data in fuzzy SQL language. In [35], Zemankova proposes a fuzzy intelligent information system. In [16], Kacprzyk *et al.* developed a "human-consistent" database querying system based on fuzzy logic with linguistic quantifiers.

In this chapter, we propose a method based on the α-cuts operations for translating fuzzy queries into precise queries in a distributed relational databases environment. We also propose a method for estimating incomplete data when one of the relations failed to access in the distributed relational databases environment. Based on the proposed methods, we also implement a system for translating fuzzy SQL queries into precise queries in the distributed relational databases environment. The proposed methods allow the users to access the distributed relational databases in a more flexible manner.

This paper is organized as follows. In Section II, we briefly review some basic concepts of fuzzy set theory from [33]. In Section III, we briefly review the fuzzy query translation method for relational database systems from [8]. In Section IV, we introduce a method for fuzzy query translation in the distributed relational databases environment based on [8]. In Section V, we propose a method for dealing with fuzzy query translation in which some relations in the distributed databases environment failed to access. Based on the proposed method, we also implement a system for estimating the values of the attributes in the relations that failed to access in the distributed relational databases environment. The conclusions are discussed in Section VI.

II. FUZZY SET THEORY

In traditional crisp sets, an element in a set is definitely included or excluded in the set. According to this feature, some applications are limited to dealing with vague and imprecise information about the real world. Since Zadeh proposed the fuzzy set theory [33], it has been widely used to express uncertain and imprecise knowledge. The fuzzy set theory has been successfully applied in many kinds of fields, such as automatic control, decision making, pattern recognition, psychology, economics, and medical diagnosis. In the following, we briefly review some basic concepts of fuzzy set theory.

DEFINITION 1. Let U be the universe of discourse. A fuzzy set A of the universe of discourse U can be defined as

$$A = \{(u_i, \mu_A(u_i)) \mid u_i \in U\}, \tag{1}$$

where μ_A, $\mu_A: U \to [0, 1]$, is the membership function of the fuzzy set A, and $\mu_A(u_i)$ is the membership grade in which the element u_i belongs to the fuzzy set A.

If the universe of discourse U is a finite set, $U = \{u_1, u_2, \ldots, u_n\}$, then the fuzzy set A can be expressed as

$$A = \sum_{i=1}^{n} \mu_A(u_i)/u_i$$
$$= \mu_A(u_1)/u_1 + \mu_A(u_2)/u_2 + \cdots + \mu_A(u_n)/u_n, \tag{2}$$

where "+" means "union" and the symbol "/" means the separator.

If the universe of discourse U is an infinite set, then the fuzzy set A can be expressed as

$$A = \int_U \mu_A(u)/u, \quad u \in U. \tag{3}$$

There are three basic operations between fuzzy sets, i.e., intersection, union, and complement. Let A and B be two fuzzy sets of the universe of discourse U, $U = \{u_1, u_2, \ldots, u_n\}$, and let μ_A and μ_B be the membership functions of the fuzzy sets A and B, respectively, where

$$\mu_A : U \to [0, 1],$$
$$\mu_B : U \to [0, 1],$$
$$A = \{(u_i, \mu_A(u_i)) \mid u_i \in U\},$$
$$B = \{(u_i, \mu_B(u_i)) \mid u_i \in U\}.$$

The three basic operations of the fuzzy sets are reviewed from [33] as follows.

DEFINITION 2. Let $A \cap B$ be the intersection of the fuzzy set A and B defined as

$$\mu_{A \cap B}(u_i) = \min(\mu_A(u_i), \mu_B(u_i)), \quad \forall u_i \in U. \tag{4}$$

DEFINITION 3. Let $A \cup B$ be the union of the fuzzy set A and B defined as

$$\mu_{A \cup B}(u_i) = \max(\mu_A(u_i), \mu_B(u_i)), \quad \forall u_i \in U. \tag{5}$$

DEFINITION 4. Let $\overline{A}$ be the complement of the fuzzy set A defined as

$$\mu_{\overline{A}}(\mu_i) = 1 - \mu_A(u_i), \quad \forall u_i \in U. \tag{6}$$

One of the most important applications of fuzzy sets is the computational linguistics. In [34], Zadeh proposed the concept of a linguistic variable and its application to approximate reasoning. A linguistic variable is a variable whose values are linguistic terms. For example, in natural language, we use "old" or "young" to describe someone's age. Thus, we can say that "age" is a linguistic variable. In this case, the words, "old" and "young" are called fuzzy terms. The meaning of a fuzzy term is subjectively defined, and it depends on the problem domain. We can use a fuzzy membership function to represent a fuzzy term. A linguistic hedge can perform a modification on a fuzzy term. It modifies the meaning of a fuzzy set. For example, "very" and "slightly" are the linguistic hedges. After we add "very" before the fuzzy term "young," it becomes a composite fuzzy term "very young." If a fuzzy term contains an "AND" or "OR" connector, then it is called a compound fuzzy term.

There are some commonly used operations on fuzzy sets. Assume that A is a fuzzy set of the universe of discourse U and μ_A is the membership function of the fuzzy set A, then

(1) Concentration CON(A):

$$\mu_{\text{CON}(A)}(x) = (\mu_A(x))^2, \quad \forall x \in U. \tag{7}$$

Figure 1 illustrates the concentration operation. This operator can be used to approximate the effect of the linguistic modifier "very." That is, for any fuzzy set A,

$$\text{very } A = A^2.$$

(2) Dilation: DIL(A)

$$\mu_{\text{DIL}(A)}(x) = (\mu_A(x))^{0.5}, \forall x \in U. \tag{8}$$

Figure 2 illustrates the dilation operation. It is obvious that

$$A = \text{DIL}(\text{CON}(A)) = \text{CON}(\text{DIL}(A)). \tag{9}$$

The dilation operator can be used to approximate the effect of the linguistic modifier *More or Less*. Thus, for any fuzzy set A,

$$\text{More or Less } A = A^{0.5} = \text{DIL}(A). \tag{10}$$

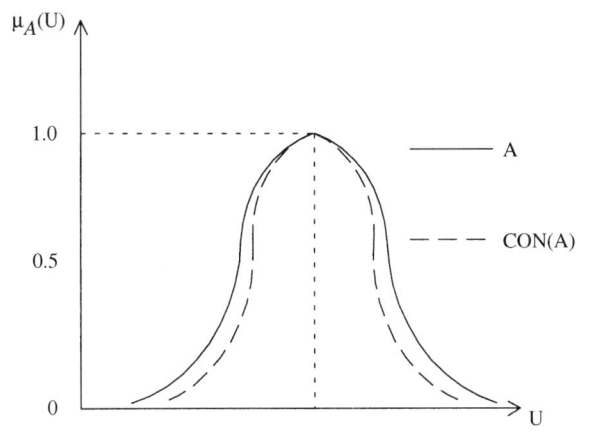

FIGURE 1 Concentration of a fuzzy set.

III. FUZZY QUERY TRANSLATION BASED ON THE α-CUTS OPERATIONS OF FUZZY NUMBERS

In this section, we briefly review a method for translating fuzzy queries into standard SQL queries from [8]. Based on [8], we will present a method for processing fuzzy queries in the distributed relational databases environment.

A fuzzy number [18] is a fuzzy set defined on the universe of discourse U that is both convex and normal. We can say that a fuzzy set A is convex if and only if for all u_1, u_2 in U,

$$\mu_A(\lambda u_1 + (1 - \lambda)u_2) \geq \text{Min}(\mu_A(u_1), \mu_A(u_2)), \tag{11}$$

where $\lambda \in [0, 1]$. A fuzzy set A of the universe of discourse U is called a normal fuzzy set if there exists $u_i \in U$ such that $\mu_A(u_i) = 1$. A fuzzy number M of the universe of discourse U may also be parametrized by a quadruple (a, b, c, d) as shown in Fig. 3.

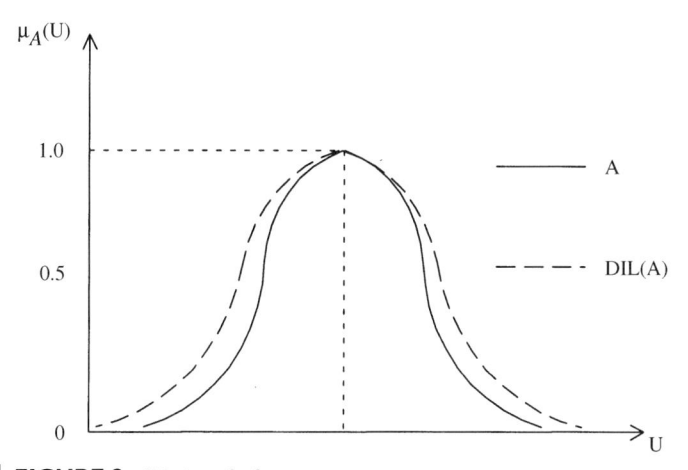

FIGURE 2 Dilation of a fuzzy set.

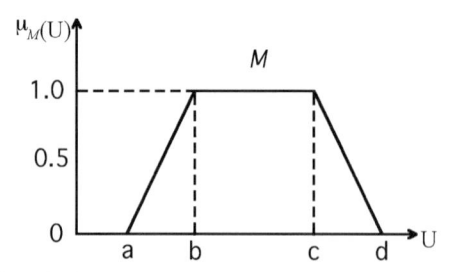

FIGURE 3 A trapezoidal fuzzy number.

We also can express the trapezoidal fuzzy number shown in Fig. 3 by the membership function shown as

$$\mu_M(x : a, b, c, d) = \begin{cases} \dfrac{x-a}{b-a}, & a \leq x \leq b, \\ 1, & b \leq x \leq c, \\ \dfrac{x-d}{c-d}, & c \leq x \leq d. \end{cases} \quad (12)$$

We can regard each part of this function as a linear function. Thus, if we perform the α-cuts operation on this trapezoidal membership function as shown in Fig. 4, we can obtain the α-cut range $[u_{1\alpha}, u_{2\alpha}]$ by the formulas

$$\begin{aligned} u_{1\alpha} &= \alpha(b-a) + a, \\ u_{2\alpha} &= \alpha(c-d) + d, \end{aligned} \quad (13)$$

where $\alpha \in [0, 1]$.

In this section, we briefly review a method from [8] for translating a fuzzy query into a standard query based on α-cuts operations of trapezoidal fuzzy numbers. First, we define the syntax of Fuzzy Structural Query Language (Fuzzy SQL) used in this section. It is shown as

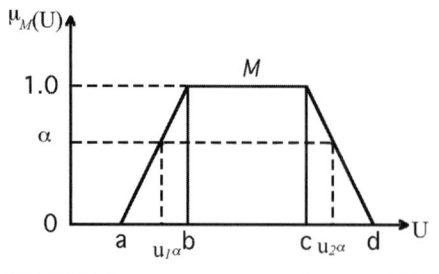

$$\begin{array}{ll} \text{SELECT} & \langle \text{attributes} \rangle \\ \text{FROM} & \langle \text{relations} \rangle \\ \text{WHERE} & \langle \text{query conditions} \rangle \\ \text{WITH} & \text{RSV} = \langle \text{retrieval threshold value} \rangle, \end{array} \quad (14)$$

FIGURE 4 α-cuts operations of a trapezoidal fuzzy number.

FUZZY QUERY PROCESSING

where

⟨attributes⟩: List the attributes to be projected.
⟨relations⟩: Identify the tables where attributes will be projected and possibly will be joined.
⟨query condition⟩: Include the conditions for tuple/row selection within a single table or between tables implicitly joined. It may contain either standard query conditions or fuzzy query conditions.
⟨retrieval threshold value⟩: A retrieval threshold value between 0 and 1.0.

Assume that a user submits a query shown as

$$\begin{array}{ll} \text{SELECT} & A \\ \text{FROM} & T \\ \text{WHERE} & A = C \\ \text{WITH} & \text{RSV} = \alpha, \end{array}$$

where C is either a simple fuzzy term, a composite fuzzy term, or a compound fuzzy term, and α is a retrieval threshold value, where $\alpha \in [0, 1]$. We consider the following cases [8]:

Case 1. If C is a simple fuzzy term represented by a fuzzy number in the universe of discourse U, then

Step 1: Find the meaning $M(C)$ of the fuzzy term C as

$$M(C) = \{(u_i, \mu_C(u_i)) \mid u_i \in U\}. \tag{15}$$

Step 2: Perform the α-cuts operation $M(C)_\alpha$ on $M(C)$ as

$$M(C)_\alpha = \{u_i \mid \mu_C(u_i) \geq \alpha, u_i \in U, \text{and } \alpha \in [0, 1]\}. \tag{16}$$

Step 3: If $M(C)_\alpha = [u_a, u_b]$, then the original query can be translated into the statements

$$\begin{array}{ll} \text{SELECT} & A \\ \text{FROM} & T \\ \text{WHERE} & A \geq u_a \text{ AND } A \leq u_b \\ \text{WITH} & \text{RSV} = \alpha. \end{array} \tag{17}$$

If $M(C)_\alpha = \phi$, then print "No tuples selected."

Case 2. If C is a composite fuzzy term (i.e., $C = m_1 m_2 \ldots m_k C_j$), where $m_1, m_2 \ldots, m_k$ are some hedges and C_j is a simple fuzzy term, then:

Step 1: Find the meaning $M(C_j)$ of the fuzzy term C_j as

$$M(C_j) = \{(u_i, \mu_{C_j}(u_i)) \mid u_i \in U\}. \tag{18}$$

Step 2: Apply the semantic rules to find the meaning $M(C)$ of the composite fuzzy term C as

$$M(C) = \{(u_i, \mu_C(u_i)) \mid u_i \in U\}. \tag{19}$$

Step 3: Perform the α-cuts operation $M(C)_\alpha$ on $M(C)$ as

$$M(C)_\alpha = \{u_i \mid \mu_C(u_i) \geq \alpha, u_i \in U, \alpha \in [0, 1]\}. \tag{20}$$

Step 4: If $M(C)_\alpha = [u_a, u_b]$, then the original query can be translated into the statements

$$\begin{array}{ll} \text{SELECT} & A \\ \text{FROM} & T \\ \text{WHERE} & A \geq u_a \text{ AND } A \leq u_b \\ \text{WITH} & \text{RSV} = \alpha. \end{array} \quad (21)$$

If $M(C)_\alpha = \phi$, then print "No tuples selected."

Case 3. If C is a compound fuzzy term composited by fuzzy terms $C_1, C_2, \ldots, C_n$ connected by AND operators (i.e., $C = C_1$ AND C_2 AND $\ldots$ AND C_n), then

Step 1: Find the meaning $M(C_j)$ of the fuzzy term C_j as

$$M(C_j) = \{(u_i, \mu_{C_j}(u_i)) \mid u_i \in U\}, \text{where } 1 \leq j \leq n. \quad (22)$$

Step 2: Perform the intersection operation on $M(C_1), M(C_2), \ldots, M(C_n)$ to obtain the result $M(C)$, where

$$M(C) = M(C_1) \cap M(C_2) \cap \ldots \cap M(C_n) \quad (23)$$
$$= \{(u_i, \mu_C(u_i)) \mid \mu_C(u_i) = \text{Min}(\mu_{C_1}(u_i),$$
$$\mu_{C_2}(u_i), \ldots, \mu_{C_n}(u_i)), u_i \in U\}.$$

The symbol "$\cap$" is the intersection operator between fuzzy numbers.

Step 3: Perform the α-cuts operation $M(C)_\alpha$ on $M(C)$ as

$$M(C)_\alpha = \{u_i \mid \mu_C(u_i) \geq \alpha, u_i \in U, \alpha \in [0, 1]\}. \quad (24)$$

Step 4: If $M(C)_\alpha = [u_a, u_b]$, then the original query can be translated into the statements

$$\begin{array}{ll} \text{SELECT} & A \\ \text{FROM} & T \\ \text{WHERE} & A \geq u_a \text{ AND } A \leq u_b \\ \text{WITH} & \text{RSV} = \alpha. \end{array} \quad (25)$$

If $M(C)_\alpha = \phi$, then print "No tuples selected."

Case 4. If C is a compound fuzzy term composited by fuzzy terms $C_1, C_2, \ldots, C_n$ connected by OR operators (i.e., $C = C_1$ OR C_2 OR $\ldots$ OR C_n), then

Step 1: Find the meaning $M(C_j)$ of the fuzzy term C_j as

$$M(C_j) = \{(u_i, \mu_{C_j}(u_i)) \mid u_i \in U\}, 1 \leq j \leq n. \quad (26)$$

Step 2: Perform the union operation on $M(C_1), M(C_2), \ldots, M(C_n)$ to obtain the result $M(C)$, where

$$M(C) = M(C_1) \cup M(C_2) \cup \ldots \cup M(C_n) \quad (27)$$
$$= \{(u_i, \mu_C(u_i)) \mid \mu_C(u_i) = \text{Max}(\mu_{C_1}(u_i),$$
$$\mu_{C_2}(u_i), \ldots, \mu_{C_n}(u_i)), u_i \in U\}.$$

FUZZY QUERY PROCESSING

The symbol "∪" is the union operator over fuzzy numbers.

Step 3: Perform the α-cuts operation $M(C)_\alpha$ on $M(C)$ as

$$M(C)_\alpha = \{u_i \mid \mu_C(u_i) \geq \alpha, u_i \in U, \alpha \in [0, 1]\}. \tag{28}$$

Step 4: If $M(C)_\alpha = [u_a, u_b]$, then the original query can be translated into the statements

$$\begin{aligned}&\text{SELECT} &&A\\&\text{FROM} &&T\\&\text{WHERE} &&A \geq u_a \text{ AND } A \leq u_b\\&\text{WITH} &&\text{RSV} = \alpha.\end{aligned} \tag{29}$$

If $M(C)_\alpha = \phi$, then print "No tuples selected."

Step 5: If $M(C)_\alpha = [u_a, u_b] \cup [u_c, u_d]$, then the original query can be translated into the statements

$$\begin{aligned}&\text{SELECT} &&A\\&\text{FROM} &&T\\&\text{WHERE} &&A \geq u_a \text{ AND } A \leq u_b \text{ OR } A \geq u_c \text{ AND } A \leq u_d\\&\text{WITH} &&\text{RSV} = \alpha.\end{aligned} \tag{30}$$

If $M(C)_\alpha = \phi$, then print "No tuples selected."

In the following we use two examples to illustrate the fuzzy query translation process of a relational database system. Assume that the fuzzy terms for the linguistic variable "SALARY" are "high," "medium," and "low," and each of them are expressed by trapezoidal membership functions as shown in Fig. 5. We can subjectively define the membership functions of the fuzzy terms as

$$\text{high} = (50000, 60000, 70000, 70000),$$
$$\text{medium} = (25000, 35000, 45000, 55000),$$
$$\text{low} = (0, 0, 23000, 30000).$$

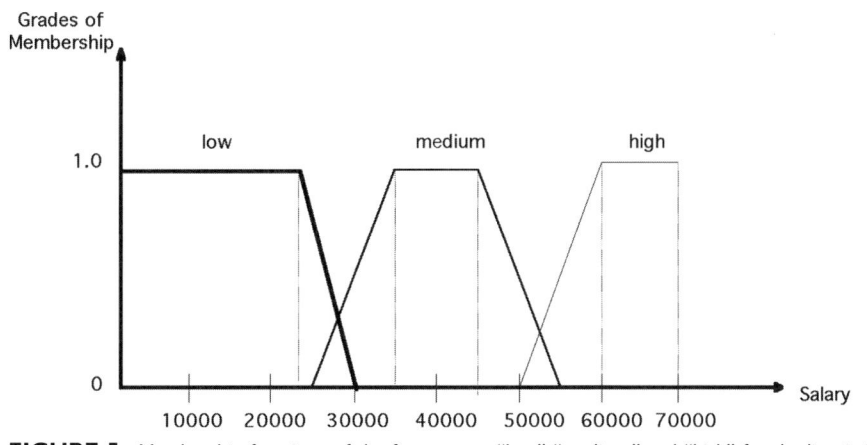

FIGURE 5 Membership functions of the fuzzy terms "low," "medium," and "high" for the linguistic variable "SALARY."

EXAMPLE 1. Assume that the user issues the fuzzy SQL query

SELECT ID, SALARY
FROM   EMPLOYEE
WHERE SALARY = medium OR high
WITH   RSV = 0.95.

In the condition part of the above fuzzy SQL query, we can see that it is a compound fuzzy query, where "medium" and "high" are the fuzzy terms of the linguistic variable "SALARY." The meanings of "medium" and "high" for the attribute SALARY are

$$M(\text{high}) = (50000, 60000, 70000, 70000),$$
$$M(\text{medium}) = (25000, 35000, 45000, 55000),$$

and the retrieval threshold value 0.95 is defined in the "WITH" clause. Thus, we can perform the union operation on $M(\text{high})$ and $M(\text{medium})$ to get $M(C)$ as shown in Fig. 6.

After performing the 0.95-cut operation on $M(C)$, we can get two intervals. We can calculate each interval by formula (13), respectively, shown as

$$u_{M(\text{medium})\_1\_0.95} = 0.95 * (35000 - 25000) + 25000 = 34500,$$
$$u_{M(\text{medium})\_2\_0.95} = 0.95 * (45000 - 55000) + 55000 = 45500,$$
$$u_{M(\text{high})\_1\_0.95} = 0.95 * (60000 - 50000) + 50000 = 59500,$$
$$u_{M(\text{high})\_2\_0.95} = 0.95 * (70000 - 70000) + 70000 = 70000.$$

Then, we can translate the user's original fuzzy query into the statements

SELECT   ID, SALARY
FROM   EMPLOYEE

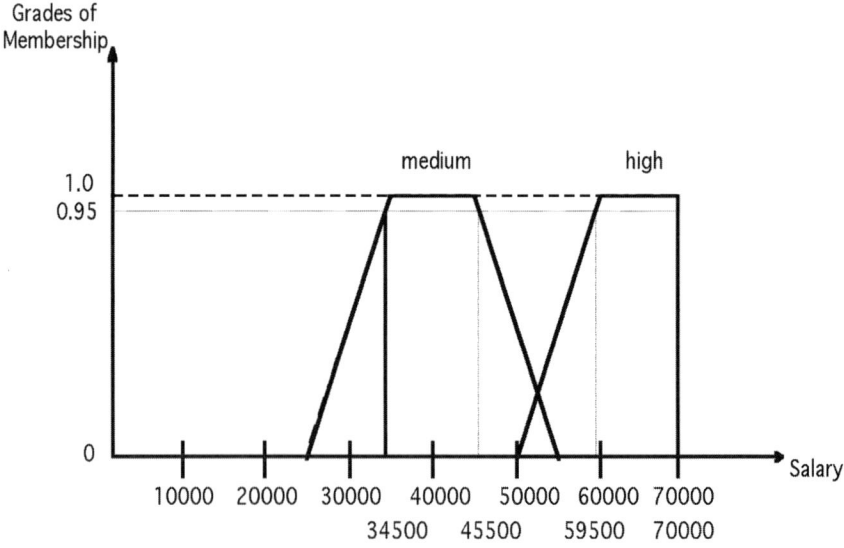

FIGURE 6 0.95-cut operations for Example 1.

FUZZY QUERY PROCESSING 213

```
WHERE   SALARY ≥ 34500 AND SALARY ≤ 455000 OR
        SALARY ≥ 59500 AND SALARY ≤ 70000.
WITH    RSV = 0.95.
```

EXAMPLE 2. Assume that the user issues the fuzzy SQL query:

```
SELECT  ID, NAME, SALARY
FROM    EMPLOYEE
WHERE   SALARY = very high
WITH    RSV = 0.95.
```

In the condition part of the above fuzzy SQL query, we can see that it is a composited fuzzy query; "high" is a fuzzy term of the linguistic variable "SALARY," and "very" is a linguistic hedge to modify the fuzzy term "high". The meaning of "high" is shown as

$$M(high) = (50000, 60000, 70000, 70000).$$

After we perform the linguistic hedge "very" on the fuzzy term "high", we can obtain the meaning M(very high) of the fuzzy term "very high" as shown in Fig. 7.

After performing 0.95-cut on M(very high), we can obtain an interval [59746, 70000] shown in Fig. 7. Then we can translate the user's original fuzzy query into the statement

```
SELECT  ID, NAME, SALARY
FROM    EMPLOYEE
WHERE   SALARY ≥ 59746 AND SALARY ≤ 70000.
WITH    RSV = 0.95.
```

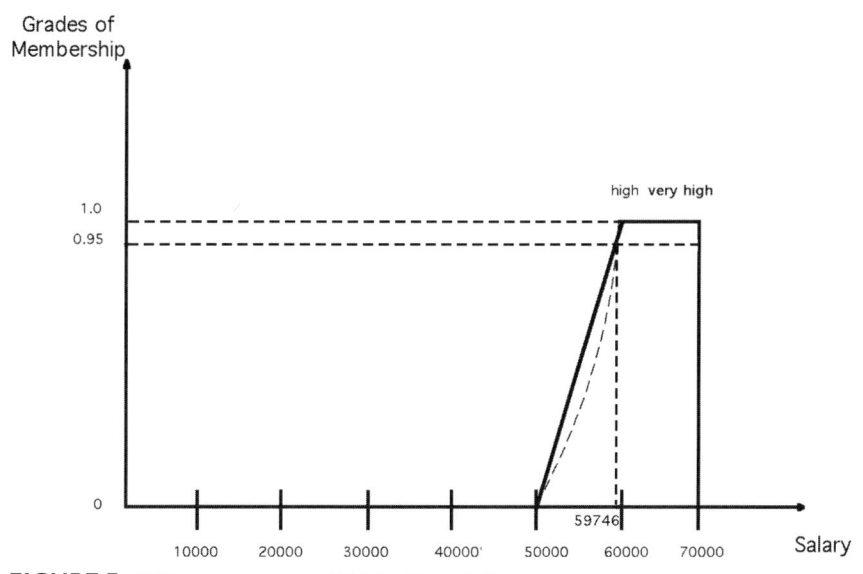

FIGURE 7 0.95-cut operation on $M(C)$ for Example 2.

IV. FUZZY QUERY TRANSLATION IN THE DISTRIBUTED RELATIONAL DATABASES ENVIRONMENT

In this section, we briefly introduce the developing tools that we use to implement the distributed relational databases query environment, Borland Delphi [22] and ODBC, and then we will present the architecture and our distributed relational databases query environment.

Delphi is a new-generation developing tool in the Windows environment. It represents a new way of developing applications for Windows. It combines the speed and ease of use of a visual development environment with the power, flexibility, and reusability of a fully object-oriented Pascal language. Briefly speaking, application developers can develop very beautiful, highly complicated, and more user-friendly applications within a very short time.

All Windows API (Application Programming Interface) are encapsulated as components in Delphi. Components are the building blocks of Delphi applications. Although most components represent visible parts of the user interface, components can also represent nonvisual elements in a program, such as timers and databases. Application developers design their applications just via the assembly of the components and within very few codes. A RAD (Rapid Application Development) developing environment is one of the powerful features of Delphi. This feature shortens all aspects of the application development cycle, and it also provides an enhanced interface and many automated features that make it easier for the application developers to develop application software.

Another feature of Delphi is that it can let application developers build sophisticated client/server applications in a short time. This is a relatively new area of DBMS programming, where large companies need to downsize those huge databases installed on mainframe computers.

The Open Database Connectivity (ODBC) interface allows applications to access data in database management systems (DBMS) using Structured Query Language (SQL) as a standard for accessing data.

The ODBC architecture has four components:

1. *Application:* It performs processing and calls ODBC functions to submit SQL statements and retrieve results.
2. *Driver manager:* It loads drivers according to the behavior of an application.
3. *Driver:* It processes ODBC function calls, submits SQL requests to a specific data source, and returns results to the application. If necessary, the driver modifies an application's request such that the request conforms to the syntax supported by the associated DBMS.
4. *Data source:* It consists of the data which the user wants to access and of its associated operating system, DBMS, and network platform (if any) used to access the DBMS.

The hierarchy of the ODBC architecture is shown in Fig. 8.

There are four parts of components in our architecture as shown in Fig. 9. We describe these components as follows.

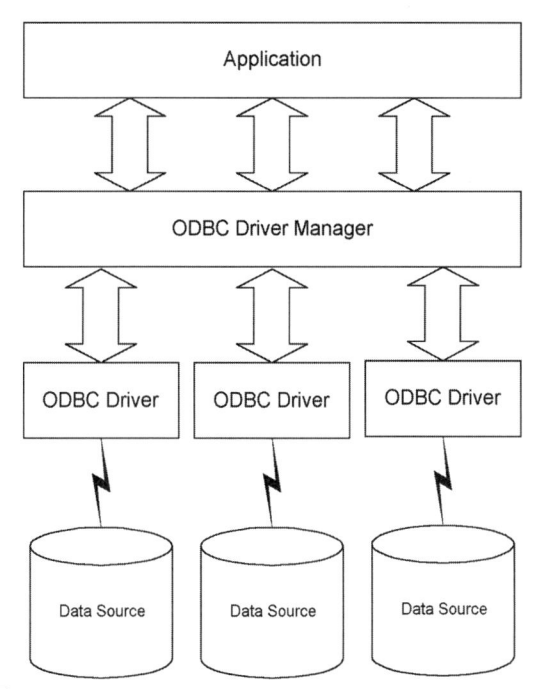

FIGURE 8 The hierarchy of the ODBC architecture.

1. *Fuzzy SQL statements:* This component contains the SQL statements that are issued by the users. The statements can be either standard SQL statements or fuzzy SQL statements.

2. *Fuzzy SQL translator:* This component parses the query statements issued from the component Fuzzy SQL statements and performs the following operations:

(1) When the query statement is not the legal SQL statement or fuzzy SQL statement that we define in Section III, this component will reject this query statement.

(2) If the query statement is a fuzzy SQL statement, this component will translate it into a standard SQL statement. According to the fuzzy term corresponding to the attribute in the condition part and the retrieve threshold value written in the query statement, the translator will perform the α-cut operation on the fuzzy term and translate the condition part into the precise SQL statement, and then pass this translated query statement to the next component. The technique used in this operation has been described in Section III.

(3) If the query statement is a standard SQL statement, this component just passes the whole SQL statement to the next component without any modification.

The membership function library is used in this component. It keeps the membership functions which are used when doing the α-cuts operations.

3. *SQL-type database management environment:* This component takes charge of access data from data sources. Database operations are actually

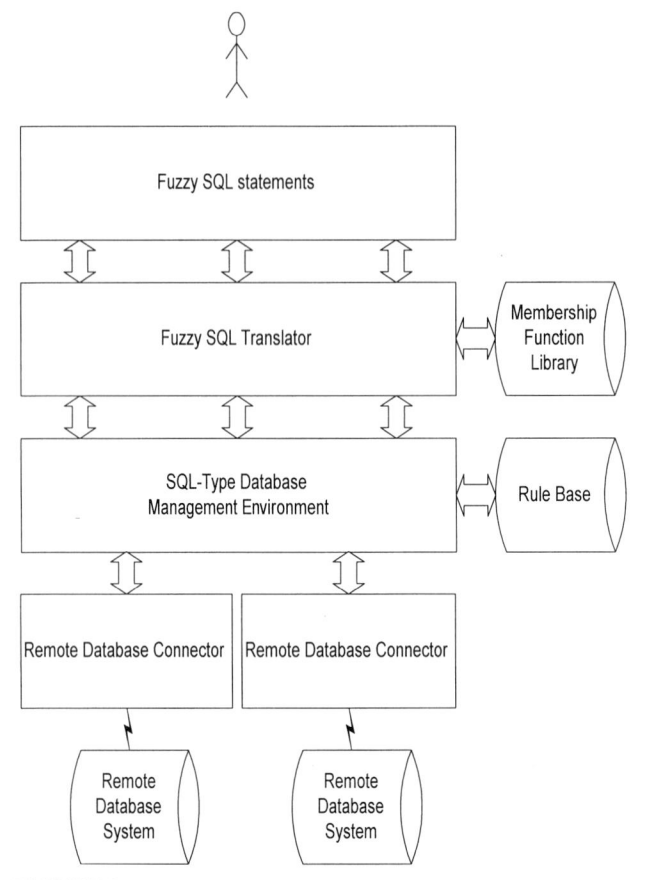

FIGURE 9 Fuzzy query translation in the distributed relational databases environment.

performed by this component. When the fuzzy SQL translator passes the precise SQL statement to this component, it will take some necessary operations to deal with this query statement. For example, if there are some databases residing in remote sites, this component maintains the communication links between the remote databases and the local program to ensure the successful access to the databases.

4. *Remote database connectors:* These components serve as the communication devices between the local program and the remote database servers. These remote database connectors are database dependent; i.e., each type of database has its specific driver. Through these drivers, the program will not necessarily decide what kind of database system it will deal with. Therefore, the methods for accessing databases are totally transparent to the program.

The architecture of this system is based on the client/server database operating environment. This system resides at the user's local site as a client. The databases can be located either in the local site or in the remote site. These two database servers act as the server sites. In our implementation, we distribute the environment to a system and two databases as shown in Fig. 10.

FUZZY QUERY PROCESSING 217

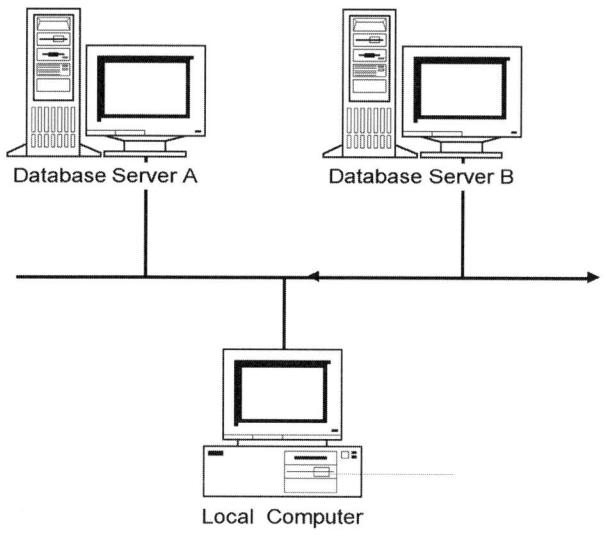

FIGURE 10   The environment of the implementation.

V. DATA ESTIMATION IN THE DISTRIBUTED RELATIONAL DATABASES ENVIRONMENT

A distributed relational database environment is a new trend for business data processing. Sometimes a business distributes its data to each related department. Each department manages its own data. This is for the convenience of speed and management. However, there are some cases where database servers fail when end users are querying databases. In this situation, we must provide a method for estimating the data stored in the failed server to approach the original values.

In the following, we use a fuzzy similarity matrix to represent a fuzzy relation. Suppose that we define a linguistic variable V that contains linguistic terms $v_1, v_2, \ldots, v_n$. Then we can make a fuzzy relation matrix for the linguistic variable V as shown in Fig. 11, where u_{ij} is the closeness degree between v_i and v_j, $u_{ij} \in [0, 1]$, $1 \leq i \leq n$, and $1 \leq j \leq n$.

We can say that the closeness degree $CD(v_i, v_j)$ between the fuzzy term v_i and the fuzzy term v_j is u_{ij}, denoted as

$$CD_v(v_i, v_j) = R_v[v_i][v_j] = u_{ij}, \tag{31}$$

where each value of u_{ij} in the fuzzy relation matrix V is defined by an experienced database administrator.

	v_1	v_2	...	v_n
v_1	1	u_{12}	...	u_{1n}
v_2	u_{21}	1	...	u_{2n}
⋮	⋮	⋮	⋮	⋮
v_n	u_{n1}	u_{n2}	...	1

FIGURE 11   A fuzzy relation matrix for the linguistic variable V.

	Ph.D.	Master	Bachelor
Ph.D.	1.0	0.7	0.4
Master	0.7	1.0	0.6
Bachelor	0.4	0.6	1.0

FIGURE 12 A fuzzy relation for the linguistic variable "DEGREE".

For example, in Fig. 12, "DEGREE" is a linguistic variable. Suppose this linguistic variable contains fuzzy terms {Ph.D., Master, Bachelor}. We can construct the fuzzy relation matrix shown in Fig. 12 for the linguistic variable "DEGREE."

We can construct the fuzzy relation matrix illustrated in Fig. 12 by using the fuzzy relation table shown in Fig. 13.

From Fig. 13, we can see the closeness degree between the fuzzy terms "Master" and "Ph.D." is CD_{degree} (Master, Ph.D.) = 0.7.

We also define a fuzzy term ranking function to keep the ranks of each fuzzy term in the same linguistic domain. Suppose the linguistic term V contains fuzzy term $\{v_1, v_2\}$, and fuzzy term v_1 is prior to fuzzy term v_2; then it can be defined as

$$\text{Rank}(v_1) > \text{Rank}(v_2).$$

A rule base is used for keeping relationships in which one attribute determines other attributes. Each rule in the rule base is given by the experts according to their experiences of the data. For example, if the attributes $A_1, A_2, \ldots,$ and A_n determine the attribute AA, then we can construct a set of fuzzy rules as shown in Fig. 14, where we can see that a_{ij} denotes the attribute value, w_{ij} is the weight for each attribute in the antecedent part of the rule, and each w_{ij} is assigned by an experienced expert, where $w_{ij} \in [0, 1], 1 \leq i \leq M$, and $1 \leq j \leq n$. For example, in a relation EMPLOYEE, we can define that the attribute "DEGREE" and the attribute "EXPERIENCE" determine the attribute "SALARY," and we can assign each weight value to the attributes "DEGREE" and "EXPERIENCE", then we can have the rules for the attribute "SALARY" as shown in Fig. 15.

The rule base shown in Fig. 15 stores important information about estimating null values. We will use it to estimate failed attribute values of a relation in the distributed relational databases environment.

X	Y	CD(X,Y)
Ph.D.	Ph.D.	1.0
Master	Ph.D.	0.7
Bachelor	Ph.D.	0.4
Ph.D.	Master	0.7
Master	Master	1.0
Bachelor	Master	0.6
Ph.D.	Bachelor	0.4
Master	Bachelor	0.6
Bachelor	Bachelor	1.0

FIGURE 13 A fuzzy relation table.

Rule 1: IF $A_1 = a_{11}$ (W=w_{11}) AND $A_2 = a_{12}$ (W = w_{12}) AND ...   AND $A_n = a_{1n}$ (W = w_{1n}) THEN AA = t_1

Rule 2: IF $A_1 = a_{21}$ (W=w_{21}) AND $A_2 = a_{22}$ (W = w_{22}) AND ...   AND $A_n = a_{2n}$ (W = w_{2n}) THEN AA = t_2

$\vdots$

Rule m: IF $A_1 = a_{m1}$ (W=w_{m1}) AND $A_2 = a_{m2}$ (W = w_{m2}) AND...   AND $A_n = a_{mn}$ (W = w_{mn}) THEN AA = t_m

FIGURE 14 Rules for determining the attribute AA.

Sometimes we may partition a relation into two or more related relations by the method of the relation normalization [3]. Moreover, we may distribute them to different locations in the business, just for convenient management of the database. These relations are obtained by vertically partitioning the original relation. It might happen that one of the relations fails when a query is submitted. In such a case, we propose a method for estimating the failed attribute value of a relation in the distributed relational database environment.

Consider the relation EMPLOYEE shown in Fig. 16. We can vertically partition this relation into two relations EMP_INFO and EMP_SALARY as shown in Fig. 17 and Fig. 18. Then we can join these two relations (i.e., EMP_INFO and EMP_SALARY) into the original relation EMPLOYEE with the SQL statements

    SELECT   ID, DEGREE, EXPERIENCE, SALARY
    FROM   EMP_INFO, EMP_SALARY
    WHERE   EMP_INFO.ID = EMP_SALARY.ID.
    WITH   RSV = 0.90.

Suppose these two relations are distributed into two different locations. Then we can create a view called EMP by the SQL statements

    CREATE   VIEW EMP AS
    SELECT   ID, DEGREE, EXPERIENCE, SALARY
    FROM   EMP_INFO, EMP_SALARY
    WHERE   EMP_INFO.ID = EMP_SALARY.ID.
    WITH   RSV = 0.90.

We know that the results of the relation EMPLOYEE and the view EMP will be identical. Now, suppose the relation EMP_SALARY failed to access when the query is submitted as

    SELECT   *
    FROM   EMP
    WHERE   ID = "S1".
    WITH   RSV = 0.90.

IF DEGREE = Master (W = 0.6) AND EXPERIENCE = 3.6 (W = 0.4)	THEN SALARY = 41000
IF DEGREE = Ph.D. (W = 0.6) AND EXPERIENCE = 7.8 (W = 0.4)	THEN SALARY = 65000
IF DEGREE = Bachelor (W = 0.65) AND EXPERIENCE = 5 (W = 0.35)	THEN SALARY = 36000

FIGURE 15 Rules for determining the attribute "SALARY".

where attribute A_k may be either a numerical or a nonnumerical domain, where $1 \leq k \leq n$. We consider these two cases:

1. A_k is in a numerical domain. If A_k is in a numerical domain, we can directly compute its closeness degree by the formula

$$CDv_{ji}(r_j.A_k, T_i.A_k) = \frac{T_i.A_k}{r_j.A_k}. \tag{32}$$

2. A_k is in a nonnumerical domain. If A_k is in a nonnumerical domain and the linguistic term rank Rank $(T_i.A_k) >$ Rank $(r_j.A_k)$, then we can look up the closeness degree $CDv_{ji}(r_j.A_k, T_i.A_k)$ from the fuzzy relation matrix shown in Fig. 12, where

$$CDv_{ji}(r_j.A_k, T_i.A_k) = \frac{1}{R_{\text{domain}}[r_j.A_k][T_i.A_k]}. \tag{33}$$

If A_k is in a nonnumerical domain and the linguistic term priority Rank$(T_i.A_k) \leq$ Rank(r_j, A_k), then we can look up the closeness degree $CDv_{ji}(r_j.A_k, T_i.A_k)$ from the fuzzy relation matrix shown in Fig. 12, where

$$CDv_{ji}(r_j.A_k, T_i.A_k) = R_{\text{domain}}[r_j.A_k][T_i.A_k]. \tag{34}$$

The total closeness degree between tuple T_i and Rule r_j is

$$CD(r_j, T_i) = \sum_{k=1}^{n} CDv_{ji}(r_j.A_k, T_i.A_k)^* w_{jk}. \tag{35}$$

After we compute all closeness degrees between tuple T_i and all rules r_j, we choose the closest rule to T_i. Suppose the following rule is the closest one to tuple T_i:

IF $A_1 = A_{j1}(W = w_{j1})$ AND $A_2 = A_{j2}(W = w_{j2})$

AND ... AND $A_n = A_{jn}(W = W_{jn})$ THEN $B_2 = N_j$.

Then we can estimate the attribute value of B_2 in tuple T_i by the calculation

$$T_i.B_2 = CD(r_j, T_i)^* N_j. \tag{36}$$

Repeat each tuple T_i until all failed attributes have been estimated.

Case 2. If the failed attribute B_2 is in a nonnumerical domain, we can also compute the closeness degree between tuple T_i and the chosen rule according to the rules that determine attribute B_2. If rule r_j is the closest to T_i, then we pick that rule as the base rule, where Rule r_j is shown as

IF $A_1 = A_{j1}(W = w_{j1})$ AND $A_2 = A_{j2}(W = w_{j2})$ AND ... AND

$A_n = A_{jn}(W = w_{jn})$

THEN $B_2 = W_j$

where attribute A_k may be either a numerical or a nonnumerical domain, where $1 \leq k \leq n$. We consider these two cases:

1. A_k is in a numerical domain. If A_k is in a numerical domain, we can directly compute its closeness degree by the formula

$$\text{CD}v_{ji}(r_j.A_k, T_i.A_k) = \frac{T_j.A_k}{r_j.A_k}. \tag{37}$$

2. A_k is in nonnumerical domain. If A_k is in a nonnumerical domain and the linguistic term rank Rank $(T_i.A_k) > $ Rank $(r_j.A_k)$, then we can look up the closeness degree $\text{CD}v_{ji}(r_j.A_k, T_i.A_k)$ from the fuzzy relation matrix shown in Fig. 12, where

$$\text{CD}v_{ji}(r_j.A_k, T_i.A_k) = \frac{1}{R_{\text{domain}}[r_j.A_k][T_i.A_k]}. \tag{38}$$

If A_k is in a nonnumerical domain and the linguistic term priority Rank$(T_i.A_k)$ < Rank$(r_j.A_k)$, then we can look up the closeness degree from the fuzzy relation matrix

$$\text{CD}_{ji}(r_j.A_k, T_i.A_k) = R_{\text{domain}}[r_j.A_k][T_i.A_k]. \tag{39}$$

The total closeness degree between tuple T_i and Rule r_j is

$$\text{CD}(r_j, T_i) = \sum_{k=1}^{n} CD_{ji}(r_j.A_i, T_k.A_k)^* w_{jk}. \tag{40}$$

After we compute the all closeness degrees between tuple T_i and all rules, we choose the closest rule to T_i. Suppose the following rule is the closest one to tuple T_i:

IF $A_1 = A_{j1}(W = w_{j1})$ AND $A_2 = A_{j2}(W = w_{j2})$ AND ... AND

$A_n = A_{jn}(W = w_{jn})$ THEN $B_2 = W_j$.

Then the estimated attribute value of B_2 is W_j, where

$$T_i.B_2 = W_j \tag{41}$$

Repeat each tuple T_i until all failed attributes have been estimated.

EXAMPLE 3. Consider the relation EMPLOYEE shown in Fig. 16. We can vertically partition this relation into two relations EMP_INFO and EMP_SALARY as shown in Fig. 17 and Fig. 18.

Then we can join these two relations into the original relation EMPLOYEE with the SQL statements

```
SELECT   ID, DEGREE, EXPERIENCE, SALARY
FROM     EMP_INFO, EMP_SALARY
WHERE    EMP_INFO.ID = EMP_SALARY.ID
WITH     RSV = 0.90.
```

Suppose these two relations are distributed in two different locations. Then we create a view called EMP by the SQL statements

```
CREATE   VIEW EMP AS
SELECT   ID, DEGREE, EXPERIENCE, SALARY
```

ID	DEGREE	EXPERIENCE	SALARY
s1	Ph.D.	7.2	?????

FIGURE 19 A failed join result.

```
FROM    EMP_INFO, EMP_SALARY
WHERE   EMP_INFO.ID = EMP_SALARY.ID.
WITH    RSV = 0.90.
```

We can see that the results of the relation EMPLOYEE and the view EMP are identical. Now suppose the relation EMP_SALARY failed to access when a query is submitted shown as

```
SELECT  *
FROM    EMP
WHERE   ID = "S1".
WITH    RSV = 0.90.
```

In this case, the query cannot be processed correctly. Thus, we must estimate the attributes in the failed relation. According to the problem described above, when the database system that stores the relation EMP_SALARY failed, the query submitted by the user cannot be executed. In this case, the join result may be like the failed result shown in Fig. 19.

Now, we will estimate all the data in the relation EMP_SALARY. We scan every tuple in the relation EMP_INFO. First, we pick the first tuple in the relation EMP_INFO. From the rules for the attribute "SALARY," we know that the attribute "DEGREE" and the attribute "EXPERIENCE" determine the attribute "SALARY." Thus, we calculate the closeness degree between the first tuple of the relation EMP_SALARY to each rule for the attribute "SALARY." For example, we choose the first rule (i.e., Rule 1) in the rule base shown in Fig. 15 as

IF DEGREE = "Master" ($W = 0.6$) AND EXPERIENCE = 3.6 ($W = 0.4$)

THEN SALARY = 41000.

In the condition part of this rule, we can see that "DEGREE = "Master"" is a nonnumerical domain. We cannot directly calculate the closeness degree between "Master" and "Ph.D." We can see that Rank(Ph.D.) > Rank(Master). Therefore, we compute their closeness degree using formula (33):

$$\mathrm{CD}_{\mathrm{degree}}(\mathrm{Master}, \mathrm{Ph.D.}) = \frac{1}{R_{\mathrm{degree}}[\mathrm{Master}][\mathrm{Ph.D.}]}$$

$$= \frac{1}{0.7}$$

$$= 1.428571428571.$$

For the attribute "EXPERIENCE," we can see that it is a numerical domain attribute. According to formula (32), we can directly calculate their closeness degree:

$$CD_{experience}(3.6, 7.2) = \frac{7.2}{3.6} = 2.$$

From Rule 1 shown in Fig. 15, we can see that that the weights for the attributes "DEGREE" and "EXPERIENCE" are 0.6 and 0.4, respectively. Then we calculate the total closeness degree between the first tuple of the relation EMP_INFO and Rule 1 using formula (35):

$$CD(Rule1, EMP.T_1) = 1.428571428571 * 0.6 + 2 * 0.4 = 1.6571428.$$

Again, we calculate the closeness degree between the first tuple of the relation EMP_INFO and the rest rules in the rule base for the attribute "SALARY." We use the same method described above to calculate each CD value:

$$CD(Rule2, EMP.T_1) = 1 * 0.6 + 0.9230769230769 * 0.4 = 0.969230769,$$

$$CD(Rule3, EMP.T_1) = 2.5 * 0.65 + 1.44 * 0.35 = 2.129.$$

In this case, we choose the closest rule to estimate the value of the attribute "SALARY," say, Rule 2. By formula (36), we can estimate the first tuple of the relation of the failed attribute "SALARY" as

$$EMP.T_1.SALARY = 0.969230769 * 65000 = 63000.$$

After scanning the rest of the tuples in the relation to estimate the values for the failed attribute "SALARY," we can get the estimated relation shown in Fig. 20.

Compared to the original relation, the estimated values and the estimation errors are shown in Fig. 21.

From Fig. 21, we can see that the average estimated error between the original value and the estimated value is 0.061.

EXAMPLE 4. Consider the relation EMPLOYEE shown in Fig. 16. We can vertically partition this relation into two relations EMP_INFO and EMP_SALARY as shown in Fig. 17 and Fig. 18. Then we can join these two relations into the original relation EMPLOYEE with the SQL statements

```
SELECT   ID, DEGREE, EXPERIENCE, SALARY
FROM     EMP_INFO, EMP_SALARY
WHERE    EMP_INFO.ID = EMP_SALARY.ID.
WITH     RSV = 0.90.
```

Suppose these two relations are distributed in two different locations. Then we create a view called EMP by the SQL statements

```
CREATE   VIEW EMP AS
SELECT   ID, DEGREE, EXPERIENCE, SALARY
FROM     EMP_INFO, EMP_SALARY
WHERE    EMP_INFO.ID = EMP_SALARY.ID.
```

Estimated Relation for EMP_INFO

ID	DEGREE	EXPERIENCE	SALARY (ESTIMATED)
s1	Ph.D.	7.2	63000
s2	Master	2.0	33711
s3	Bachelor	7.0	46648
s4	Ph.D.	1.2	36216
s5	Master	7.5	56200
s6	Bachelor	1.5	27179
s7	Bachelor	2.3	29195
s8	Ph.D.	2.0	39861
s9	Ph.D.	3.8	48061
s11	Master	3.5	40544
s10	Bachelor	3.5	32219
s12	Master	3.6	41000
s13	Master	10.0	64533
s14	Ph.D.	5.0	55666
s15	Bachelor	5.0	35999
s16	Master	6.2	51866
s17	Bachelor	0.5	24659
s18	Master	7.2	55200
s19	Master	6.5	52866
s20	Ph.D.	7.8	65000
s21	Master	8.1	58200
s22	Ph.D.	8.5	67333

FIGURE 20 An estimated relation for the relation EMP_INFO.

ID	DEGREE	EXPERIENCE	SALARY (ORIGINAL)	SALARY (ESTIMATED)	ESTIMATED ERROR
s1	Ph.D.	7.2	63000	63000	+0.00
s2	Master	2.0	37000	33711	-0.09
s3	Bachelor	7.0	40000	46648	+0.17
s4	Ph.D.	1.2	47000	36216	-0.23
s5	Master	7.5	53000	56200	+0.06
s6	Bachelor	1.5	26000	27179	+0.05
s7	Bachelor	2.3	29000	29195	+0.01
s8	Ph.D.	2.0	50000	39861	-0.20
s9	Ph.D.	3.8	54000	48061	-0.11
s10	Bachelor	3.5	35000	32219	-0.08
s11	Master	3.5	40000	40544	+0.01
s12	Master	3.6	41000	41000	+0.00
s13	Master	10.0	68000	64533	-0.05
s14	Ph.D.	5.0	57000	55666	-0.02
s15	Bachelor	5.0	36000	35999	-0.00
s16	Master	6.2	50000	51866	+0.04
s17	Bachelor	0.5	23000	24659	+0.07
s18	Master	7.2	55000	55200	+0.00
s19	Master	6.5	51000	52866	+0.04
s20	Ph.D.	7.8	65000	65000	+0.00
s21	Master	8.1	64000	58200	-0.09
s22	Ph.D.	8.5	70000	67333	-0.04

FIGURE 21 An estimated relation compared to the original relation.

FUZZY QUERY PROCESSING

We can see that the results of the relation EMPLOYEE and the view EMP are identical. Now suppose the relation EMP_SALARY failed to access when a query is submitted as

SELECT　*
FROM　EMP
WHERE　ID = "S1".
WITH　RSV = 0.90.

In this case, the query cannot be processed correctly. Thus, we must estimate the attributes in the failed relation. When the database system that stores the relation EMP_INFO failed, the query submitted previously cannot be processed. In this case, the join result may be like the failed result shown in Fig. 22.

We can see that the attribute "DEGREE" failed in the relation EMP. Therefore, we must estimate the values in the attribute "DEGREE" in the relation EMP. We scan every tuple in the relation EMP, and pick the first tuple in the relation EMP. From the rules for the attribute "DEGREE," we know that the attribute "EXPERIENCE" and the attribute "SALARY" determine the attribute "DEGREE". Thus, we calculate the closeness degree between the first tuple of the relation EMP and each rule. Suppose we define the rules for estimating the attribute "DEGREE" as shown in Fig. 23.

We choose the first rule in the rule base shown in Fig. 23 as

IF EXPERIENCE = 5.0 ($W = 0.2$) AND SALARY = 57000 ($W = 0.8$)

THEN DEGREE = Ph.D.

Relation EMP

ID	DEGREE	EXPERIENCE	SALARY
s1	???	7.2	63000
s2	???	2.0	37000
s3	???	7.0	40000
s4	???	1.2	47000
s5	???	7.5	53000
s6	???	1.5	26000
s7	???	2.3	29000
s8	???	2.0	50000
s9	???	3.8	54000
s10	???	3.5	35000
s11	???	3.5	40000
s12	???	3.6	41000
s13	???	10.0	68000
s14	???	5.0	57000
s15	???	5.0	36000
s16	???	6.2	50000
s17	???	0.5	23000
s18	???	7.2	55000
s19	???	6.5	51000
s20	???	7.8	65000
s21	???	8.1	64000
s22	???	8.5	70000

FIGURE 22 A failed join result in the relation EMP.

IF EXPERIENCE = 5.0 (W = 0.2) AND SALARY = 57000 (W =0.8) THEN DEGREE = Ph.D.
IF EXPERIENCE = 3.5 (W = 0.2) AND SALARY = 40000 (W =0.8) THEN DEGREE = MASTER
IF EXPERIENCE = 2.3 (W = 0.2) AND SALARY = 29000 (W =0.8) THEN DEGREE = Bachelor

FIGURE 23 Rules for determining the attribute "DEGREE."

For the attribute "EXPERIENCE," we can see that it is a numerical domain attribute. According to formula (37), we can directly calculate its closeness degree:

$$CD_{experience}(5.0, 7.2) = \frac{7.2}{5.0} = 1.44.$$

For the attribute "SALARY," we can see that it is also a numerical-domain attribute. According to formula (37), we can directly calculate its closeness degree:

$$CD_{salary}(57000, 63000) = \frac{63000}{57000} = 1.105263158.$$

From Rule 1 of the rule base shown in Fig. 23, we can see that the weights for the attributes "EXPERIENCE" and "SALARY" are 0.2 and 0.8, respectively. Then we calculate the total closeness degree between the first tuple of the relation EMP and Rule 1 using formula (40):

$$CD(Rule1, EMP.T_1) = 1.44 * 0.2 + 1.105263158 * 0.8 = 1.088.$$

Again, we can calculate the closeness degree between the first tuple of the relation EMP and the rest rules in the rule base for the attribute "DEGREE." We can use the same method described above to calculate each CD value:

$$CD(Rule2, EMP.T_1) = 2.05714 * 0.2 + 1.575 * 0.8 = 1.2114,$$

$$CD(Rule3, EMP.T_1) = 3.13043 * 0.2 + 2.172 * 0.8 = 2.2261.$$

In this case, we choose the closest rule to estimate the value of the attribute "DEGREE," i.e., Rule 1. By formula (41), we can estimate the failed attribute "DEGREE" as

$$EMP.T_1.DEGREE = Rule1.Degree = Ph.D.$$

After scanning the rest of the tuples in the relation to estimate the values for the failed attributes "DEGREE," we can get the estimated relation shown in Fig. 24.

The estimated values and the estimated errors are compared to the original relation in Fig. 25.

The architecture of the implemented system based on the proposed methods is shown in Fig. 26. There are five parts of components in the implemented system, i.e., fuzzy SQL statements, fuzzy SQL translator, SQL-type database management environment, remote database connectors, and failed data generator.

The components of fuzzy query statements, fuzzy SQL translator, SQL-type database management environment, and remote database connector have already been described in Section IV, while the failed data generator is based

FUZZY QUERY PROCESSING

Relation EMP

ID	DEGREE (ESTIMATED)	EXPERIENCE	SALARY
s1	Ph.D.	7.2	63000
s2	Bachelor	2.0	37000
s3	Master	7.0	40000
s4	Bachelor	1.2	47000
s5	Master	7.5	53000
s6	Bachelor	1.5	26000
s7	Bachelor	2.3	29000
s8	Bachelor	2.0	50000
s9	Master	3.8	54000
s10	Bachelor	3.5	35000
s11	Master	3.5	40000
s12	Master	3.6	41000
s13	Ph.D.	10.0	68000
s14	Ph.D.	5.0	57000
s15	Bachelor	5.0	36000
s16	Master	6.2	50000
s17	Bachelor	0.5	23000
s18	Master	7.2	55000
s19	Master	6.5	51000
s20	Ph.D.	7.8	65000
s21	Ph.D.	8.1	64000
s22	Ph.D.	8.5	70000

FIGURE 24 An estimated relation for the relation EMP.

on the method presented in this section. Again, we briefly describe these components as follows:

1. *Fuzzy SQL statements:* It contains the SQL statements that are issued by the users.

2. *Fuzzy SQL translator*: It parses the query statements issued from the component fuzzy SQL statement and performs the syntax checking and the

ID	DEGREE (ORIGINAL)	EXPERIENCE	SALARY	DEGREE (ESTIMATED)
s1	Ph.D.	7.2	63000	Ph.D.
s2	Master	2.0	37000	Bachelor
s3	Bachelor	7.0	40000	Master
s4	Ph.D.	1.2	47000	Bachelor
s5	Master	7.5	53000	Master
s6	Bachelor	1.5	26000	Bachelor
s7	Bachelor	2.3	29000	Bachelor
s8	Ph.D.	2.0	50000	Bachelor
s9	Ph.D.	3.8	54000	Master
s10	Bachelor	3.5	35000	Bachelor
s11	Master	3.5	40000	Master
s12	Master	3.6	41000	Master
s13	Master	10.0	68000	Ph.D.
s14	Ph.D.	5.0	57000	Ph.D.
s15	Bachelor	5.0	36000	Bachelor
s16	Master	6.2	50000	Master
s17	Bachelor	0.5	23000	Bachelor
s18	Master	7.2	55000	Master
s19	Master	6.5	51000	Master
s20	Ph.D.	7.8	65000	Ph.D.
s21	Master	8.1	64000	Ph.D.
s22	Ph.D.	8.5	70000	Ph.D.

FIGURE 25 An estimated relation compared to the original relation.

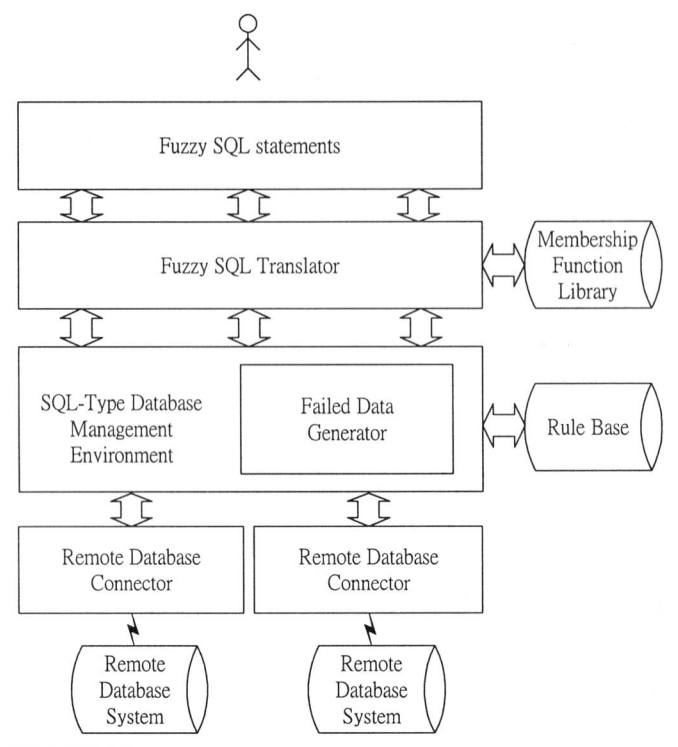

FIGURE 26 Fuzzy query translation in the distributed relational databases environment including the failed data generator.

fuzzy query statement translation. The membership function library is used in this component. It also keeps the membership functions that are used when doing the α-cut operations.

3. *SQL-type database management environment:* It offers data access from the data sources. Database operations are actually performed by this component.

4. *Failed data generator:* If one of the remote databases failed when users submit query statements, the failed data generator component will be activated to perform the failed data generation based on the proposed method described previously. These data are all estimated to the original data as close as possible. When the estimated data are generated, the other part of the fuzzy query translation process in the SQL-type database management environment component will be continued until the whole process of the fuzzy query translation is performed completely. The rule base is used in the failed data generator component. It provides any necessary information for estimating the failed data.

5. *Remote database connectors:* These components communicate between the local program and remote database servers. ODBC and BDE serve as this function. These components make database access transparent to the program.

VI. CONCLUSIONS

We have presented a method for dealing with fuzzy query translation based on the α-cuts operations of trapezoidal fuzzy numbers for the distributed relational databases environment. It allows the users to access the information in the distributed relational databases environment in a more flexible manner. It also allows the users to submit fuzzy SQL queries and to translate the fuzzy SQL queries into standard SQL queries. We also present a method for estimating incomplete data when one of the relations failed to access in the distributed relational databases environment. Based on the proposed methods, we have implemented a system on a Pentium PC by using the Borland Delphi version 3.0 developing environment to translate fuzzy SQL queries into precise SQL queries. It is transparent to the user who submits fuzzy queries to the relational database system, and it also provides a method for null values estimation when the queried relations failed to access in the distributed relational databases environment. The proposed methods allow the users to deal with fuzzy information retrieval in a more flexible manner in the distributed relational databases environment.

REFERENCES

1. Bosc, P., Galibourg, M., and Hamon, G. Fuzzy querying with SQL: Extensions and implementation aspects. *Fuzzy Sets Systems* 28(3): 333–349, 1988.
2. Bosc, P., and Pivert, O. SQLf: A relational database language for fuzzy querying. *IEEE Trans. Fuzzy Systems* 3(1): 1–17, 1995.
3. Codd, E. F. Normalized data base structure: a brief tutorial. In *Proceedings of 1971 ACM SIGFIDET Workshop on DATA Description, Access, and Control*, San Diego, CA, November 1971.
4. Chang, S. K., and Ke, J. S. Database skeleton and its application to fuzzy query translation. *IEEE Trans. Software Engrg.* 4(1): 31–43, 1978.
5. Chang, S. K., and Ke, J. S. Translation of fuzzy queries for relational database systems *IEEE Trans. Pattern Anal. Mach. Intell.* 1(3): 281–294, 1979.
6. Chen, H. H., and Chen, S. M. Fuzzy query translation for information retrieval in the distributed relational database environment. In *Proceedings of the 6th National Conference on Science and Technology of National Defense*, Taoyuan, Taiwan, Republic of China, vol. 2, pp. 433–439, 1997.
7. Chen, S. M. Using fuzzy reasoning techniques for fault diagnosis of the J-85 jet engines. In *Proceedings of the Third National Conference on Science and Technology of National Defense*, Taoyuan, Taiwan, Republic of China, vol. 1, pp. 29–34, 1994.
8. Chen, S. M., and Jong, W. T. Fuzzy query translation for relational database systems. *IEEE Trans. Systems Man Cybern et. Part B* 27(4): 714–721, 1997.
9. Chen, S. M., Ke, J. S., and Chang, J. F. Techniques of fuzzy query translation for database systems. In *Proceedings of 1986 International Computer Symposium*, Tainan, Taiwan, Republic of China, vol. 3, pp. 1281–1290, 1986.
10. Date, C. J. *An Introduction to Database Systems*, 6th ed. Addison-Wesley, Reading, MA, 1995.
11. Grant, J. Null values in a relational data base. *Inform. Process. Lett.* 6(5): 156–157, 1977.
12. Huemer, C., Happel, G., and Vieweg, S. Migration in object-oriented database systems - a practical approach. *Software—Practice Exper.* 25:1065–1096, 1995.
13. Jeng, B., and Liang, T. Fuzzy indexing and retrieval in case-based systems. In *Proceedings of 1993 Pan Pasific Conference on Information Systems*, Taiwan, Republic of China, pp. 258–266, 1993.

14. Hou, Y. C., and Chen, C. M., Apply the fuzzy set theory to the structural query language of database. In *Proceedings of International Joint Conference of CFSA/IFIS/SOFT'95 on Fuzzy Theory and Applications*, Taipei, Taiwan, Republic of China, pp. 107–113, 1995.
15. Hou Y. C., and Wu, W. T. Fuzzy query processing in fuzzy database. In *Proceedings of International Joint Conference of CFSA/IFIS/SOFT'95 on Fuzzy Theory and Applications*, Taipei, Taiwan, Republic of China, pp. 114–120, 1995.
16. Kacprzyk, J., Zadrozny, S, and Ziokkowski, A. FQUERY III +: A "human-consistent" database querying system based on fuzzy logic with linguistic quantifiers. In *Proceedings of the Second International Fuzzy Systems Association Congress*, Tokyo, Japan, pp. 443–453, 1987.
17. Kacprzyk, J., and Zadrozny, S. Fuzzy query in Microsoft Access V.2. In *Proceedings of the FUZZ-IEEE/IFES'95 Workshop on Fuzzy Database Systems and Information Retrieval*, Yokohama, Japan, pp. 61–66, March 1995.
18. Kaufman, A., and Gupta, M. M. *Introduction to Fuzzy Arithmetic*. Van Nostrand Reinhold, New York, 1985.
19. Kaufmann, A., and Gupta, M. M. *Fuzzy Mathematical Models in Engineering and Management Science*. North-Holland, Amsterdam, 1988.
20. Kim, W. Object-oriented database systems: promises, reality and future. In *Proceedings of the 19th International Conference on Very Large Data Bases*, pp. 676–687, 1994.
21. Motro, A. VAGUE: A user interface to relational database that permits vague queries. *ACM Trans. Office Inform. Systems* 187–214, 1988.
22. Mueller, J. *Peter Norton's Guide To Delphi 2*, premier ed. Sams, Indianapolis, IN, 1996.
23. Nakajima, H., and Senoh, Y. Development of fuzzy add-in macros with spread sheet. In *Proceedings of the FUZZ-IEEE/IFES'95 Workshop on Fuzzy Database Systems and Information Retrieval*, Yokohama, Japan, pp. 61–66, 1995.
24. Nakajima, H., Sogoh, T., and Arao, M. Operations on fuzzy data in fuzzy SQL language. In *Proceedings of 1993 Pan Pacific Conference on Information Systems*, Taiwan, Republic of China, pp.1–6, 1993.
25. Prade, H. Lipski's approach to incomplete information databases restated and generalized in the setting of Zadeh's possible theory. *Inform. Systems* 9(1): 27–42, 1984.
26. Prade, H., and Testemale, C. Generalizing database relational algebra for the treatment of incomplete or uncertain information and vague queries. *Inform. Sci.* 115–143, 1984.
27. Umano, M., Hatono, I., and Tamura, H. Fuzzy database systems. In *Proceedings of the FUZZ-IEEE/IFES'95 Workshop on Fuzzy Database Systems and Information Retrieval*, Yokohama, Japan, pp. 35–36, 1995.
28. Vassiliadis, S. A fuzzy reasons database question answering system. *IEEE Trans. Knowledge Data Engrg.* 6(6): 868–882, 1994.
29. Vila, M. A., Cubero, J. C., Medina, J. M., and Pons, O. "A logic approach to fuzzy relational databases. *Int. J. Intell. Systems* 9(5): 449–460, 1994.
30. Vila, M. A., Medina, J. M., Pons, O., and Cubero, J. C. Toward the computer implementation of fuzzy relational and deductive database system. In *Proceedings of the FUZZ-IEEE/IFES'95 Workshop on Fuzzy Database Systems and Information Retrieval*, Yokohama, Japan, pp. 67–73, March 1995.
31. Yeh. M. S., and Chen, S. M. A new method for fuzzy query processing using automatic clustering techniques, *J. Computers* 6(1): 1–10, 1994.
32. Yen, S. J. Neighborhood/conceptual query answering with imprecise/incomplete data. Master Thesis, Institute of Computer Science, National Tsing Hua University, Hsinchu, Taiwan, R. O. C., June 1993.
33. Zadeh, L. A. Fuzzy sets. *Inform. Control* 8: 338–353, 1965.
34. Zadeh, L. A. The concept of a linguistic variable and its application to approximate reasoning *Inform. Sci.* 8(3): 199–249, 1975 (part I); 8, no. (4): 301–357, 1975 (part II); 9(1): 43–80, 1975 (part III).
35. Zemankova, M. FIIS: A fuzzy intelligent information system. *Data Engrg.* 11(2): 11–20, 1989.
36. Zemankova, M., and Kandel, A. Implementing imprecision in information systems. *Inform. Sci.* 37:107–141, 1985.
37. Zimmermann, H. J. *Fuzzy Set Theory and Its Applications*, 2nd ed. Kluwer Academic, Boston, 1991.

7 DATA COMPRESSION: THEORY AND TECHNIQUES

GÁBOR GALAMBOS
JÓZSEF BÉKÉSI

Department of Informatics, Teacher's Training College, University of Szeged, Szeged H-6701, Hungary

I. INTRODUCTION 233
II. FUNDAMENTALS OF DATA COMPRESSION 235
   A. Information Theoretical Background 236
   B. Models 239
III. STATISTICAL CODING 243
   A. Shannon–Fano Coding 244
   B. Huffman Coding 245
   C. Redundancy of Huffman Codes 248
   D. Arithmetic Coding 250
   E. Adaptive Techniques 254
IV. DICTIONARY CODING 255
   A. Methods Using a Static Dictionary 256
   B. Adaptive Methods 265
V. UNIVERSAL CODING 269
VI. SPECIAL METHODS 271
   A. Run Length Encoding 271
   B. Algorithms Based on List Update 272
   C. Special Codes and Data Types 273
VII. CONCLUSIONS 273
   REFERENCES 273

I. INTRODUCTION

Despite continuing improvements in storage and transmission technology the rapidly growing amount of information stored on and transmitting between computers has increased the need for text compression. A huge amount of information can be stored on a single CD but sometimes this is not enough to avoid multivolume applications. It is known that a simple ad hoc method can compress an English text to around 70% of its original size, and the best techniques have a compression ratio about 25%. In case of Braille the used compression processes can reduce the size of books by 20%. For computers, compression can increase the amount of information stored on a disk. If archive—and compressed—data are stored on magnetic tapes not only fewer tapes are needed, but fewer shelves are used to store them and less time is taken to read them. The compression of transmitted data has another benefits: the cost of transmission is reduced and the effective speed of transmission also increases.

Data compression has a side effect for secret services: using compression some encryption is achieved because the lack of redundancy in a compressed file removes the opportunity to use statistical regularities to break a code. Some schemes generally change their coding after each character is transmitted, so the codebreaker's task is compounded.

Since the pioneer work of Shannon [60] it has been known that most of the data are represented by more bits than the minimal needed considering its information contents. In other works we can say that the description has a redundancy. In a data compression process the aim is to decrease the redundancy of a given data description. The standard processes that use this information in a computer system require standard forms e.g., ASCII and BMP. Despite the fact that computer storage capacity and the speed of a transmission line are growing extraordinary rapidly, it seems to be evident that these two fields of computer science are the most common applications of data compression processes. In both cases first we compress the data, so either we use smaller space to store the data in a secondary storage equipment or we need to transmit a decreased amount of bytes through a transmission channel. Thereafter, for further processing we decompress them again for getting the earlier standard form.

Information can appear in different forms like text, image, or voice. From a data compression point of view there is a fundamental difference among them: In case of a textual information performing a compression/decompression process we must recover exactly the original data, while in the case of pictures or voices—without getting into deep trouble—it is allowed to get an approximation of the original information. In this chapter we deal with the textual data compressions; i.e., we consider only the so-called lossless techniques.

Intuitively, it is not difficult to see that if we know the relative frequencies of each character—i.e., we know the distribution of the characters—in a given text, then using a compression process the shorter the codes we can order of the more frequently appearing characters, the better the result is. In other words we can say: if we can give a good prediction for the next character then we can reach a better compression. This prediction can be made in a model where we estimate the probability distribution for the next character. The more the model resembles the source of the text, the better the messages can be compressed. The task of finding a suitable model for text is an extremely important problem in compression, and a lot of work has been done in this direction. A good overview of the different models can be found in [10]. Separating the compression process into two parts—predicting by a model and encoding the text into binary digits by an encoder—is one of the major advances in the theory of data compression over the past years. In practice we encode a given text by a model and after transmitting the compressed text through a communication channel we decode the text. It is very important that in this later process we must use the same model. If we use a fixed model for different texts then the transmission may become inefficient because the model is not appropriate for the text. Such a problem can occur if we use a Morse code handling numeric data only. There are different ways to maintain a model in a compression process:

- In a *static modeling* the encoder and decoder use a fixed model, regardless of the text to be encoded.
- In a *semiadaptive scheme* before sending the text the encoder checks it and prepares a "codebook." Then he transmits the codebook, followed by the coded text. The decoder first gets this codebook and then uses it to decode the text. This technique has two disadvantages: firstly, the encoder must see the entire text before transmitting it, and secondly, we must send the codebook for each text, which could take a substantial amount of time. So, two passes are required for encoding.
- If we use an *adaptive model* then the encoder sends a text character by character. By agreement, when a part of the text (we can refer to it as "word") has been transmitted—and also received—twice, then both the decoder and encoder add it to the codebook. In the future that word can be transmitted using the new code. So, if we use adaptive coding, then the code of a particular character (or word) is based on the text already transmitted.

There is another possibility to distinguish different techniques. Certain classical statistical methods use static models, and they transmit texts character by character. Unfortunately, sometimes we do not know the whole text in advance, so we need one of the other techniques to perform a compression. On the other hand, there are such methods that use the so-called set of dictionary coding techniques. They use a—static or adaptive—dictionary in which they correspond different parts of the source text to other—coded—sequences. In the following firstly we overview the information theoretical backgrounds and the basic definitions of the data compression. Section III deals with the different statistical coding methods. Some dictionary coding techniques are considered in Section IV. In Section V we discuss some universal coding methods, and further special techniques are mentioned in Section VI.

II. FUNDAMENTALS OF DATA COMPRESSION

DEFINITION 1. Compression refers to a process that produces a shorter $\Delta(D)$ information from a given source information D.

DEFINITION 2. Lossless compression is a procedure in which D can be exactly restored from $\Delta(D)$. We call lossy compression such a method in which the original information can be decoded only approximately.

In case of lossless compression the later decompressed data must be identical to the original source code. In this paper we deal only with lossless compression methods, so we always assume that our aim is the exact reconstruction. Usually this kind of method can be used in the cases of database, text, and other data files. The efficiency of the compression method is significantly affected by the characteristic of the source information and the applied technique.

From an information theoretical point of view, if we talk about compression the most important factor is the information content of the data we would like to compress. Usually the real amount of storage occupied by the information does not reflect this. Many times data contain some redundancy and require more storage than their real information content would contain. The main aim of the compression is to remove this redundancy from the information. Before the detailed description of compression methods we would like to mention a simple theorem and also present a very short proof. This theorem is very important and determines many investigations into the theory and techniques of compression methods.

THEOREM 2.1 [48]. *There is no such lossless compression method that compresses each data.*

Proof. Suppose we have such an algorithm, and for a given string S_i we denote the compressed string by $\Delta_A(S_i)$. We also suppose that the length of S_i is n bits. We know that the total number of different binary series with length n is 2^n.

Take now all the binary series of length less than n. The total number of such series is

$$1 + 2 + 2^2 + \cdots + 2^{n-1} = 2^n - 1.$$

So there are at least two different strings S_i and S_j for which $\Delta_A(S_i) = \Delta_A(S_j)$. Decoding these coded-strings we cannot distinguish between S_i and S_j, which is a contradiction. ∎

A. Information Theoretical Background

The theoretical background of data compression is mainly based on some results of information theory. The fundamental of this theory was worked out by Claude Shannon more than 50 years ago [60], and later many books and publications appeared in this topic (see, e.g., [1,28,33]). This theory investigates questions of information storage and communication, too, and data compression became one of its most important application. Before overviewing these important results in information theory that have been used in the field of data compression we introduce some definitions and basic theorems. As we mentioned, in this chapter we are dealing only with text compression. So, to be precise we need to introduce a model. The model is based on the fact that a letter in a text has been chosen from an alphabet.

DEFINITION 3. We refer to a nonempty set $A_n = \{a_1, \ldots, a_n\}, \infty > n \geq 1$, as an alphabet and the elements of A_n are called characters or symbols. A series of characters of A_n is called a string. Usually we assume that the length of a string is also finite.

DEFINITION 4. We call the source of such a procedure F_n, which emits the characters of A_n. A source is called first order if we can order to the characters of

A_n some independent probabilities $p_1, \ldots, p_n$, where $p_i > 0, i = 1, \ldots, n$ and $\sum_{i=1}^{n} p_i = 1$. We refer to the p_i's as the emitting probabilities of the characters.

DEFINITION 5. Let $K_n = \{\alpha_1, \ldots, \alpha_n\}$ be a set of binary series of finite length where the lengths of certain series can be different. We call such a procedure character coding, which orders a binary series $\alpha_i \in K_n$ to each character of an alphabet A_n. K_n is called the code and the elements $\alpha_1, \ldots, \alpha_n$ are called the code-words. The binary series of α_i will be denoted by $\omega_1 \omega_2 \cdots \omega_{l_i}$ where $\omega_k \in \{0, 1\}$.

DEFINITION 6. A code K_n is called uniquely decipherable, if an arbitrary binary series can be uniquely divided into products of code-words. (Here product means the concatenation of the code-words).

It is clear that in the case of text compression we are interested in only uniquely decipherable codes. Before thinking on how we can produce a compression method we must decide whether the text in hand is compressible. This raises the first questions: how can we measure the information content of a text, or how can we decide whether a message has redundancy?

Shannon investigated the idea of *entropy* to answer the above questions. Suppose we have a first-order source F_n, which emits the characters of alphabet A_n with probability $p_i, i = 1, \ldots, n$. Suppose that we have coded the symbols of alphabet A_n by the—not necessarily binary—code K_n. Then Shannon introduced the following.

DEFINITION 7. $H(F_n) = -k \sum_{i=1}^{n} p_i \log p_i = k \sum_{i=1}^{n} p_i \log \frac{1}{p_i}$ is the entropy of the source F_n, where k is a positive integer governing the units in which we measure the entropy. Usually, the units are bits, where k = 1, and so—for binary coding—the entropy is $H(F_n) = \sum_{i=1}^{n} p_i \log \frac{1}{p_i}$.

Shannon proved that the function of entropy satisfies the following requirements, and he also demonstrated that it is the only function which does so:

- $H(F_n)$ is a continuous function of the probabilities $p_1, \ldots, p_n$.
- In the case of uniform distributions if $n_1 > n_2$ then $H(F_{n_1}) > H(F_{n_2})$.
- If S_1 and S_2 are two stages with probability p_1 and p_2 respectively, and F_n^1 and F_n^2 are the sources belonging to the stages, then $H(F_n) = pH(F_n^1) + p_2 H(F_n^2)$.

From the above definition it is clear that more likely messages that appear with greater probability contain less informations; i.e., the more surprising the message, the more information content it has.

Now, to measure the goodness of code K_n we introduce the following.

DEFINITION 8. For the source F_n the expression $L(K_n) = \sum_{i=1}^{n} p_i l_i$ is the cost of the code K_n.

As we showed above, the entropy applies only to a probability distribution, and it gives us the average information content of a given text emitted by a source F_n. However, we are often more interested in qualifying the entropy of a particular choice from the text. Supposing that the probability of this event is p_i, we can get the desired entropy using the definition $H_i(F_n) = \log \frac{1}{p_i}$. Now, making n subsequent decisions with probabilities $p_1, \ldots, p_n$ we get that the average entropy of the earlier processed decisions is $H(F_i) = \sum_{i=1}^{n} p_i H_i(F_n) = \sum_{i=1}^{n} p_i \log \frac{1}{p_i}$, which is the overall entropy.

Now, performing a compression step by step we will get an "entropy-like" coding process if after having compressed the text for each individual choice of an arbitrary string (or a letter) its compressed length $t_i = \log \frac{1}{p_i}$. So, the only question remaining is to decide whether this result can be beaten.

DEFINITION 9. A uniquely decipherable code K_n^0 is optimal for the source F_n, if for any uniquely decipherable code K_n for F_n, $L(K_n) \geq L(K_n^0)$.

Our aim is to find such a code, which is optimal, i.e., has a minimal cost, considering the given probabilities. (Of course we would like to assure the recoverability using uniquely decipherable codes.) The next theorems present that we can answer the above raised question negatively.

THEOREM 2 [1]. *For an arbitrary uniquely decipherable code K_n for F_n, the relation $L(K_n) \geq H(F_n)$ holds.*

Abramson also proved that there exists a type of coding that produces a very good compression. In [1] he introduced the following.

DEFINITION 10. We say that a code-word $\alpha_i = \omega_1 \omega_2 \cdots \omega_{l_i}$ is a prefix of another $\alpha_j = \omega_1' \omega_2' \cdots \omega_{l_j}'$ if $l_i \leq l_j$ and there exists a $l_s \leq l_i$, such that $\omega_k = \omega_k'$, if $k \leq l_s$. A code K_n is a prefix, if no code-word is a real prefix of another.

The prefix codes have great importance, since it is easy to see that if we use a prefix code, then the decoding process can be done uniquely.

THEOREM 3 [1]. *Each prefix code is uniquely decipherable.*

THEOREM 4 [1]. *For an arbitrary source F_n there exists an optimal prefix code.*

By Theorem 4 there exists an optimal prefix code for a given source F_n. The following—so-called Noiseless Coding Theorem—gives an interesting upper bound on the cost of such a code.

THEOREM 5 [60]. *Let K_n^0 be the optimal prefix code for a given source F_n. Then the relation $L(K_n^0) \leq H(F_n) + 1$ holds.*

From Theorems 2 and 5 it follows that the cost of an optimal prefix code is very close to the entropy of the given source. So, this theorem shows us that an entropy-like coding process gives us an optimal coding method. So, the next question is in hand: can we produce such a code?

Because of the above theorem, as a first step of our investigations we can concentrate on the existence of prefix codes. Taking into account the following theorem we can get two important results: On the one hand, the constraint gives us an exact bound for constructing a prefix code. On the other hand, if we have a code in our hand we can decide easily whether it is a prefix one.

THEOREM 6 [44]. *For any sequence $l_1, \ldots, l_n$ of natural numbers, there is a prefix code K_n with code-words of length $l_1, \ldots, l_n$ if and only if*

$$\sum_{i=1}^{n} 2^{-l_i} \leq 1. \qquad (1)$$

Inequality (1) is known as the Kraft Inequality.

B. Models

As we saw earlier, the entropy of a given text depends on the probabilities of the symbols being coded. Similarly, the average length of the compressed text (or as we called it, the cost of a code) is also a function of the probabilities. It is also obvious that we can state certain models to compute the probabilities, and in different models these values would be different. Since the entropy serves a lower bound for the average length of the compressed text it is important to use the adequate model in our process.

The fundamental role of a model is to supply probabilities for the message. In a model—usually—we do not calculate the probabilities in one step. Instead, they are built up incrementally, starting at the beginning of the text, and processing through it character by character. Depending on this criterion we can distinguish between static and adaptive models. In the following we will show the most popular models used in connection with the data compression.

1. Static Models

In the case of a static model we calculate explicitly the probabilities in advance, we fix them, and we supply them for each example. So, we need a preprocessing step before starting the compression itself, and it supposes a deeper—and longer—statistical investigation for the structure of the text being later compressed. The deeper the investigation is, the better the model is.

Finite-Context Models

One of the simplest models for counting the probabilities is what allocates a fixed probability to each character irrespective of its position in the text. To do this we need to know all characters that may occur in a message. It is so in the case of different natural languages. A collection of American English text is known as the Brown corpus, and it has been widely used in investigating different language statistics. It based on 500 separate 2000-word samples of natural language text representing a wide range of styles and authors. The alphabet of the corpus contains 94 symbols. The first 15 most frequent characters is shown by Table 1. By analyzing a given English text one can estimate for example the probability of the word "∘for" (here the symbol "∘" means the space character) as follows: One can find the probabilities of each character in Table 1, which are ∘ = 0.1741, f = 0.0176, o = 0.059, and r = 0.0474. So the probability of the entire text-fragment is

$$0.1741 \times 0.0176 \times 0.059 \times 0.0474 = 4.515 \times 10^{-5} = 2^{-14.435},$$

TABLE I Letter Statistics from the Brown Corpus*

Letter	Prob. (%)	Letter	Prob. (%)	Letter	Prob. (%)
o	17.41	i	5.51	l	3.19
e	9.76	n	5.50	d	3.05
t	7.01	s	4.94	c	2.30
a	6.15	r	4.77	u	2.10
o	5.90	h	4.15	m	1.87

*Ref. 10. Reprinted by permission of Pearson Education, Inc., Upper Saddle River, NJ.

so the optimum coding of the string in hand is 14.435 bits in this simple model. In this model we did not take into account the preceding characters while having to calculate the probabilities. In this case we refer to the model as an *order-0 model*. It is easy to recognize that the probability of a character will differ depending on the symbols that precede it. So, we can generalize the above idea: we will say that a model is an *order-k* model if it considers k preceding characters while determining the probability of the next symbol. If we want to use an order-k model we will have some difficulties at the beginning of the text: there will be an insufficient number of characters to supply our formula. In that case some ad hoc solution is used: either we assume that the text is primed with a k-length sequence of default characters or we use an order-0 model for the first $k-1$ characters.

Models of up to order 11 have been reported in the book of [10]. It is a natural feeling that we must use a high-order model to get good estimations for the probabilities. This is true but it is also easy to see that the number of possible contexts increases exponentially with the order of the model. Thus larger and larger samples are needed to make the estimates and so, we may need a huge amount of memory to store them. This will destroy all of the advantages of any compressing procedure.

Markov Models

Natural languages are good examples to use with a finite-context model, but there are other strings for which this type of model is not usable. The most relevant example for this type of string is DNA, in which four type of bases (A,C,G, or T) can occur in triplets. The probability of one of the bases occurring within a triplet is strongly influenced by its position. Unfortunately, any knowledge about the previous base or even a number of previous bases does not help much to estimate the probabilities, and a position can only be decided by counting back to the beginning of the DNA sequence.

Final-state probabilistic models are good tools for handling such type of strings. Because of the probabilistic theory background these models are often referred to as Markov models. For a given alphabet A_n one can imagine such a model as a finite-state machine with n different states denoted by S_i, $i = 1, 2, \ldots, n$. In each state we can give a set of transition probabilities p_{ij}, which gives the transition probability from the current state S_i to the state S_j. (It is clear that $\sum_{j=1}^{n} p_{ij} = 1$.) Using this model for a given string we get a unique path through the model, and the probability of any string can be computed by multiplying the probabilities out of each state.

Markov models are very useful for modeling natural languages, and they are widely used for this purpose.

Some of the state models are *nonergodic* in the sense that in these models there are states from which parts of the system are permanently inaccessible. All state models used in connection with natural languages are ergodic.

Grammar Models

For those types of strings which represent a part of any language with strong syntactic rules, the above models are not usable. For example, in computer algebra (like MAPLE or MATHEMATICA) if the parentheses are balanced in a formula, the next character may not be a")". Similarly, for those of computer languages where the delimiter is a special character (e.g., "." or ";") this character may not occur "inside" a statement. For the above type of strings with—theoretically—infinite nesting possibilities, the so-called grammar models are adequate. In a grammar model we have well-defined productions (e.g., conditional or unconditional jump statements and subroutine calling sequences), and we can decide the probabilities of each subproduction in a given production. This gives us a multilevel hierarchy, containing in each level a discrete probability distribution. Now, if we have a string to be modeled by a grammar model it is parsed according to the grammar, and its probability may be computed by multiplying together the probability of each production that is used.

The use of grammars—principally for compressing Pascal programs—has been explored by Katajainen *et al.* [39] and Cameron [14]. Compressing strings from a formal—computer—language, this type of model is very successful, but it is almost usable for natural languages. It follows from pragmatic reasons that it is almost impossible to find a grammar for natural languages: their syntactic rules are very complicated and are not modelable "by hand." Constructing them mechanically from samples is also impossible because we cannot decide the exact boundary of the given language. It is worth mentioning that some heuristics are useful for modeling natural languages.

The Problem of Conditioning Classes

As we have seen, in a finite-context model there is a possibility of using an order-k model to count more precisely the probability of certain parts of a given text. Unfortunately, to get a good estimation a lot of different conditional probabilities must be considered. This problem was solved first by Rissanen and Langdon in [56], by introducing the *conditional classes*. Before giving a formal description we need to introduce some notations: a substring of length $k - i + 1$ in a given text $S = s_1 s_2 \ldots s_n$ from the position i to the position k will be denoted by $s_i s_{i+1} \ldots s_k$. The probability of a text S is denoted as usual by $p(S)$, and $p'(S)$ is the probability that the string S is the prefix of any message. If Λ is the empty message then it is easy to see that

$$p(S) = p(s_1 s_2 \ldots s_n) = \frac{p'(s_1)}{p'(\Lambda)} \frac{p'(s_1 s_2)}{p'(s_1)} \cdots \frac{p'(s_1 s_2 \ldots s_n)}{p'(s_1 s_2 \ldots s_{n-1})} \frac{p(s_1 s_2 \ldots s_n)}{p'(s_1 s_2 \ldots s_n)}.$$

If we realize that each fraction is a conditional probability, i.e.,

$$\frac{p'(s_1 s_2 \ldots s_i)}{p'(s_1 s_2 \ldots s_{i-1})} = p(s_i | s_1 s_2 \ldots s_{i-1}),$$

then the probability of the entire message is reduced to a sequence of choices, one for each symbol in the text. This reformulation can help only if we can calculate the conditional probabilities easier than the overall probability of the string. Usually, this is not the situation, but we can approximate the conditional probabilities. A common way to do that is to ignore a part of the message seen so far. For example, if we consider the last two characters instead of counting the whole formula then the probability $p(s_i|s_1 s_2 \ldots s_{i-1})$ can be substituted with $p''(s_i|s_{i-2} s_{i-1})$, where this last probability means that the character s_i follows the symbols s_{i-2} and s_{i-1} in this order. This simplified formula results in an approximation for the right probability, so the overall message cannot always be compressed optimally, but the estimation will be satisfactory in most cases. As Rissanen and Langdon pointed out in [56] this "two character estimation" can be generalized if we assign each possible context string to some conditioning class. So, we can use the estimation

$$p(s_i|s_1 s_2 \ldots s_{i-1}) \approx p''(s_i|U(s_1 s_2 \ldots s_{i-1})),$$

where $U(s_1 s_2 \ldots s_{i-1})$ is the *conditioning class* of the string $s_1 s_2 \ldots s_{i-1}$. It is worth mentioning that—despite the fact that any computable function can be used to calculate the conditioning classes—in practice the above type of estimation is common; i.e., a finite number of symbols can be considered to be formulating a class. The interesting reader can find a good survey for the techniques in [4].

2. Adaptive Models

In the case of static models—based on some theoretical background—we produce a model in advance, and we supply it for any string having been generated from a given alphabet. In a static model we need to know the entire text being compressed in advance; otherwise we are not able to count the relative frequencies of the characters. *Adaptive models* have many advantages since usually they start with no statistical information and the model is built up from this initial state. So, we do not have to spend a lot of time checking whether the sender and the receiver have the same initial model, and we can use an adaptive model for any type of text. This flexibility is very important in applications of adaptive models where there is no possibility of seeing ahead of time what is likely to be transmitted.

Since the adaptive models do not know the message in advance we expect that they behave worse than the static ones. One can suppose that this is the price we need to pay for being on-line. On the other hand one can say that the adaptive model will fit step by step to the actual situation, and therefore an adaptive coding scheme must be better than a nonadaptive one. There is no general theorem that proves this latter conjecture, but there are nice theorems that state the opposite: an adaptive model will be only slightly worse than any static model:

THEOREM 7 [10]. *Given a set of conditioning classes with K members, an alphabet with q symbols, and a message of length n, there are adaptive models that will take at most Kq log n bits more than the best possible nonadaptive model.*

We remind the reader that in the case of semi-adaptive models the model must be sent with the message, and coding the model requires approximately $Kq \log n$ bits, so about the same number of bits will be used as for a fully adaptive model. Intuitively, it is also expected that for an adaptive model a "well-suited" message will be excellent compressible. However, what is the worst-case situation?

THEOREM 8 [10]. *There is an adaptive model where the compressed string will be at most $(q+1)/2 \log n$ bits longer than the original string.*

After this surprising result one can say that an adaptive model may not be a good choice for processing a compression. Fortunately, there is another theorem that states that for any text there exists a static model that can expand it arbitrarily. So the consequence is nice:

COROLLARY 9. *There is a message where an adaptive code will do asymptotically better than the static model.*

So we can prefer an adaptive model in practice. However, there are two problems using this model that we need to face. The first is the *zero-frequency problem*. This is rooted in the fact that every time a character is encoded, all symbols that can possibly occur at that point must be predicted with a nonnegative probability, and this must be valid, even those symbols that have never occurred before the actual position of the coding. (If a symbol would have a zero probability then its code-length would be –log 0, which is infinite.) This problem can be solved if we assign a very small probability to each nonoccurring symbol, and—at the same time—we adjust the other probabilities. Of course, this will deform the distribution and so, the compression may not be optimal.

The second problem is connected with counting the *conditioning classes*. In the literature there are two contrasting approaches. In the first one while estimating the probabilities one counts as much as possible attempts to minimize the statistical errors. If we apply the second method then we try to define a lot of conditioning classes that may result in a model in which the probabilities will accurately reflect the current context. A detailed discussion of these approaches for different adaptive models can be found in [10].

III. STATISTICAL CODING

Compression is usually made by coding. Character coding—as a special kind of coding—was defined in the previous section. Generally a code is a mapping from some source strings to some code words. Depending on the sizes of the source words and the code-words, codings can be categorized into different classes. If the lengths of all source words are equal and the lengths of all code words are also constant—where the two lengths are not necessarily the same—we say that the coding is block-to-block type.

EXAMPLE 1. A block-to-block coding is as follows:

Source words	Code words
a	011
b	010
c	110
d	111

Similarly we can speak about block-to-variable, variable-to-block, and variable-to-variable codings. In each coding on the variable side the length of the codes can be varied. In the case of variable-to-block coding the length of the code words are fixed, but the lengths of the source words can be different. In variable-to-variable coding both of them can vary.

EXAMPLE 2. A variable-to-variable coding is as follows:

Source words	Code words
ab	11
b	010
cbd	101
dc	011

Statistical compression methods are based on the information theoretical results mentioned in the previous section. These algorithms try to give such a uniquely decipherable code, which has an optimal cost or its cost is close to the optimal. By Theorem 4 there exists such a code. By Theorem 2 the codes belonging to the symbols should be chosen in such a way that their lengths should be close to the logarithm of the reciprocal value of the probability of the symbol. If the relative frequency of the characters of the source string can be computed, then the optimal code lengths could be derived. In practice the problem is that the logarithm values are usually not integers. Many algorithms were developed to solve this problem. The most popular ones are Shannon–Fano coding [27], Huffman coding [35], and Arithmetic coding [32,54,55]. These methods always assume that the probabilities of the symbols are given. In practice the easiest method for evaluating the probabilities is to calculate the relative frequencies. So, usually these methods are not on-line in the sense that before using the coding technique we need to count the relative frequencies in a preprocessing step, and so we need to know the whole string in advance. In the following we present the most widely used statistical compression methods.

A. Shannon–Fano Coding

This technique was independently discovered in the late 1940s by C. E. Shannon and R. M. Fano. Shannon–Fano coding [27] is a block-to-variable coding, where code words are assigned to the symbols of a given alphabet. The algorithm divides recursively the symbols of the alphabet into some groups until each group contains only one symbol. During the division a 0 or 1 digit is ordered to each group, which will form the code. It is easy to see that this process

DATA COMPRESSION

e:0.35	0	00	
a:0.25		01	
d:0.15	1	10	
b:0.14		11	110
c:0.11			111

FIGURE 1 Shannon–Fano code of Example 3.

always produces a prefix code. An exact description of the procedure is the following:

- Suppose the probabilities of the symbols are given.
- List the symbols in decreasing order due to their probabilities.
- Divide the set of symbols into two parts such that each part has an equal or approximately equal probability.
- Assign to the code of the first part a 0 bit and to the code of the second part a 1 bit.
- Continue the division of both parts recursively until each subdivision contains only one symbol.
- The code of each symbol will be a series of 0's and 1's assigned to it.

EXAMPLE 3. Suppose we have five symbols in our alphabet. These are a, b, c, d, e. The probabilities of the symbols in a source are given in the table

Symbols	c	b	d	a	e
Probabilities	0.11	0.14	0.15	0.25	0.35

The construction of Shannon–Fano code for this example is represented by Fig. 1.

Shannon–Fano coding was the first attempt to solve the optimal statistical coding problem. Because the dividing step is not defined clearly, its optimality does not hold. However, in practice Shannon–Fano code is not too far from the optimum. As we saw above, this coding scheme strives to give high-probability characters short codes and low-probability ones longer codes. However, in fact, Shannon–Fano coding sometimes assigns a longer code to a more probable character than it does to a less probable one. The following coding does not suffer from this deficiency.

B. Huffman Coding

Huffman coding is also a block-to-variable coding technique. It lists the symbols in increasing probabilities, and gathers them into some sets recursively, assigning to each set the sum of the probabilities of the symbol in the set. At each step a bit is appended to the code of the symbols in the set. The algorithm can be implemented using a tree data structure. The exact method is the following:

- Suppose the probabilities of the symbols are given.
- List the symbols in increasing order due to their probabilities.
- Consider the symbols with the two least probabilities.

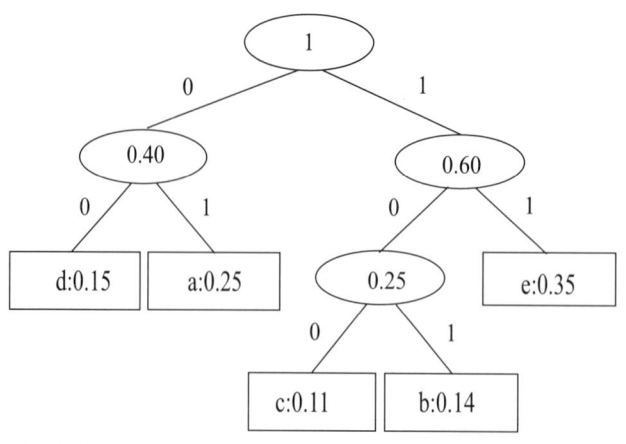

FIGURE 2 Huffman tree of Example 3.

- Substitute these symbols with a set, whose probability is the sum of the two probabilities. We order a bit of value 0 to the code of the first symbol and a bit of value 1 to the other.
- For these newly constrained sets repeat the previous three steps until we get a list containing only one element.

Using the above algorithm the following Huffman code can be constructed for Example 3. The symbols and the sets are represented by a tree, which is a usual technique in the implementations of the method (see Fig. 2). The code words for Example 3 are

Symbols	a	b	c	d	e
Code words	01	101	100	00	11

Huffman coding is one of the most popular compression methods. Many authors investigated the characteristics of the method from several points of view: Karp [38], Krause [45], and later Cot [22] and Mehlhorn [49] considered the case where the characters of the code alphabet have nonequal costs. Gilbert investigated the construction of Huffman codes based on inaccurate source probabilities [30].

In honor of the twenty-fifth anniversary of Huffman coding Gallager presented an interesting property of the Huffman trees [29]. This property is the so-called sibling property.

DEFINITION 11. *A binary code tree has the sibling property if each node (except the root) has a sibling and if the nodes can be listed in order of nonincreasing probability with each node being adjacent in the list to its sibling.*

The next theorem helps to decide whether a binary prefix code is a Huffman code.

THEOREM 10 [29]. *A binary prefix code is a Huffman code if and only if the code tree has the sibling property.*

Another interesting problem is to determine the maximum length of the Huffman codes. This problem was investigated by Buro [13]. He gave an upper bound on the maximum length of a binary Huffman code and on the sum of the length of all code words. In the following we present some of his results.

DEFINITION 12. *The external path length of a Huffman tree is the sum of all path lengths from the root to the leaves.*

THEOREM 11 [13]. *Assume that we have a source alphabet consisting of $n > 1$ symbols. Denote the probabilities of the symbols by $p_1, \ldots, p_n$ and suppose that $p_i \leq p_{i+1}$ for all $1 \leq i \leq n-1$. Denote the length of the longest code word of the corresponding Huffman code by L. Then*

$$L \leq \min\left\{\left\lfloor \log_\Phi\left(\frac{\Phi+1}{p_1\Phi+p_2}\right)\right\rfloor, n-1\right\},$$

where $\Phi = \frac{1+\sqrt{5}}{2}$.

COROLLARY 12 [13]. *The external path length of a Huffman tree is at most*

$$\min\left\{\left\lfloor \log_\Phi\left(\frac{\Phi+1}{p_1\Phi+p_2}\right)\right\rfloor \cdot n, \frac{(n+2)(n-1)}{2}\right\}.$$

Because of the construction none of the assigned code words are a prefix of another in the Huffman code. So the derived code is a prefix and Theorem 3 holds. As a consequence decoding can be done easily: we search for the first matching code word in the compressed data, then we substitute it with the corresponding symbol, and we continue this process until the end of the compressed file.

The main problem with decoding is that storing the Huffman tree may require large memory. In the original paper the array data structure was used to implement the complete binary tree. Later Hashemian [34] presented an efficient decoding algorithm using a special array data structure. In the following we present a memory-efficient array data structure to represent the Huffman tree. This was published by K.-L. Chung in [19]. The memory requirement of this representation is $2n-3$ where n is the size of the basic alphabet. Based on this implementation a fast decoding is possible. The following algorithm creates the array structure H:

• Traverse the Huffman tree in a preorder way. For each left edge record the number of edges E and leaf nodes L in the subtree of that edge. Assign the $E + L + 1$ value to the node whose left edge has been investigated.

• Traverse again the Huffman tree in a preorder way. At each time emit the assigned value when a left edge is encountered, or a "1" when a right edge is encountered. Emit the source symbol when a leaf edge is encountered.

• Save the ordered emitted values in H.

EXAMPLE 4. For the Huffman tree in Example 3, H is the following:

$$H: 2, e, 1, 5, 2, c, 1, b, 1, 2, d, 1, a.$$

Now we present the Chung decoding algorithm [19]. The algorithm uses two pointers. One pointer points to the Huffman code C, the other to the array H. The pointers are denoted by cp and ap, respectively. In the code $len(C)$ denotes the length of the corresponding Huffman code C. Using the construction of the H array, the algorithm moves the pointers in such a way that if *cp* points to the end of a code word in C then *ap* points exactly to the corresponding source symbol in the H array. Using this process, decoding the next symbol can be done easily outputting $H[ap]$. The pseudo-code looks like this:

```
ap := 1; cp := 1;
while cp < len(C) do
    begin
    if H[cp] = 0 then
        begin
        cp := cp + 1;
        ap := ap + 1;
        end
    else
        begin
        cp := cp + 1;
        ap := H[ap] + 1;
        if not eof (C) then
            begin
            if H[cp] = 1 then
                begin
                cp := cp + 1;
                ap := H[ap] + 1;
                end
            else
                begin
                cp := cp + 1;
                ap := ap + 1;
                end
            end
        end
    Output H[ap]
    end
```

There are other approaches in the practice: in [50] a VLSI implementation of Huffman encoding and decoding was considered. Teng [62] presents a $O(\log(n)^2)$ parallel algorithm for constructing a Huffman tree with n leaves. Some years later in [46] an off-line construction was investigated for those types of Huffman codes where the depth of leaves is limited.

C. Redundancy of Huffman Codes

It is well known that the Huffman code is an optimal prefix code; i.e., its cost is minimal among the prefix codes of the given alphabet and probabilities. The question is how close is the code to the entropy of the given source? The difference between the entropy and the cost of the Huffman code is characterized by its *redundancy*. Given that each character in an alphabet must occupy an integral number of bits in the encoding, Huffman coding achieves a "minimum redundancy"; i.e., it performs optimally if all probabilities are exact powers of $\frac{1}{2}$. Unfortunately, this is not the case usually in practice. Huffman codes—like the Shannon–Fano process—can take up one extra bit for each character.

DEFINITION 13. *Let F be a given source and denote the Huffman code for F by K_H. Then the value*

$$R = H(F) - L(K_H)$$

is the redundancy of the Huffman code.

When the Noiseless Channel Theorem is used, it immediately follows that $R \leq 1$ for all sources. Many authors investigated the problem of finding tight upper bounds for R. The first results were given by Gallager [29].

THEOREM 13 [29]. *Let p_1 be the probability of the most likely letter in a source. Then*

$$R \leq p_1 + \sigma,$$

where $\sigma = 1 - \log_2 e + \log_2(\log_2 e) \approx 0.086$.

THEOREM 14 [29]. *Let p_1 be the probability of the most likely letter in a source. If $p_1 \geq 0.5$, then*

$$R \leq 2 - \kappa(p_1) - p_1,$$

where κ is the binary entropy function, i.e.,

$$\kappa(x) = -x \log_2(x) - (1-x) \log_2(1-x).$$

The above bound is tight.

Later Johnsen [37], Capocelli *et al.* [15], and Capocelli and de Santis [16] proved some further results on the redundancy.

THEOREM 15 [37]. *Let p_1 be the probability of the most likely letter in a source. If $0.5 > p_1 \geq 0.4$, then*

$$R \leq \begin{cases} 1 + 0.5(1 - p_1) - \kappa(p_1) & \text{if } 0.4 \leq p_1 \leq \delta \\ 3 - 5p_1 - \kappa(2p_1) & \text{if } \delta \leq p_1 \leq 0.5, \end{cases}$$

where $\delta \approx 0.4505$. The above bounds are tight.

THEOREM 16 [15]. *Let p_1 be the probability of the most likely letter in a source. If $\delta > p_1 \geq \frac{1}{3}$, then*

$$R \leq 1 + 0.5(1 - p_1) - \kappa(p_1).$$

The above bound is tight.

THEOREM 17 [16]. *Let p_1 be the probability of the most likely letter in a source. Then*

$$R \leq \begin{cases} \frac{3}{4} + \frac{5p_1}{4} - \kappa(p_1) & \text{if } \frac{2}{9} < p_1 < \theta \\ 3 - (3 + 3\log 3)p_1 - \kappa(3p_1) & \text{if } \theta \leq p_1 \leq \frac{1}{3}, \end{cases}$$

where $\theta \approx 0.3138$. The above bounds are tight.

THEOREM 18 [16]. *Let p_1 be the probability of the most likely letter in a source. If for some $l \geq 3$*

$$\frac{2}{2^{l+1}+1} < p_1 < \frac{1}{2^l-1},$$

then

$$R \leq \begin{cases} 3 - \kappa(p_1) - (1-p_1)(2\log 3 - \frac{5}{9}) & \text{if } \frac{2}{17} < p_1 < \gamma \\ 4 - 7(1+\log 7)p_1 - \kappa(7p_1) & \text{if } \gamma < p_1 < \frac{1}{7} \\ 1 - \kappa(p_1) - (1-p_1)A_{2^l-1} & \text{if } l \geq 4, \end{cases}$$

where $\gamma \approx 0.1422$, $A_j = \min_{w_j \in W_j} \{H(W_j) - w_j\}$ and $W_j, j \geq 2$ is the set of positive real numbers $w_1, w_2, \ldots, w_j$ that satisfy $w_1 \geq w_2 \geq \cdots \geq w_j \geq \frac{w_1}{2}$ along with $\sum_h w_h = 1$. The above bounds are tight.

The above theorems cover all the cases when we know the largest symbol probability. There are some other results on the redundancy of Huffman codes with some other assumptions. For example we assume that we know the largest and the smallest probabilities. Details can be found in [15,17]. In addition to the redundancy, another similar notion was introduced in the literature. This is the *maximum data expansion*.

DEFINITION 14. Assume we are given a code $K = \{\alpha_1, \ldots, \alpha_n\}$ and denote $l_1, \ldots, l_n$ as the lengths of the $\alpha_1, \ldots, \alpha_n$ code words. Let the probabilities of the characters of the alphabet be $p_1, \ldots, p_n$. The maximum data expansion $\delta(K)$ of the code K is defined as

$$\delta(K) = \sum_{\{i \mid l_i > \log n\}} (l_i - \log n) p_i.$$

As presented before, Huffman coding uses two phases to compress a source word. First it calculates the relative frequencies that approach the symbol probabilities. Then the compression algorithm substitutes each symbol with its code word. During this phase the size of the file may grow temporarily when the symbols with low probabilities are placed at the beginning of the file. The maximum data expansion gives some estimation on the ratio of this growth. Its notion was introduced by Cheng et al. [18]. It is an interesting question to give some upper bound on $\delta(K)$. The most recently known best result is due to De Prisco and De Santis [23].

THEOREM 19 [23]. *The maximum data expansion $\delta(K_H)$ of a Huffman code is bounded by*

$$\delta(K_H) < 1.39.$$

It is not known, whether the above bound is tight.

D. Arithmetic Coding

Beyond Huffman coding, arithmetic coding is one of the most known statistical coding algorithms (see [32,54,55]). This method represents the input text by a number between 0 and 1. The subsequent symbols divide a previously defined interval due to their probabilities. The symbols with small probability decrease

DATA COMPRESSION

the length of the interval more significantly, giving more bits to the representation, while the symbols with higher probability decrease less the length of the interval.

The algorithm works in the following way:

- Let the starting interval be [0,1].
- Divide the corresponding interval due to the probabilities of the symbols.
- Consider the next symbol of the text and take the corresponding subinterval as the next interval.
- Repeat the previous two steps until we reach the end of the text. An arbitrary number from the last interval can represent the text.

EXAMPLE 5. Consider again the symbols and probabilities given in Example 3. Suppose that the input string is *deec*. The change of the intervals is the following:

$$\begin{array}{ll} \text{first} & [0, 1) \\ \text{after } d & [0.60, 0.75) \\ \text{after } e & [0.60, 0.6525) \\ \text{after } e & [0.60, 0.618375) \\ \text{after } c & [0.61635375, 0.618375) \end{array}$$

Figure 3 shows another representation of the coding process of Example 5. The greatest problem of the algorithm is that as the length of the text increases, the required accuracy of the number belonging to it increases, using more and more bits.

Decoding is also easy in this case. We consider the compressed form and the representing number. We divide the starting interval [0, 1) due to the probabilities. The first symbol of the source will be that character whose interval contains the number. Then we take the subinterval of this character and repeat the process until we decode the last character of the source.

In the implementation of the arithmetic coding usually integer arithmetic is used. To avoid overflow the bits that are not necessary for further coding should be sent to the output immediately. A C language implementation of arithmetic coding can be found in [10,70].

It is a well-known fact that arithmetic coding is optimal; i.e., its coding result is arbitrarily close to the entropy. For Huffman coding, the redundancy

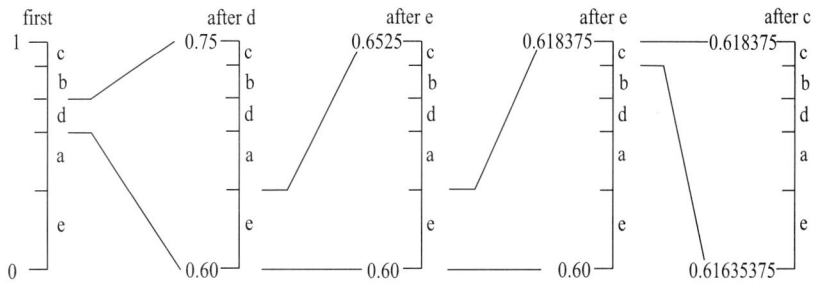

FIGURE 3 Arithmetic coding process for Example 5.

TABLE 2 Compression of Natural Language Alphabets by Huffman and Arithmetic Coding [12]*

Language	Huffman	Arithmetic	Huffman cost (%)
English	4.1854	4.1603	0.6
Finnish	4.0448	4.0134	0.8
French	4.0003	4.0376	0.9
German	4.1475	4.1129	0.8
Hebrew	4.2851	4.249	0.8
Italian	4.0000	3.9725	0.7
Portuguese	4.0100	3.9864	0.6
Spanish	4.0469	4.0230	0.6
Russian	4.4704	4.4425	0.6
English-2	7.4446	7.4158	0.4
Hebrew-2	8.0370	8.0085	0.4

*With permission from Springer-Verlag.

bounds show that this is not always true. So for a given example, it is a natural question as to whether arithmetic coding is superior to Huffman coding. Bookstein and Klein investigated this problem by comparing the two methods from several points of view [12]. They stated the most important advantages and disadvantages of arithmetic coding relative to Huffman codes. The advantages are optimality, efficient encoding if the alphabet or its characteristics are changing over the file, and simple extensibility to infinite alphabet. The disadvantages are slowness, complexity, and only small savings in realistic situations. Some other comparisons were based on the size of the alphabet. For large alphabets it can be stated that in general the probability of the most frequent character is close to 0, so the cost of the Huffman code is close to the entropy and the difference between the two methods is not significant. Bookstein and Klein compared the algorithms for natural language alphabets. Here we present their results in Table 2. The first column contains the name of the language, the next two columns give the average code-word lengths for the two methods, and the fourth gives the increase of the Huffman value over the value for arithmetic coding in percent.

Unfortunately, Huffman coding can work poorly for small alphabets. For example, in the pathological case when we have a binary alphabet with probabilities ε and $1 - \varepsilon$. Then the length of each code word is 1 bit with Huffman coding. Arithmetic coding will reach the entropy, which is $\varepsilon \log_2 \frac{1}{\varepsilon} + (1 - \varepsilon) \log_2 \frac{1}{1-\varepsilon}$. The entropy tends to 0 if $\varepsilon \to 0$. It shows that Huffman coding is a poor choice in such cases. It is also stated in [12] that arithmetic coding gives better compression in case of inaccurate probabilities. Time comparisons present that arithmetic coding consumes much more time than Huffman coding.

Some variants of arithmetic coding appeared in the literature too. A modification was proposed by Teuhola and Raita [63]. They found some disadvantages of arithmetic coding, like nonpartial decodability, vulnerability, i.e., strong effect of small (for example, one-bit) errors, etc. To avoid these problems, they

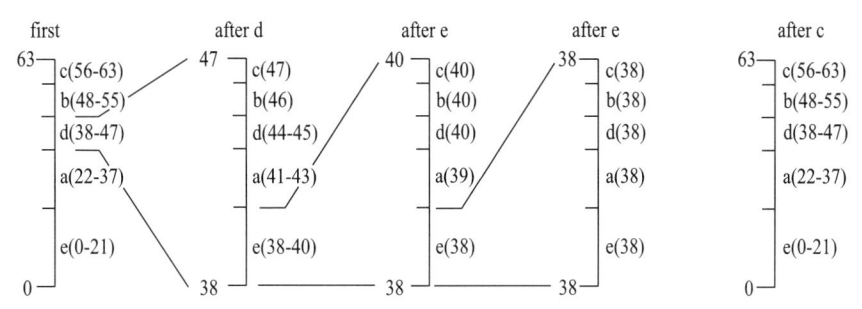

FIGURE 4 Coding steps of Example 3 using the fixed-length arithmetic algorithm.

proposed a modified version of arithmetic coding that produces fixed-length code words. The idea of their algorithm is to apply arithmetic coding repeatedly to some substrings, so that each substring produces a fixed-length code word. The technique is similar to the original arithmetic coding. However instead of the interval [0, 1) the range [0, $2^n - 1$] is considered, where n is a fixed integer. A code word will be an integer from this range. The algorithm works the same way as arithmetic coding: first it divides the range [0, $2^n - 1$] into some parts in accordance with the symbol probabilities. Then it chooses the subinterval corresponding to the next symbol. This technique is repeated recursively. If the range gets so small that the current symbol does not fall into a unique range, then the code is ready.

EXAMPLE 6. Take again the symbols and probabilities in Example 3. Let $n = 8$, so the code range is [0,63]. Suppose we have the same source word *deec*. Figure 4 shows the coding steps. The corresponding codewords can be 38 and 60.

The main difference between this fixed-length arithmetic coding and the original one is that in this case some collisions happen, i.e., some symbols can fall into the same range after the division, if the original range is narrow. Because this collision information is not utilized, the algorithm would not be optimal. To avoid this problem, the modified version of the algorithm use this information. This means that if a collision happens, both the encoder and the decoder know the symbols that are taking part in the collision. In the next step the algorithm reduces the alphabet to these symbols. This can be done, because in the case of a collision the next symbol is always restricted to one of the symbols of the collisions. The main disadvantage of this algorithm is that the successive code words are not independent and not separately decodable. The experimental results in [63] showed that these variants of arithmetic coding are rather practical and their redundancy is very small for some longer code words.

At the end of this section we refer back to the modeling step. Those models that have been introduced are suitable for supplying probabilities to such types of encoder like the Huffman code or the Arithmetic code. In the later case a coder is able to compress strings in that number of bits that are indicated by the entropy of the model being used, and this is the minimum size possible for the model chosen. Unfortunately, in the case of Huffman coding this lower bound can be achieved only under special conditions. This implies the importance of modeling and underlines the two-phase process that we need to follow in a compression procedure.

E. Adaptive Techniques

If we consider a generic model for a natural language, or pick up an order-0 statistic for any binary code and we compare these statistics to a particular message we can easily realize that the general models rarely represent these examples exactly. Earlier, we mentioned those adaptive techniques which we can use to fit the model dynamically to the message to be transmitted. The main idea for using the adaptive techniques is to change the symbol frequencies so far in the message. At the beginning the frequencies are equal, and they must be updated as the subsequent symbol arrives to approximate the observed frequencies. Of course both the encoder and the decoder start with the same initial values and they must use the same update algorithm. This ensures us that the model remains in step: getting the next symbol the encoder encodes it and fits the frequencies, and the decoder first identifies the character according to the actual model and then it also updates the model.

It is easy to see that each of the above static models can be changed to use an adaptive technique. When using a particular coding procedure such as the Huffman or Arithmetic coding the most exciting task is always to find the best implementation and to use the most adequate data structure for the technique being used. In the next part of the chapter we will review some known adaptive techniques.

1. Adaptive Huffman Coding

It is evident to proceed with Huffman coding adaptively by recalculating the Huffman tree step by step. However, it is also easy to see that such a procedure cannot be very efficient since updating the frequencies for an alphabet that contains q different characters can take–in the worst case–$q \log q$ operations, and it is very expensive. So, certain approaches for solving this problem more effectively have been investigated:

A. The *incremental-method* was introduced by Faller [26] and Gallager [29] independently. We can succinctly describe the method as follows: getting the subsequent character in the message we increment the count of the appropriate node. This can result in a rearrangement of the tree. In the simplest case it is merely an exchange of two nodes in the tree with incrementations of their parents', grandparents', etc. node counts to the root. Unfortunately, sometimes it is not enough, and the update operation may require rearranging further nodes' positions too. This can be implemented effectively by rippling up the tree and/or swapping some nodes as appropriate.

B. The *aging technique* is based on the fact that if we increment a node count, then it may overflow. So, we attempt to keep the counts within an interval, keeping in mind that our statistic must remain relevant to the portion of text being encoded. To avoid the overflow, the simplest technique is to halve all counts, but we can rescale the counts by any constant less than 1 (see [21,43]). The advantage of this method is that the relative frequencies stay the same, so we do not need to reorganize the Huffman tree. Different aging techniques are considered in [10]. We may have certain problems with this technique:

- The larger the time constant for aging, the slower the adaptation of the model, which may result in a better estimate for slowly varying statistics, but it can be irrelevant for rapidly varying statistics.
- Rescaling can create fractional parts, and the incremental update tree algorithm cannot handle these type of counts. So we need either to round or to truncate them to the nearest integer, which can change the structure of the Huffman tree dramatically.

Improvements and generalizations were considered in [20,43,64]. Finally, Lelewer and Hirschberg [47] summarized the improvements proposed by Vitter [64]. Weyland and Pucket [67] considered an adaptive technique for Huffman-like trees for compression of a Gaussian source of fixed and floating point numbers.

At the end of this subsection we must mention that the key of this technique is always the recreation of the Huffman tree. Since it may be time-consuming the resulting algorithm could be unsatisfactory for on-line coding.

2. Adaptive Arithmetic Coding

Using the Arithmetic coding we have counts for each symbol, and so we can count the total as well. Normalizing the counts we can get the relative frequencies of the symbols. It is easy to see that such a model can be updated simply by incrementing the count of the subsequent character. The only problem is the implementation. We must distinguish techniques developed for binary alphabets from those effective for large alphabets. For binary alphabets the first method was developed by Rissanen and Langton [56]. Efficient implementations for adaptive arithmetic coding both for binary and large alphabets are discussed in [10]. Further implementation can be find in [36,51] for large alphabets. It is interesting that there are experimental results for measuring the efficiency of some implementations; for example in [56] it has been pointed out that the method examined method has a very good efficiency (about 98.5%). In [70] the authors gave an implementation for the adaptive arithmetic coding, and a detailed discussion of its performance was given.

IV. DICTIONARY CODING

The basic idea of textual substitution or dictionary coding is to substitute the subsequent word fragments by a pointer or an index to a given dictionary. A *dictionary* is a finite set of ordered pairs (*source word, code word*), where the source word is a string from a finite alphabet and the code words are used to substitute the corresponding parts of the source text with the code word belonging to the matching source word. The dictionary coding methods can be divided into three groups. These are static, semiadaptive, and adaptive methods.

A. Methods Using a Static Dictionary

A static coding method uses always the same (static) dictionary given in advance, independently from the source text. The disadvantage of this model is based on the fact that if the dictionary does not fit the source text then we can get an extremely wrong compression ratio. On the other hand, if the dictionary contains too many words or word fragments then its size becomes too large, resulting in problems in both storing and searching. Static dictionaries are definitely useful in those cases when we must compress records of a database and some words (or word fragments) occur repeatedly. For example when we would like to compress the records of a library catalog containing as the words authors, titles, ISBN-s, books, etc. Supposing that we use a static dictionary; we can start compression with any record of the database. In the next part of the chapter we deal with these methods in detail.

1. Further Definitions

As was proved by Schuegraf and Heaps [58] compressing a given source string optimally is equivalent to the problem of finding a *shortest path* in a related directed, edge-weighted graph. For a source string $S = s_1 s_2 \ldots s_n$ we define a graph $N = (V, A)$ on the vertex set $V = \{v_0, v_1, \ldots, s_n\}$. The edge $(v_i, v_{i+d}) \in A$ exists iff there exists a pair of codes—(source word, code word)—such that the source word contains d characters that exactly match the original source string in positions $i + 1, \ldots, i + d$. The weight of this edge is the number of bits in the corresponding code word. It is easy to see that a shortest path from v_0 to v_n in the graph N corresponds to an optimal compression of the source string S.

EXAMPLE 7. To illustrate the above graph take the following string and dictionary

$$S = THIS\_IS\_AN\_EXAMPLE!$$

Source word	A	E	H	I	L	M	N	P	S
Code word	a	b	c	d	e	f	g	h	i
Weight	x	x	x	x	x	x	x	x	x

Source word	T	X	!	IS	_EX	XAM	THI	MPLE	MPLE!
Code word	j	k	l	m	n	o	p	q	r
Weight	x	x	x	x	x	x	x	x	x

The corresponding graph of Example 7 can be seen in Fig. 5.

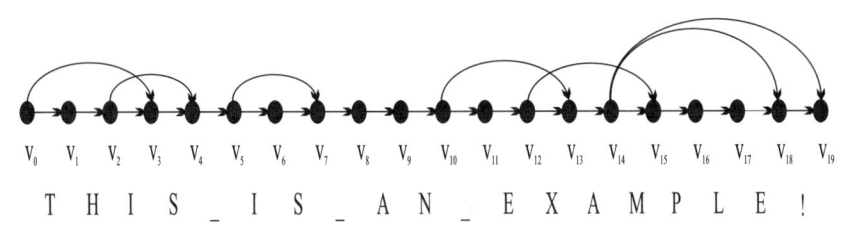

FIGURE 5 The edge-weighted graph of Example 7.

If we suppose that the weights of the edges are equal, then the shortest path from v_0 to v_{19} is the path

$$v_0 v_3 v_4 v_5 v_7 v_8 v_9 v_{10} v_{13} v_{14} v_{19}.$$

Using the above model the solution of the problem becomes easy, since we can apply one of the shortest-path algorithms for a directed, weighted graph. These algorithms run always in polynomial time. If the corresponding graph has many *cut vertices* (i.e., vertices that divide the original problem into independent subproblems) and if these subproblems are reasonably small, we can indeed solve the problem efficiently and can compute the *optimal* encoding. Unfortunately, in practice this will not be the case and a shortest-path algorithm cannot be applied since it takes too much time and space to compute an *optimal* solution for very long strings. Similarly, we have difficulties in case of *on-line* compression, where we must compress a source string block by block (where a block is a segment of the given string). Therefore, *heuristics* have been developed to derive near optimal solutions.

The earlier developed heuristics (for example, the *longest fragment first heuristic* (LFF) cf. Schuegraf and Heaps [59]) have not been deeply analyzed and only experimental results on their performance have been reported. Later, when the worst-case analysis became more popular these—and other newly created—algorithms were analyzed also from a worst-case point of view. Most of these algorithms are *on-line*. An *on-line data compression algorithm* starts at the source vertex v_0, examines all outgoing edges, and chooses one of them according to some given rule. Then the algorithm continues this procedure from the vertex reached via the chosen edge. There is no possibility of either undoing a decision made at an earlier time or backtracking.

Of course, usually an on-line heuristic will generate only a suboptimal compression. One possibility for measuring the "goodness" of an algorithm is to analyze its *worst-case behavior*. This is generally measured by an *asymptotic worst-case ratio*, which is defined as follows: Let $D = \{(w_i, c_i) : i = 1, \ldots, k\}$ be a static dictionary and consider an arbitrary data compression algorithm A. Let $A(D, S)$, respectively $OPT(D, S)$, denote the compressed string produced by algorithm A, respectively, the optimal encoding for a given source string S. The length of these codings will be denoted by $\|A(D, S)\|$, respectively $\|OPT(D, S)\|$. Then the *asymptotic worst-case* ratio of algorithm A is defined as

$$R_A(D) = \lim_{n \to \infty} \sup \left\{ \frac{\|A(D, S)\|}{\|OPT(D, S)\|} : S \in S(n) \right\},$$

where $S(n)$ is the set of all text strings containing exactly n characters.

The first worst-case analysis for an on-line data compression method was performed by Katajainen and Raita [41]. They analyzed two simple on-line heuristics, the *longest matching* and the *differential greedy* algorithm, which will be defined exactly later.

Four parameters have been used in the literature to investigate the asymptotic worst-case ratios:

$Bt(S) =$ length of each symbol of the source string S in bits

$lmax(D) = \max\{|w_i| \, i = 1, \ldots, k\}$

$$cmin(D) = \min\{\|c_i\| \, i = 1, \ldots, k\}$$
$$cmax(D) = \max\{\|c_i\| \, i = 1, \ldots, k\},$$

where $|w_i|$ denotes the length of a string w_i in characters and $\|c_i\|$ the length of a code word c_i in bits. If the meaning is clear from the context, we will simply denote the bit length of each input character by Bt and also omit the reference to the dictionary by using *lmax* instead of *lmax(D)*.

Not surprisingly, the worst-case behavior of a heuristic strongly depends on the features of the available dictionary. The following types of dictionaries have been examined in different papers:

A dictionary is called *general* if it contains all of the symbols of the input alphabet as source words (this ensures that every heuristic will in any case reach the sink of the underlying graph and thus will terminate the encoding with a feasible solution). In this paper we will only deal with general dictionaries. A general dictionary is referred to as follows:

1. **code-uniform** dictionary, if all code words are of equal length (i.e., $\|c_i\| = \|c_j\|, 1 \leq i, j \leq k$),
2. **nonlengthening** dictionary, if the length of any code word never exceeds the length of the corresponding source word (i.e., $\|c_i\| \leq |w_i| Bt, 1 \leq i \leq k$),
3. **suffix** dictionary, if with every source word w also all of its proper suffixes are source words (i.e., if $w = \omega_1 \omega_2 \ldots \omega_q$ is a source word $\Rightarrow$ $\omega_h \omega_{h+1} \ldots \omega_q$ is a source word for all $2 \leq h \leq q$), and
4. **prefix** dictionary, if with every source word w also all of its proper prefixes are source words i.e., if $w = \omega_1 \omega_2 \ldots \omega_q$ is a source word $\Rightarrow$ $\omega_1 \omega_2 \ldots \omega_h$ is a source word for all $1 \leq h \leq q - 1$).

2. Optimal and Approximation Algorithms

Consider again now the original problem, i.e., when we want to find an optimal encoding of a source text assuming that we have a static dictionary. There were known results for solving this problem even at the beginning of the 1970s [57,65,66]. As was mentioned before, Schuegraf and Heaps [58] showed that this question is equivalent to the problem of finding a *shortest path* in a related directed edge-weighted graph.

Later Katajainen and Raita [40] presented an optimal algorithm, which can be considered as a refinement of the above methods. Their algorithm is based on the general shortest-path method, but it uses cut vertices to divide the problem into smaller parts. The authors used the graph model to describe the steps of the algorithm. The dictionary is stored in an extended trie. A trie is a multiway tree, where each path from the root to a node represents an element from the dictionary. The extended trie was introduced by Aho and Corasick [3], and it allows fast string matching. In an extended trie each node contains a special pointer—called a failure transition—which points to the node whose associated string is the longest proper suffix of the string associated to the given node. Using these pointers a linked list is ordered to each node, and this list contains the nodes associated to the string itself and to those strings of the dictionary that are proper suffixes of it. Figure 6 illustrates the extended trie of

DATA COMPRESSION

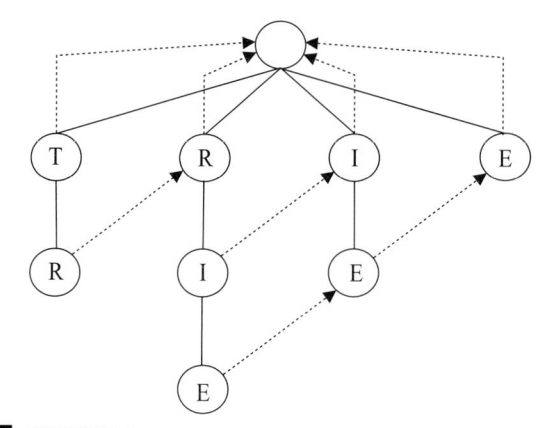

FIGURE 6 An extended trie. The dashed lines represent failure transition pointers.

the dictionary given as follows:

Source word	T	R	I	E	IE	TR	RIE
Code word	a	b	c	d	e	f	g

Using the notations given in the Introduction, a formal description of the algorithm is the following:

Let $S = s_1 s_2 \ldots s_n$ be a source string and $D = \{(w_i, c_i) : i = 1, \ldots, k\}$ a static dictionary;

Create an extended trie and add the dictionary strings $w_1, w_2, \ldots, w_k$ to it;

Create an empty output buffer B;
$d(v_0) := 0; p(v_0) := 0; cp := 0;$
for each character s_j in S **do**
    begin
    Using the extended trie find the set I of indices which defines those dictionary strings which match with the original text and end at position j;
    $d(v_0) := \infty.;$
    for each index i in I **do**
        begin
        $p := |w_i|; q := \|c_i\|;$
        if $d(v_j) > d(v_{j-p}) + q$ **then** $d(v_j) := d(v_{j-p}) + q; p(v_j) := i;$
        end
    if $j - lmax > cp$ **then**
        begin
        put $p(v_{j-lmax})$ to B;
        if v_{j-lmax} is a cut vertex **then**
            begin
            Traverse the shortest path in the buffer B
            Encode the contents of B
            Reset B
            $cp := j - lmax;$
        end
    end

    for $j := lmax - 1$ **downto** 0 **do**
        put $p(v_{n-j})$ to B;
    Traverse the shortest path in the buffer B
    Encode the contents of B
end

It is easy to see that the d and p arrays contain the set of the last *lmax* distance and parent values. The distance value is always the actual value of the shortest path and the parent pointer points to the previous node in the shortest path. The processed parent values are always sent to the output buffer. Unfortunately the necessary size of the output buffer is not known before the algorithm starts. The algorithm checks whether we have a cut vertex. If this occurs, then the contents of the buffer can be encoded. Unfortunately it is possible that there is no cut vertex at all. In this case the size of the output buffer can be arbitrary large. Of course this happens rarely in practice, but theoretically it is possible.

Raita and Katajainen showed that the time complexity of this shortest-path algorithm is $O(n+m)$, while the total time complexity of the extended trie construction and processing is $O(Wc \log_2 c + n \log_2 c + m)$ if it is implemented as a binary tree. Here W denotes the sum of the lengths of the dictionary source words, c is the maximal number of children of a node, n is the number of vertices and m is the number of edges of the graph.

The authors also analyzed the effect of a fixed-length output buffer on the compression ratio. They proved the following theorems, assuming that the length of the output buffer is $|B|$ and this approximation algorithm is denoted by A.

THEOREM 20 [40]. *Let D be a* **general** *dictionary. Then*

$$R_A(D) \leq 1 + \frac{lmax(lmax-1)}{|B|} \frac{cmax}{cmin}.$$

THEOREM 21 [40]. *Let D be a* **code-uniform** *dictionary. Then*

$$R_A(D) \leq 1 + \frac{lmax(lmax-1)}{|B|}.$$

THEOREM 22 [40]. *Let D be a* **nonlengthening** *dictionary. Then*

$$R_A(D) \leq \begin{cases} 1 + \dfrac{lmax(lmax-1)}{|B|} \dfrac{Bt}{cmin} & \text{if } cmin \leq Bt < cmax \\ 1 + \dfrac{lmax(lmax-1)}{|B|} \dfrac{cmax}{cmin} & \text{if } cmin < cmax \leq Bt. \end{cases}$$

THEOREM 23 [40]. *Let D be a* **suffix** *dictionary. Then*

$$R_A(D) \leq 1 + \frac{lmax}{|B|} \frac{cmax}{cmin}.$$

In Table 3 we summarize the results for this approximation algorithm.

TABLE 3 Summary of the Results on the Behavior of the Approximation Algorithms A

⟨Dictionary D⟩			
Suffix	CU	NL	$R_A(D)$
—	—	—	$1 + \dfrac{lmax\,(lmax - 1)}{\|B\|}\dfrac{cmax}{cmin}$
x	—	—	$1 + \dfrac{lmax}{\|B\|}\dfrac{cmax}{cmin}$
—	x	—	$1 + \dfrac{lmax\,(lmax - 1)}{\|B\|}$
—	—	x	$1 + \dfrac{lmax\,(lmax - 1)}{\|B\|}\dfrac{\min(Bt, cmax)}{cmin}$
x	x	—	$1 + \dfrac{lmax}{\|B\|}$
x	—	x	$1 + \dfrac{lmax}{\|B\|}\dfrac{cmax}{cmin}$
—	x	x	$1 + \dfrac{lmax(lmax - 1)}{\|B\|}$
x	x	x	$1 + \dfrac{lmax}{\|B\|}$

3. On-line Heuristic Algorithms

In this section we review the most important on-line heuristics and compare them from worst-case points of view. First of all we give the exact definitions.

The **longest matching** heuristic LM chooses at each vertex of the underlying graph the *longest* outgoing arc, i.e., the arc corresponding to the encoding of the longest substring starting at the current position. Ties can be broken arbitrary.

Katajainen and Raita [41] analyzed the worst–case behavior of LM for dictionaries that are code uniform/nonlengthening/suffix and they derived tight bounds for all eight combinations of these properties.

The *greedy* heuristic, which we will call **differential greedy** DG (introduced by Gonzalez–Smith and Storer [31]) chooses at each position the arc implied by the dictionary entry (w_i, c_i) yielding the maximal "local compression," i.e., the arc maximizing $|w_i|Bt - \|c_i\|$. Ties are broken arbitrarily. The **fractional greedy algorithm** (introduced by Békési et al. [7]) takes at any actual position in the source string the fractionally best possible local compression, i.e., if I is the set of indices of the arcs emanating from the current node of the corresponding graph then an arc i_0 will be chosen such that

$$i_0 = \arg\min_{i \in I} \frac{\|c_i\|}{|w_i|Bt}.$$

Obviously, although each heuristic is locally optimal, globally they can give a rather poor result. On the other hand it is possible that some heuristic compresses optimally such inputs, for which another gives the worst possible result and reverse.

It is intuitively clear that in many cases greedy type heuristics will perform better than the LM heuristic, which does not care about code lengths at all. There are also differences between the greedy methods. This is illustrated by the following example (let $a^1 = a$, $a^{i+1} = aa^i$, $i \in \mathbb{N}$, for any character a):

EXAMPLE 8. Let us consider the following nonlengthening dictionary with $cmax = 4$, $cmin = 1$ and, as usual for ASCII encodings, $Bt = 8$.

Source word	u	v	uv	$v^{lmax-1}u$
Code word	10	1101	1100	0
Weight	2	4	4	1

Compressing the source string $S_i = u(v^{lmax-1}u)^i$ consisting of $8(lmax \cdot i + 1)$ bits with the LM or the DG algorithm in both cases yields the code string $(1100(1101)^{lmax-2})^i 10$ with $4(lmax - 1)i + 2$ bits. Applying the FG heuristic to the same problem generates the code string $10(0)^i$, which is only $i + 2$ bits long.

Although Example 8 is based on a very special dictionary, it demonstrates the differences between the algorithms. The following theorems give a short summary of the most important results for the different heuristics.

THEOREM 24 [7,41]. *For a* **general** *dictionary D*

$$R_{\mathrm{LM}}(D) = R_{\mathrm{FG}}(D) = (lmax - 1)\frac{cmax}{cmin},$$

$$R_{\mathrm{DG}}(D) = \begin{cases} \dfrac{cmin + (lmax - 1)cmax}{cmin + (lmax - 1)Bt} & \text{if } (lmax - 1)^2 cmax\, Bt \leq cmin^2 \\ & \text{and } \left\lfloor \dfrac{cmax - cmin}{Bt} \right\rfloor \geq lmax - 1 \\ \dfrac{(lmax - 1)cmax}{cmin} & \text{otherwise.} \end{cases}$$

The above result presents that from worst-case point of view the three methods work very similar. Only the ratio of the DG algorithm differs a little in a special case.

Another interesting problem may be to analyze the heuristics for different types of dictionaries. First we will investigate suffix dictionaries and present the most important results.

THEOREM 25 [6,7,41]. *Let D be a* **suffix** *dictionary. Then*

$$R_{\mathrm{LM}}(D) = \frac{cmax}{cmin},$$

$$R_{\mathrm{DG}}(D) = \begin{cases} \dfrac{cmin + (lmax - 1)cmax}{cmin + (lmax - 1)Bt} & \text{if } (lmax - 1)^2 cmax\, Bt < cmin^2 \\ & \text{and } \lfloor (cmax - cmin)/Bt \rfloor \geq lmax - 1 \\ \dfrac{(lmax - 1)cmax}{cmin} & \text{otherwise,} \end{cases}$$

$$R_{\mathrm{FG}}(D) \leq \frac{cmax(\ln(lmax - 1) + 1)}{cmin}$$

and there exists a suffix dictionary D_0, for which

$$\frac{cmax(\ln(lmax - 1) + 1 - \ln 2)}{cmin} < R_{\mathrm{FG}}(D_0).$$

What is interesting for suffix dictionaries is that LM works much better than the greedy algorithms. If the dictionary is also nonlengthening, then LM is even optimal. DG can reach the worst possible ratio, while FG is somewhere between LM and DG. Prefix property is similar to the suffix one; therefore one would expect similar results. The following theorems shows that this is not the case.

THEOREM 26 [6,7]. *Let D be a **prefix** dictionary. Then*

$$R_{LM}(D) = R_{FG}(D) = \frac{(lmax - 1)cmax}{cmin},$$

$$R_{DG}(D) = \begin{cases} \dfrac{cmin + (lmax - 1)cmax}{cmin + (lmax - 1)Bt} & \text{if } (lmax - 1)^2 cmax\, Bt \leq cmin^2 \\ & \text{and } \lfloor \dfrac{cmax - cmin}{Bt} \rfloor \geq lmax - 1, \\ \dfrac{(lmax - 1)cmax}{cmin} & \text{otherwise.} \end{cases}$$

We can conclude that prefix property does not help at all in the worst case, because our results are the same as those in the general case. Finally we compare the three heuristics for nonlengthening dictionaries. This case may be interesting, because all heuristics give the same worst-case ratio.

THEOREM 27 [6,7,41]. *Let D be a **nonlengthening** dictionary and S be a string. Then* $R_{LM}(D) = R_{DG}(D) = R_{FG}(D)$, *and*

$$R_{LM}(D) = \begin{cases} \dfrac{(lmax - 1)cmax}{cmin} & \text{if } cmax \leq Bt \\ \dfrac{(lmax - 2)Bt + cmax}{cmin} & \text{if } Bt < cmax < 2Bt \\ \dfrac{lmax\, Bt}{cmin} & \text{if } 2Bt \leq cmax. \end{cases}$$

4. Almost On-line Heuristics

More than twenty years ago Shuegraf and Heaps [59] introduced the *longest fragment first (LFF)* heuristic. They supposed that the file we want to compress is divided into records of the same lengths. The idea is the following: the longest word fragment—within the actual record—which matches a word from the dictionary is chosen and encoded. Then the overlapping matches are eliminated and the algorithm works repeatedly.

Later Stauffer and Hirschberg [61] presented the so-called LFF parsing algorithm, which was based on the above idea. However they described the algorithm for a parallel architecture. In this model a processor is assigned to each character of the input string and these processors can work in parallel. First each processor calculates the list of the lengths of matches between the dictionary and the input string beginning at its position. Then the algorithm determines the maximum match length. Starting from this match length, the algorithm goes down to length 1, and in each step it finds the maximum collection of nonoverlapping matches of the given length. These matches will be selected for coding. Finally the algorithm eliminates all the matches overlapping the selected ones. A formal description of the algorithm is the following:

Compute the list of the length of matches at each position of the source string S.
Compute the maximum match length, L
for $l := L$ downto 1 do
  begin
  Find a maximum collection C of nonoverlapping matches of length l
  Select the elements of C for coding
  Eliminate the elements overlapping the matchings of C from the match lists
  end

Of course this parallel algorithm can be implemented on a normal computer architecture too. The only problem is that this algorithm is an off-line one in this form, since we must know the total source string to compute the list of match lengths. To avoid this problem Nagumo et al., defined the on-line version of the above algorithm [52], which can be effective for conventional computer architectures. They use a lookahead of length $\frac{1}{2}(lmax - 1)(lmax - 2) + lmax$. The basis of the algorithm is the same as that of the Stauffer and Hirschberg algorithm, but they use a modified selection and elimination procedure. Their algorithm is the following:

$p := 1$;
while $p \leq $ Length(S) do
  begin
  for $l := 1$ to $lmax$ do
    begin
    let d_l be the distance of the closest match of length l to p;
    if $d_l > \frac{1}{2}(lmax - 1)(lmax - 2) + lmax$ then $d_l := \infty$;
    end
  $l := lmax$;
  $t := d_l$;
  while $d_l > 0$ do
    begin
    if $d_l + (l - 1) - 1 \geq t$ then $d_{l-1} := \infty$;
    else $t := d_{l-1}$;
    $l := l - 1$;
    end
  encode substring $S_i \ldots S_{i+l-1}$;
  $p := p + l$;
  end

The proof of the correctness of the algorithm is given in [52].

A variation of the above-mentioned longest fragment first parsing algorithm is when the remaining part of the record is compressed with an on-line algorithm (the LM heuristic can be chosen, for example). If the file has no record structure, we can consider a buffer, which always contains the actual part of the text (so we will talk about buffers instead of records). Now, before reading the next part of the file into the buffer, the algorithm always encodes the whole buffer. We will refer to a whole buffer-coding procedure as a *step*. We will denote this algorithm by LFF$_{LM}$. To avoid double indexing, instead of $R_{LFF_{LM}}(D)$ we write $R_{LFF}(LM, D)$.

As one can see algorithm LFF$_{LM}$ gives up the strict on-line property, because it looks ahead in the buffer, getting more information about its content. One has a feeling that the more information about the text to be compressed, the better worst-case behavior of a good algorithm. This suggests to us that this algorithm behaves better than the on-line ones. The experimental results showed [59] that the LFF-type algorithms give a compression ratio better than that of the longest matching or the differential greedy heuristics. In the paper [8] we presented some theoretical results on the behavior of the algorithm LFF$_{LM}$. Here we mention the most important theorems.

THEOREM 28 [8]. *Let D be a* **general** *dictionary. Then*

$$R_{LFF}(LM, D) = \frac{(t-1)lmax - (t-3)}{t} \frac{cmax}{cmin}.$$

THEOREM 29 [8]. *Let D be a* **nonlengthening** *dictionary. Then*

$$R_{LFF}(LM, D) = \begin{cases} \frac{(t-1)lmax - (t-3)}{t} \frac{cmax}{cmin} & \text{if } cmax \leq Bt \\ T & \text{if } Bt < cmax < 2Bt \\ \frac{(t-1)lmax\, Bt + cmax}{t\, cmin} & \text{if } 2Bt \leq cmax, \end{cases}$$

where

$$T = \frac{(t-1)lmax\, Bt - t(2Bt - cmax) + 4Bt - cmax}{t\, cmin}.$$

THEOREM 30 [8]. *Let D be a* **prefix** *dictionary. Then*

$$R_{LFF}(LM, D) = \frac{(t-1)lmax - (t-3)}{t} \frac{cmax}{cmin}.$$

THEOREM 31 [8]. *Let D be a* **suffix** *dictionary. Then*

$$R_{LFF}(LM, D) = \begin{cases} \left(1 + \frac{2(lmax - 1)}{t}\right) \frac{cmax}{cmin} & \text{if } t \geq 3 \\ \left(\frac{lmax + 1}{2}\right) \frac{cmax}{cmin} & \text{if } t = 2. \end{cases}$$

B. Adaptive Methods

1. The LZ77 Algorithm

This algorithm maintains a window and a lookahead buffer. The window contains some characters backwards, i.e., the last coded characters. The lookeahed buffer contains some characters to be coded. The pointers of the LZ77 method point to the occurrences of the substrings from the lookeahed buffer to the occurrences of the same substring in the window. Since it is possible that only one character match can be found, the output can contain individual characters too. Denote the length of the lookeahed buffer by L_S. The algorithm can work on a buffer of length n, which contains always a part of the source text. The length of the window is $n - L_S$. In the current step we find the longest substring in the windows that match for the lookahead buffer starting from the beginning. The two matching substrings can overlap, but they cannot be the same. This match is coded by a triplet $\langle i, j, a \rangle$, where i is the index of the found substring in the window, j is its length, and a is the first character that has not matched. Then we move the buffer right on the text by $j + 1$ characters and continue the process. Putting the character a to (i, j) ensures the working of the algorithm in the case when we have no match at all.

More formally the algorithm works as follows. First we introduce some notations. Let n be the length of the applied buffer, A is the basic alphabet, and S is the source string. As mentioned before denote by L_S the length of the window and by n the length of the buffer, and let $L_C = 1 + \lceil \log(n - L_S) \rceil + \lceil \log(L_S) \rceil$, where the basis of the logarithm is $|A|$. L_C means the fixed length of the codes, which are created from alphabet A too. Let $S(1, j)$ be a real prefix of the string S, and let i, $1 \leq i \leq j$ a given integer. Let $L(i) = \max \{l : S(i, i + l - 1) = S(j + 1, j + l)\}$, and $L(p) = \max_{1 \leq i \leq j} L(i)$. We refer to the $S(j + 1, j + L(p))$ string as a reproducible extension of $S(1, j)$ into S. It can be seen that $S(j + 1, j + L(p))$ is the longest substring among the matching substrings of S beginning in $S(1, j)$.

EXAMPLE 9. Let $S = 01101101$ and $j = 4$. Then $L(1) = 0, L(2) = 4$, $L(3) = 1, L(4) = 0$. So $S(4 + 1, 4 + 4) = 1101$ is the reproducible extension of $S(1, 4)$ into S with $p = 2$.

The LZ77 algorithm [71] is as follows:

- Let $B_1 = 0^{n-L_s} S(1, L_S)$, where 0^{n-L_s} means the all-zero string of length $n - L_S$, and let $i = 1$.
- Consider the buffer B_i, $i \geq 1$, and let $S_i = B_i(n - L_S + 1, n - L_S + l_i)$, where the length of $l_i - 1$ prefix of S_i is the reproducible extension of $B_i(1, n - L_S)$ into $B_i(1, n - 1)$.
- Let p_i be the index of the above reproducible extension. Then the code word C_i for S_i is $C_i = C_{i1} C_{i2} C_{i3}$, where, C_{i1} and C_{i2} are $|A|$-radix representations of $p_i - 1$, and $l_i - 1$ respectively, while C_{i3} is the last symbol of S_i.
- Modify the contents of B_i that we leave the first l_i, and load the next l_i characters. Increase the value of i by 1, and continue the algorithm with Step 2.

EXAMPLE 10. Consider the following binary series ($|A| = 2$)

$$S = 0010101101101111011011100$$

$$L_S = 8, n = 16 \Rightarrow L_C = 1 + \log_2(16 - 8) + \log_2 8 = 6.$$

$B_1 = 00000000|00101011 \qquad p_1 = 8, l_1 = 3 \qquad C_1 = 111|010|1$
$B_2 = 00000001|01011011 \qquad p_2 = 7, l_2 = 5 \qquad C_2 = 101|100|1$
$B_3 = 00010101|10110111 \qquad p_3 = 4, l_3 = 4 \qquad C_3 = 011|011|1$

TABLE 4 Dictionary for Example 11

Dictionary	0	01	010	1	10	11	011	101	1011	100
Number	1	2	3	4	5	6	7	8	9	10
Output	0, 0	1, 1	2, 0	0, 1	4, 0	4, 1	2, 1	5, 1	8, 1	5, 0

EXAMPLE 11. Consider again the same binary series as in the case of the LZ77 algorithm

$$S = 0010101101101111011011100.$$

Table 4 shows the dictionary generated by LZ77 for S. Figure 7 illustrates the dictionary trie.

Decoding of an LZ78 compressed code starts with an empty dictionary. In each step a pair of codes is read from the input. This code word refers to an existing dictionary string or if it is zero, it contains only one symbol. Then this new string is added to the dictionary in the same way as in the encoding process. This way during the decoding the dictionary changes the same way as in the case of encoding. So we get the proper source string.

4. The LZW Algorithm

LZW is a similar modification of LZ78 as LZSS is of LZ77. It was proposed by Welch [68]. The algorithm modifies as follows:

- Let $B_1 = S(1, n)$, where n is the length of the buffer and let $i = 1$. Construct a dictionary D that contains all the characters of the input alphabet using the trie data structure.
- Consider the buffer $B_i, i \geq 1$, and let $S_i = B_i(1, l_i)$, where the length of $l_i - 1$ prefix of S_i is the longest prefix of $B_i(1, n-1)$ which matches a dictionary item in D. Add S_i to the dictionary D with a new node index.

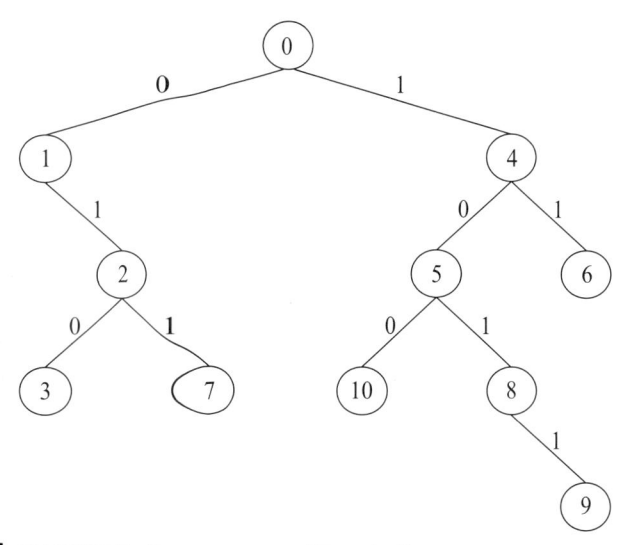

FIGURE 7 Dictionary trie of Example 11.

Decoding of the compressed texts is easy. The a
the same way as during the encoding process.
$C_i = C_{i1}C_{i2}C_{i3}$ is read from the input. Then the $
and C_{i2}, and the character C_{i3} is sent to the outpu

Ziv and Lempel proved [71] that using algo
as good a result as using another special adaptive
the buffer is large enough. The problem is that i
the buffer, then searching becomes slow and the
can overcome this problem by using special data
quire more storage. Detailed information can be
in [10].

2. The LZSS Algorithm

The LZSS algorithm is a slight modification o
by Bell [9]. It eliminates some redundant inforrr
example in the case if there is no match in the win
a pointer if it is not longer than the length of th(
LZ77 modifies as follows, all the other steps being

- Let p_i be the index of the given reproc
C_{i1}, C_{i2}, C_{i3}, where C_{i1} and C_{i2} are $|A|$-radix re[
$l_i - 1$ respectively, while C_{i3} is the last symbol of
$C_i = C_{i1}C_{i2}$: else let $C_i = C_{i3}$ and $l_i = 1$.

3. The LZ78 Algorithm

The LZ78 algorithm is a simple variation of
vious that the size of the window gives some restr
in the coded part of the text. LZ78 eliminates tl
all the previous matchings in an explicit dictiona
can contain many words, if we compress a large
good data structure for making searching efficient
the trie contains the number of the represented d
is used for coding. Because of this representatior
dictionary requires only creating a new child fro
longest match. Formally the LZ78 algorithm is as

- Let $B_1 = S(1, n)$, where n is the length of tl
  Construct an empty dictionary D using the
- Consider the buffer $B_i, i \geq 1$, and let $S_i = $,
  $l_i - 1$ prefix of S_i is the longest prefix of B_i
  dictionary item in D. Add S_i to the dictiona
- Let p_i be the index of the above matching (
  if there is no match at all. Then the code w
  where C_{i1} is some representation of p_i, whi
- Modify the contents of B_i that we leave the
  characters. Increase the value of i by 1, and
  Step 2.

- Let p_i be the index of the above matching dictionary item. Then the code word C_i for S_i is some representation of p_i.
- Modify the contents of B_i that we leave the first $l_i - 1$, and load the next $l_i - 1$ characters. Increase the value of i by 1, and continue the algorithm with Step 2.

V. UNIVERSAL CODING

The Noiseless Coding Theorem gives a relation between the cost of the optimal prefix code and the entropy of the given source. It is always assumed that the probability distribution is explicitly given. Unfortunately sometimes this distribution is unknown or it is impossible to determine the characteristics of the source. A natural question is whether it is possible to find such a code that is optimal for any probability distribution instead of a particular one. This kind of code is called universal.

Many authors investigated the problem of finding universal codes [24,25,42,69]. Universal codes can be classified into two classes. Some kind of universal coding techniques are similar to statistical coding methods; i.e., they order a code to the characters of the basic alphabet. Other codes are based on dictionary technique. A "statistical" universal code was introduced by Elias [24,25]. The idea of the Elias codes is to represent each source string by integers and then order to each integer a code. This code is given explicitly and can be applied for each message. Calculating the code of an integer x consists of two phases. First we consider the binary representation of x, prefaced by $\lfloor \lg x \rfloor$ zeros. The binary value of x is expressed in the least possible bits, so it begins with 1. Therefore the prefix property is held. In the second phase this code is calculated for the integer $\lfloor \lg x \rfloor + 1$. Then the binary value of x is appended to this code without the leading 1. This way the resulting code word has length $\lfloor \lg x \rfloor + 2\lfloor \lg(1 + \lfloor \lg x \rfloor) \rfloor + 1$. Elias proved the following theorem:

THEOREM 32 [25]. *The Elias code is asymptotically optimal, i.e.,*

$$\lim_{n \to \infty} \frac{E(n)}{H(F)} = 1,$$

where $E(n)$ is the expected code word length for a source word of length n divided by n and $H(F)$ is the entropy of the source.

Table 5 summarizes the Elias codes of the first 8 integers.

EXAMPLE 12. Consider an alphabet that contains four symbols a, b, c, d. Let S be *bbaaadccd*. The Elias code of S can be constructed as

Symbol	Frequency	Rank	Code word
a	3	1	1
b	3	2	0100
c	2	3	0101
d	2	4	01100

The complete coded form of S is

010001001110110001010101011100.

TABLE 5   Elias Codes

Number	Code
1	1
2	0100
3	0101
4	01100
5	01101
6	01110
7	01111
8	00100000

A similar universal coding technique was found by Apostolico and Fraenkel [5]. The method is based on the well-known standard Fibonacci numbers, which are defined by the recurrence

$$F_0 = 1,$$
$$F_1 = 1,$$
$$F_k = F_{k-1} + F_{k-2} \text{ for } k \geq 2.$$

The series looks like this: 1, 1, 2, 3, 5, 8, 13, 21, 34, 55, ...

It is also known that each positive integer I has a unique Fibonacci representation in the form

$$I = \sum_{i=0}^{k} d_i F_i,$$

where $d_i \in \{0, 1\}, k \leq I$.

Using this representation the Fibonacci code of the integer I can be easily defined. Simply we consider the Fibonacci representation of I with the binary symbols $d_0, d_1, \ldots, d_k$. To get the Fibonacci code of I we reserve the order of the symbols in the representation and append 1 to it. It can be seen that the code is a prefix, because it terminates with two consecutive 1's, which cannot appear anywhere else in a code word because of the property of the Fibonacci representations. Table 6 summarizes the Fibonacci codes of the first 8 integers.

EXAMPLE 13. Consider again the same alphabet and source word as in Example 12. The Fibonacci code of S can be constructed as

Symbol	Frequency	Rank	Codeword
a	3	1	11
b	3	2	011
c	2	3	0011
d	2	4	1011

The complete coded form of S is

$$01101111111101100110011011.$$

TABLE 6 Fibonacci Codes

Number	Fibonacci representation	Fibonacci code
1	1	11
2	10	011
3	100	0011
4	101	1011
5	1000	00011
6	1001	10011
7	1010	01011
8	10000	000011

It is also interesting to find a very simple code that still has the universal property. One of the simplistic universal code was discovered by Neuhoff and Shields [53]. The idea of the encoding is based on a simple dictionary coding technique. The dictionary is formed where the original source is divided into some blocks of a given length l. The dictionary will contain these l-blocks as source words. The code word of a given dictionary source word is its location in the dictionary using fixed-length encoding. To get universal code all possible block lengths should be investigated and the one that produces the shortest code should be chosen. Denote the length of this shortest code by L_n for a source word of length n. Neuhoff and Shields proved the following theorem.

THEOREM 33 [53]. *For any stationary, ergodic source F with alphabet A and entropy $H(F)$ the encoding rate $\frac{L_n}{n}$ converges to entropy $H(F)$ in both expected value and almost surely as $n \to \infty$.*

This theorem shows that a real simple algorithm can be universal. It is a nice theoretical result. Unfortunately it is complicated to use this algorithm in practice, because finding the optimal block length is very time consuming. Especially for long source strings—when one can get a good approximation of the entropy—many different block lengths should be tried to get the best one.

VI. SPECIAL METHODS

A. Run Length Encoding

Run length encoding is one of the simplest compression methods. It tries out some special properties of the source string. Run length encoding replaces the sequences of repeated characters by their lengths. For a given sequence a character and the length of the sequence is stored as the code. This algorithm is effective, if the data contains long sequences of repeated symbols. For example, some multimedia data like images can have these characteristics. The method is particularly useful when the size of the alphabet is small. It was shown before that in this case classical methods, like Huffman coding, can work poorly, while run length encoding can give good compression, depending on the structure of the data.

EXAMPLE 14. Consider an image whose alphabet contains only 0 and 1 values. 0 means white (w) pixel and 1 means black (b). A part of the image and its run length code would look like this:

Data	Run length code
00000000111111111100000000000011111111	$w8b11w11b10$

B. Algorithms Based on List Update

The idea of applying list update methods for data compression originates from Bentley *et al.* [11]. They showed how a list update algorithm can be used for compression. List update or self-organizing sequential search problem is widely investigated in combinatorial optimization. We are given a set of items $x_1, \ldots, x_n$. The items are unsorted and stored in a linked list. We are also given a sequence of requests. Each request specifies an item from $x_1, \ldots, x_n$. The algorithm must serve each request by accessing the give item. This can be done with linear search, and in the case of the serving item x_i has a cost of i. After the search the requested item may be moved to another location in the list at no extra cost. This may decrease the cost of the subsequent requests. The goal is to serve the given sequence of requests at the smallest total cost. Different kinds of on-line algorithms exist to solve this problem. A well-known one is the Move to Front (MTF) method. This algorithm moves the requested item to the front of the list. Bentley *et al.* proposed the following idea to use MTF for compressing data. Both the encoder and the decoder have a list of symbols. The encoder is given a source string S of these symbols. For each character of S the encoder searches for the character in its list and outputs the position where the symbol is found. After that the encoder updates its list using MTF. When the decoder receives the compressed message, for each code i it reads the symbol at the position i, outputs it, and update the list using MTF strategy.

EXAMPLE 15. Consider an alphabet that contains four symbols a, b, c, d. Let S be *bbaaadccd*. MTF coding works as follows

Character	MTF code	List
		a, b, c, d
b	2	b, a, c, d
b	1	b, a, c, d
a	2	a, b, c, d
a	1	a, b, c, d
b	2	b, a, c, d
d	4	d, b, c, a
c	3	c, d, b, a
c	1	c, d, b, a
d	2	d, c, b, a

Bentley *et al.* showed that for arbitrary probabilities of symbols, the expected number of bits to encode one symbol of S using MTF coding is linear in the entropy of the source.

Recently Albers and Mitzenmacher [2] presented a new list update algorithm that can be applied for data compression. They called it the Timestamp ($TS(0)$) algorithm. $TS(0)$ inserts the requested item x in front of the first item in the list that has been requested at most once since the last request to x. If x has not been requested so far, it leaves the position of x unchanged. Albers and Mitzenmacher proved that for $TS(0)$ the expected number of bits to encode one symbol of a source string is also linear in the entropy of the source, and the constant is slightly better than that of the MTF coding.

C. Special Codes and Data Types

Sometimes using some special coding can compress data. For example, English text can be coded where each character is represented by a 7-bit ASCII code. This technique is widely used to save storage. Binary coded decimal (BCD) is a way of storing integers. Using this, four bits represent each digit. This way we can store 100 different numbers in one byte. Some other similar techniques for saving space also exist, see [10] for details.

VII. CONCLUSIONS

In this chapter we gave a review of the most important data compression techniques and some issues of the theories behind them. In the first part of the chapter we presented some classical information theoretical theorems. These results give the basis of many data compression methods, especially for statistical algorithms. The methods in the chapter can be divided into four groups. These are statistical coding, dictionary coding, universal coding, and some special techniques. Statistical coding methods assume *a priori* knowledge of some statistical characteristics of the data to be compressed. This information is usually the relative frequency of the symbols of the data. The most well-known methods and the corresponding theory were presented in the chapter. Dictionary coding uses a completely different idea. In this case fragments of the data are substituted with some code words ordered to these fragments by a given dictionary. The dictionary can be static or can change dynamically during the coding process. We presented many theoretical results for different static dictionary algorithms. Classical methods were also given in the chapter. Universal coding is useful if we do not have any information on the characteristics of the source data. So it is possible that they give worse results than some statistical methods. Some simple universal coding methods were also described. Finally we gave some well-known special methods. These techniques can be efficiently applied for data with special properties.

REFERENCES

1. Abramson, N. *Information Theory and Coding*. McGraw-Hill, New York, 1963.
2. Albers, S., and Mitzenmacher, M. Average case analyses of list update algorithms with application to data compression. *Algorithmica* 21: 312–329, 1998.
3. Aho, A. V., and Corasick, M. J. Efficient string matching: An aid to bibliographic search. *Commun. ACM* 18(6): 333–340, 1975.
4. Angluin, D., and Smith, C. H. Inductive inference: Theory and methods. *Comput. Surveys* 15(3): 237–269, 1983.

5. Apostolico, A., and Fraenkel, A. S. Robust transmission of unbounded strings using Fibonacci representations. Tech Rep. CS85-14, Department of Applied Mathematics, Weizmann Institute of Science, Rehovot, 1985.
6. Békési, J., Galambos, G., Pferschy, U., and Woeginger G. J. Greedy algorithms for on-line data compression. *J. Algorithms* 25: 274–289, 1997.
7. Békési, J., Galambos, G., Pferschy, U., and Woeginger G. J. The fractional greedy algorithm for on-line data compression. *Computing* 56(1): 29–46, 1996.
8. Békési, J., Galambos, G., and Raita, T. Longest fragment first algorithms for data compression. In *New Trends in Mathematical Programming* (Eds.: F. Gianessi, T. Rapcsák. and S. Komlósi, Eds.), pp. 13–28. Kluwer Academic Dordrecht, The Netherlands, 1998.
9. Bell, T. C. Better OPM/L text compression. *IEEE Trans. Commun.* 34(12): 1176–1182, 1986.
10. Bell, T. C., Cleary, G., and Witten, I. H. *Text Compression*. Prentice–Hall, Englewood Cliffs, NJ, 1990.
11. Bentley, J. L., Sleator, D. S., Tarjan, R. E., and Wei, V. K. A locally adaptive data compression scheme. *Commun. ACM* 29: 320–330, 1986.
12. Bookstein, A., and Klein, S. T. Is Huffman coding dead? *Computing* 50(4): 279–296, 1993.
13. Buro, M. On the maximum length of Huffman codes. *Inform. Process. Lett.* 45: 219–223, 1993.
14. Cameron, R. D. Source encoding using syntactic information source models, LCCR Technical Report 86-7. Simon Fraser University, Burnaby, BC, Canada.
15. Capocelli, R. M., Giancarlo, R., and Taneja, I. J. Bounds on the redundancy of Huffman codes. *IEEE Trans. Inform. Theory* 32(6): 854–857, 1986.
16. Capocelli, R. M., and De Santis, A. Tight upper bounds on the redundancy of Huffman codes. *IEEE Trans. Inform. Theory* 35(5): 1084–1091, 1989.
17. Capocelli, R. M., and De Santis, A. New bounds on the redundancy of Huffman codes. *IEEE Trans. Inform. Theory* 37(4): 1095–1104, 1991.
18. Cheng, J.-F., Dolinar, S., Effros, M., and McEliece, R. Data expansion with Huffman codes. In *Proc. of ISIT'95*, pp. 325–332, 1995.
19. Chung, K. Efficient Huffman decoding. *Inform. Process. Lett.* 61: 97–99, 1997.
20. Cormack, G. V., and Horspool, R. N. Algorithms for adaptive Huffman. codes. *Inform. Process. Lett.* 18: 159–166, 1987.
21. Cormack, G. V., and Horspool, R. N. Data compression using dynamic Markov modelling. *Computer J.* 30: 541–550, 1987.
22. Cot, N. *Characterization and Design of Optimal Prefix Code*. Ph. D. Thesis, Computer Science Department, Stanford University, 1977.
23. De Prisco, R., and De Santis, A. A new bound for the data expansion of Huffman codes. *IEEE Trans. Inform. Theory* 43(6): 2028–2032, 1997.
24. Elias, P. Universal code word sets and representations of the integere. *IEEE Trans. Inform. Theory* 2: 194–203, 1975.
25. Elias, P. Interval and recency rank source coding: Two on-line adaptive variable-length schemes. *IEEE Trans. Inform. Theory* 33(1): 3–10, 1987.
26. Faller, N. An adaptive system for data compression. In *Conference Record of Seventh IEEE Asilomar Conference on Circuits and Systems*, pp. 593–597, 1973.
27. Fano, R. *Transmission of Information*. M.I.T. Press, Cambridge, MA, 1949.
28. Gallager, R. *Information Theory and Reliable Communication*. Wiley, New York, 1968.
29. Gallager, R. Variations on a theme by Huffman. *IEEE Trans. Inform. Theory* 24(6): 668–674, 1978.
30. Gilbert, E. N. Codes based on inaccurate source probabilities. *IEEE Trans. Inform. Theory* 17(3): 304–314, 1971.
31. Gonzalez-Smith, M., and Storer, J. Parallel algorithms for data compression. *J. Assoc. Comput. Mach.* 32: 344–373, 1985.
32. Guazzo, M. A general minimum-redundancy source-coding algorithm. *IEEE Trans. Inform. Theory* 26(1): 15–25, 1980.
33. Hamming, R. *Coding and Information Theory*. Prentice–Hall, Englewood Cliffs, NJ, 1980.
34. Hashemian, R. Memory efficient and high-speed search Huffman coding. *IEEE Trans. Commun.* 43: 2576–2581, 1995.

35. Huffman, D. A method for the construction of minimum-redundancy codes. In *Proc. Inst. Electr. Electron. Engineers* **40**(9): 1098–1101, 1952.
36. Jones, D. W. Application of splay trees to data compression. *Commun. ACM* **3**: 280–291, 1988.
37. Johnsen, O. On the redundancy of binary Huffman codes. *IEEE Trans. Inform. Theory* **26**(2): 220–222, 1980.
38. Karp, R. M. Minimum-redundancy coding for the discrete noisless channel. *IRE Trans. Inform. Theory* **7**: 27–39, 1961.
39. Katajainen, J., Pentonnen, N., and Teuhola, J. Syntax-directed compression of program files. *Software-Practice Exper.* **16**(3): 269–276, 1986.
40. Katajainen, J., and Raita, T. An approximation algorithm for space-optimal encoding of a text. *Computer J.* **32**(3): 228–237, 1989.
41. Katajainen, J., and Raita, T. An analysis of the longest matching and the greedy heuristic in text encoding. *J. Assoc. Comput. Mach.* **39**: 281–294, 1992.
42. Kieffer, J. C. A survey of the theory of source coding. *IEEE Trans. Inform. Theory* **39**: 1473–1490, 1993.
43. Knuth, D. E. Dynamic Huffman coding. *J. Algorithms* **6**: 163–180, 1985.
44. Kraft, L. G. A device for quantizing, grouping, and coding amplitude modulated pulses. M. Sc. Thesis, Department of Electrical, Engineering, MIT, Cambridge, MA, 1949.
45. Krause, R. M. Channels which transmit letters of unequal duration. *Inform. Control* **5**: 13–24, 1962.
46. Larmore, L. L., and Hirschberg, D. S. A fast algorithm for optimal length-limited codes, Technical report, Department of Information and Computer Science, University of California, Irvine, CA, 1990.
47. Lelewer, D. A., and Hirschberg, D. S. Data compression. Technical Report, 87-10, Department of Information and Computer Science. University of California, Irvine, CA, 1987.
48. Lovasz, L. Personal communication, 1995.
49. Mehlhorn, K. An efficient algorithm for constructing nearly optimal prefix codes. *IEEE Trans. Inform. Theory* **26**(5): 513–517, 1980.
50. Mukherjee, A., and Bassiouni, M. A. On-the fly Algorithms for data compresion. In *Proc. ACM/IEEE Fall Joint Computer Conference.* 1987.
51. Moffat, A. A data structure for arithmetic encoding on large alphabets. In *Proc. 11th. Australian Computer Science Conference.* Brisbane, Australia, pp. 309–317.
52. Nagumo, H., Lu, M., and Watson, K. On-line longest fragment first parsing algorithm. *Inform. Process. Lett.* **59**: 91–96, 1996.
53. Neuhoff, D. L., and Shields, P. C. Simplistic universal coding. *IEEE Trans. Inform. Theory* **44**(2): 778–781, 1998.
54. Rissanen, J. J. Generalized Kraft inequality and arithmetic coding. *IBM J. Res. Develop.* **20**(3): 198–203, 1976.
55. Rissanen, J. J., and Langdon, G. G. Arithmetic coding. *IBM J. Res. Develop.* **23**(2): 149–162, 1979.
56. Rissanen, J. J., and Langdon, G. G. Universal modeling and coding. *IEEE Trans. Inform. Theory* **27**(1): 12–23, 1981.
57. Rubin, F. Experiments in text file compression. *Commun. ACM* **19**(11): 617–623, 1976.
58. Shuegraf, E. J., and Heaps, H. S. Selection of equifrequent word fragments for information retrieval. *Inform. Storage Retrieval* **9**: 697–711, 1973.
59. Shuegraf, E. J., and Heaps, H. S. A comparision of algorithms for database compression by use of fragments as language elements. *Inform. Storage Retrieval* **10**: 309–319, 1974.
60. Shannon, C. E. A mathematical theory of communication. *Bell System Tech. J.* **27**: 398–403, 1948.
61. Stauffer, L. M., and Hirschberg, D. S. PRAM algorithms for static dictionary compression. In *Proc. 8th International Parallel Processing Symposium*, pp. 344–348, 1994.
62. Teng, S. H. The construction of Huffman-equevalent prefix code in NC. *ACM SIGACT News* **18**: 54–61, 1987.
63. Teuhola, J., and Raita, T. Arithmetic coding into fixed-length code-words. *IEEE Trans. Inform. Theory* **40**(1): 219–223, 1994.

64. Vitter, J. S. Design and analysis of dynamic Huffman coding. *J. Assoc. Comput. Mach.* **34**: 825–845, 1987.
65. Wagner, R. Common phrases and minimum-space text storage. *Commun. ACM* **16**(3): 148–152, 1973.
66. Wagner, R. An algorithm for extracting phrases in a space optimal fashion. *Commun. ACM* **16**(3): 183–185, 1973.
67. Weyland, N., and Puckett, P. Optimal binary models for the Gaussian source of fixed precision numbers. Technical Report, Mitre Corporation, Bedford, MA, 1986.
68. Welch, T. A. A technique for high-performance data compression. *IEEE Computer* **17**(6): 8–19, 1984.
69. Willems, F. M. J. Universal data compression and repetition times. *IEEE Trans. Inform. Theory* **35**: 54–58, 1989.
70. Witten, I. H., Neal, R., and Cleary, J. G. Arithmetic coding for data compression. *Commun. ACM* **30**(6): 520–540, 1987.
71. Ziv, J., and Lempel, A. An universal algorithm for sequential data compression. *IEEE Trans. Inform. Theory* **23**(3): 337–343, 1977.
72. Ziv, J., and Lempel, A. Compression of individual sequences via variable-rate coding. *IEEE Trans. Inform. Theory* **24**(5): 530–536, 1978.

8
GEOMETRIC HASHING AND ITS APPLICATIONS

GILL BAREQUET

The Technion—Israel Institute of Technology, Haifa 32000, Israel

I. INTRODUCTION 277
II. MODEL-BASED OBJECT RECOGNITION 278
III. PRINCIPLES OF GEOMETRIC HASHING 279
IV. EXAMPLES 281
V. IMPLEMENTATION ISSUES 284
    A. Footprint Quality and Matching Parameter 284
    B. Rehashing 284
VI. APPLICATIONS 284
    A. Molecular Biology 285
    B. Medical Imaging 286
    C. Other Applications 286
    REFERENCES 286

I. INTRODUCTION

The *Geometric Hashing* technique was introduced, about a decade ago, as an efficient method for object recognition in computer vision. Since then it has been applied in many other fields, e.g., in medical imaging, molecular biology, and computer-aided design. The underlying idea of Geometric Hashing is using a database for storing pieces of information (features) of known geometric objects, in such a way that will allow a fast recognition of an unknown query object.

The main advantage of this technique is its ability to perform *partial* matching between geometric objects, e.g., for recognizing objects in an image which are partially occluded or have undergone some transformation. It does not depend on the existence of any particular predefined features in the matched objects. It is usually very easy to implement, and it performs fast and accurately.

The Geometric Hashing technique is an indexing-based approach, where local features of objects are encoded and stored in a database. Such approaches are now widely recognized as the method of choice for implementing reliable recognition systems that handle large model databases.

II. MODEL-BASED OBJECT RECOGNITION

As mentioned above, the Geometric Hashing technique was first introduced in the context of model-based object recognition. Object recognition is an important and extensively studied problem in robotics applications of computer vision, including robot task and motion planning, and automatic image understanding and learning. Given a 2- or 3-dimensional image of a scene, we wish to identify in it certain types of objects (which may be only partially visible), and for each identified object to determine its position and orientation in the scene. Many approaches were developed for object recognition. These include *pose clustering* [27] (also known as *transformation clustering* and *generalized Hough transform* [1,22]), *subgraph isomorphism* [7], *alignment* [18], *iterative closest point* [9], and many *indexing* techniques (including Geometric Hashing). There is an enormously extensive literature on this subject. See, for example, the two comprehensive surveys given by Besl and Jain [8] and by Chin and Dyer [11]. One of the basic approaches to this problem is *model-based* object recognition. In order to identify objects that participate in a given scene, this approach assumes some prior knowledge about them, already stored efficiently in a *model database*. This technique first applies a "learning" process, in which the model objects are analyzed and preprocessed, which enables us to later perform the recognition task on-line, and usually very fast. The typical running time of the recognition step does not depend on the number of stored objects and on their complexities, but only on the complexity of the given scene (under some assumptions about the performance of the database, as detailed below).

The matching between a given image and a known (already processed) model is carried out by comparing their *features*. The database contains for each preprocessed model a set of features encoded by some function, which is *invariant* under the class of transformations by which the model objects are assumed to be placed in the scene. Such typical classes include translations, rigid motions, rigid motions and scalings, and affine or perspective transformations. In order to identify the query model, its features are encoded by the same function and compared to the contents of the database. A database model matches the query model if they have a sufficiently large number of features in common and if these corresponding features match each other under the same transformation. Many recognition systems use encoding functions that are invariant under rotation and translation, since they aim to identify objects subject to rigid motions, but, as just noted, other classes of transformations may also be considered.

The recognition task usually requires the ability to perform only a partial matching between objects. This is either because only portions of the objects may match or, more typically, because the query object may be partially occluded in a composite scene. In addition, the recognition system is usually expected to tolerate some amount of noise, either because the input image is obtained with some inaccuracy or because the objects to be matched are only similar but not identical to those in the model database, or simply because the encoding function is not a one-to-one mapping.

A major contribution to automatic object recognition was made by the *partial curve matching* technique, which was first suggested by Kalvin *et al.* [19]

and by Schwartz and Sharir [26]. This technique, which uses the Geometric Hashing method, originally solved the curve matching problem in the plane, under the restrictive assumption that one curve is a proper subcurve of the other one, namely: Given two curves in the plane, such that one is a (slight deformation of a) proper subcurve of the other, find the translation and rotation of the subcurve that yields the best least-squares fit to the appropriate portion of the longer curve.

This technique was extended (by removing the curve-containment restriction) and used in computer vision for automatic identification of partially obscured objects in two or three dimensions. The Geometric Hashing technique was applied [17,20,21,28] in various ways for identifying partial curve matches between an input scene boundary and a preprocessed set of known object boundaries. This was used for the determination of the objects participating in the scene, and the computation of the position and orientation of each such object.

III. PRINCIPLES OF GEOMETRIC HASHING

Geometric Hashing is a general model-based recognition technique that can be applied in any dimension under different classes of transformations. It identifies efficiently partial matches between objects in a given scene and objects stored in a model library. In a nutshell, the method consists of two steps. In the first off-line step features of some given model objects are analyzed, encoded by some transformation-invariant function, and stored in a database (usually an efficient hashing table). In the second step, a query object is analyzed on-line, and the database is scanned for locating features of the model objects that match (or are similar to) those of the query object. Such matching features suggest partial matches between the query object and the model objects, and also the respective geometric transformation between them. A voting scheme is then applied for identifying candidate partial matches between the query object and some of the model objects (and the respective transformations).

There are three basic aspects to the Geometric Hashing technique:

1. Representation of the object features using transformation invariants, to allow recognition of an object subject to any allowed transformation;
2. Storage of these invariants in a hashing table to allow efficient retrieval, which is (nearly) independent of the complexity of the model database; and
3. Robust matching scheme that guarantees reliable recognition even with relatively small overlap and in the presence of considerable noise.

The original variant of this technique aimed to find partial matches between curves in the plane. We first describe the technique in this context. We assume that some collection of "known" curves is preprocessed and stored in a database, and that the actual task is to find matches between *portions* of a composite query curve and portions of the curves stored in the database, subject to a rigid motion in the plane.

In the preprocessing step, features of all the curves are generated, encoded, and stored in a database. Each curve is scanned and *footprints* are generated at equally spaced points along the curve. Each point is labeled by its sequential number (proportional to the arclength) along the curve. The footprint is chosen so that it is invariant under a rigid motion of the curve. A typical (though certainly not exclusive) choice of a footprint is the second derivative (with respect to arclength) of the curve function; that is, the *change* in the direction of the tangent line to the curve at each point. Each such footprint is used as a key to a hashing table, where we record the curve and the label of the point along the curve at which this footprint was generated. The (expected) time and space complexity of the preprocessing step is linear in the total number of sample points on the curves stored in the database. Since the processing of each curve is independent of the others, the given curves can be processed in parallel. Moreover, adding new curves to the database (or deleting curves from it) can always be performed without recomputing the entire hashing table. The construction of the database is performed off-line before the actual matching.

In the recognition step, the query curve is scanned and footprints are computed at equally spaced points, with the same discretization parameter as for the preprocessed curves. For each such footprint we locate the appropriate entry in the hashing table, and retrieve all the pairs (curve,label) stored in it. Each such pair contributes one vote for the model curve and for the relative shift between this curve and the query curve. The shift is simply the difference between the labels of the matched points. That is, if the footprint of the ith sample point of the query curve is close enough to the footprint of the jth point of model curve c, then we add one vote to the curve c with the relative shift $j - i$. In order to tolerate small deviations in the footprints, we do not fetch from the hashing table only the entry with the same footprints as that of the point along the query curve, but also entries within some small neighborhood of the footprint. A commonly used implementation of this process is by range-searching (see, e.g., [23, p. 69] or [10]). The major assumption on which this voting mechanism relies is that real matches between long portions of curves result in a large number of footprint similarities (and hence votes) between the appropriate model and query curves, with almost identical shifts. By the end of the voting process we identify those (curve,shift) pairs that got most of the votes, and for each such pair we determine the approximate endpoints of the matched portions of the model and the query curves, under this shift. It is then straightforward to compute the rigid transformation between the two curves, with accuracy that increases with the length of the matched portions. The running time of the matching step is, on the average, linear in the number of sample points generated along the query curve. This is based on the assumptions that on the average each access to the hashing table requires constant time, and that the output of the corresponding range-searching queries has constant size. Thus, the expected running time of this step does not depend on the number of curves stored in the database and on the total number of points on the curves.

Many generalizations and applications of the Geometric Hashing technique have appeared in the literature. These include different choices of the allowed transformations, specific domains in which the technique is used (e.g., locating an object in a raster image, registration of medical images, molecule docking),

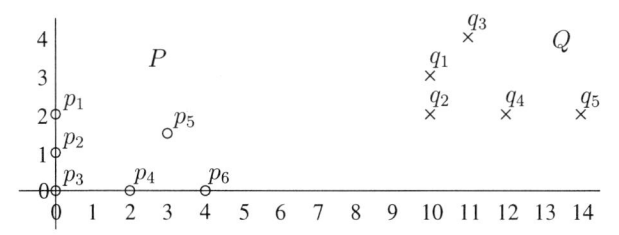

FIGURE 1 Two point sets.

and generalizations to higher dimensions. We note that in most cases the key to success is defining a good footprint system (in the sense detailed above), so that the "correct" solutions manifest themselves by sufficiently many correct votes. In practice, every application of the Geometric Hashing technique has its own special footprint setting, which strongly depends on the nature of the problem in question.

IV. EXAMPLES

Let us illustrate the course of Geometric Hashing by a simple example of matching the two planar point sets shown in Fig. 1. The two sets, denoted by P and Q, contain six and five points, respectively.

In the first matching experiment we allow only translations, and we assume the availability of only the point coordinates. Here every pair of matched points, one of each set, defines uniquely the translation that maps P to Q. (Specifically, if the point $p \in P$ matches the point $q \in Q$, then the sought translation is simply $\vec{q} - \vec{p}$.) Thus the matched feature is a point, and in the absence of any additional information, each pair of points (p, q) (where $p \in P$ and $q \in Q$) contributes one vote for the translation $\vec{q} - \vec{p}$. (In situations where we trust some of the matching pairs, we can weigh the votes.) The resulting voting table, which is also a detailed description of the Minkowski difference between the sets Q and P (denoted as $Q \ominus P$), is shown in Fig. 2. Indeed, the "correct" translation (10,2) received the largest number of votes (4). This is because four pairs of points, one of each set (namely, (p_2, q_1), (p_3, q_2), (p_4, q_4), and (p_6, q_5)) casted votes for this translation. All the other 26 votes were (luckily) spread in the voting table so that no other translation received four or more votes. Geometric Hashing is thus a viable method when the number of "correct" votes (compared to a

4		1		1		1		
3	1		2		1	1		
2	1	1	2		4	1	2	1
1		1		1	2	1	1	1
0					1		1	1
	6	7	8	9	10	11	12	13	14

FIGURE 2 Voting table for $Q \ominus P$.

usually much higher number of "incorrect" votes) is sufficient for identifying the sought transformation, or at least for including it in the first few candidate solutions which receive the largest numbers of votes. The leading candidates are then transferred to a secondary validation process, which applies other methods for determining whether a candidate solution is correct.

In the second matching experiment we allow translations and rotations between the two sets. Formally, the set P is assumed to have undergone a rotation by some angle θ around the origin $(0, 0)$, followed by some translation $t = (t_x, t_y)$, so as to form the set Q. Note that in this experiment the scaling of the Euclidean plane is not allowed. A natural choice of the matched feature is an *ordered pair* of points (in the same set). For each ordered pair of points (p_{i_1}, p_{i_2}) (where $p_{i_1}, p_{i_2} \in P$, $1 \leq i_1, i_2 \leq 6$, and $i_1 \neq i_2$), and for each ordered pair of points (q_{j_1}, q_{j_2}) (where $q_{j_1}, q_{j_2} \in Q$, $1 \leq j_1, j_2 \leq 5$, and $j_1 \neq j_2$), we first check whether the lengths of the line segments defined by the two pairs of points are similar. For practical reasons (noisy input data, approximate matching, etc.) we tolerate some deviation between the two segment lengths. Namely, we check whether $||\overline{p_{i_1} p_{i_2}}| - |\overline{q_{j_1} q_{j_2}}|| \leq \varepsilon$, where ε is some tuning parameter of the algorithm, usually specified by the user. (This parameter represents the user's *a priori* estimation of the maximum matching error between the sets P and Q.) If the two lengths are not identical (or not approximately the same), then no rotation and translation can map the first pair of points to the second pair. In such case we proceed to checking the next match between two pairs of points. However, in case the two lengths are similar, we compute the unique rotation and translation that realize the match between the two pairs. Denote the point coordinates by $p_{i_1} = (x_{i_1}, y_{i_1})$, $p_{i_2} = (x_{i_2}, y_{i_2})$, $q_{j_1} = (x_{j_1}, y_{j_1})$, and $q_{j_2} = (x_{j_2}, y_{j_2})$. A simple calculation shows that the sought transformation is

$$\theta = \arctan((y_{j_2} - y_{j_1})/(x_{j_2} - x_{j_1})) - \arctan((y_{i_2} - y_{i_1})/(x_{i_2} - x_{i_1})),$$
$$t_x = x_{j_1} - \cos\theta \cdot x_{i_1} + \sin\theta \cdot y_{i_1}, \quad \text{and}$$
$$t_y = y_{j_1} - \sin\theta \cdot x_{i_1} - \cos\theta \cdot y_{i_1}.$$

Obviously every match between (p_{i_1}, p_{i_2}) and (q_{j_1}, q_{j_2}) is also reflected by the match between (p_{i_2}, p_{i_1}) and (q_{j_2}, q_{j_1}). We avoid this redundancy by requiring that $j_1 < j_2$. In this example there are 30 matches between pairs of points, where each pair consists of two points of the same set. The two leading transformations in the voting table are

1. 6 votes: $\theta = 0°, t = (10, 2)$;
2. 3 votes: $\theta = 180°, t = (14, 2)$.

All the other 21 candidate matches receive only one vote each. Fig. 3 shows the two best solutions by superimposing the transformed set P with the set Q.

So far in our matching experiments the points had no additional information attached to them (except, of course, their coordinates). Assume now that each point is also attributed by some value which we denote as its *footprint*. This value can be a number, a vector of numbers, color, or any other property that is invariant under the mapping that transformed P into Q. In this setting, matching pairs of features (one of each set) should have similar footprints (up to some predefined tolerance), while features that should not match should

GEOMETRIC HASHING AND ITS APPLICATIONS

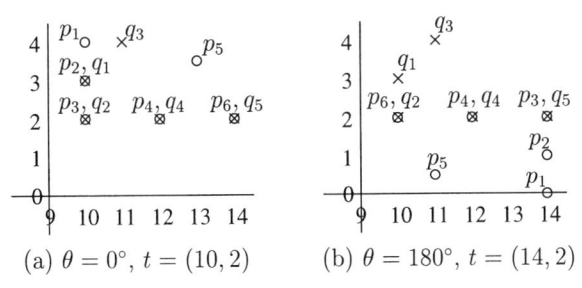

(a) $\theta = 0°$, $t = (10, 2)$ (b) $\theta = 180°$, $t = (14, 2)$

FIGURE 3 Matching by rotating and translating.

have significantly different footprints. This assumption allows us to significantly speed up the matching process by storing each set in a database (usually a hashing table) whose keys are the footprints. As noted above, the database implementation should allow not only fetching the entry (or entries) that match a given key, but also fetching all the entries whose keys are close to the given key up to some specified tolerance. This is usually achieved by implementing a data structure that allows range-searching queries. In our example it suffices to store only the set P in a database. For matching under translation only, each point $q \in Q$ (or, rather, its footprint) is used as a key for a range-searching query in the database that contains the set P. Each point $p \in P$ returned by the query then casts a vote for $\vec{q} - \vec{p}$ in the voting table, and the matching proceeds as described above.

Refer again to the matching experiment in which we allowed rotations and translations. In this experiment the matched feature was a *pair* of points. Assuming that each set contains n points, each set has $O(n^2)$ pairs and we now potentially have $O(n^4)$ candidate matches. An alternative used in many Geometric Hashing works (e.g., [14]) is to use every pair of points as a *basis* of a coordinate system, to specify the coordinates of all the other points of the same set with respect to that system, and to store all the points in the database in a redundant manner, so that each point is specified in terms of all the bases in which it does not take part. The matching feature in this variant is a single point: points are matched according to their basis-defined coordinates. The information given by the match (namely, the two bases—one of each set, and the translation between the two matched points) is enough for casting a vote for a unique rotation and a unique translation. Asymptotically we do here the same amount of work. Each point appears (redundantly) $O(n)$ times in the database, so the number of stored points is now $O(n^2)$. Then the matching step considers every pair of points, one of each database, giving us a total of $O(n^4)$ work.

The same ideas work for higher dimensions. In a 3-dimensional space, for example, we can consider triples of points. For every pair of congruent triangles, one defined by three points of the first set and the other defined by three points of the other set, we cast a vote for the transformation that maps the first triple to the second triple. Alternatively, we can have every three noncollinear points define a basis for a coordinate system and redundantly represent each point by its coordinates with respect to all the bases. In the matching step each pair of points, together with their respective coordinates according to some basis, casts a vote for the appropriate transformation. In both methods we may use footprints that depend on the application for pruning the matched pairs of features.

V. IMPLEMENTATION ISSUES

A. Footprint Quality and Matching Parameter

The success of the Geometric Hashing technique crucially relies on the "descriptiveness" of the footprint system. That is, we expect features that should match to have similar footprints, and expect features that should not match to have footprints that differ significantly enough. In practice, the amount of incorrect votes usually dominates the amount of correct votes, but when the distribution of the incorrect votes does not have too-high random peaks, the correct votes still exhibit an "accumulation point" in the voting table, which suggests the correct solution for the matching problem.

As mentioned earlier, the running time of the matching step is, on average, linear in the total number of features in the two sets. This is based on the assumptions that on average each access to the hashing table requires constant time, and that the output of the corresponding queries has constant size. This is due to the nature of hashing and does not assume anything about the input to the algorithm. Nevertheless, it requires a reasonable choice of the proximity parameter ε, which should yield on average a constant number of output points for each range-searching query. Improper choice of ε, say, equal to the size of the entire set, will result in a running time that is quadratic in the complexity of the input.

B. Rehashing

Even when the footprint quality is satisfactory, it is desirable to have the distribution of footprints (in the space of invariants) as uniform as possible. This is for optimizing the performance of the hashing table. A highly nonuniform distribution interferes with the balance of the hashing bins that store the footprints, while the most occupied bin determines the worst-case performance of the hashing table. When the probability density function of the footprints is known, one can transform the input point coordinates so as to make the *expected* distribution of footprints uniform (see Figs. 5a and 6a of [29, p. 16]. If the rehashing function is chosen carefully, the new hashing table can have the same number of bins as that of the original table.

VI. APPLICATIONS

As noted earlier, the first application of Geometric Hashing was for partial curve matching in the plane [19,26]. This application was later extended in [17,20, 21,28] for identifying objects participating in a scene. (In fact the silhouettes of the objects and of the scene were used to solve a 2-dimensional matching problem.) In addition to these object-recognition problems, Geometric Hashing was used in several other domains, some of which are detailed below.

A. Molecular Biology

Geometric Hashing was used to solve surface and volume matching problems that arise in molecular biology. One such typical problem is to find a "docking" of two molecules (or subunits of the same molecule). Here one seeks a rigid motion of one molecule relative to the other, which creates a good geometric fit between large portions of the molecule boundaries, so that the molecules themselves remain disjoint; that is, one seeks surface matching and volume complementarity. (In practice, the docking of molecules may depend also on a good chemical/electrical fit between the atoms participating in the docking. The purely geometric statement of the problem is thus only an approximation of the problem, but it is appropriate in many cases.) Another typical problem is to detect similar 3-dimensional structural motifs in macromolecules. Here one also seeks a rigid motion that creates a good fit between large portions of the molecule surfaces, but now one wants their volumes to overlap near this fit. The standard representation of a molecule is just a list of its atoms and their spatial positions. Consequently, a major difficulty in studying molecule docking and structural motifs is in the definition and computation of the molecule boundary. We do not elaborate here on available techniques for overcoming this difficulty.

First attempts to solve the molecule docking problem, which are based on energy minimization, were only partially successful. Geometric approaches were much more successful, but (at least the earlier ones) were not reliable enough, and suffered from unacceptedly long computation time. Some geometric methods use clique-search algorithms in graphs; other methods perform a brute-force search over all the discretized 3-dimensional rotations, while using a secondary method for identifying the appropriate translation. Traditional methods for detecting structural motifs in proteins usually employ string-matching algorithms. A survey of these methods, most of which are based on dynamic programming, is found in [25].

A major contribution to the problems of detecting structural motifs and of molecule docking was achieved by applying Geometric Hashing. In this application, the method proceeds by assigning footprints to the molecule atoms, then by matching the footprints and by voting for the relative transformation (rigid motion) of one molecule relative to the other. For the motif detection, Nussinov and Wolfson [24] define the footprint of each atom as its coordinates in systems defined by any three noncollinear atoms (thus each atom has $O(n^3)$ footprints, where n is the number of atoms in the molecule). Similar ideas are presented in [13]. Fischer *et al.* [14] take a similar approach for the molecule docking problem. In one variant, each pair of atoms defines a basis (whose length is the distance between the two atoms), and the footprint of every atom is defined as the distances from the atom to the endpoints of every basis, coupled with the length of the basis (thus each atom has $O(n^2)$ footprints). In another variant, the angles between the normal to the surface (at the candidate atom) and the normals at the endpoints of the basis, as well as a knob/hole label of the atom (obtained in a preprocessing step), are also considered. In all cases, the footprints are stored in a hashing table, which makes it possible to retrieve entries with some tolerance. Here this is needed not just because of the noisy footprints, but also because of the conformational changes that might occur in the molecule structures during the reaction between them.

B. Medical Imaging

The topic of medical image matching has attracted a lot of attention in the medical literature. The problem arises when complementary information about some organ is obtained by several imaging techniques, such as CT (computed tomography) and MRI (magnetic resonance imaging). The goal is to match (register) the various models of the same organ obtained by these methods, in order to obtain a single improved and more accurate model. Such a registration is needed because the orientations of the organ usually differ from one model to another.

Many methods, which are similar to the methods for object recognition, were proposed for the solution of this organ registration problem. These include, among many others, approximated least-squares fit between a small number of markers, singular-value decomposition for matching point pairs, high-order polynomials for a least-squares fit, "thin-plate spline" for registering intrinsic landmarks or extrinsic markers, parametric correspondence, chamfer maps, partial contour matching, moments and principal axes matching, and correlation functions. Detailed reviews of image-registration techniques are given in [6,12]. Geometric Hashing was also exploited for alignment of medical data by Barequet and Sharir [5] and by Guéziec et al. [16]. The former work matched 3-dimensional point sets (voxels), while the latter work registered 3-dimensional curves extracted from the data.

C. Other Applications

Geometric Hashing has been applied to other matching problems as well. Germain et al. [15] use this technique for matching real (human) fingerprints for noncriminal identification applications. Barequet and Sharir [2,3] apply Geometric Hashing to solve a computer-aided design problem, namely, for detecting and repairing defects in the boundary of a polyhedral object. These defects, usually caused by problems in CAD software, consist of small gaps bounded by edges that are incident to only one face of the model. Barequet and Sharir [4] apply a similar technique to the reconstruction of a three-dimensional surface (bounding a human organ) from a series of polygonal cross sections.

REFERENCES

1. Ballard, D. H. Generalizing the Hough transform to detect arbitrary shapes. *Pattern Recognit.* 13 (2): 111–122, 1981.
2. Barequet, G. Using geometric hashing to repair CAD objects. *IEEE Comput. Sci. Engrg.* 4 (4): 22–28, 1997.

3. Barequet, G. and Sharir, M. Filling gaps in the boundary of a polyhedron. *Comput. Aided Geom. Design* **12** (2): 207–229, 1995.
4. Barequet, G. and Sharir, M. Piecewise-linear interpolation between polygonal slices. *Comput. Vision Image Understanding*, **63** (2): 251–272, 1996.
5. Barequet, G. and Sharir, M. Partial surface and volume matching in three dimensions. *IEEE Trans. Pattern Anal. Mach. Intell.* **19** (9): 929–948, 1997.
6. Brown, L. G. A survey of image registration techniques. *ACM Comput. Surveys* **24**: 325–376, 1992.
7. Bolles, R. C. and Cain, R. A. Recognizing and locating partially visible objects: The local-feature-focus method. *Int. J. Robot. Res.* **1** (3): 637–643, 1982.
8. Besl, P. J. and Jain, R. C. Three-dimensional object recognition. *ACM Comput. Surveys* **17** (1): 75–154, 1985.
9. Besl, P. J. and McKay, N. D. A method for registration of 3-D shapes. *IEEE Trans. Pattern Anal. Mach. Intell.* **14** (2): 239–256, 1992.
10. Chazelle, B. A functional approach to data structures and its use in multidimensional searching. *SIAM J. Comput.* **17** (3): 427–462, 1988.
11. Chin, R. T. and Dyer, C.R. Model-based recognition in robot vision. *ACM Comput. Surveys* **18** (1): 67–108, 1986.
12. van der Elsen, P. A. Pol, E. J. D., and Viergever, M. A. Medical image matching—A review with classification. *IEEE Engrg. Med. Biol.* **12** (1): 26–39, 1993.
13. Fischer, D., Bachar, O., Nussinov, R., and Wolfson, H. J. An efficient computer vision based technique for detection of three dimensional structural motifs in proteins. *J. Biomolec. Structure Dynam.* **9**: 769–789, 1992.
14. Fischer, D., Norel, R., Nussinov, R., and Wolfson, H. J. 3-D docking of protein molecules. In *Proc. 4th Symp. on Combinatorial Pattern Matching*, Lecture Notes in Computer Science 684, pp. 20–34. Springer-Verlag, Berlin, 1993.
15. Germain, R. S., Califano, A., and Colville, S. Fingerprint matching using transformation parameter clustering. *IEEE Comput. Sci. Engrg.* **4** (4): 42–49, 1997.
16. Guéziec, A. P., Pennec, X., and Ayache, N. Medical image registration using geometric hashing. *IEEE Comput. Sci. Engrg.* **4** (4): 29–41, 1997.
17. Hong, J. and Wolfson, H. J. An improved model-based matching method using footprints. In *Proc. 9th Int. Conf. on Pattern Recognition*, Rome, Italy, November 1988, pp. 72–78.
18. Huttenlocher, D. P. and Ullman, S. Recognizing solid objects by alignment with an image. *Int. J. Comput. Vision* **5** (2): 195–212, 1990.
19. Kalvin, A., Schonberg, E., Schwartz, J. T., and Sharir, M. Two-dimensional, model based, boundary matching using footprints. *Int. J. Robot. Res.* **5** (4): 38–55, 1986.
20. Kishon, E., Hastie, T., and Wolfson, H. 3-D curve matching using splines. *J. Robot. Systems* **8** (6): 723–743, 1991.
21. Lamdan, Y., Schwartz, J. T., and Wolfson, H. J. Affine invariant model-based object recognition. *IEEE Trans. Robot. Automat.* **6** (5): 578–589, 1991.
22. Linnainmaa, S., Harwood, D., and Davis, L. S. Pose determination of a three-dimensional object using triangle pairs. *IEEE Trans. Pattern Anal. Mach. Intell.* **10** (5): 634–647, 1988.
23. Mehlhorn, K. *Data Structures and Algorithms 3: Multi-Dimensional Searching and Computational Geometry* (Brauer, W., Rozenberg, G., and Salomaa, A. Eds.). Springer-Verlag, Berlin, 1984.
24. Nussinov, R. and Wolfson, H. J. Efficient detection of three-dimensional structural motifs in biological macromolecules by computer vision techniques. *In Proc. Natl. Acad. Sci. USA* **88**: 10,495–10,499, 1991.
25. Sankoff, D. and Kruskal, J. B. *Time Warps, String Edits and Macromolecules*. Addison-Wesley, Reading, MA, 1983.
26. Schwartz, J.T. and Sharir, M. Identification of partially obscured objects in two and three dimensions by matching noisy characteristic curves. *Int. J. Robot. Res.* **6** (2): 29–44, 1987.
27. Stockman, G. Object recognition and localization via pose clustering. *Comput. Vision Graphics Image Process.* **40** (3): 361–387, 1987.
28. Wolfson, H. J. On curve matching. *IEEE Trans. Pattern Anal. Mach. Intell.* **12** (5): 483–489, 1990.
29. Wolfson, H. J. and Rigoutsos, I. Geometric hashing: An overview. *IEEE Comput. Sci. Engrg.* **4** (4): 10–21, 1997.

9
INTELLIGENT AND HEURISTIC APPROACHES AND TOOLS FOR THE TOPOLOGICAL DESIGN OF DATA COMMUNICATION NETWORKS

SAMUEL PIERRE

Mobile Computing and Networking Research Laboratory (LARIM), and Department of Computer Engineering, École Polytechnique de Montréal, Montréal, Quebec, Canada H3C 3A7

I. INTRODUCTION   289
II. BASIC CONCEPTS AND BACKGROUND   291
   A. Acronyms, Notation, and Basic Assumptions   291
   B. Definitions and Problem Statement   293
III. CHARACTERIZATION AND REPRESENTATION OF DATA COMMUNICATION NETWORKS   294
   A. Network Characterization   295
   B. Network Representation   297
   C. DESNET: An Example of a Design Tool   300
IV. INTELLIGENT AND HYBRID APPROACHES   305
   A. Basic Principle of the AI-Based Approach   305
   B. Basic Concepts and Background   306
   C. The Inductive Learning Module   307
   D. Numerical Applications with SIDRO   310
V. HEURISTIC APPROACHES   312
   A. Conventional Heuristics and Meta-heuristics   312
   B. Implementation of the Tabu Search Approach   315
   C. Numerical Applications with Heuristic Methods   317
   REFERENCES   325

I. INTRODUCTION

A typical data communication network essentially consists of a set of nodes representing workstations, switches, routers, and so on, linked to each other by means of communication links. As shown in Fig. 1, such a network is generally

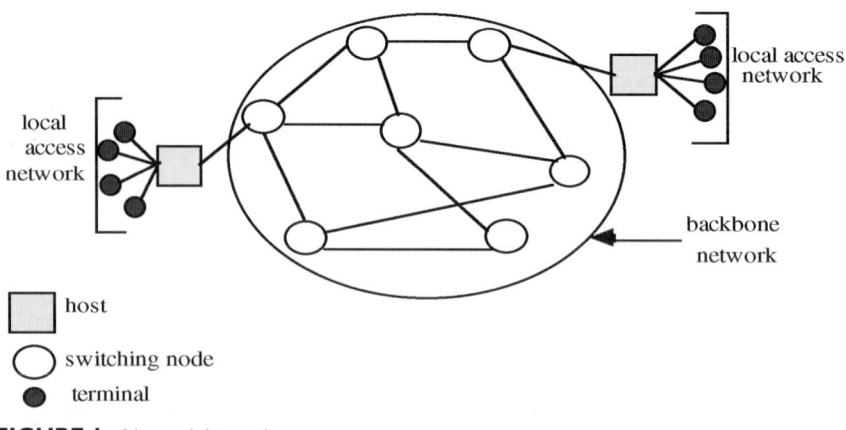

FIGURE 1 Network hierarchy.

considered as a hierarchical structure integrating two levels: the backbone network at the first level, and the local access networks at the second level. The backbone network is dedicated to the delivery of information from source to destination. The local access networks are typically centralized systems that essentially allow users to access hosts or local servers. In this chapter, the focus is on the backbone network design considered as a distributed network.

The topological design of data communication networks consists essentially of finding a network topology that satisfies at the lowest possible cost some constraints related to quality of service and reliability [6,9,12,19,28,29,46]. Traditionally formulated as an integer programming problem and for various reasons discussed and reported elsewhere [3,9–12,39,45], it is considered to be a very difficult optimization problem [20]. In fact, if n indicates the number of nodes, the maximum number of links is given by $n(n-1)/2$, and therefore the maximum number of topological configurations of n nodes is $2^{n(n-1)/2}$. For instance, if $n = 11$, the number of topological configurations that can be exhaustively explored is 3.603×10^{13}; at the generation speed of 10^6 configurations per second, the overall CPU time required for such an exploration is 1,142.46 years. Even by taking into account only the configuration aspect of this problem, the risk of combinatorial explosion is already obvious.

In order to facilitate its resolution, the topological design problem is usually divided into three subproblems: (1) topological configuration taking into account reliability aspects, (2) routing or flow assignment, and (3) capacity assignment [43]. Nevertheless, this division does not enable one to solve the overall problem in a reasonable CPU time. As a result, this problem is realistically solved by means of heuristic methods that attempt to reduce the search space of candidate topologies, even if that possibly leads to suboptimal solutions. Clearly, determining the optimal size of such a search space would be a compromise between the exploration time and the quality of the solution. This observation led many researchers to develop heuristic approaches leading to "good" solutions, instead of optimal solutions [35,37,40,45].

The range and the nature of the heuristics vary widely [17]. Some of them are inspired by formal optimization approaches [10,11]. Linear programming methods (without constraints involving integer variables) can take advantage of convexity; unfortunately this is not the case with integer programming methods, which are characterized by nonconvex solution spaces. The exploration of such spaces by local search methods leads to minima that may only be local. For that reason, over the past ten years, many researchers have opted for meta-heuristics such as simulated annealing, genetic algorithm, tabu search, and artificial neural networks, in order to solve network design problems by generalizing and improving conventional local search methods [23,24,32–35,38]. On the other hand, several other researchers, looking for solution efficiency, transparency, and user-friendliness have adopted artificial intelligence (AI) approaches, particularly knowledge-based systems [9,36,37,40]. Dutta and Mitra [9] have proposed a hybrid method that integrates both the algorithmic approach and a heuristic knowledge system. This method builds a solution by subdividing the network design problem into modules that can be individually solved by applying either optimization models or heuristic methods. Furthermore, it integrates the partial solutions to obtain a global solution of the design problem.

This chapter presents and analyzes some intelligent and heuristic approaches and tools that have been used for designing distributed data communication networks. Section II presents basic concepts and discusses related work and background. Section III analyzes network characterization and representation issues considered as fundamental aspects of network planning. Section IV studies some design approaches based on the artificial intelligence concepts of knowledge-based system and machine learning. Section V presents heuristic design appraoches, with a particular emphasis on tabu search and some comparisons with other meta-heuristics such as simulated annealing and genetic algorithms.

II. BASIC CONCEPTS AND BACKGROUND

The topological design problem of computer networks can be considered as part of the overall network planning. It consists of finding a network topology configuration that minimizes the total communication cost, taking into account some constraints such as delay and reliability. In this section, we first present some basic definition needed to formulate the problem, then discuss other approaches and related work.

A. Acronyms, Notation, and Basic Assumptions

Acronyms/Abbreviations

AI	Artificial intelligence
BXC	Branch X-change
CBE	Concave branch elimination
CS	Cut saturation
FD	Flow deviation
GA	Genetic algorithm
MENTOR	Mesh network topology optimization and routing

SA	Simulated annealing
TS	Tabu search
WAN	Wide-area network
MAN	Metropolitan-area network
LAN	Local-area network

Notation

G	A graph
N	Set of nodes of a graph
A	Set of edges of a graph
n	Number of nodes of a network
m	Number of links of a network
m_{max}	Maximum number of links
R	Diameter of the network, that is, the length of the longest of the shortest paths over all node pairs in the network
K	Connectivity degree of a network
C_k	Capacity of link k, that is, the maximum data rate in bits per second (bps) carried by this link
f_k	Flow of link k, that is, the effective data rate in bps on this link
U_k	Utilization of link k, that is, the ratio f_k/C_k
L_k	Length of the link k
L_{max}	Maximum Euclidean distance between any node pair of the network
$d(i)$	Incidence degree of a node i, that is, the number of links connected to it
d_G	Degree of a graph G, that is, the degree of the node having the smallest degree among all the nodes
$C = (C_k)$	link capacity vector
$f = (f_k)$	Link flow vector
γ_{ij}	Traffic (number of packets per second exchanged) between nodes i and j
γ	Total traffic in a network
$r_{aver} = \gamma/m_{max}$	Average traffic between all the node pairs
$I_{ij} = \gamma_{ij}/r_{aver}$	Index traffic of link (i, j)
Γ	Traffic matrix
T	Average packet delay in a network
T_{max}	Maximum acceptable delay
$T_n = T/T_{max}$	Normalized average delay
$d_k(C_k)$	Cost capacity function of link k
Variable unit cost	Cost in \$/month/km for a given link capacity
Fixed cost	Cost in \$/month for a given link capacity
CMD_{ij}	The most economical path between two nodes i and j

Assumptions

- Poisson distribution of the traffic between node pairs
- Exponential distribution of packet size with a mean of $1/\mu$ bits/packet

- Infinite nodal memory
- Independence and identical distribution of interarrival times
- Independence and identical distribution of transmission times on each link.

B. Definitions and Problem Statement

Quality of service in a data communication network is usually measured by the average packet delay T. Based on the set of assumptions of the previous section and according to Little's rules, the average packet delay can be expressed as [12,13]

$$T = \frac{1}{\gamma} \sum_{k=1}^{m} \frac{f_k}{C_k - f_k}. \tag{1}$$

The average delay T given by (1) must be less than or equal to the maximum acceptable delay $T_{\max}$.

Equation (1) does not take into account the propagation delay and the nodal processing time. These factors play a more important role in high-speed networks where it is unrealistic to neglect them. Furthermore, the validity of the previous assumptions (Section A) has been tested by simulation studies on a variety of applications [12]. Results confirm the robustness of the model. Thus, the average packet delay obtained under these assumptions is realistic for medium-speed packet-switched networks. However, such assumptions can be unrealistic if one is interested in estimating the delay of a particular packet or the delay distribution rather than just the average value.

The cost d_k of the link k is generally a function of the link length and capacity. Therefore, the total link cost D is given by

$$D = \sum_{k=1}^{m} d_k(C_k). \tag{2}$$

The techniques used to solve the problem of the capacity assignment essentially depends on the nature of the cost capacity functions $d_k(C_k)$, which can be linear, concave, or discrete [12]. In practice, the cost of the link k includes two components: a fixed part and a variable part which depends on the physical length L_k of this link:

$$d_k(C_k) = (\text{Variable unit cost})_k L_k + (\text{Fixed cost})_k. \tag{3}$$

Variable unit cost represents the price structure for leased communications links; the fixed cost refers to a constant cost associated with a given link and represents the cost of a modem, interface, or other piece of equipment used to connect this link to its end nodes.

The flow assignment consists of determining the average number of packets λ_k on each link k [43]. For this purpose, a routing policy that determines the route to be taken by packets between each source–destination pair is needed. Routing strategies are generally classified into fixed, adaptative, and optimal routing. In this chapter, for sake of simplicity, we adopt the fixed routing based on the Euclidean distance between nodes.

Given:

- the number of nodes n and their location (X_i, Y_i), with $i=1, 2, ..., n$
- the traffic requirements $\Gamma = (\gamma_{ij})$, with $i, j=1, 2, ..., n$ and $i \neq j$
- the capacity options and their costs
- the maximum acceptable delay T_{max} in (ms)
- the desired level of reliability (K-node-connectivity)

Minimize

the network cost D

Subject to:

- Network delay constraint: $T \leq T_{max}$
- Reliability constraint : K-node-connectivity
- Capacity constraint : $f \leq C$

Design variables:

- topological configuration
- routing strategy
- capacity assignment.

FIGURE 2 General formulation of the topological design problem.

The reliability of a data communication network depends on the availability and the reliability of their components. For this reason, it is necessary to evaluate the overall network reliability by taking into account in the design phase the possibility of link or node failures [18]. Many reliability measures have been proposed for computer communication networks. The most popular among these is the concept of K-connectivity, which integrates both arc-connectivity and node-connectivity [41]. A graph is said to be K-arc-connected if and only if all pairs of nodes are connected by at least K arc-disjoint paths. Similarly, a graph is said to be K-node-connected if and only if any node pair is connected by at least K node-disjoint paths. If C_a denotes the arc-connectivity degree and C_n the node-connectivity degree, it is obvious that $C_n \leq C_a \leq d_G$. As a result, for a strong topological design, node-connectivity appears to be more relevant than arc-connectivity for measuring network reliability as well as for providing a certain level of network survivability and fault-tolerance. For large networks with high failure rates, a high level of node-connectivity is required (3-connectivity and more) in order to ensure an adequate level of reliability. For smaller networks, 2-connectivity has been suggested as a reliable measure [12].

Various formulations of the topological design problem can be found in the literature [9–13,21,18]. Generally, they correspond to different choices of performance measures, design variable, and constraints. Common formulations search either to minimize the average packet delay given the network cost or to maximize the network throughput given the network cost and the admissible average delay [10]. This chapter adopts the general formulation shown in Fig. 2.

III. CHARACTERIZATION AND REPRESENTATION OF DATA COMMUNICATION NETWORKS

The network design problem raises three kinds of questions: What is the usefulness of designing a model for representing data communication networks? How could these models be used to improve the network performance? What degree of manoeuvrability must these models have? This section identifies the main characteristics of a typical data communication network, then analyzes some issues related to its representation, and finally presents some existing network representation or design tools.

A. Network Characterization

A data communication network is characterized by different structures, types, topologies, components, performance indexes, and management strategies. Regarding structures, one can distinguish between the distributed and centralized networks. In centralized networks, terminals or workstations are related to a single data source called a *server* through a variety of communication links. Conversely, distributed networks are characterized by the multiplicity of routes that link each source to a given destination.

Generally, three types of network should be distinguished: local-area network, metropolitan-area network, and wide-area network. A LAN is a local communication system connecting several computers, servers, and other network components; it makes possible high-speed data transfer (1 to 100 Mbps) through short distances, in small areas such as organizations, campuses, and firms. A MAN essentially serves a large city; it also regroups several computers with more or less reduced data throughput and makes it possible to link several enterprises in one city. WANs are used to connect several cities located at some tens of kilometers apart. Usually, the data throughput of a WAN is less than 100 Mbps.

The topology of a network informs on its configuration, that is, the way in which its nodes are linked to each other; it also indicates the capacity of each link in the network. If communication is established between two nodes through a direct link, one can speak of a point-to-point link; every network consisting of a point-to-point link is called a *point-to-point network*. Conversely, with a *multipoint link*, communication is rather broadcasted from one node to several nodes; every network consisting of multipoint links is a *multipoint network* or *general broadcasting network*.

Point-to-point networks can have a star, tree, ring, or mesh topology. In a star topology, all nodes are related by a point-to-point link to a common central node called the *star center*. All communications placed in this type of network must go through this node. In a tree topology, the network has a directory structure that is hierarchically structured. The principal node of this topology through which all applications pass is called a *tree root*. In this structure, the common link takes the form of a cable (with several branches) to which one or several stations are attached. In a ring topology, all the nodes are related to form a closed ring, which, in its turn, takes a point-to-point form. A mesh topology is formed by a number of links such that each node pair of the network is linked by more than one path. Generally, a mesh topology is used with WAN.

In multipoint networks, there are two types of topologies: the bus topologies and the ring topologies. In a bus topology, each network node is set linearly on a cable which constitutes a common physical link. The information is transmitted by any node through the entire bus in order to reach the other nodes of the network. In a ring configuration, all the nodes are set on a closed circuit formed by a series of point-to-point links. These nodes form a ring; the information within the ring is transmitted in one sense.

The main components of a network are nodes and links. The nodes represent more or less advanced units, which could be terminals, servers, computers, multiplexers, concentrators, switches, bridges, routers, or repeaters. Each of these units has its own attributes. In the framework of topological design, the most relevant factors are cost, capacity, availability, compatibility, and reliability [22].

The cost of a node includes purchasing and maintenance, as well as the cost of related software. The capacity of a node refers to the speed of its processor, the size of both programs and available memories. Availability is defined by the percentage of time during which a node is usable, or else, as the probability that a node could be available in a given instant. The compatibility of a node can be defined as the concordance between the types of traffic which the node manages and the types of links to which that node could be attached.

The reliability of a node is considered as the probability that it correctly functions under given conditions. This means that the node is not a subject of repair nor of any intervention other than that predicted in the technical manuals.

A link or a transmission support refers to a set of physical means put in place in order to propagate electromagnetic signals that correspond to messages exchanged between an emitter and a receiver. There exist several types of transmission support. Each type has its distinct physical features, the way it carries data, and its realm of use. Most known and used transmission supports are twisted pairs, coaxial cables, electromagnetic waves, fiber-optic, and satellite links.

Like the nodes, each type of link has its own characteristics, which are attributes that could be taken into account during the topological design process. The most important attributes are the following: length, capacity, cost, flow, delay, and utilization. These attributes have been defined in Section A (Notation) of Section II.

The most usual indexes for measuring the performance of a network are the following: response time, data throughput, stability, easiness of extension, information security, reliability, availability, and cost. Response time can be defined as the time delay between the emission of a message by a node and the receipt of an answer. An efficient data throughput is the useful average quality of information processed by a unit of time and evaluated under given conditions and time period.

The stability of a network refers to its capacity to absorb a realistic traffic pattern. It can be defined as the number of tasks that the system can perform and the time needed to process each of these tasks in different instants, while the network is functioning. For a given network, the easiness of extension represents the capacity of this network to accept new users, or its capacity to be modified without structural changes. Information security includes both the information protection that restricts users' access to a part of the system, and the notion of information integrity, which depends on the capacity of the system to alter or lose information.

The reliability of a network can be defined as its ability to continue functioning when some of its nodes or links fail. It is often linked to the notion of network connectivity [31,34]. The availability of a network refers to the probability that this network is usable during a period of time, given redundancies, breakdown detection, and repair procedures, as well as reconfiguration mechanisms.

Networks could assume several functions which could differ by their importance and use. Among these functions, one can mention routing, flow control, congestion control, configuration management, performance management, error and breakdown handling, security, and accounting information management. Figure 3 synthesizes the characteristics of data communication networks.

B. Network Representation

The purpose of the network representation is to find the most efficient way to model networks in order to make easier their design and analysis. To achieve this objective, the representation must be based on the use of data structures being sufficiently efficient (i.e., neither congested or complex) for minimizing the execution times or optimizing the data storage process. A good representation facilitates the implementation of both analysis and design algorithms [22].

There exist two types of representation: external and internal. The external representation of a network deals with aspects related to data display. In a design and analysis tool, external representation plays the important role of taking into account the data supplied by the user, controlling their integrity and organization, and storing in a manner that facilitates their use and update. At the level of this representation, the user specifies the number of nodes, the location of each node, the choice of links, and related characteristics as well as the traffic requirements. Internal representation has the purpose of facilitating the implementation of design and analysis algorithms. It also makes the latter efficient in terms of memory consumption and execution times.

Ag Rhissa *et al.* [1] describe two types of network representation: the inheritance tree and the content tree. The inheritance tree defines the hierarchical organization of the network's components and the administrative element included in these components. Such a representation can be transformed into an object structure whose route is a superclass that contains information regarding all the objects.

The content or instance tree defines the physical or logical relationships between the different elements of the network; it allows us to identify, in an unequivocal manner, an element from its positioning in the tree. This tree can also be transformed into an object structure and makes it possible to model the relationships between different objects in the form of an information management tree. The content tree essentially supplies information regarding the management of configurations [42].

Users still suffer from difficulties while they manipulate the design and representation models available in the marketplace. Their work is often constrained by the lack of flexibility of such models. Hence, it is necessary to provide for a generic representation model. By *generic model,* we refer to the capacity of representing a variety of types of networks and aspects related to their performance and management. Therefore, the following questions can be raised: What are the functions a representation model could offer to the user? What data structure could one use in order to be able to take into account all

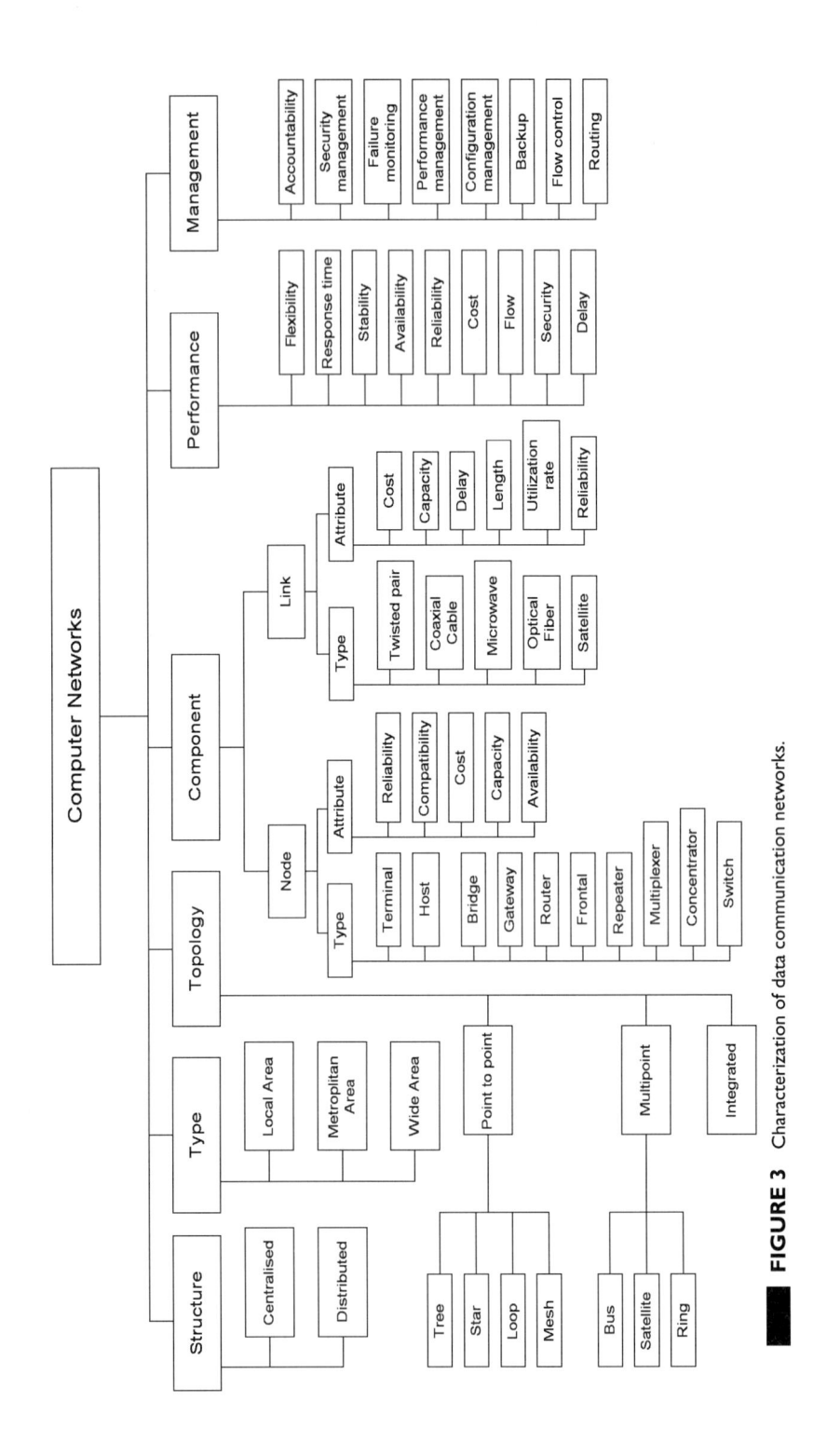

FIGURE 3 Characterization of data communication networks.

the aspects of a data communication network under design? How does one implement and validate such a model by taking into account the diversity of topologies, structures, and management mechanisms associated with the concept of a network?

The representation of networks is considered an important aspect of topological design. Most models and tools were rather devoted to the aspects of routing, evaluation, and optimization of performance. In these models, a network representation is often limited to capturing incomplete data and displaying the network in a graphical mode. Tools and models presented in this section are not contradictory to these observations.

Dutta and Mitra [9] have designed a hybrid tool that integrates formal models for specifying problems (Lagrangian formulation), and heuristic models for evaluating and optimizing network performance. This leads to the most needed flexibility in both the processing of data and the application of constraints. For this purpose, this tool first divides the network into a core part (Backbone) and several other access networks. After this procedure, the designer limits their work to the topological design of the backbone only. They consider as data the following items: the location of the nodes, traffic between each node pair, allowed maximum delay, reliability, and cost requirements. From this information, the tool decides the topological configuration, routing, flow, and capacity assignment. All this is done by taking into account the constraints of the problem.

In this approach, the network representation has been practically neglected for the benefit of other topological design aspects. This is explained by the fact that the objective of the designers was essentially the optimization of network performance. Therefore, the resulting tool lacks both universality and interactive capabilities.

AUTONET [2] is a tool for analyzing the performance of a WAN that interconnects local networks. It is among the few tools that pay special attention to network representation. In fact, AUTONET provides the users with sophisticated means to design networks and perform modifications and adjustments required at any moment. It also offers a user-friendly interface suitable for various levels of users. One of its inconveniences remains the fact that it is dedicated exclusively to the modeling and representation of WAN, without taking into account other types of networks. Thus, the local networks, which could be linked to WAN, are considered as forming a single entity, and therefore their specific characteristics are neglected. The other inconvenience is that the capture of data is essentially oriented in performance evaluation, which is not necessarily compatible with the requirements of network representation. As a result, these data are incomplete and insufficient for adequately representing networks.

COMNET III [7] is the latest version of a series of tools produced by the CACI Products Company. This tool simulates and analyzes the performance of telecommunication networks, and offers the advantage of modeling and representing all types of network. COMNET III also integrates sophisticated graphical display options, allowing users to represent networks with a greater flexibility. It is available to users of all levels, from beginners to experts. In terms of universality, COMNET III is certainly better than the other tools previously mentioned. However, like AUTONET, it has some inconveniences.

For instance, it could be improved by both introducing other representation modes than graphical representation, and by adding data control procedures and user-customized representations.

OPNET (Optimized Network Engineering Tools), produced by MIL3 [26], is a simulation and analysis tool that allows, among other things, the simulation of large networks and detailed modeling of related protocols. It integrates several characteristics such as the specification of graphical models, dynamic simulation based on events, integrated data analysis, and hierarchical and object modeling. The specification domain offers several editors that allow the user to specify graphically the different components of a network. It also supplies an editor for programming finite states and specification parameters. The simulation domain is a library of procedures that facilitates the processing of packets to be transmitted. Finally, the analysis domain supplies the users with several tools including those that collect, graphically represent, and analyze data.

C. DESNET: An Example of a Design Tool

DESNET (*des*ign of *net*work) is a design tool developed by Pierre and Gharbi [30] for personal computers in a Windows environment. It offers the users the possibility of processing several design aspects such as routing, flow and capacity assignment, and calculation of network's cost and delay. It also integrates data manipulation interfaces that are understandable and accessible by any user who has a minimum knowledge of topological design.

1. Description of Functions

DESNET provides the user with a large number of functions. Its flexibility and simplicity facilitate adding several functions without affecting the robustness and reliability of the system. For organization reasons, we have decided to regroup the functions offered by DESNET in three classes according to their type, extent, and domains of application. We have defined a class for the definition of networks, another to represent them, and another for their handling.

Network Definition

This class of functions regroups all the applications that act as a single entity. The functions allow the user to select the network to be processed and permit the introduction of a new network in the system, or the deletion of an existing network.

Network Representation

The class of functions that describe network representation has the role of representing the network and its components in several manners, according to the user's needs. The user has the choice among a graphical representation, a matrix, or a list.

Network Management

This is the most important class of functions offered by DESNET. As shown in Fig. 4, this class regroups the most specific functions of the tool. Certain functions of this class are accessible at any time, when a network is open or

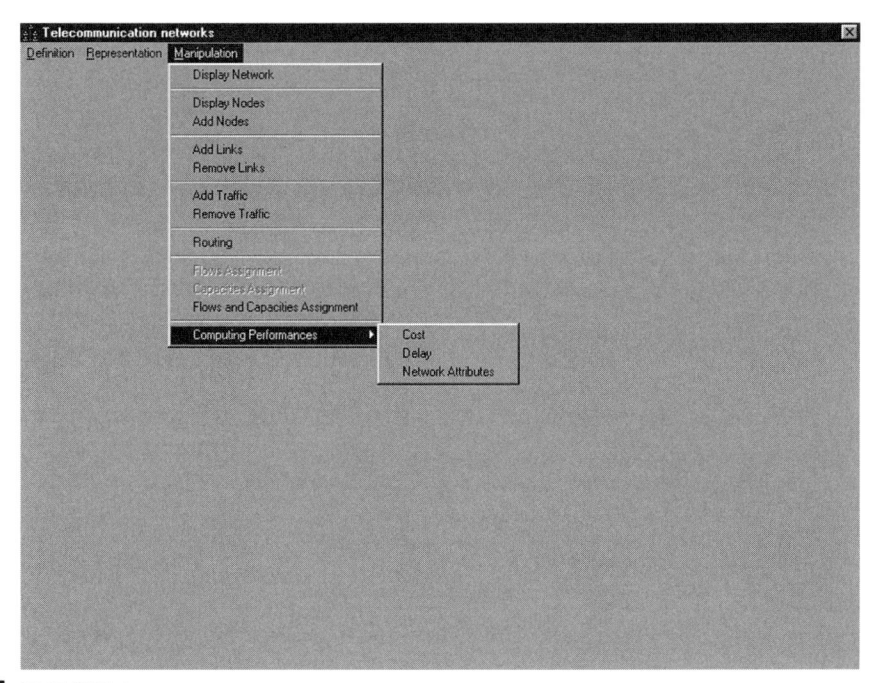

TOPOLOGICAL DESIGN OF DATA COMMUNICATION NETWORKS
301

FIGURE 4 Network manipulation.

captured: this is the case of those related to network, nodes, links, and traffic. There are also certain other functions that are accessible once the routing is calculated: this is the case of flow and capacity assignment, and calculation of network performance.

2. Example of DESNET's Working

Let us consider a network that has 9 nodes representing 8 American cities and 12 links [22]. The coordinates of the nodes are represented in Table 1; they have been fixed according to a reference point on the upper left part of the screen. As shown in Fig. 5, this network is a WAN with a mesh topology. After the capture of data related to the network and its topological configuration, we have started to capture the network's nodes. Figure 6 illustrates the capture of the first node (NYK); one should note the presence of the *principal node* domain, reserved to a network configured as a star or a tree. In both cases, it is important for the system to know the main node of the star and the root of the tree. Because our network has a mesh configuration, this field is automatically disactivated by the system.

TABLE 1 Cartesian Coordinates of the 8 Nodes [22]

NODE	NYK	LSA	CHI	DAL	BAL	SFO	MIA	DEN
Abscissa	92	12	64	56	86	2	99	36
Ordinate	12	98	26	90	25	90	89	61

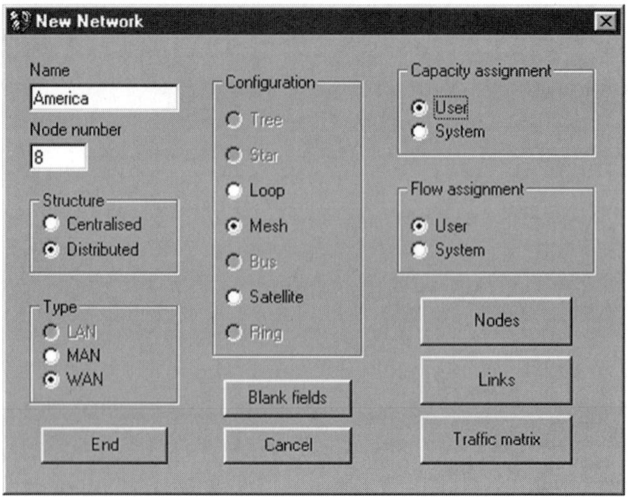

FIGURE 5 Data capture of network features and topological configuration.

Figure 7 represents the screen that captures a link. One should note on this screen that the domain *Cost* is not activated, because the cost of a link is calculated automatically and should be captured by the user. Similarly, for the nodes, DESNET does allow the user to capture the same link twice. After the capture of nodes and links, the user has the following choices: to capture the traffic, to confirm the capture, or to quit the system. For this example, we have chosen the capture of the traffic matrix. We have supposed that the traffic matrix is uniform with a constant value of 5 packets/s; the average size of packets is equal to 1000 bits. Figure 8 represents the capture of traffic between the nodes NYK and BAL.

Having confirmed the capture of these data, we can then access the data processing part. Figure 9 shows the graphical representation of this network. The numbers that appear beside the links represent their length in kilometers.

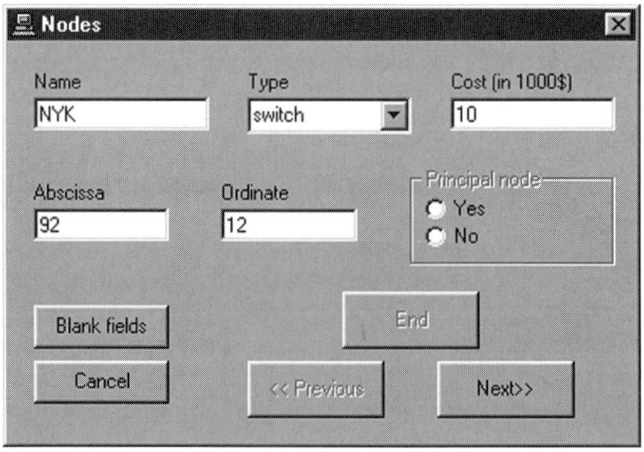

FIGURE 6 Data capture of the first node.

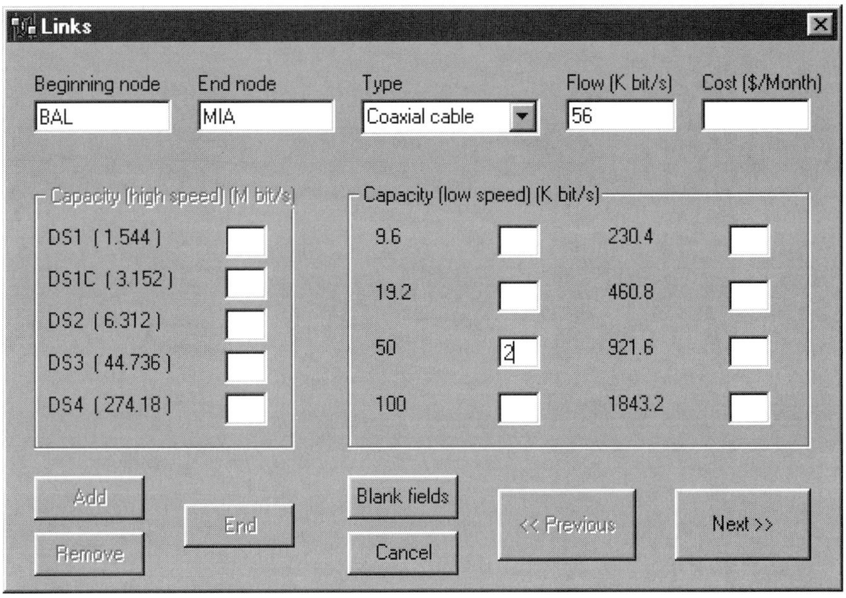

TOPOLOGICAL DESIGN OF DATA COMMUNICATION NETWORKS 303

FIGURE 7 Data capture of the link BAL–MIA.

Furthermore, we have added to this network two new links called SEA and CANADA5. The node SEA has 5 and 20 as coordinates, while the coordinates of CANADA5 are 45 and 15. During the addition of one or several nodes, DESNET allows the user to choose the network's new name and to determine exactly the number of nodes needing to be added. The addition of a node is realized exactly in the same manner to that of the capture a node.

To link two new nodes added to an existing network, we have decided to add four links, which are in this case the links between SEA and SFO, SEA and CHI, SEA and CANADA5, and CANADA5 and NYK. As shown in Fig. 10, the addition of a link is considered a data capture. In effect, all control operations regarding the network's connectivity and integrity of data used by DESNET during the capture of links are also applicable upon the addition. The user has

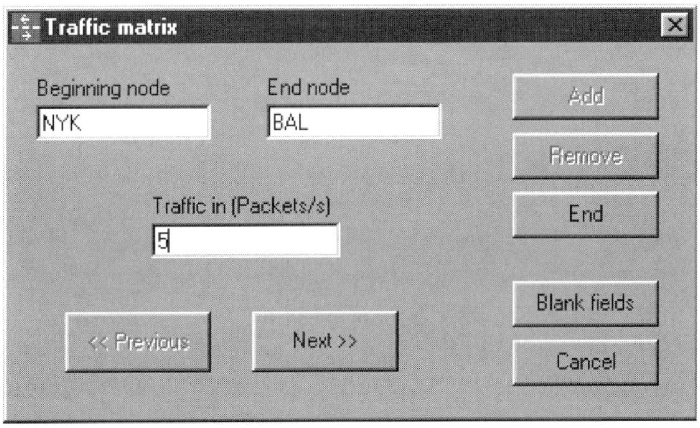

FIGURE 8 Data capture of the traffic between NYK and BAL.

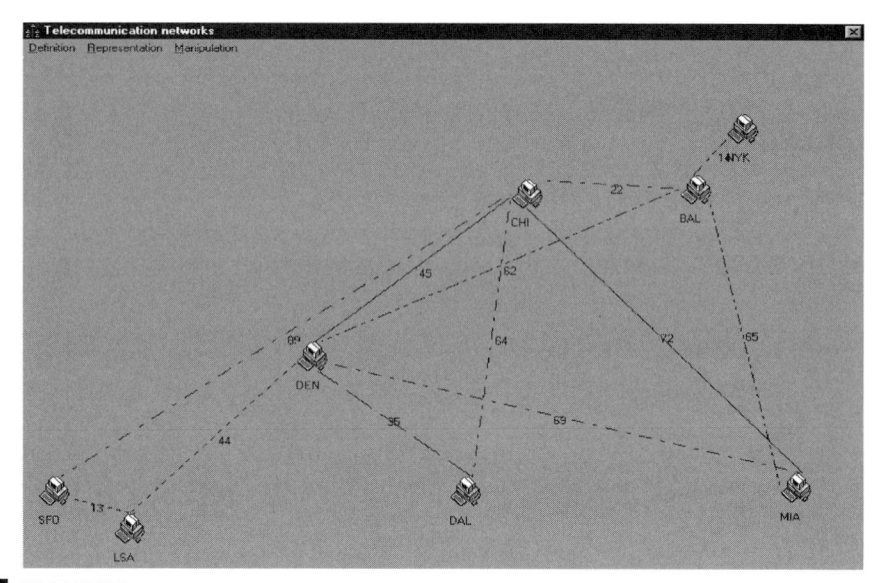

FIGURE 9 Graphical representation of the network.

the right to add as many links as she/he likes, provided that the maximum number of links m_{max} is not exceeded. For the current example, there are a maximum of 45 links.

After adding the nodes, it is convenient to add the traffic between these new nodes and the remaining network nodes. In order to uniformly maintain the traffic matrix, the traffic between each new node pair is maintained at 5 packets/s; the average size of packets is still 1000 bits. Figure 11 represents the network obtained after the addition of SEA and CANADA5 nodes. The new network contains 10 nodes and 16 links.

FIGURE 10 Addition of a link between SEA and CHI.

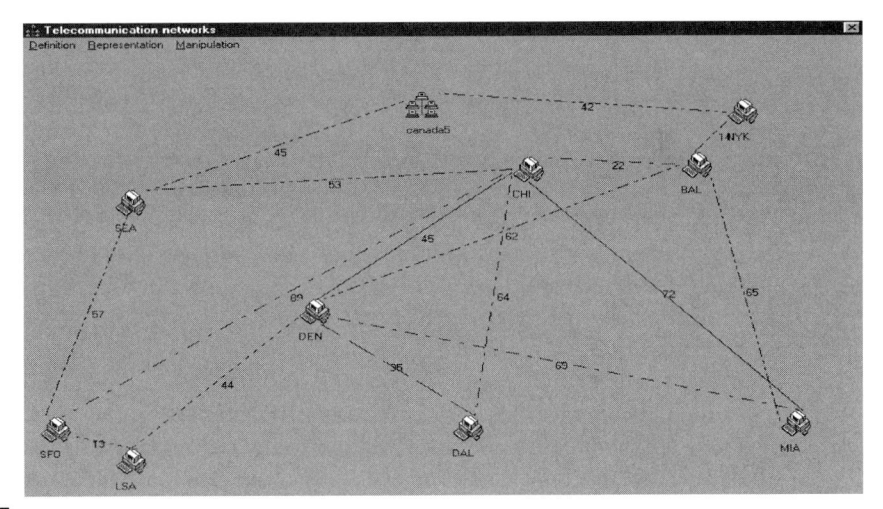

TOPOLOGICAL DESIGN OF DATA COMMUNICATION NETWORKS 305

FIGURE 11 New network graphical representation.

IV. INTELLIGENT AND HYBRID APPROACHES

A new tendency emerges in the use of AI approaches for designing data communication network topologies. Among others, Pierre [37] proposed the system called SIDRO, which starts with an initial topology according to user specifications. This initial topology is then submitted to a set of rules that determine the choice of perturbation types in order to reduce the total link cost or the average delay. According to this choice, SIDRO applies perturbation rules for generating examples that are kept in an example base and used elsewhere by a learning module to generate new rules.

A. Basic Principle of the AI-Based Approach

The approach presented in this section consists of perturbating a starting topology by applying sequences of rules and metarules, handled by an example generator, in order to reduce the total cost of the links and/or to improve the average delay of this network topology [36,37]. This *example generator* consists of a rule base, an inference engine, and an example base. For efficiency and performance purposes, the rule base component is subdivided into three hierarchical levels: (1) perturbation selecting rules (PSR), (2) perturbation rules (PR), and finally (3) positive or negative example defining rules (PNR). A perturbation selecting rule is a metarule that indicates the type of perturbation rule to be applied, depending on the specific context described by the premises of this rule. It is also a generic concept employed to point out a link addition rule, a link deletion rule, or a link substitution rule.

A perturbation cycle can be defined as the process by which positive and negative examples are generated by applying all the perturbation rules corresponding to a given perturbation selecting rule to a specific starting topology. After each perturbation cycle, positive or negative example defining rules are then used for labeling the examples generated by perturbation: positive examples (e^+) are feasible topologies in the sense they satisfy all the specified constraints, whereas negative examples (e^-) refer to topologies where only the delay constraint is not satisfied. The solution of the current problem is then the least-cost positive example, which has been generated up to the last perturbation cycle. In this way, perturbation cycles that aim at improving the current solutions can be viewed as a method for generalizing a local search process. After a certain number of perturbation cycles, feasible solutions or improvements to current solutions cannot be obtained by starting new cycles. As a result, refining current perturbation rules and discovering new ones from examples that have been previously generated constitute the only ways for improving solutions. This can be done by means of machine learning mechanisms [4,5,8,27]. The integration of an inductive learning module into the basic knowledge-based system has been considered as an extension of the example generator. In this chapter, we are interested in the specific problem of inferring new design rules that could reduce the cost of the network, as well as the message delay below some acceptable threshold.

B. Basic Concepts and Background

A network topology can be characterized by three types of descriptors: local, global, and structural [31]. These descriptors will be used either to state the topological design problem or to describe the machine learning module integrated into SIDRO.

1. Local Descriptors

A *local descriptor* essentially characterizes one node or one link of a network. This category of descriptors includes the length of a link, the incidence degree of a node, the traffic index of a link, the flow of a link, the capacity of a link, the utilization ratio of a link, and the excess cost index of a link. Except for the last one, all these concepts have already been defined in Section A of Section II.

The excess cost of a link k can be defined as $E_k = d_k(C_k - f_k)/C_k$. This relation can be rewritten as $E_k = d_k(1 - U_k)$. The average excess cost E of a network can be defined as $E = D_m(1 - U)$, where D_m is the average cost of the links, and U a mean utilization ratio. The *excess cost index* P_k can now be defined, for each link k of a given network topology, as

$$P_k = E_k/E = [d_k(1 - U_k)]/[D(1 - U)].$$

Clearly, if the excess cost index P_k of a link is greater than 1, the excess cost of that link is greater than the average excess cost of the network.

2. Some Global and Structural Descriptors

Global descriptors are features whose scope covers the whole network. For instance, the following parameters are global descriptors: number of nodes, number of links, total cost of the links, connectivity degree, normalized average delay, diameter, incidence degree of the network, and average traffic of the network.

Structural (or semantic) descriptors essentially consist of classic concepts derived from graph theory or conventional network design techniques [12,13].

Stated at an intermediary level of characterization between local and global descriptors, the structural descriptors refer to features shared by a subset of nodes or links. This category of descriptors includes a subgraph of a given degree, a subgraph of a given diameter, a saturated cut set, the least loaded path between two nodes, the fastest path between two nodes, and the most economical path between two nodes.

The structural descriptor *subgraph with a given degree* is obtained by associating the descriptors' *set of links incident on a node* and *subgraph* with the global descriptor *incidence degree of a graph*. The structural descriptor *subgraph of diameter R_S* is obtained by combining the descriptors *subgraph* and *diameter*; it is very relevant in a process of average delay reduction. A *saturated cut* is the minimal set of highly utilized links ($U_k > 0.9$) such that the removal of these links will split the network into two connected components.

The residual capacity of a link k is defined as the difference between the flow and the capacity of this link ($C_k - f_k$). It follows that the residual capacity of a path corresponds to the minimum residual capacity measured over the links of this path. Therefore, the structural descriptor *least loaded path between two nodes* can be defined as the path having the highest residual capacity between these two nodes. On the other hand, each link k of a path introduces a specific mean delay. The delay of a path is obtained by summing the mean delay values of its links. Thus, the *fastest path between two nodes* corresponds to the path having the lowest delay between these nodes. This structural descriptor can be computed using a shortest path search procedure, which takes the mean link delay as metric. Finally, the cost of a path is simply the total cost of the links belonging to this path. Therefore, the structural descriptor *most economical path between two nodes* can be computed using a shortest path search procedure, by taking the link cost as metric.

C. The Inductive Learning Module

Inductive learning is defined as the acquisition of knowledge by means of inductive inference performed from facts that are provided by a teacher or by the environment. It is often considered as a heuristic search through a space of symbolic descriptions called inductive assertions [8,27]. The inductive learning module developed in this section aims at inferring new perturbation rules from examples stored in the example base of SIDRO [37].

1. Syntax of the Perturbation Rules

Perturbation rules to be inferred are structured according to one of the following two formats [37]:

Format 1.   Cost reduction objective:

If   (1) $P_1(x_1)$
       (2) $P_2(x_2)$
       (3) $P_3(x_3)$
       (4) $P_4(x_4)$
       (5) $P_5(x_5)$

Then $Q_i(h_{ij}, O)$ can lead to a cost reduction (CV: α).

Format 2. Delay constraint restoration objective:

If (1) $P_1(x_1)$
    (2) $P_2(x_2)$
    (3) $P_3(x_3)$
    (4) $P_4(x_4)$
    (5) $P_5(x_5)$

Then $Q_i(h_{ij}, O)$ can lead to the delay constraint restoration (CV: α).

$P_i(x_i)$ denotes a premise built with some descriptors, and $Q_i(h_{ij}, O) = p_k$ a perturbation operator built with a hypothesis h_{ij}, where $i = 1$ for a link addition, $i = 2$ for a link deletion, and $i = 3$ for a link substitution operator. The index j specifies a hypothesis, that is, a basic criterion or a combination of basic criteria that can be used for selecting potential links to be perturbed. Clearly, because of the great number of possible ways to perturb a network topology, it is unrealistic to adopt an exhaustive approach.

Once a perturbation operator $Q_i(h_{ij}, O)$ is applied to an example in a learning process, the objective indicator O takes the value 1 if the aimed objective is reached, and 0 otherwise. This operation is successively applied to a great deal of examples. The likelihood factor CV is then computed as the success rate of applying this perturbation operator to all the considered examples. For a CV greater than or equal to 0.85, a new rule is inferred and built with the specific operator $Q_i(h_{ij}, O)$.

For the same i in h_{ij}, it can happen that more than one hypothesis leads to the searched objective: cost reduction or delay constraint restoration. As a result, a hypothesis preference criterion is needed for selecting only one hypothesis from the appropriate space indexed by i. In the context of topological design, the hypothesis preference criterion (HPC) chosen is the *best cost-performance ratio*; it implies choosing the hypothesis leading to the greatest total link cost reduction, while restoring or maintaining the delay constraint. According to this HPC, with a positive example as seed (cost reduction objective), the only hypothesis h_{ij} that can be selected is the one that enables the best cost reduction and preserves delay constraint. Conversely, with a negative example as seed (delay constraint restoration objective), HPC allows only the hypothesis enabling the restoration of the delay constraint and the highest cost reduction.

2. Notation Used for Describing the Learning Algorithm

Here is the list of notations used to describe the learning algorithm, which intrinsically attempts to infer new perturbation rules leading to cost reduction or delay constraint restoration:

- E Current example base related to a given problem being solved; it is also called *short-term example base*.
- X Example base related to all problems already solved by the example generator; it is also called *long-term example base*.
- X_c Compressed long-term example base resulting from removing superfluous or redundant examples from X.

e_g Example (positive or negative) extracted from E and used as the starting example for the learning process; it is also called a *seed*.
R_b Current rule base.
r_t Tentative rule inferred (not validated yet).

This learning algorithm is inspired by the well-known Star methodology [27] and described by the following steps:

Step 0. Initialization:
$$X = X \cup E$$
$$X_c = \phi.$$

Step 1. Select at random in E a seed e_g.

Step 2. From the number of nodes n, the degree of connectivity K, the normalized average delay T_n, and the diameter R of the seed e_g, obtain the premises $P_1(x_1)$, $P_2(x_2)$, $P_3(x_3)$, $P_4(x_4)$.

Step 3. Determine (i, j), with $i = 1, 2, 3$ and $j = 1, 2, \ldots, q_i$ (q_i = number of hypotheses of type i) such that applying the operator $Q_i(h_{ij}, O)$ to e_g results in a cost reduction if e_g is a positive example, or in the restoration of the delay constraint if e_g is a negative example.

Step 4. In the case of more than one acceptable operator $Q_i(h_{ij}, O)$, turn to the hypothesis preference criterion (the best cost-performance ratio) to select the best conclusion for a new rule. Then infer from this the value of $x_5(x_5 = i)$ specifying the premise $P_5(x_5)$, together with the tentative rule $r_t = (P_1, P_2, P_3, P_4, P_5, i, j, Q_i(h_{ij}, O), 1)$.

Step 5. Apply r_t to examples stored in X in order to validate this tentative rule, that is, to verify that its application effectively results in a cost reduction or in the delay constraint restoration, depending on the features of the considered seed e_g. Then compute the value of the likelihood factor CV as the ratio v_s/v_t, where v_s denotes the number of successful applications of r_t, and v_t the total number of applications of this tentative rule to the suitable examples taken from X.

Step 6. If r_t covers at least 85% of examples considered in X (CV ≥ 0.85), then it becomes a valid discovered rule to be inserted in the rule base R_b, and go to Step 8.

Step 7. Reduce the short-term example base E to the only examples not covered by the tentative rule r_t and return to Step 1.

Step 8. Update the long-term example base by keeping only nonredundant examples which constitute X_c ($X = X_c$).

3. Illustrative Example

Once the seed e_g is selected at Step 1, a premise-building procedure is used at Step 2 for extracting the number of nodes n, the connectivity degree K, the normalized average delay T_n, and the diameter R. For instance, for a seed e_g characterized by the values of parameters $n = 20$, $K = 5$, $T_n = 0.7$, $R = 0.95 L_{\max}$, this procedure builds the following premises:

(P_1) The topology has a number of nodes greater than 7
  ($K \leq n - 1 \Rightarrow n > K + 2 = 7$)
(P_2) The degree of connectivity is equal to 5 ($K = 5$)
(P_3) The normalized average delay is less than or equal to 1
  ($T_n = 0.7 < 1$)
(P_4) The diameter of the topology is less than or equal to L_{max}
  ($R = 0.95 L_{max} < L_{max}$).

Since the normalized average delay T_n is less than 1, the seed e_g is a positive example: only cost reduction constitutes a relevant objective. Specifically, Step 3 consists of searching heuristicly through the hypothesis spaces H_i for the hypothesis h_{ij}, with $i = 1, 2, 3$ and $j = 1, 2, \ldots, q_i$, such that applying operator $Q_i(h_{ij})$ to the seed e_g leads to a cost reduction. Assume that the preferred hypothesis is

$$h_{29} = (k \in \text{CMD}_{ij}) \wedge ([k = (i, j)] \wedge [d(i) > K] \wedge [d(j) > K]).$$

In accordance with Step 4, the result is $i = 2$ and $j = 9$. It follows that $x_5 = 2$, $r_t = (P_1, P_2, P_3, P_4, P_5, 2, 9, Q_2(h_{29}, 0), 1)$. Since $i = 2$, (P_5) can be paraphrased as follows: "The envisioned perturbation is a link deletion."

At Step 5, the tentative rule r_t is applied to examples stored in X in order to compute the likelihood factor CV. In accordance with Step 6, if the success rate is at least equal to 85%, the tentative rule is considered as a valid rule discovered by the inductive learning module. Otherwise, the short-term example base is updated by removing all examples covered by r_t.

In a postprocessing phase, the rule r_t is paraphrased as follows:

(r_t) IF   (1) THE TOPOLOGY HAS A NUMBER OF NODES GREATER THAN 7
       (2) THE DEGREE OF CONNECTIVITY IS EQUAL TO 5
       (3) THE NORMALIZED AVERAGE DELAY OF THE TOPOLOGY IS LESS THAN OR EQUAL TO 1
       (4) THE DIAMETER OF THE TOPOLOGY IS LESS THAN OR EQUAL TO L_{max}
       (5) THE ENVISIONED PERTURBATION IS A LINK DELETION
    THEN   THE DELETION OF LINKS $k = (i, j)$ BELONGING TO THE LEAST LOADED PATH BETWEEN i AND j, SUCH THAT $d(i)$ AND $d(j)$ REMAIN GREATER THAN OR EQUAL TO 5 AFTER THE DELETION, CAN LEAD TO A COST REDUCTION (CV:0.85)

Table 2 summarizes and paraphrases a sample of rules discovered by the inductive learning module, according to a process detailed in [36].

D. Numerical Applications with SIDRO

Consider the problem of finding a 3-connected topology which guarantees a maximum allowable delay of 50 ms per packet, starting from the 20-node initial topology shown in Fig. 12. The traffic between each node pair is equal

TABLE 2 Sample of Inferred Rules

(r_5)   IF   (1) THE TOPOLOGY HAS A NUMBER OF NODES GREATER THAN 6
(2) THE DEGREE OF CONNECTIVITY IS EQUAL TO 4
(3) THE NORMALIZED AVERAGE DELAY IS LESS THAN OR EQUAL TO 1
(4) THE DIAMETER OF THE TOPOLOGY IS LESS THAN OR EQUAL TO L_{max}
(5) THE ENVISIONED PERTURBATION IS A LINK DELETION
  THEN   THE DELETION OF LINKS $k = (i, j)$ SUCH THAT $L(k) > 0.6*L_{max}$, k BEING IN A SUBGRAPH OF WHICH THE DEGREE IS GREATER THAN 3, $d(i)$ AND $d(j)$ REMAINING GREATER OR EQUAL TO 3 AFTER THE LINK DELETION, CAN LEAD TO A COST REDUCTION (CV: 0.85).

(r_{11})   IF   (1) THE TOPOLOGY HAS A NUMBER OF NODES GREATER THAN 5
(2) THE DEGREE OF CONNECTIVITY IS EQUAL TO 3
(3) THE NORMALIZED AVERAGE DELAY IS GREATER THAN 1
(4) THE DIAMETER OF THE TOPOLOGY IS LESS THAN OR EQUAL TO L_{max}
(5) THE ENVISIONED PERTURBATION IS A LINK ADDITION
  THEN   THE ADDITION OF LINKS $k = (i, j)$ INCIDENT TO A NODE BELONGING TO THE SATURATED CUT-SET, AND SUCH THAT ITS TRAFFIC INDEX IS GREATER THAN 1, CAN LEAD TO THE DELAY CONSTRAINT RESTORATION (CV: 0.88).

(r_{18})   IF   (1) THE TOPOLOGY HAS A NUMBER OF NODES GREATER THAN 7
(2) THE DEGREE OF CONNECTIVITY IS EQUAL TO 5
(3) THE NORMALIZED AVERAGE DELAY IS GREATER THAN 1
(4) THE DIAMETER OF THE TOPOLOGY IS GREATER THAN L_{max}
(5) THE ENVISIONED PERTURBATION IS A LINK SUBSTITUTION
  THEN   THE REPLACEMENT OF LINKS $k = (i, j)$ SUCH THAT $L(k) > 0.7*L_{max}$, BY TWO OTHER LINKS $v = (i, p)$ AND $w = (j, q)$ BOTH INCIDENT TO NODES BELONGING TO THE FASTEST PATH BETWEEN i AND j, WITH $L(v)$ AND $L(w)$ BOTH LESS THAN $0.8*L(k)$, CAN LEAD TO THE DELAY CONSTRAINT RESTORATION (CV:0.92).

(r_{19})   IF   (1) THE TOPOLOGY HAS A NUMBER OF NODES GREATER THAN 5
(2) THE DEGREE OF CONNECTIVITY IS EQUAL TO 3
(3) THE NORMALIZED AVERAGE DELAY IS LESS THAN OR EQUAL TO 1
(4) THE DIAMETER OF THE TOPOLOGY IS LESS THAN OR EQUAL TO L_{max}
(5) THE ENVISIONED PERTURBATION IS A LINK SUBSTITUTION
  THEN   THE REPLACEMENT OF LINKS $k = (i, j)$ OF WHICH UTILIZATION RATIO IS LESS THAN 0.8, BY TWO OTHER LINKS $v = (i, p)$ AND $w = (j, q)$, THE SHORTEST POSSIBLE, BOTH HAVING THEIR TRAFFIC INDICES GREATER THAN 1 CAN LEAD TO A COST REDUCTION (CV: 0.87).

(r_{23})   IF   (1) THE TOPOLOGY HAS A NUMBER OF NODES GREATER THAN 7
(2) THE DEGREE OF CONNECTIVITY IS EQUAL TO 5
(3) THE NORMALIZED AVERAGE DELAY IS LESS THAN OR EQUAL TO 1
(4) THE DIAMETER OF THE TOPOLOGY IS LESS THAN OR EQUAL TO L_{max}
(5) THE ENVISIONED PERTURBATION IS A LINK DELETION
  THEN   THE DELETION OF LINKS $k = (i,j)$ SUCH THAT $L(k) > 0.7*L_{max}$, $d(i)$ AND $d(j)$ REMAINING GREATER OR EQUAL TO 5 AFTER THE LINK DELETION, AND THE EXCESS COST INDEX OF k IS LESS THAN 1, CAN LEAD TO A COST REDUCTION (CV: 0.87).

to 10 packets/s, and the average packet length has been taken to be 1000 bits. Table 3 gives the Cartesian coordinates of the 20 nodes. Table 4 shows the costs associated with the link capacity options. The total link cost D of this topology is equal to \$197,776/month. Figure 13 shows the solution resulting from the application of some addition and deletion rules of Table 2 during three perturbation cycles. We observe a cost reduction of 9.2% per month, whereas the delay constraint has been preserved.

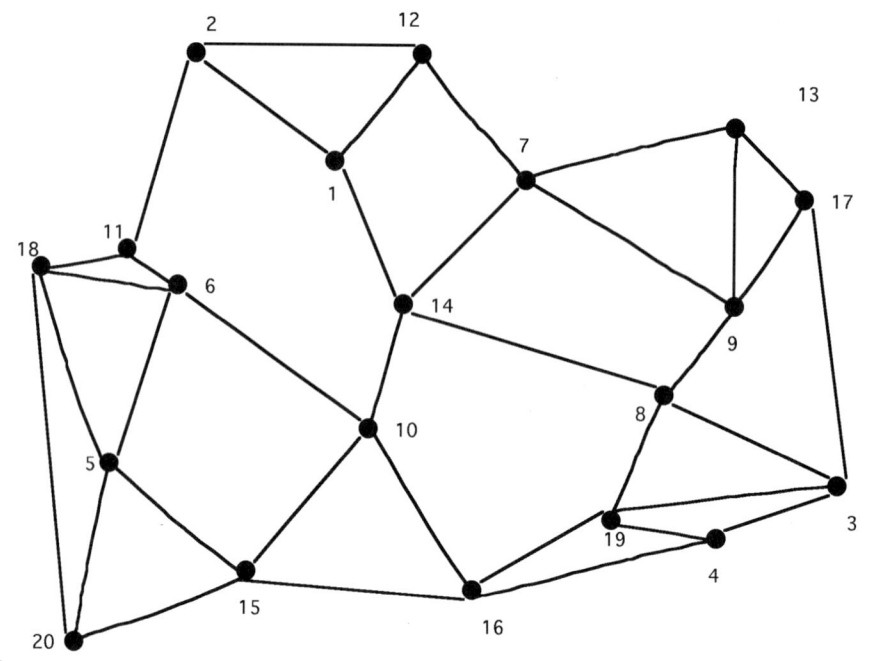

FIGURE 12 A 20-node initial topology ($D = \$197,776$/month and $T = 42.4$ ms).

V. HEURISTIC APPROACHES

Various heuristic methods for solving the topological design problem, in the context of packet-switched networks, have been proposed. These methods are generally incremental in the sense that they start with an initial topology and perturb it repeatedly until they produce suboptimal solutions.

A. Conventional Heuristics and Meta-heuristics

BXC starts from an arbitrary topological configuration generated by a user or a design program to reach a local minimum by means of local transformations.

TABLE 3 Cartesian Coordinates of the Nodes (X_i, Y_i)

i	X_i	Y_i	i	X_i	Y_i
1	250	360	2	165	420
3	600	100	4	480	55
5	90	130	6	150	250
7	400	325	8	435	185
9	530	250	10	275	165
11	100	300	12	350	420
13	550	360	14	320	240
15	205	85	16	365	40
17	595	310	18	15	260
19	415	80	20	50	25

TABLE 4 Costs Associated with the Link Capacity Options

Capacity (Kbps)	Variable cost (($/month)/Km)	Fixed cost ($/month)
9.6	3.0	10.0
19.2	5.0	12.0
56.0	10.0	15.0
100.0	15.0	20.0
200.0	25.0	25.0
560.0	90.0	60.0

A local transformation often called *Branch X-change* consists of the elimination of one or more old links and the insertion of one or more new links to preserve the 2-connectivity. This technique requires an exhaustive exploration of all local topological exchanges and tends to be time consuming when applied to networks with more than 20 or 30 nodes [12].

CBE starts with a fully connected topology using concave costs and applies the FD algorithm until it reaches the local minimum [12]. The FD algorithm eliminates uneconomical links and strongly reduces the topology. This algorithm is terminated whenever the next link removal violates the constraint of 2-connectivity: the last 2-connected solution is then assumed to be the local minimum. CBE can efficiently eliminate uneconomical links, but does not allow for the insertion of new links. In order to overcome such limitations, the

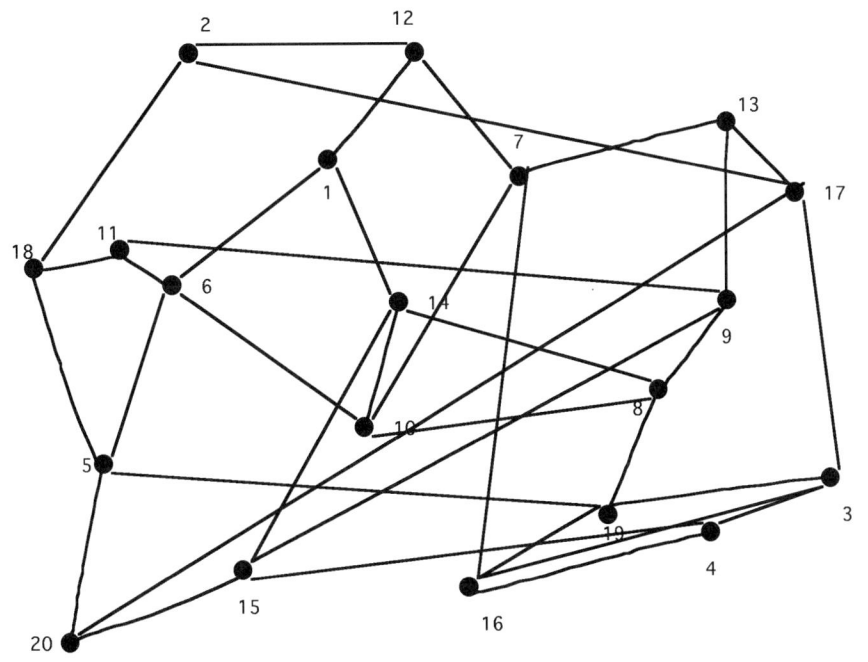

FIGURE 13 New topology generated by SIDRO ($D = \$179,620$/month and $T = 44.76$ ms).

CS method has been proposed [13]. This method is iterative and consists of three main steps:

1. Find the saturated cut, that is, assess the minimal set of the most utilized links that, if removed, leaves the network disconnected.
2. Add new links across the cut in order to connect the two components.
3. Allow the removal of the least utilized links.

CS can be considered as an extension of BXC, in the sense that, rather than exhaustively performing all possible branch exchanges, it selects only those exchanges that are likely to improve throughput and cost.

MENTOR has been proposed by Kershenbaum *et al.* [21]. It essentially tries to find a distributed network with all the following characteristics: (i) traffic requirements are routed on relatively direct paths; (ii) links have a reasonable utilization; (iii) relatively high-capacity links are used, thereby allowing us to benefit from the economy of scale generally present in the relationship between capacity and cost. These three objectives are, to some extent, contradictory. Nevertheless, the MENTOR algorithm trades them off against one another to create low-cost networks.

Another solving approach consists of using combinatorial optimization meta-heuristic methods, such as SA and GA. The SA method starts by choosing an arbitrary initial solution, then searches, in the set of neighbor solutions, a new solution that, hopefully, improves the cost.

SA is a process whereby candidate solutions to a problem are repeatedly evaluated according to some objective function and incrementally changed to achieve better solutions [23,24,44]. The nature of each individual change is probabilistic in the sense that there is some probability it worsens the solution. In addition, an annealing schedule is followed whereby the probability of allowing a change that worsens the solution is gradually reduced to 0 [38]. If a better solution is found, then it becomes the current solution; if not, the method stops and at this step a local optima is reached [24].

This method has been applied to many combinatorial optimization problems [6]. Pierre *et al.* [35] adapted this method to solve the problem of topological design of packet-switched networks. This adaption consists of starting with an initial topology that satisfies the reliability constraint, then applying the SA algorithm with an initial high value of the temperature parameter, in order to obtain a new configuration that minimizes the total link cost or improves the mean delay.

The Genetic Algorithms (GA) have been introduced by Holland [17]. They are inspired by the Darwin's Model and based on the survival of the fittest species. Just as in nature where specimens reproduce themselves, in genetic algorithms specimens also reproduce themselves. GAs are essentially characterized by the coding of the problem parameters, the solution space, the evaluation function, and the way of choosing chromosomes to be perturbed. In practice, from a generation to another, chromosomes that form the population have a very high aptitude value. GAs start generally with a population generated randomly. To undertake an efficient search of performing structures, genetic operators are applied to this initial population in order to produce, within a time limit, successive high-quality populations. We distinguish generally four main genetic operators: reproduction, crossover, mutation, and inversion [17].

Pierre and Legault [32,33] adapted GAs for configuring economical packet-switched computer networks that satisfy some constraints related to quality of service. The adaptation results show that the GA method can produce good solutions by being applied to networks of 15 nodes and more.

An hybrid method has been introduced by Dutta and Mitra [9]. This method integrates both the algorithmic approach and a knowledge-based system. It builds a solution by subdividing the topological design problem into modules that can be individually solved by applying optimization models or heuristic methods. Furthermore, it integrates the partial solutions to obtain a global solution to the design problem. The system is made up of independent modules that share a common blackboard structure. It usually provides good solutions with minimal costs.

B. Implementation of the Tabu Search Approach

TS is an iterative improvement procedure that starts from an initial feasible solution and attempts to determine a better solution in the manner of an ordinary (descent) local method, until a local optimum is reached [14,15]. This method can be used to guide any process that employs a set of moves for transforming one solution into another; thus it provides an evaluation function for measuring the attractiveness of these moves [14,16].

1. Basic Principles

For a given combinatorial optimization problem, a solution space S may be defined as the set of all feasible solutions. TS associates with each feasible solution a numerical value that may be considered as the cost of the solution obtained by optimizing the cost function. For each solution s_i in the space solution S, there is a subset of S, say $N(s_i)$, considered as a *neigborhood* of s_i. This subset contains a set of feasible solutions that may be reached from s_i in one move. TS starts from an initial feasible solution s_i, and then moves to a solution s_j, which is also an element of $N(s_i)$. This process is repeated iteratively, and solutions that yield cost values lower than those previously encountered are recorded. The final cost recorded, when the search is interrupted, constitutes the overall optimum solution. Thus, TS can be viewed as a variable neighborhood method: each step redefines the neighborhood for which the next solution will be drawn.

A move from s_i to s_j is made on the basis that s_j ($s_i \neq s_j$) has the minimum cost among all the allowable solution in $N(s_i)$. Allowability is managed by a mechanism that involves historical information about moves made while the procedure progresses. TS is a high-level procedure that can be used for solving optimization problems; it escapes the trap of local optimality by using short-term memory recording of the most recently visited solutions [16]. The short-term memory constitutes a form of aggressive exploration that seeks to make the best move possible satisfying certain constraints. These constraints are designed to prevent repetition of some moves considered as forbidden (tabu). Such attributes are maintained in a *tabu list* (LT).

TS permits backtracking to previous solutions which may ultimately lead, via a different direction, to better solutions. This flexibility element is implemented through a mechanism called *aspiration criteria* [16]. The goal of aspiration criteria is to increase the flexibility of the algorithm while preserving the

Given

X	:	*Space of feasible solutions*
F	:	*Objective function, X→ R, defined on X*
N(s)	:	*Neighbourhood of s ∈ X*
|LT$_i$|	:	*Length of each tabu list LT$_i$*
f*	:	*Lower bound of objective function*
nbmax	:	*Maximum number of iterations between two improvements of s**

Initialization

Choose by any heuristic an initial solution $s \in X$

s* := s   (s* *best solution obtained*)

nbiter := 0   (*Iteration counter*)

bestiter := 0   (*iteration given the last s**)

Initialize LT$_i$ for each i

A$_j$(s, m) = + ∞

While (f(s) > f*) and (nbiter - bestiter < nbmax)   **DO**

nbiter := nbiter +1

generate a sample V* ⊆ N(s) of neighbour solutions

if [*one of the tabu conditions is violated*, i.e. t$_i$(s,m) ∈ LT$_i$] or [*at least one of aspiration criteria conditions is verified*, i.e. a$_j$(s,m) < A$_j$(s,m)] then

Choose the best s' ∈ V* minimizing f on V* (*by a heuristic*)

If   f(s') < f(s*)   **Then**   s* := s'

                                           bestiter := nbiter

Update of tabu lists LT$_i$

Update of threshold values A$_j$(s,m)

s := s'

Endwhile

Result s*   : best solution found after the execution of the procedure

FIGURE 14 General version of TS.

basic features that allow the algorithm to escape local optima and avoid cyclic behavior. Figure 14 presents a general version of TS.

2. Definition of the Moves

Adaptation of TS to a specific problem essentially relies on the definition of moves that describe the neighborhood to be explored. In the case of topological design of communication networks, some moves or local transformations called perturbations are applied to a starting topology in order to reduce its total link cost and/or to improve its average packet delay. These perturbations deal with *addition, removal, and substitution* of links.

The main goal of removal moves is to reduce the total link cost. If a starting topology contains the minimum number of links to preserve the K-connectivity, then it is impossible to apply to it a removal move because the connectivity constraint would be automatically violated. In our implementation, we defined three types of removal moves:

M_1^R the removal of links $k = (i, j)$ such that $L(k) > \alpha^* L_{\max}$, with $0 < \alpha \leq 1$, $d(i)$ and $d(j)$ remaining at least equal to the desired connectivity degree after the link removal;

M_2^R the removal of links $k = (i, j)$ such that the excess index cost P_k is less than 1, $d(i)$ and $d(j)$ remaining at least equal to the desired connectivity degree after the link removal;

M_3^R the removal of links $k = (i, j)$ such that the utilization rate U_k is less than α, with $0 < \alpha \leq 1$, $d(i)$ and $d(j)$ remaining at least equal to the desired connectivity degree after the link removal.

The addition moves cannot violate the connectivity constraint, but generally have negative effects on the cost. They are defined as follows:

M_1^A to each topology that has a normalized delay (T_n) greater than 1, add the links $k = (i, j)$ that have an index traffic greater than 1;

M_2^A to each topology that has a normalized delay (T_n) less than 1, add the links $k = (i, j)$ such that $L(k) < \alpha^* R$, with $0 < \alpha \leq 1$.

The substitution moves correspond to a sequence of removals and additions of links. These moves, which cannot guarantee the preservation of the connectivity degree, are defined as follows:

M_1^S the substitution of all links $k = (i, j)$ such that $L(k) > \alpha^* L_{\max}$, with $0 < \alpha \leq 1$, by two other links $v = (i, p)$ and $w = (j, q)$, with $L(v) \leq \alpha_1 L(k)$ and $L(w) \leq \alpha_2 L(k)$, $0 < \alpha_1 \leq 1$ and $0 < \alpha_2 \leq 1$;

M_2^S the substitution of all link $k = (i, j)$ such that $U_k > \alpha$, with $0 < \alpha \leq 1$, by two other links $v = (i, p)$ and $w = (j, q)$ with $I_{ip} > 1$ and $I_{iq} > 1$.

The neighborhood of a current topology s is a finite set $N(s)$ of topologies that are said to be feasible. In our implementation, this neighborhood cannot contain more than 6 topologies, each of which is obtained from the current topology by applying one move. The length of the tabu list is fixed to 7. The average packet delay is calculated using Eq. (1), and the total link cost is computed using Eqs. (2) and (3).

C. Numerical Applications with Heuristic Methods

In order to evaluate the effectiveness and efficiency of TS approach, we have considered a set of 20 nodes defined by the Cartesian coordinates given in Table 5. The node coordinates give an Euclidean representation of the network and are used to determine the distance between each pair of nodes or the length

TABLE 5   Node Coordinates

Node	1	2	3	4	5	6	7	8	9	10
Abscissa	63	22	41	33	32	40	52	80	19	15
Ordinate	8	72	45	10	84	78	52	33	35	81
Node	11	12	13	14	15	16	17	18	19	20
Abscissa	27	27	70	48	4	10	56	82	9	95
Ordinate	3	16	96	4	73	71	27	47	54	61

TABLE 6 Capacity Options and Costs

Capacity (Kbps)	Fixed cost ($/month)	Variable cost ($/month/Km)
9.60	650.00	0.40
19.20	850.00	2.50
50.00	850.00	7.50
100.00	1700.00	10.00
230.40	2350.00	30.00
460.80	4700.00	60.00
921.60	9400.00	120.00
1843.20	18800.00	240.00

of each link; the selection of moves to be performed at each step is based on the link length, among others.

The capacity options are given in Table 6, and the traffic matrix is provided in Table 7. The maximum acceptable delay is $T_{max} = 250$ ms, the degree of connectivity is equal to 3, and the average packet length is 1000 bits.

Starting with the above specification data, step 1 of this method generates an initial topology with connectivity degree at least equal to 3. In step 1, the operation that has a higher cost in terms of CPU time and memory requirements remains the computation of link lengths. The computational complexity of this step is $O(n^2)$. Figure 15 gives the initial topology, while Table 4 provides the link attribute values of this topology.

Table 8 shows that the links of the initial topology are among the shortest possible links. The total link cost of this configuration is $D = \$124,222.98$/month and its average delay is evaluated at 81.84 ms. To this

TABLE 7 Traffic Matrix

	1	2	3	4	5	6	7	8	9	10	11	12	13	14	15	16	17	18	19	20
1	0	4	7	8	6	9	5	5	9	3	9	3	6	4	3	4	1	7	7	10
2	4	0	9	3	2	8	3	1	2	9	8	10	6	10	3	6	10	2	6	3
3	7	9	0	7	10	10	6	5	5	10	6	8	8	9	1	2	4	4	10	9
4	8	3	7	0	9	6	5	4	7	3	7	6	8	5	9	4	2	10	3	5
5	6	2	10	9	0	8	1	3	8	6	6	7	6	3	3	1	6	5	4	2
6	9	8	10	6	8	0	10	9	6	7	1	5	1	5	9	6	10	5	4	2
7	5	3	6	5	1	10	0	9	7	4	7	6	2	8	5	3	8	8	3	4
8	5	1	5	4	3	9	9	0	9	4	4	4	1	5	10	9	7	7	10	3
9	9	2	5	7	8	6	7	9	0	6	7	1	4	5	10	6	6	8	8	3
10	3	9	10	3	6	7	4	4	6	0	10	2	6	5	7	2	4	8	7	8
11	9	8	6	7	6	1	7	4	7	10	0	5	4	6	10	9	8	5	6	2
12	3	10	8	6	7	5	6	4	1	2	5	0	3	6	5	6	6	3	7	7
13	6	6	8	8	6	1	2	1	4	6	4	3	0	3	9	3	4	7	1	9
14	4	10	9	5	3	5	8	5	5	5	6	6	3	0	3	4	3	4	2	4
15	3	3	1	9	3	9	5	10	10	7	10	5	9	3	0	8	5	1	9	9
16	4	6	2	4	1	6	3	9	6	2	9	6	3	4	8	0	2	1	4	7
17	1	10	4	2	6	10	8	7	6	4	8	6	4	3	5	2	0	10	10	9
18	7	2	4	10	5	5	8	7	8	8	5	3	7	4	1	1	10	0	10	6
19	7	6	10	3	4	4	3	10	8	7	6	7	1	2	9	4	10	10	0	8
20	10	3	9	5	2	2	4	3	3	8	2	7	9	4	9	7	9	6	8	0

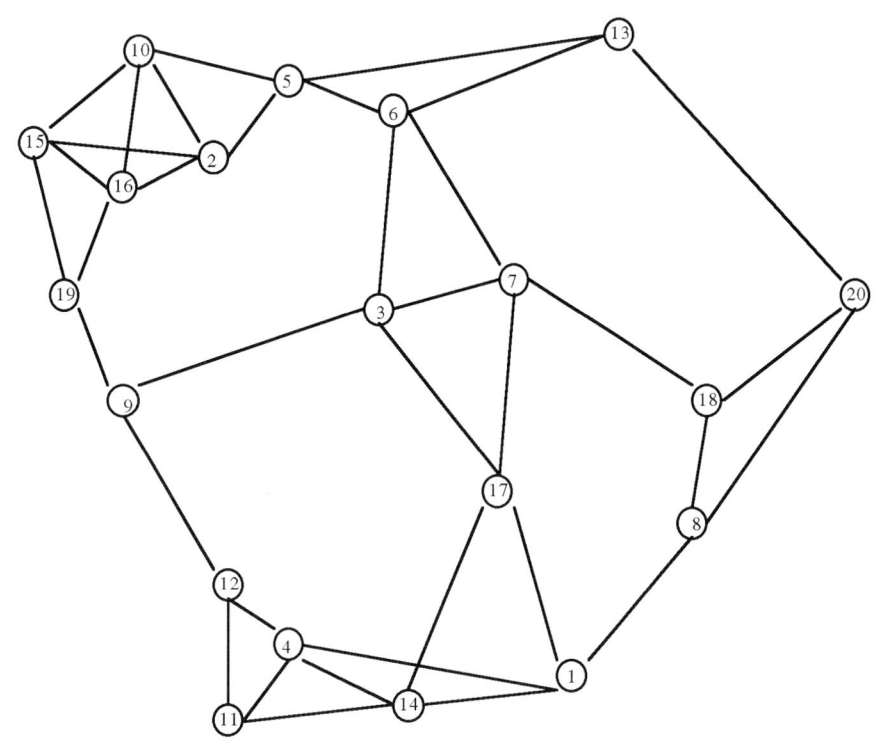

FIGURE 15 Initial topological configuration ($D = \$124{,}222.98$/month, $T = 81.84$ ms).

initial topology, the application of the third removal move links M_3^R during the first iteration cycle has generated, by deletion of links 1–14, 2–5, and 10–15, the topology specified by Fig. 16 and Table 9. The cost of this topology was checked against the cost of each topology generated from the initial topology during the current iteration cycle; this cost is found to be the lowest. Thus, it becomes the solution of the first perturbation cycle.

Therefore, iteration cycle 1 did not lead to a solution less expensive than the current initial topology. By contrast, we observe a diminution of the average delay T. In fact, this one has changed from 81.84 to 73.78 ms, that is, a diminution of 9.48%. For iteration cycle 2, this solution is kept as a new starting topology to which different moves are applied. The link removal move M_2^R led to a new topology with a total link cost $D = \$111{,}420.70$/month and an average delay $T = 95$ ms.

In iteration cycle 3, the application of the substitution move M_1^s to the starting topology shown in Fig. 15 led to the new topology specified by Fig. 17 and Table 10. The improvement percentage in terms of cost is 17.6%. By contrast, the average delay is changed from 81.84 to 133.68 ms, with an increase of 51.84 ms. This delay did not pass the maximum acceptable delay T_{max}, which is fixed in this application at 250 ms. Since we are looking for a solution that minimizes the total link cost, taking into consideration some performance constraints, this solution therefore becomes the best solution found during the overall execution of this method.

TABLE 8 Link Attributes of the Initial Topology

Link number	Link	Flow (Kbps)	Capacity (Kbps)	Utilization
3	1–4	134	230.40	0.58
7	1–8	170	230.40	0.73
13	1–14	74	100.00	0.74
16	1–17	70	100.00	0.70
22	2–5	216	230.40	0.93
27	2–10	18	19.20	0.93
32	2–15	6	9.60	0.62
33	2–16	210	230.40	0.91
40	3–6	302	460.80	0.65
41	3–7	174	230.40	0.75
43	3–9	388	460.80	0.84
51	3–17	348	460.80	0.75
61	4–11	14	19.20	0.72
62	4–12	302	460.80	0.65
64	4–14	96	100.00	0.96
71	5–6	296	460.80	0.64
75	5–10	192	230.40	0.83
78	5–13	120	230.40	0.52
86	6–7	134	230.40	0.58
92	6–13	78	100.00	0.78
110	7–18	204	230.40	0.88
121	8–17	138	230.40	0.59
122	8–18	144	230.40	0.62
124	8–20	94	100.00	0.94
127	9–12	500	921.60	0.54
134	9–19	550	921.60	0.59
140	10–15	86	100.00	0.86
141	10–16	70	100.00	0.70
146	11–12	158	230.40	0.68
148	11–14	68	100.00	0.68
169	13–20	108	230.40	0.46
172	14–17	94	100.00	0.94
176	15–16	16	19.20	0.83
179	15–19	130	230.40	0.28
183	16–19	322	460.80	0.69
189	18–20	74	100.00	0.74

Our results in terms of cost and mean delay are compared with results provided by other heuristics. First, TS is compared with CS. For both methods, the experience was based on the following choices: uniform traffic of 5 packets per second between each pair of nodes, 2-connected topologies (the CS method handles only 2-connected topologies), and the average length of packets being 1000 bits. We have used the capacity options and costs of Table 5. The Cartesian coordinates of the nodes are given in Table 11. Table 12 shows the comparative results provided by both methods. The last column of this table provides the improvement rate obtained by TS versus CS. In all cases, TS offers better solutions in terms of cost than CS. However, delays provided by CS are generally better.

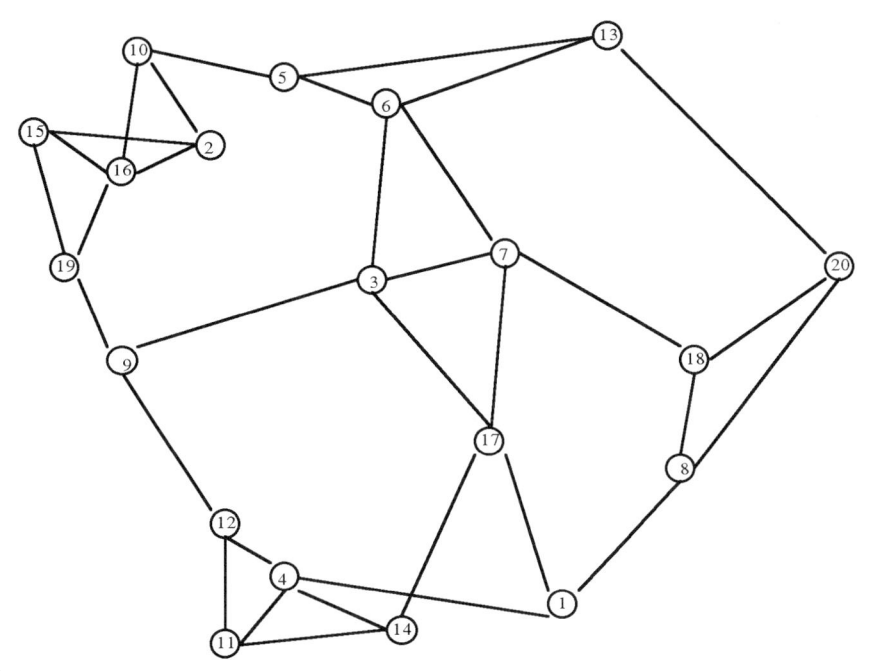

FIGURE 16 Best topology found during the first iteration cycle ($D = \$127{,}890.26$/month, $T = 73.78$ ms).

The TS approach has been also compared to the GA approach, on networks having a connectivity degree ranging from 3 to 5. The traffic between all pairs of nodes was uniform, equal to 5 packets per second, and the average length of packets was 1000 bits. We used the capacity options and costs given in Table 5. The Cartesian coordinates are similar to those shown in Table 11. Comparative results provided by both methods are given in Table 13. In almost cases

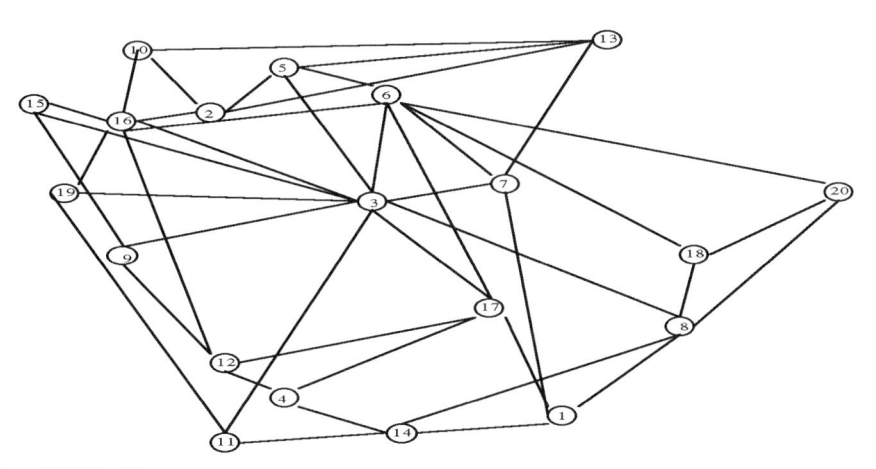

FIGURE 17 Topological configuration of the (last) final solution ($D = \$102{,}419.91$/month, $T = 133.68$ ms).

TABLE 9 Link Attributes of the Solution Obtained during the First Iteration Cycle

Link number	Link	Flow (Kbps)	Capacity (Kbps)	Utilization
3	1–4	182	230.40	0.78
7	1–8	144	230.40	0.62
16	1–17	70	100.00	0.70
27	2–10	106	230.40	0.46
32	2–15	6	9.60	0.62
33	2–16	98	100.00	0.98
40	3–6	294	460.80	0.63
41	3–7	194	230.40	0.84
43	3–9	388	460.80	0.84
51	3–17	340	460.80	0.73
61	4–11	54	100.00	0.54
62	4–12	310	460.80	0.67
64	4–14	96	100.00	0.96
71	5–6	288	460.80	0.45
75	5–10	400	460.80	0.86
78	5–13	120	230.40	0.52
86	6–7	134	230.40	0.58
92	6–13	78	100.00	0.78
110	7–18	204	230.40	0.88
121	8–17	164	230.40	0.71
122	8–18	144	230.40	0.62
124	8–20	94	100.00	0.94
127	9–12	508	921.60	0.55
134	9–19	558	921.60	0.60
141	10–16	276	460.80	0.59
146	11–12	158	230.40	0.68
148	11–14	28	50.00	0.56
169	13–20	108	230.40	0.46
172	14–17	128	230.40	0.55
176	15–16	102	230.40	0.44
179	15–19	130	230.40	0.56
183	16–19	330	460.80	0.71
189	18–20	74	100.00	0.74

(13 out of 14), costs provided by TS are better than those obtained by GA. However, delays obtained by TS are relatively less than those obtained by GA. In general, TS provides better solutions in terms of cost than GA.

We have also compared our results to those provided by SA. Our experience used the same data previously mentioned. Table 14 gives a summary of the results obtained by the two methods. These results confirm once again that TS offers better solutions than SA in terms of cost.

TABLE 10 Link Attributes of the Final Solution

Link number	Link	Flow (Kbps)	Capacity (Kbps)	Utilization
6	1–7	44	50.00	0.88
7	1–8	96	100.00	0.96
13	1–14	144	230.40	0.62
16	1–17	196	230.40	0.85
22	2–5	112	230.40	0.48
27	2–10	76	100.00	0.76
30	2–13	38	50.00	0.76
33	2–16	184	230.40	0.79
39	3–5	62	100.00	0.62
40	3–6	44	50.00	0.88
41	3–7	214	230.40	0.92
42	3–8	206	230.40	0.89
43	3–9	186	230.40	0.80
45	3–11	48	50.00	0.96
49	3–15	48	50.00	0.96
50	3–16	136	230.40	0.59
51	3–17	220	230.40	0.95
53	3–19	116	230.40	0.50
62	4–12	212	230.40	0.92
64	4–14	220	230.40	0.95
67	4–17	74	100.00	0.74
71	5–6	200	230.40	0.86
78	5–13	46	50.00	0.92
86	6–7	28	50.00	0.56
95	6–16	90	100.00	0.90
96	6–17	108	230.40	0.46
97	6–18	84	100.00	0.84
99	6–20	96	100.00	0.96
105	7–13	86	100.00	0.86
118	8–14	114	230.40	0.49
122	8–18	178	230.40	0.77
124	8–20	112	230.40	0.48
127	9–12	150	230.40	0.65
130	9–15	82	100.00	0.82
138	10–13	12	19.20	0.62
141	10–16	134	230.40	0.58
148	11–14	110	230.40	0.47
153	11–19	90	100.00	0.90
158	12–16	114	230.40	0.49
159	12–17	12	19.20	0.62
176	15–16	164	230.40	0.71
183	16–19	180	230.40	0.78
189	18–20	12	19.20	0.62

TABLE 11 Node Coordinates

Node	1	2	3	4	5	6	7	8	9	10
Abscissa	63	22	41	33	32	40	52	80	19	15
Ordinate	8	72	45	10	84	78	52	33	35	81

Node	11	12	13	14	15	16	17	18	19	20
Abscissa	27	27	70	48	4	10	56	82	9	95
Ordinate	3	16	96	4	73	71	27	47	54	61

Node	21	22	23
Abscissa	67	56	54
Ordinate	8	54	23

TABLE 12 Comparison of Results Provided by TS and CS

| | | | Cut Saturation ||| Tabu Search |||
No.	N	T_{max}	D ($/month)	T (ms)	Cap. (Kbps)	D ($/month)	T (ms)	%D
1	6	80	19972	32.73	50	8480	80	58
2	10	100	44262	37.28	100	25272	69.56	43
3	12	120	56231	109.29	100	43338	77.48	23
4	15	150	160984	17.69	230.40	65161	141.86	60
5	20	150	381278	7.16	460.80	144131	103.73	63
6	23	80	394455	10.80	460.80	210070	58.12	45

TABLE 13 Comparison of Results Provided by TS and GA

| | | | | GA || TS ||||
No.	N	K	T_{max}	D ($/month)	T (ms)	D ($/month)	T (ms)	%T	%D
1	6	3	100	10697	80.62	9867	80.89	—	8
2	6	4	100	12938	91.35	11338	78.50	15	13
3	10	3	150	27534	115.08	24322	97.12	16	12
4	10	4	150	26860	94.10	22252	94.82	—	18
5	10	5	150	30189	91.57	28407	87.20	5	6
6	15	3	200	65142	95.06	60907	78.95	17	7
7	15	4	200	63838	83.10	60013	93.10	—	6
8	15	5	200	46774	94.63	41626	90.62	5	12
9	20	3	250	113714	96.25	105495	112	—	8
10	20	4	250	110815	103.06	103524	88.02	15	7
11	20	5	250	116123	76.98	106122	83.14	—	9
12	23	3	190	162627	107.18	148340	90.67	16	9
13	23	4	190	163129	90.14	168118	113	—	-3
14	23	5	190	149522	87.13	139154	86.14	2	7

TABLE 14 Comparison of Results Provided by TS and SA

| | | | | SA || TS ||||
No.	N	K	T_{max}	D ($/month)	T (ms)	D ($/month)	T (ms)	%T	%D
1	6	3	100	11490	90.50	9867	80.89	11	15
2	6	4	100	16939	88.15	11338	78.50	11	33
3	10	3	150	30433	103.06	24322	97.12	6	20
4	10	4	150	28450	100.02	22252	94.82	5	22
5	10	5	150	33982	98.23	28407	87.20	12	17
6	15	3	200	65200	110	60907	78.95	29	7
7	15	4	200	70434	96.12	60013	93.10	4	15
8	15	5	200	54810	105	41626	90.62	14	24
9	20	3	250	132872	123.06	105495	112	10	21
10	20	4	250	151918	99.09	103524	88.02	12	32
11	20	5	250	143341	114.03	106122	83.14	28	26
12	23	3	190	174696	97.45	148340	90.67	7	15
13	23	4	190	186871	115.08	168118	113	2	11
14	23	5	190	164123	93.67	139154	86.14	9	16

REFERENCES

1. Ag Rhissa, A., Jiang, S., Ray Barman, J., and Siboni, D. Network generic modeling for fault management expert system. In *International Symposium on Information, Computer and Network Control,* Beijing, China, Feb. 1994.
2. AUTONET / *Performance-3,* Network Design and Analysis Corporation, VA, USA, 1995.
3. Boorstyn, R. R., and Frank, H. Large-scale network topological optimization. *IEEE Trans. Commun.* **25**(1): 29–47, 1977.
4. Buchanan, B. G. Some approaches to knowledge acquisition. In *Machine Learning: A Guide to Current Research* (Mitchell, T. M., Carbonell, J. G., and Michalski, R. S. Eds.), pp. 19–24. Kluwer Academic, Dordrecht, 1986.
5. Carbonell, J. G., Michalski, R. S., and Mitchell, T. M. An overview of machine learning. In *Machine Learning: An Artificial Intelligence Approach* (Michalski, R. S., Carbonell, J. G., and Mitchell, T. M. Eds.), pp. 3–23. Tioga, Portola Valley, CA, 1983.
6. Coan, B. A., Leland, W. E., Vechi, M. P., and Weinrib, A. Using distributed topology update an preplanned configurations to achieve trunk network survivability. *IEEE Trans. Reliability* **40**: 404–416, 1991.
7. COMNET III. *A Quick Look at COMNET III, Planning for Network Managers.* CACI Products Company, La Jolla, CA, 1995.
8. Dietterich, T., and Michalski, R. A comparative review of selected methods for learning from examples. In *Machine Learning: An Artificial Intelligence Approach* (Michalski, R. S., Carbonell, J. G., and Mitchell, T. M. Eds.), pp. 41–82.Tioga, Portola Valley, CA, 1983.
9. Dutta, A., and Mitra, S. Integrating heuristic knowledge and optimization models for communication network design. *IEEE Trans. Knowledge and Data Engrg.* **5**: 999–1017, 1993.
10. Gavish, B. Topological design of computer networks — The overall design problem. *Eur. J. Oper. Res.* **58**: 149–172, 1992.
11. Gavish, B., and Neuman, I. A system for routing and capacity assignment in computer communication networks. *IEEE Trans. Commun.* **37**(4): 360–366, 1989.
12. Gerla, M., and Kleinrock, L. On the topological design of distributed computer networks. *IEEE Trans. Commun.* **25**: 48–60, 1977.
13. Gerla, M., Frank, H., Chou, H. M., and Eckl, J. A cut saturation algorithm for topological design of packet switched communication networks. In *Proc. of National Telecommunication Conference,* Dec. 1974, pp. 1074–1085.
14. Glover, F. Tabu search: Improved solution alternatives for real world problems. In *Mathematical Programming: State of the Art* (J. R. Birge and K. G. Murty, Eds.), pp. 64–92 Univ. of Michigan Press, Ann Arbor, MI, 1994.
15. Glover, F. Tabu thresholding: improved search by nonmonotonic trajectories. *INFORMS J. Comput.* **7**: 426–442, 1995.
16. Glover, F., and Laguna, M. Tabu search. In *Modern Heuristic Techniques for Combinatorial Problems* (C. Reeves, Ed.), pp. 70–141. Blackwell Scientific, Oxford, 1993.
17. Holland, J. H. *Adaptation in Natural and Artificial Systems.* Univ. of Michigan Press, Ann Arbor, MI, 1975.
18. Jan, R. H., Hwang, F. J., and Cheng, S. T. Topological optimization of a communication network subject to reliability constraints. *IEEE Trans. Reliability* **42**: 63–70, 1993.
19. Kamimura, K., and Nishino, H. An efficient method for determining economical configurations of elementary packet-switched networks. *IEEE Trans. Commun.* **39**(2): 278–288, 1991.
20. Karp, R. M. Combinatorics, complexity, and randomness. *Commun. ACM* **29**(2): 97–109, 1986.
21. Kershenbaum, A., Kermani, P., and Grover, G. A. MENTOR: An algorithm for mesh network topological optimization and routing. *IEEE Trans. Commun.* **39**: 503–513, 1991.
22. Kershenbaum, A. *Telecommunication Network Design Algorithms.* IBM Thomas J. Watson Research Center, USA, 1993.
23. Kirkpatrick, S. Optimization by simulated annealing: Quantitative studies. *J. Stat. Phys.* **34**: 975–986, 1984.
24. Kirkpatrick, S., Gelatt, C. D., and Vecchi, M. P. Optimization by simulated annealing. *Science* **220**: 671–680, 1983.

25. Kleinrock, L. *Queueing Systems: Vol. II, Computer Applications.* Wiley–Interscience, New York, 1976.
26. MIL3. *The OPNET Modeler Simulation Environment,* 1997. Available at http://www.mil3.com/products/modeler/home.html.
27. Michalski, R. S. A theory and methodology of inductive learning. In *Machine Learning: An Artificial Intelligence Approach* (Michalski, R. S., Carbonell, J. G., and Mitchell, T. M. Eds.), pp. 83–134. Tioga, Portola Valley, CA, 1983.
28. Monma, C. L., and Sheng, D. D. Backbone network design and performance analysis: A methodology for packet switching networks. *IEEE J. Selected Areas in Commun.* 4(6): 946–965, 1986.
29. Newport, K. T., and Varshney, P. K. Design of survivable communications networks under performance constraints. *IEEE Trans. Reliability* 40(4): 433–440, 1991.
30. Pierre, S., and Gharbi, I. A generic object-oriented model for representing computer network topologies, *Adv. Eng. Software* 32(2): 95–110, 2001.
31. Pierre, S. Inferring new design rules by machine learning: A case study of topological optimization. *IEEE Trans. Man Systems Cybernet.* 28A (5): 575–585, 1998.
32. Pierre, S., and Legault, G. A genetic algorithm for designing distributed computer network topologies. *IEEE Trans. Man Systems Cybernet.* 28(2): 249–258, 1998.
33. Pierre, S., and Legault, G. An evolutionary approach for configuring economical packet-switched computer networks. *Artif. Intell. Engrg.* 10: 127–134, 1996.
34. Pierre, S., and Elgibaoui, A. A tabu search approach for designing computer network topologies with unreliable components. *IEEE Trans. Reliability* 46(3): 350–359, 1997.
35. Pierre, S., Hyppolite, M.-A., Bourjolly, J.-M., and Dioume, O. Topological design of computer communications networks using simulated annealing. *Engrg. Appl. Artif. Intell.* 8: 61–69, 1995.
36. Pierre, S. A new methodology for generating rules in topological design of computer networks. *Engrg. Appl. Artif. Intell.* 8(3): 333–344, 1995.
37. Pierre, S. Application of artificial intelligence techniques to computer network topologies. *Eng. Appl. Artif. Intell.* 6: 465–472, 1993.
38. Rose, C. Low mean internodal distance network topologies and simulated annealing. *IEEE Trans. Commun.* 40: 1319–1326, 1992.
39. Saksena, V. R. Topological analysis of packet networks. *IEEE J. Selected Areas Commun.* 7: 1243–1252, 1989.
40. Samoylenko, S. I. Application of heuristic problem-solving methods in computer communication networks. *Mach. Intell.* 3(4): 197–210, 1985.
41. Schumacher, U. An algorithm for construction of a K-connected graph with minimum number of edges and quasiminimal diameter. *Networks* 14: 63–74, 1984.
42. Siboni, D., Ag Rhissa, A., and Jiang, S. Une fonction intelligente de gestion globale des incidents pour un hyperviseur de réseaux hétérogènes. In *Actes des quatorzièmes journées internationales d'Avignon,* AI' 94, Paris, 30 Mai–3 Juin 1994, pp. 379–387.
43. Suk-Gwon, C. Fair integration of routing and flow control in communications networks. *IEEE Trans. Commun.* 40(4): 821–834, 1992.
44. Van Laarhoven, P. J. M., and Aarts, E. H. L. *Simulated Annealing: Theory and Applications.* Reidel, D., Dordrecht, Holland, 1987.
45. Wong, R. T. Probabilistic analysis of a network design problem heuristic. *Networks* 15: 347–362, 1985.
46. Yokohira, T., Sugano, M., Nishida, T., and Miyahara, H. Fault-tolerant packet-switched network design and its sensitivity. *IEEE Trans. Reliability* 40(4): 452–460, 1991.